ORLANDO
& Walt Disney World

© Disney

2023

Simon & Susan Veness

T0322525

foulsham
LONDON • NEW YORK • TORONTO • SYDNEY

W. Foulsham & Co. Ltd
for Foulsham Publishing Ltd
The Old Barrel Store, Drayman's Lane, Marlow, Bucks SL7 2FF

Foulsham books can be found in all good bookshops or direct
from www.foulsham.com

While every effort has been made to ensure the accuracy of all the information contained
within this book, neither the author nor the publisher can be liable for any errors. In particular,
since prices, times and any holiday or hotel details change on a regular basis, it is vital that
each individual checks relevant information for themselves.

ISBN: 978-0-572-04829-7

A CIP record for this book is available from the British Library

Our sincere thanks go to Wendy Hobson, Jane Hotson and all the hard-working people at
Foulsham who help to bring our work to life every year.

Acknowledgements: The authors wish to acknowledge the help of the following:
Visit Orlando, Experience Kissimmee, Walt Disney Attractions Inc., Universal
Orlando, SeaWorld Parks & Entertainment, Visit Florida, St Petersburg/Clearwater
Area Convention and Visitors Bureau, Seminole County Convention & Visitors
Bureau, Visit Tampa Bay, Space Coast Office of Tourism, Discover Crystal River,
Visit West Volusia, Martin County Florida, Greater Orlando Aviation Authority,
Orlando Melbourne International Airport and Alamo Rent A Car.

CONTENTS

Foreword

Simon says… The Orlando experience has become a lot more complicated in recent years thanks to the pandemic, economics and sheer demand for a Florida holiday. We saw record numbers visiting the state in 2022 and some significant changes in the way the attractions do business. While we have always stressed the importance of planning and preparation for Orlando, it is now essential to pay attention to the need to do your 'homework' in advance and have a good plan of campaign. For first-timers in particular, this is a unique and complex destination that will pull you in umpteen directions at once and leave you exhausted if you're not prepared! But fear not. This is where the *Brit Guide* comes in, your 'good companion' for all that's in store, an indispensable aid to preparing for, navigating and enjoying your holiday to the max. We have been doing this for almost 30 years and we remain fully in touch with everything that makes up this truly amazing holiday playground. Take us along for the ride and you'll have the most comprehensive and up-to-date guide available. Just make sure to read and digest before you go…!

Susan says… The key word for a 2023 visit to the theme park capital of the world is 'flexibility'. Over the course of the past year some restrictions changed, some were eliminated but some will remain in effect at least part-way through 2023, while a few are expected to last through the year. While most of Orlando feels like it's back to normal, the pandemic is not quite over, and health and safety guidance may change as needed. But the good news is (and this is BIG good news) it's okay to hug Mickey Mouse again! And that represents a huge step toward normality. So, look forward to your next Orlando holiday with great anticipation, and say 'Hi' if you see us in the parks!

And now, if you're ready, let's get on with the planning…

PS: A quick note about prices, as they have gone up noticeably in places. With some parks now charging $30/day just to park, be sure to budget accordingly. Suffice it to say, we're not impressed with what we see as some blatant profiteering, even though most attractions made significant losses during the pandemic.

Simon and *Susan Veness*
(For feedback, email **britsguide@yahoo.com** and be sure to Follow **Veness Travel Media** on Twitter, Facebook and YouTube)

1 Introduction

Or, Welcome to the Holiday of a Lifetime

Fun. Excitement. Thrills. Fantasy. Food (lots of food!). They are all waiting for you in this vast area of Central Florida we call Orlando. It is an amazing array of choice, temptation and all-out holiday appeal that has no equal anywhere else on earth. It is a fully fledged assault on the senses and it draws families, couples and singles, young and old alike. It runs the gamut from astounding theme parks to world-class shopping, superb nature and fabulous nightlife.

Most of all, though, this is a BIG venture in every sense and it's vital you do some 'homework' first. Walt Disney World is the leading attraction and is the size of a small city, plus there's a strong supporting cast with Universal Orlando, SeaWorld and LEGOLAND Florida. There's something for all tastes and ages, but it exacts a high toll. You'll walk a lot, queue a lot and probably eat a lot. You WILL have a fabulous time, but you'll probably end up exhausted, too. But stick with us, and you'll have the best possible preparation for what's in store.

Eight theme parks

In simple terms, there are eight major theme parks, and several need two days to enjoy fully. Add a day at a water park, a trip to one of the nature attractions and the lure of the Kennedy Space Center, and you already have two full weeks of pure adventure mania. Mix in the night-time fun of Disney Springs, Universal's CityWalk and a host of dinner shows, plus superb shopping, and you start to understand the awesome scope of the place. Even with two weeks, something has to give – just make sure it isn't your patience or wallet. Or your sanity.

The key to all this is Planning. We suggest drawing up a plan like our example on p 313. Note the time demands of each park and build in a quiet day by the pool or at one of the smaller attractions. Focus on the attractions that appeal to you most, try not to be too ambitious, and don't underestimate the vast scale involved – this is a *huge* area and it takes time even to get from park to park. But do stop to admire the imagination and detail of what's on offer as it is all world class.

Iron Gwazi at Busch Gardens

© Busch Gardens

Florida

0 ——————————— 50 miles

N

Amelia Island

◻ **JACKSONVILLE**

Atlantic

Ocean

← Panama City Beach

⑩

St Augustine

⑦⑤

Flagler Beach
Ormond Beach
Daytona Beach

Ocala

DeLand

New Smyrna Beach

Crystal River

Mount Dora

Sanford

④

Homosassa Springs

Apopka

Titusville

Winter Garden

Cape Canaveral
■ Kennedy Space Center

◻ **ORLANDO**

Walt Disney World 🎡

Cocoa Beach

Kissimmee

New Port Richey

Winter Haven
Legoland Florida

Melbourne

④

Lakeland

Clearwater Beach

Lake Wales
Bok Tower Gardens

⑨⑤

◻ **TAMPA**

FLORIDA

St Pete Beach

Vero Beach

Gulf of

Bradenton

FLORIDA TURNPIKE

Mexico

Sarasota

Venice

Stuart

*Lake
Okeechobee*

Charlotte Harbor

Fort Myers

Palm Beach

Captiva

Delray Beach

Sanibel

Florida

Boca Raton

How far from Orlando to . . .

Naples

Fort Lauderdale

⑦⑤

	mls	-	km
Bradenton	130	-	210
Clearwater Beach	110	-	176
Cocoa Beach	40	-	64
Daytona Beach	60	-	97
Fort Lauderdale	205	-	330
Fort Myers	190	-	306
Jacksonville	155	-	250
Key Largo	294	-	470
Key West	375	-	604
Miami	220	-	354
Naples	230	-	370
Sarasota	140	-	225
St Augustine	120	-	193
St Pete Beach	105	-	169
Tampa	75	-	120
Venice	160	-	257
Winter Haven	40	-	64

Marco Island

Everglades

◻ **MIAMI**

Key Largo

Key West

Florida Keys

© Steve Munns 2022

Orlando

In tourist terms, 'Orlando' has grown to encompass much of Central Florida, an area almost twice the size of Yorkshire. The city itself is north of the main tourist areas and many people won't even see it as they charge from park to park, which is a shame as it is a happening place. When Walt Disney's dream of a vast resort opened in 1971 with the Magic Kingdom (sadly, he never saw it realised as he died in 1966), it led to a huge and ongoing tourism boom.

There are seven counties in Central Florida. **Orange County**, home to the city of Orlando, with Walt Disney World in the south-west corner, part of which is also in **Osceola County**, with Kissimmee its main town; rural **Seminole County**, north-east of Orange; **Lake County** to the north-west, with Mount Dora its prime city; **Polk** to the south-west, home of many holiday villas and LEGOLAND Florida; and east to **Brevard** and **Volusia**, where you'll find the Kennedy Space Center, Daytona Beach and new Melbourne Orlando International Airport.

Orlando typically hosts 70 million visitors a year, and the area boasts some 129,000 hotel rooms, 30,000 vacation homes, 5,000 places to eat and 30 shopping centres. Here are the highlights.

Walt Disney World

This is where the magic really starts. This vast resort consists of four separate theme parks, 22 themed hotels, a camping ground, two water parks, a sports complex, four golf courses, mini-golf and a huge shopping and entertainment district (Disney Springs). It covers 47ml^2/122km^2 and Alton Towers and Thorpe Park would comfortably fit into its car parks! At peak periods, it holds over 200,000 visitors. It maintains a high level of customer service, where everyone who works for them is a Cast Member, not just staff, and they take that ethos to heart.

Magic Kingdom: The essential Disney, with the magic of its wonderful films, the adventures of the Wild West and Africa, the excitement of thrill rides like Space Mountain (an indoor roller-coaster), the eye-catching Fantasyland and splendid parades and fireworks.

> **BRITTIP**
>
> Although it started in 2021, Walt Disney World's park-wide 50th anniversary celebration lasts a full 18 months to the end of March 2023.

Look out for character and celebrity appearances at the Magic Kingdom

© Disney

EPCOT: Disney's revamped four-part park, featuring tech-inspired attractions and a vivid journey round the globe in World Showcase. Slightly more geared for adult sensibilities, it still has some memorable rides, including the new Guardians of the Galaxy: Cosmic Rewind, plus great dining.

Disney's Hollywood Studios: Ride the movies in style, including the new (in 2019) Star Wars: Galaxy's Edge area that still draws HUGE crowds, along with Toy Story Land, Indiana Jones, the Muppets, and much, much more.

Disney's Animal Kingdom: Realistic animal habitats, including a 100acre/40.5ha safari savannah, captivating shows and terrific rides, like the grand Expedition Everest. Newest 'land' Pandora is a brilliant recreation from the film *Avatar*.

Disney's Typhoon Lagoon Water Park: Splash down waterslides and learn to surf in the world's biggest man-made lagoon.

Disney's Blizzard Beach Water Park: The big brother of all the water parks, with a massive spread of rides in a 'snowy' environment.

Disney Springs: Almost a mile of themed restaurants, bars, shops, a cinema multiplex, bowling centre, House of Blues music venue and the Cirque du Soleil theatre.

Wedding Pavilion: A fairytale venue overlooking Seven Seas Lagoon.

Guardians of the Galaxy: Cosmic Rewind

© Disney

ESPN Wide World of Sports: A huge sporting venue to both play and watch top events.

The other parks

If you think Orlando is only about Disney, prepare to be amazed.

Universal Orlando: The other main resort has two theme parks, an entertainment district, themed water park, **Volcano Bay**, and seven themed hotels. At **Universal Studios** you encounter The Simpsons, the Rip Ride Rockit roller-coaster, The Fast and the Furious, TRANSFORMERS: The Ride – 3D and the Wizarding World of Harry Potter – Diagon Alley. At **Islands of Adventure**, experience another Wizarding World area, plus a superb blend of thrill rides, family attractions, shows, great design and high-tech features such as the stunning new VelociCoaster ride.

SeaWorld: THE place for creatures of the deep, with killer whales, dolphins and penguins, a refreshing atmosphere, great shows, fabulous Antarctica attraction, thrill rides like Manta, Kraken, Mako and the new Ice Breaker, a Sesame Street area of rides and activities just for kids, and vital animal rescue facilities.

Discovery Cove: Its exclusive neighbour offers the chance to swim with dolphins, among other things.

Aquatica: A fab water park providing even more fun and animal encounters in a colourful South Seas setting.

BRITTIP

Be realistic when buying tickets. You simply won't get full use out of, say, a 14-day Disney ticket, a Universal 3-Park Explorer ticket AND a 3-Park SeaWorld ticket in a two-week holiday.

Busch Gardens: In nearby Tampa, SeaWorld's sister park offers creatures of the land, plus great rides and shows. Highlights are coasters Cheetah Hunt, SheiKra, Cobra's Curse, Tigris and new Iron Gwazi, plus the Edge of Africa 'safari' experience and extensive Sesame Street play area. A family treat and a must for coaster fans.

Other key attractions

These include the **Kennedy Space Center**, with its superb Space Shuttle Atlantis exhibit; the surprisingly fun and humorous **Gatorland**; **LEGOLAND Florida** for the 2–12 age group, plus the new **Peppa Pig** theme park; **ICON Park**, featuring the 400ft/120m The Wheel; and **Wild Florida**, for a close-up with Kissimmee nature. Plus there's mini-golf almost everywhere and other attractions along International Drive.

Disney tickets

This is where things get complicated and it's important to work out what tickets you need. Most people buy one of two multi-day passes aimed at the UK market that allow visits to more than one park a day. They are great value for a two or three-week visit and provide full flexibility. But they aren't cheap and, if you want only two or three of the Disney parks, you have to buy a Magic Your Way ticket in Orlando. Be aware you can't walk between the parks (they are up to 6 miles apart) and trying to do more than one a day is hard work, especially in summer.

BRITTIP

Once you've bought your Disney tickets (ideally in advance), be ready to make daily park reservations online if the 2022 requirements are still in place, as seems likely to be the case.

Disney's standard ticket system can be horribly complicated (although there is a simplified choice for UK visitors; see below). The 2–10-day tickets offer savings against one-day tickets but unused days expire from 4–14 days after first use.

Standard Tickets: If you just turn up at the ticket booths (or buy in advance from a US broker), you must choose:

- The number of days you want (up to 10).
- If you want the **Park Hopper** option (giving you the ability to move between parks on the same day) for an extra $65–85/ticket.

- If you want the **Water Park & Sports** option, which adds 2–10 visits to the water parks, ESPN Wide World of Sports™, Winter-Summerland or Fantasia Gardens mini-golf, or the nine-hole Oak Trail golf course (book in advance on 407 939 4653; club hire NOT included) for $75/ticket.
- You can also bundle the Park Hopper and Water Park options together for a significant saving.

Per-day ticket savings increase with the more days you buy: 1 day = $109–136 plus tax; 10 days = $550–670 plus tax, or $55–67/day (depending on the time of year, as prices go up at peak periods).

UK tickets: In the UK, there are two tickets on offer: the 7 and 14-day Disney Magic tickets (see chart p11).

Other tickets

The choice is equally complicated for Universal Orlando, SeaWorld, Busch Gardens and Aquatica. Do check periodic special offers (see **AttractionTickets.com**, p10).

- **1, 2, 3, 4 or 5-day Tickets:** For Universal, for one, two or three parks each day.
- **2 and 3-Park Explorer Ticket:** 14 consecutive days at Universal Studios and IoA, or those two plus Volcano Bay (sold in UK only).
- **1, 2, 3 or 4-Park Tickets:** To any combination of SeaWorld, Busch Gardens, Aquatica and Adventure Island water park, valid for 1, 2 or 3 visits, or, with the 4-Park ticket, for 14 consecutive days and free parking. UK ticket brokers have **2 and 3-Park** tickets valid for 14 consecutive days with parking.
- **Discovery Cove:** Bought in the UK, a day ticket includes a 14-Day Pass for SeaWorld and Aquatica. The Ultimate Package adds Busch Gardens for an extra £20 (plus free parking at all 4 parks).
- **14-Day Combo Ticket:** Offered by many UK brokers, for Disney & Universal, plus a **Freedom** ticket (or similar) that includes the SeaWorld parks. This is NOT one ticket but a bundle of two or three.

- **Go Orlando Pass:** A money-saving digital pass for the likes of Kennedy Space Center, The Wheel at ICON Park, LEGOLAND Florida, Fun Spot, WonderWorks, airboat rides and mini-golf ($149–269 adults, $129–239 3–12s; days must be used within 14 days); or **Explorer Pass,** with even more choices for two to five attractions valid for up to 60 days ($54–104; **gocity.com/orlando/en-us**).

- **Eat and Play Card:** A money-saving destination pass for dining, shops and attractions, it comes in a handy digital form, with the bonus of interactive map and 'Near Me' search functions, plus built-in links for advance bookings and other promo codes. The well-established (since 2010) card can be bought and used almost immediately, is always up to date and stays securely on your mobile device. It has 150 places to save at, averaging 18% off the total price, and PLAY category discounts at more than 20%. It includes Orlando Magic tickets, LEGOLAND Florida, Madame Tussauds, WonderWorks, SeaLife Aquarium, Wild Florida Airboats, Denny's, Margaritaville, Red Lobster, Carrabba's, Pizza Hut, Macy's, Bloomingdale's, Tommy Hilfiger and many more, valid for six months from activation at a bargain $25 (1888 680 7109, **eatandplaycard.com**).

With regular price rises, try to buy tickets as soon as you can, but be aware some must be used for the first time in the year of purchase (e.g. 'first use by 31 Dec 2022'). Shop around; many outlets have special offers, but use a reputable agent and use your credit card for added security. The following companies all come highly recommended.

AttractionTickets.com: Britain's top direct-sell Florida ticket broker, with a sharp bookings team, no credit card fees, free delivery in seven days and a promise to match any UK brochure price, plus a huge range of dinner shows, excursions, sports, theme park backstage tours and special offers (0800 223 0324, **attractiontickets.com**).

FloridaTix: Independent ticket specialist featuring all the theme parks, plus the likes of Kennedy Space Center, dinner shows, many tours and excursions, no credit card fees and a £20 deposit ticket offer (0330 100 3130, **floridatix.com**).

Ocean Florida: Another independent specialist that also offers a well-priced ticket service, featuring all the theme parks, plus Kennedy Space Center, Clearwater Beach, dining experiences and more (0208 131 4731, **ocean-florida.co.uk**).

Orlando Attractions: A UK-owned all e-ticket service based in Orlando, it offers all the parks, airboat rides, fishing and other activities, plus well-priced combo tickets. Fully ABTA-bonded and prices include tax and no credit card fees (0800 294 9458, **orlandoattractions.com/tickets**).

BRITTIP

Be sure to download the Orlando Attractions App, from the Apple Store or Google Play, for up-to-the-minute info on ride wait times, maps, special deals, local news and more.

There are others, including the main tour operators (p19), but beware offers for 'free' tickets as these are purely timeshare lures. And NEVER buy resale tickets from a booth in Orlando – they are often unusable. Stick with the main brokers, who offer good products, service and local knowledge.

Millennium Falcon: Smuggler's Run

© Disney

Choosing a ticket

Ticket type	Park	Allowance
1-Day Ticket	Any Disney park, Universal Orlando parks, SeaWorld or Busch Gardens	Access to one park ONLY for one day; not available in advance. Advance reservations may be necessary.
7 and 14-day Disney Magic ticket	All Disney parks	7 or 14 days access to all Disney parks, including water parks. A starting date must be selected, then tickets are valid for 7 or 14 days within a 15 or 18-day period respectively. Available only in advance in the UK.
Disney Incredi-Pass	*Magic Kingdom Park, EPCOT, Disney's Hollywood Studios, Disney's Animal Kingdom;* plus discounts for shops, dining and tours	Unlimited admission and *free parking* for 365 days after purchase date. If ordered online, you get a voucher that must be activated at a park; the 365 days start on the day you activate the pass. NB: This was still suspended in 2022.
Disney Incredi-Pass Plus	All Disney parks; plus numerous discounts for shops, dining and tours	On top of the new Incredi-Pass, you can add the Water Parks & Sports option for an extra $99, and add PhotoPass downloads for a further $99. NB: This was still suspended in 2022
2, 3, 4 or 5-Day 1-Park Ticket	Universal Studios, Islands of Adventure	Access to one of the Universal parks each day for 2–5 days
2, 3, 4 or 5-Day 2 or 3-Park Ticket	Universal Studios and Islands of Adventure, or those two plus Volcano Bay	Access to the parks each day
2 and 3-Park Explorer Ticket	Universal Studios and Islands of Adventure, or those 2 and Volcano Bay	14 consecutive days' access to 2 or 3 of the Universal parks sold in UK only
2 or 3-Park Ticket; Unlimited ticket	SeaWorld, Busch Gardens, Aquatica and Adventure Island water park	2 or 3 visits to any of the 4 SeaWorld parks; Unlimited Ticket offers admission to all 4, and free parking, for 14 consecutive days
2-Park Ticket and 3-for-2 Ticket	Either SeaWorld and Aquatica or SeaWorld and Busch Gardens; or all 3	14 consecutive days' access to each of the 2 parks; or access to all 3 for 14 days with free parking (available in UK only)

Mickey's Philharmagic

© Disney

The climate

Sub-tropical Florida can be seriously hot May–Oct, with temperatures above 33°C/92°F and high humidity that makes it feel even hotter. Add fierce – but short – thunderstorms, with lots of lightning (Florida is the lightning capital of the world), and the weather can be a challenge in summer. However, Mar/Apr and Nov/Dec can be close to idyllic, while it is occasionally possible for Jan–Feb to see night-time temps hit freezing. It's rare to go more than 24 hours without a healthy dose of sunshine, though. Winter sees the biggest temperature range, sometimes from 30°C/86°F down to barely 7°C/45°F at night. Rain rarely lasts for long but can be extremely heavy (be careful when driving on the motorways). If you are governed by school holidays, late Aug is your best bet.

Tipping

Seeing as this is America, there are definitely cultural differences, like tipping. With the exception of fast-food restaurant servers, just about everyone who serves in hotels, bars, restaurants, taxis, airports and public amenities will expect a tip, not least because all service industry workers are taxed on the basis of receiving 15% in tips, whether they're given or not.

Bars, restaurants and taxis: 15%.

Porters: $1/bag.

Housekeeping: $1/day per adult.

BRITTIP

Tipping guide

Bill	Suggested tip
$15	$2.25
$20	$3.00
$25	$3.75
$30	$4.50
$40	$6.00
$50	$7.50

ESTA and immigration

Anyone flying to the USA on the Visa Waiver Programme MUST register online via the Electronic System for Travel Authorization (ESTA) no later than three days before departure.

ESTA: ESTA is a pre-authorisation process prior to arriving at US immigration. The fee is $14 per person and is valid for any visits in a two-year span (so you do NOT pay the $14 fee again in that time).

Apply at **bit.ly/brit-esta** and fill in your basic immigration info – passport, address in the USA, flight and employment details (where necessary), email address and a few security questions. Have your holiday address available for the ESTA and your Advance Passenger Information for your flight online.

Ask your tour operator if you don't have a specific address (e.g. for a villa allocated on arrival) as it will have a formula for this. Your application should generate an immediate response of 'Authorization Approved' or 'Pending'. If you get 'Travel Not Authorized', the applicant is unable to travel under the Visa Waiver Programme and must apply for a visa in advance. Remember to record or print your Application Number so you can amend it for future visits within two years.

BRITTIP

If you need to fill in the white I-94 immigration form for visa holders, do so carefully in block capitals. Mistakes are often sent to the back of the queue. Please be courteous to immigration officials – they do a difficult job in demanding circumstances.

The ESTA speeds up the immigration process and cuts out most form-filling. An ESTA must be completed for each member of your group or family travelling under the Visa Waiver Programme. Those who have a US visa because they are not eligible to travel under the Visa Waiver Programme (see opposite) still need to fill in a white I-94 form en route (fill in the front only) but they do NOT pay the $14 ESTA fee. However, anyone with a US work visa and who is travelling to America for a holiday WILL need to fill in an ESTA and pay the fee.

Customs: You still need to complete a white customs form en route (it'll be given to you on the plane or at check-in and it's best to complete it in advance). Fill in one customs form per family, with some of the same basic info but also the value of any goods that will stay in the USA (put $0 unless you are arriving with gifts for friends). Hand the documents with your passports to the immigration official who checks you through and takes a fingerprint scan and photo. The customs form will be handed back to you to present to another official when you exit the baggage hall.

Visa requirements

Holiday visitors to America do not need a visa providing they hold a valid machine-readable British passport (MRP). Each family member must have their own passport, valid for the FULL duration of the holiday. However, British subjects, those without an MRP or those who fail to meet the photo/biometric data criteria DO need a visa ($160), and should apply at least two months in advance to the US Embassy.

US immigration requires ALL visitors aged 14–79 to give fingerprint and photo ID on arrival. First put the four fingers and thumb of one hand, and then the other on the plate, then stand still for the camera.

Some travellers may NOT be eligible under the Visa Waiver Programme and will have to apply for a special restricted visa or they may be refused entry. This applies to those who have been arrested (even if it did not result in a conviction), have a criminal record (the Rehabilitation of Offenders Act does not apply to US visa law), have a serious communicable illness (but no longer including AIDS/HIV), or

have previously been refused admission into, been deported from, or have overstayed in the US on the Visa Waiver Programme. Minor traffic offences do not count. Visa appointments can be arranged online at **bit.ly/brit-visa** or call 020 3608 6998.

Contacts
- **England, Scotland and Wales:** Visa Office, US Embassy, 33 Nine Elms Lane, London SW11 7US (020 7499 9000).

- **Northern Ireland:** US Consulate General, Danesfort House, 223 Stranmillis Road, Belfast BT9 5GR (028 9038 6100).

- **Detailed advice: uk.usembassy.gov/**

Travel information

Luggage is liable to random searches in the US so do NOT lock your suitcases at check-in for the flight home as TSA officials have the authority to break into them. Using zip-lock seals that can be snipped open is okay and some airlines provide them free, or you can also buy TSA-approved reusable locks at some travel shops. Leave any gifts you are taking home unwrapped, and put scissors and other sharp items in checked bags, never in your hand luggage.

The Wheel at Icon Park

© Icon Park

What's new?

The last two years have felt like writing this guide was a job for Mystic Meg. The constant pandemic-induced changes in the world of travel have made forward-looking topics a lottery, while creating no end of challenges for airlines, tour operators, hotels and attractions. With that in mind, we're kicking off our annual look ahead with a retrospective of how things have changed, and what *might* be on the cards for 2023!

Just to start with, 2022 began with the return of most flights from the UK to the USA, but it still took six months before regular capacity was restored, while we also went from face masks fully mandated to masks being optional. In June 2022, the US axed its requirement for a negative pre-flight Covid-19 test, but you still had to be fully vaccinated, hence the need to check the CDC website (p13). Happily, there were plenty of positive developments, and most attractions were working normally.

Walt Disney World: the resort's ongoing 50th anniversary has ensured plenty of razzmatazz around the House of Mouse, including the opening in May 2022 of the eagerly anticipated **Guardians of the Galaxy: Cosmic Rewind** ride at Epcot. Following the 2021 debut of Remy's Ratatouille Adventure, this has given the park two headline new attractions, while the park's current transformation – including the **World Celebration** area and **Journey of Water, Inspired by** *Moana* – should be complete in 2023. Over at the Magic Kingdom, the New Year is due to mark the debut of the long-awaited **TRON Lightcycle/Run** coaster. **Disney Springs** is busier, too, with the addition of gourmet ice-cream shop Salt & Straw, while the chic Summer House On The Lake should open in 2023. **Disney's Boardwalk** has seen a major upgrade with the arrival of a new ice cream parlour, bakery and, in 2023, the fancy desserts of the award-winning Cake Bake Shop. The dramatic **Galactic Starcruiser** resort/experience also opened to rave reviews (and high prices!). For regular visitors,

the replacement of the free FastPass+ system with the paid-for **Genie+** (p86) remains a bone of contention, but we ARE seeing shorter wait times in the stand-by queues in general terms. 2022 also saw the debut of the **MagicBand+**, with even more interactive features, and the Alexa-like **Hey Disney!** at their hotels.

Universal Orlando: The 2022 closure of the Shrek 4-D attraction has led to strong rumours that this will be transformed into a Minions attraction for 2023/24, while the CityWalk area is undergoing some significant alterations. Gone are nightclubs Red Coconut Club and the groove; their replacements will be The Great Movie Escape game (in late 2022), plus a new restaurant concept (in 2023).

SeaWorld and **Busch Gardens** both opened a major coaster in 2022, and will also have new rides in 2023, with the Surf Coaster at the former for the summer, and the latter debuting giant swing attraction Serengeti Flyer in the spring, which will reach 135ft above the Serengeti Plain at up to 68mph – the tallest and fastest of its kind in the world. **LEGOLAND Florida** will open the fun Pirate River Quest ride in early 2023.

In the meantime, we continue to recommend visitors check the latest travel requirements on **gov.uk/foreign-travel-advice/usa**, as well as the websites for the major attractions for any health and safety requirements. In this era of lingering COVID, it pays to stay informed of our sensitive travel landscape, and feel free to keep in touch with us at **facebook.com/VenessTravelMe1**.

Plan your visit

Okay, enough of the travel worries! The next few chapters will tell you all you need to know to plan the ideal holiday. Make a rough itinerary and then fine tune it with this book.

Ice Breaker at SeaWorld

© SeaWorld

2 Planning and Practicalities

Or, How to *Almost* Do It All and Live to Tell the Tale

There is one simple key to a memorable Orlando holiday: planning. There are no short-cuts here, you simply have to do some 'homework' in advance, or risk being frustrated and/or exhausted!

This huge, demanding place can pull you in a dozen directions, with a dazzling array of options. Nowhere else in the world can be so complex to navigate, so it's vital to plan your visit in advance.

Start with WHEN you want to go; WHERE you'd like to stay; WHAT sort of holiday you want; WHO to book with; and finally HOW MUCH to try to do.
Just remember there's no way you will be able to do it all in 2 or 3 weeks.

When to go

To avoid the worst of the crowds, the best times to go are Oct–Dec (but not Thanksgiving week or Christmas); mid-Jan–mid-Mar; and the week after Easter to the end of May.

Busiest times: Orlando is seldom quiet but is absolutely packed at:

- Christmas/New Year period (about 17 Dec–12 Jan).

- Mid-Mar through to Easter.

- From Memorial Day weekend (the last Mon in May, the start of the summer season) to mid-Aug, especially around 4 July.

- Labor Day weekend in early Sept, the last holiday of summer.

- Thanksgiving week (Wed–Sun).

The parks can even close to new arrivals by mid-morning during the Christmas period.

Space Mountain at the Magic Kingdom Park

Brit Guide touring plans

Due to the constantly fluctuating theme park conditions and restrictions brought about by the pandemic, the Brit's Guide touring plans service has been suspended. Be sure to monitor the Brit Guide website – **www.britguideorlando.net** – and our social media, including **www.facebook.com/VenessTravelMe1/**, for the latest information about their status and return to regular service.

– Susan & Simon

BRITTIP

Thanksgiving is the 4th Thurs in Nov; George Washington's birthday, or President's Day, is the 3rd Mon in Feb, and both make for above-average long-weekend crowds.

Best times: The best combination of good weather and smaller crowds are in Apr (after Easter) and Oct. Rain isn't a big factor (although outdoor rides and water parks will close if lightning threatens), but the crowds will noticeably thin out when it does rain and you can take advantage by bringing waterproofs or buying a plastic poncho (cheaper from local supermarkets than at the parks). In the colder months, take warm layers for early morning queues. When it heats up, leave them in the park lockers. When it gets really hot, seek out the air-conditioned attractions. The humidity alone will knock you sideways in summer and it's vital to drink plenty of water.

BRITTIP

Beware holiday homes (and some hotels) that insist they are 'just minutes from Disney World' – which may actually mean 30mins or more from the parks. Check the exact address.

Hurricane alert?

June–Nov is hurricane season, but it is not anything to worry about. Major storms hit the area in 2004, 2005 and 2017, plus 2022's Hurricane Ian, but the main attractions are rarely impacted significantly beyond being closed for a day or two. In the event of a hurricane, keep your TV tuned to local news stations WESH, WFTV, WKMG or Spectrum 13 and follow their advice.

Simon & Susan's 10 Commandments

1. Drink water frequently
2. Use sunscreen regularly
3. Bring a lightweight rain jacket
4. Pre-book Disney dining
5. Use the new **Disney Genie** service
6. Slow down
7. Remember: you can't do it all
8. Wear comfortable walking shoes
9. Be sure to see some of Florida
10. Don't forget to tip

Where to stay

This is absolutely vital, and there is a huge choice. As a rough guide, four main areas make up the great Orlando tourist conglomeration.

Walt Disney World: Some of the most sophisticated, convenient and fun places to stay are Disney's own hotels, built with the same imagination that created the theme parks. They all feature free transport, early park entry and put you in the heart of the magic. However, with the exception of Disney's All-Star, Pop Century and Art of Animation Resorts, its hotels are among the most expensive, especially to eat in, and are not close to the other attractions, but they make a good one-week base.

Lake Buena Vista: On the eastern edge of Walt Disney World and along I-4, this features a good mix of hotels. It is handy for Disney (and slightly cheaper), with most hotels offering free transport to the parks, plus there is good dining and shopping.

Dining Plan option

Most tour operators offer the Disney Dining Plan as an optional extra with Disney hotel packages and it can be good value if you spend ALL your time in Walt Disney World, where there are few cheap dining outlets. But, because ALL members of the family must be included for the FULL length of your stay, even the Quick Service plan adds around £1,700 for a family of four (with children 3–9) staying for two weeks; the main Dining Plan would be £2,300; and the Deluxe Plan a huge £3,500. It is a LOT of food, and, these days, you need to book all full-service restaurants in advance. The option was still suspended in summer 2022 as a lasting effect of the pandemic, so look up disneyworld.co.uk or call 0800 169 0730 for the latest info. You *can* eat cheaper elsewhere, so don't book unless you're sure. Tour operators occasionally offer the Dining Plan as a free perk, which then adds great value to your holiday. See more on p53.

International Drive: The big tourist corridor of I-Drive lies mid-way between Disney and downtown Orlando, running parallel to I-4, and is an excellent central location about 20mins drive from Disney and close to Universal and SeaWorld. It is a well-developed area, with great shops, restaurants and attractions like ICON Park, Ripley's Believe It Or Not, WonderWorks and iFLY Orlando, plus its own transport service, the I-Ride Trolley. The downside is it gets congested in peak times, but it is good value and one of the few areas with extensive pavement, making it easy to explore on foot. A sub-district off I-Drive is the Universal area of Kirkman Road and Major Boulevard.

Kissimmee: Budget holiday-makers flock to the tourist sprawl of Highway 192 (the Irlo Bronson Memorial Highway), an almost unbroken 20ml/32km strip of hotels, motels, restaurants and shops. It offers some of the best economy accommodation and is handy for Disney, though further from Universal and SeaWorld. A car is advisable, although there's extensive pavement, landscaping, bus shelters and benches. **Highway 27** is often referred to as 'Kissimmee' but is actually either in Lake County (north) or Polk County (south). This is prime holiday-home and villa territory.

Split holidays

Florida has so much to offer, many opt to spend a week in Orlando and a week somewhere else. The Atlantic and west coasts have great beaches and the Everglades are 3-4 hours to the south. There's excellent shopping almost everywhere and plenty of sports activities, including superb golf, fishing, biking and kayaking. The tour operators offer a huge variety of packages, plus cruise-and-stay options. Budget permitting, the ideal is two weeks in Orlando then a week relaxing on a beach. A two-week, 50/50 split is popular; just try not to pack too much into your Orlando week! Fly-drives are flexible, but there is a lot to tempt you and you may find it better to book a two-centre stay that includes a car and accommodation so you can still travel but avoid too much packing and unpacking (see also Chapter 9).

BRITTIP

I-Drive south of Sand Lake Road offers some of the best hotels and restaurants. To the north, it is more budget hotels, fast food and gift shops.

Wheezy in Toy Story Land

© Disney

Booking your holiday

The big question is whether to book a package or book the flight, accommodation, car hire, etc, separately. The DIY approach can pay dividends but, at peak periods, a package may still be cheaper. Shop around, and use the internet. Increasingly, it pays to book early, especially for the summer and Christmas, while the pandemic has highlighted the value of using an ABTA-bonded travel agent and ensuring your flights are ATOL licensed. Start by looking at prices with the Big Boys (Virgin, TUI, etc) then compare with online specialists like Expedia and Opodo and look up 'aggregator' websites like Skyscanner and Kayak that check flights/hotels/car hire from a number of sources.

The big boys: You'll find a good range of holidays, featuring Orlando, the Gulf Coast, Miami and the Florida Keys from **British Airways Holidays** (**bit.ly/brit-ba**); **TUI** (**tui.co.uk**); and **Virgin Holidays**, who remain Britain's top tour operator for Florida, with the widest array of choice, including for 2022/23 a Florida Fun Card on arrival (offering discounts on a variety of shops, restaurants and even some attractions), as well as wedding services and exclusive options in Miami, Marco Island and Key West (**virginholidays.co.uk**). **Thomas Cook** has returned with a full Florida programme (using flights by TUI, BA or Virgin), albeit under new ownership (**thomascook.com**). TUI also offers flights-only seasonally (from Birmingham, Bristol, Doncaster Sheffield, Edinburgh, Glasgow, Gatwick, Manchester and Newcastle) but they are now using Melbourne Orlando International Airport, some 70mls away from Disney.

The specialists: There's also a variety of smaller operators specialising in Florida and the US. Take a look at:

- **Florida First** (**florida-first.com**)
- **James Villa Holidays** (**jamesvillas. co.uk**)
- **Kuoni** (**kuoni.co.uk**)
- **Ocean Florida** (**ocean-florida.co.uk**)
- **Trailfinders** (**trailfinders.com**)
- **Travelbag** (**travelbag.co.uk**)
- **USAirtours** (**usairtours.co.uk**)

BRITTIP

For a genuine tailor-made choice of Florida options, be sure to check out the specialists of Florida First, who can offer a fully customised and individual travel service.

Online agents: You can also price-check with a variety of online agencies who provide packages, flights, hotels and car hire.

- **Cheap Flights** (**cheapflights.co.uk**)
- **Dial A Flight** (**dialaflight.com**)
- **eBookers** (**ebookers.com**)
- **Expedia** (**expedia.co.uk**)
- **Flight Centre** (**flightcentre.co.uk**)

Kumba at Busch Gardens

- **Kayak (kayak.co.uk)**
- **(netflights.com)**
- **Opodo (opodo.co.uk)**
- **Sky Scanner (skyscanner.net)**
- **Travel Supermarket (travelsupermarket.com)**

Scheduled flights

For DIY, book your flights first. These airlines offer scheduled, year-round services to Orlando.

Aer Lingus: Direct flights from Dublin (**aerlingus.com**).

British Airways: Flies direct daily from Gatwick and Heathrow to Orlando and Gatwick to Tampa, plus twice daily from Heathrow to Miami (**britishairways.com**).

Icelandair: Fly via Keflavik, Iceland, from Heathrow, Glasgow or Manchester (**icelandair.co.uk**).

PLAY!: This new Icelandic low-cost airline was due to start services from Stansted and Liverpool to Orlando, via Keflavik, in October 2022 with some seriously competitive prices if you don't mind breaking the journey in Iceland. Beware all the 'extras' for baggage, seat choice, etc, though (**flyplay.com**).

Virgin Atlantic: Multiple direct flights each week from Heathrow and Manchester, plus seasonally from Edinburgh, as well as Heathrow to Miami and, from 2022, to Tampa (**virginatlantic.com**).

Another new start-up airline, **Norse Atlantic**, started an Oslo–Orlando route in July 2022, with plans to add flights from London to Orlando and Fort Lauderdale in future.

Indirect flights: You can often save money on indirect flights, the obvious drawback being the extra journey time, and the connecting flight may land you in Orlando late in the evening. However, it does break the journey and places like Detroit and Dallas often process international passengers quicker than Orlando, meaning less hassle when you arrive.

American Airlines: From Heathrow, Manchester, Edinburgh or Dublin via Boston, Chicago, Charlotte, Dallas, New York, Philadelphia, Raleigh Durham and Miami (0844 369 9899, **americanairlines.co.uk**).

Delta/KLM: Gatwick, Glasgow, Heathrow, Manchester or Edinburgh via Boston, Atlanta, Minneapolis, Detroit or New York (020 7660 0293, **klm.com**).

United: Heathrow, Belfast, Dublin, Manchester, Birmingham, Glasgow or Edinburgh via Washington, Houston, New York or Chicago (0845 607 6760, **united.com**).

What to see when

The best way to end up exhausted is to head for one theme park after another. Take advantage of quieter park days and include rest days. If you have only a week, drop Busch Gardens and focus on Disney, Universal and SeaWorld. Kennedy Space Center is also hard to miss.

- **Magic Kingdom:** 2 days – the biggest hit with young children.
- **EPCOT:** 2 days – one day is not really enough, but there are fewer rides to amuse children.
- **Animal Kingdom:** 1 day – a little short on appeal for the youngest but with lots of live entertainment.
- **Disney's Hollywood Studios:** 1 day – plus two evening shows.
- **SeaWorld:** 1–2 days.
- **Islands of Adventure:** 1–2 days.
- **Universal Studios:** 1–2 days.
- **Busch Gardens:** 1 day – popular with Brits, 75mins away in Tampa.

LEGOLAND Florida: is also a full day's outing, while **ICON PARK** can be fitted around the main parks. Use the detail in Chapters 5–8 to plan.

BRITTIP

You can sometimes get cash back on travel purchases including flights and hotels from websites such as topcashback.co.uk and quidco.com. Consult Martin Lewis's MoneySavingExpert.com, too.

A princess waves to the Cavalcade!

Our must-do experiences

- Soarin' and World Showcase (EPCOT)
- Wizarding Worlds of Harry Potter and new VelociCoaster at Universal Orlando
- Wild Florida (Kissimmee)
- Pandora: The World of Avatar (Animal Kingdom)
- Disney Enchantment fireworks, Pirates of the Caribbean and Haunted Mansion rides (Magic Kingdom)
- Star Wars: Galaxy's Edge (Disney's Hollywood Studios)
- Shopping!
- Infinity Falls, Ice Breaker and Mako rides (SeaWorld)
- Cheetah Hunt, Iron Gwazi and SheiKra coasters (Busch Gardens)
- Space Shuttle Atlantis & new Gateway exhibit (Kennedy Space Center)
- A Disney character meal
- A trip to Winter Park
- A day at a water park

Smaller attractions

Smaller-scale attractions can be fitted around your Big Eight itinerary. The **water parks** or the quieter **Bok Tower Gardens** make for a relaxing half-day, while **Gatorland** (at least half a day) is a unique look at some of Florida's oldest inhabitants and is a good combination with **Boggy Creek Airboats** or **Wild Florida**. Then there are the likes of **Ripley's Believe**

It Or Not museum, **ICON Park** and the **WonderWorks** house of fun, all offering hours of entertainment, the thrills of **iFLY Orlando** (an indoor 'sky-diving' wind tunnel) and the lure of old-fashioned go-karts and other fairground-type rides at **Fun Spot, Andretti Indoor Karting** and **Magical Midway**. Many stay open after the parks close.

Each main area is also well served with creatively designed **mini-golf** courses (p249).

Evenings

The evening entertainment features a similarly wide choice. By far the best, and worth at least one evening each, are **Disney Springs** and Universal's **CityWalk** – the latter will keep you busy until the early hours! Dinner shows provide a lot of fun: two-hour cabarets based on themes such as medieval knights, pirates, Al Capone and murder mysteries that all include a hearty meal. Downtown Orlando (the actual city centre) is also well worth a visit (see Chapter 10).

Guardians of the Galaxy: Cosmic Rewind

Shopping

Shopping in Orlando is world class (see Chapter 12) and your plan should include at least a day to visit the spectacular malls and discount centres, like the two **Orlando Premium Outlets** centres, **Lake Buena Vista Factory Stores**, **Mall at Millenia** and the **Florida Mall**. Busy at weekends, but handy if it rains.

What to do when

There are several guidelines for avoiding the worst of the tourist hordes, even in high season.

Avoid busy days: Most Americans arrive at weekends and head for the main theme parks first, so Sun and Mon are often bad times to visit the Magic Kingdom, while Tues is usually also busy at EPCOT. New rides like Guardians of the Galaxy (at EPCOT) and the VelociCoaster (IoA) also create longer queues, notably at weekends, when Universal Orlando is also generally busiest. Animal Kingdom is the hardest to navigate when crowded, while EPCOT handles the crowds best. Blizzard Beach and Typhoon Lagoon water parks hit high tide at weekends, and Thurs and Fri in summer; avoid Volcano Bay and Aquatica at weekends, too. If Disney is busy early in the week, visit SeaWorld, Busch Gardens or Kennedy Space Center.

BRITTIP

If your hotel is close by, take a break from the park for an afternoon siesta or swim. Your car park ticket is valid all day, and the parks are pleasant in the evening.

The Space Shop at Kennedy Space Center

© Kennedy Space Center

Arrive early: Getting the most out of your days at the parks is another art form, and there are several options.

The opening times can be as early as 8am in peak season, and arriving at least 30mins before opening time (or an hour at peak periods) is advisable. You will also be better placed to park in the huge car parks and catch the tram to the main gates.

Prioritise: Once you are in pole position, don't waste time on the shops, scenery and other frippery that will lure the unprepared first-timer. Head straight for some of the main rides and get a few big-time thrills under your belt before the hordes arrive. You will quickly work out where the most popular attractions are as the majority of early birds will flock to them. Use Chapters 5 and 6 to plan your park strategies.

Pace yourself: Disney's parks, notably the Magic Kingdom, stay open until 10 or 11pm at peak periods, and that's a l-o-n-g day for kids. It's vital to pace yourself, especially if you arrive early. There are plenty of options to take time off for a drink or a rest somewhere air-conditioned, which is vital in summer.

Disney Genie (and **Genie+**): Make *sure* you study this in advance and use it to your advantage (p85).

Meal breaks: Benefit from the American habit of dining at lunchtime (midday–1.30pm) and dinner (5.30–7pm) by planning your meals outside those times. It pays to take an early lunch (before noon), snack in mid-afternoon and then enjoy a relative drop-off in crowds in late afternoon. Try not to have all your meals in the parks; eating here can be expensive ($16–20/person for a basic meal). A good breakfast before you arrive and a light lunch will save you $$$s!

BRITTIP

The water IS safe to drink in the US, but it might not taste great as it's heavily fluoridated. If you buy bottled water, do so at supermarkets, not at the parks, where it is exorbitantly expensive.

Baby zebra at Animal Kingdom

Footy frenzy

You don't need a specialist sports bar for most British football on TV. The Premier League is extensively covered by NBC, while the Champions League is on CBS Sports. Check if your villa/hotel has NBC and CBS Sports, as they are cable channels that not everyone gets. The FA Cup is only offered online on ESPN+. And don't forget to check out our own team – Orlando City – at **orlandocitysc.com** (p250).

Comfort and clothing

Avoid alcohol and coffee on the plane and drink plenty of water to help reduce jetlag during the first day or so after arrival.

Shoes: These are the most important part of your holiday wardrobe – you'll be on your feet a LOT, even at off-peak periods. The smallest park is 'only' 100acres/40ha, but that is irrelevant to the time spent queuing. This is not the time to break in new sandals or trainers. Comfortable, well-worn shoes or trainers are essential (many rate Croc-type shoes as ideal park footwear).

BRITTIP

Look after your feet and avoid the onset of blisters by buying some moleskin footpads from a supermarket or 'drug-store' like Walgreens and CVS.

Casual clothes: Casual dress is fine in parks and nearly all restaurants, but swimwear is not acceptable away from pool areas. If you want a change of clothes or a sweater for the evening, use the park lockers (unlimited use all day for a small fee).

Measurements

US clothes sizes are smaller than ours, hence a US size 12 dress is a UK 14, or an American jacket sized 42 is a 44. Shoes are the opposite: a US 10 should fit a British size 9 foot. The measuring system is imperial, not metric.

BRITTIP

Don't be tempted to pack a lot of smart or formal clothing – you really won't need it in hot, informal Florida.

Baby services: All the parks are well equipped with pushchairs, or 'strollers', for hire (although it pays to have your own), and baby services are located at regular intervals. You can even hire pushchairs for your full holiday period from Orlando Stroller Rentals from $110 for two weeks (**orlandostrollerrentals.com**).

Sunscreen: It is VITAL to use high-factor sun creams (30-plus) at all times, even during the winter when the sun may not feel strong but can still burn. Orlando has a subtropical climate so you need the high factor, waterproof if you are swimming. Use sun block on sensitive areas like nose and ears, and splash on the after-sun liberally at the end of the day. Skincare products are widely available and usually inexpensive (at Wal-Mart, Publix or Target). Wear a hat during the day, and avoid alcohol, coffee and fizzy drinks until the evening as they are dehydrating and make you liable to heatstroke. You must increase your fluid intake SIGNIFICANTLY in the summer, with lots of water.

Disney's Riviera Resort

Medical help

Should you need medical treatment consult your tour operator's info. In the event of an emergency, dial **911** as you would 999 in Britain. It cannot be overstressed, however, you should take out comprehensive travel insurance (p25) for any trip to America, as there is NO NHS and any form of medical treatment is expensive. Keep all the receipts and put in a claim on your return home.

BRITTIP

If a medical emergency arises and you need urgent treatment, head straight for the ER (Emergency Room) at a major hospital like the Dr Phillips Hospital on Turkey Lake Road.

Emergency outpatients: These can be found with AdventHealth Centra Care in more than 20 Central Florida locations (407 200 2273: **centracare. org/florida**), as well as full family and paediatric care.

Open 8am–8pm (5pm at weekends), there are several locations open to midnight Mon–Fri, including at 12500 S Apopka-Vineland Road near the Disney Springs entrance at Lake Buena Vista (8pm Sat and Sun; 407 934 2273). Other notable tourist area locations are: 8201 West Irlo Bronson Memorial Highway (192), by Orange Lake Resort (407 465 0846); on Sand Lake Road, between John Young Parkway and Orange Blossom Trail (9am–5pm Sat and Sun; 407 851 6478); and 4320 West Vine Street, near Medieval Times (407 390 1888).

BRITTIP

Look for local insect-repellent brands Cutter, Repel and Off! and use them when outdoors away from the parks.

Medical Concierge®: This has doctors throughout the tourist areas, making house calls to hotels and villas 24/7. They also have a clinic at 6000 Turkey Lake Road (near Universal) 8am–8pm Mon-Fri, but you must call for an appointment. Doctors have mobile pharmacies and even X-ray units and they specialise in healthcare for overseas visitors. They can often arrange same-day dental and other specialist care and take many UK travel insurance policies, dealing directly with the insurance company. Their switchboard is manned around the clock (1855 932 5252, **themedicalconcierge.com**).

If you need an emergency dentist, **Mobile Dental ER** has a mobile facility that can visit anywhere in the Orlando area, 7 days a week (9am–5pm). Pay with all major credit cards (but save receipts for your insurance). (407 955 0743; **mobiledentaler.com**).

BRITTIP

If you take regular prescription drugs, find out the different UK and US names from your doctor or pharmacist and carry the info with you (e.g. adrenaline is known as epinephrine, paracetamol is acetaminophen).

The Dr P Phillips Hospital, 9400 Turkey Lake Road, also has an emergency outpatients (the Emergency Room, or ER) open 24hrs (407 351 8500).

Chemists: The largest chemists ('drug stores') are Walgreens (**walgreens.com**) and CVS (**cvs.com**), and the Walgreens at 12100 S Apopka-Vineland Road (near Disney Springs), 5935 W Irlo Bronson Memorial Highway (Highway 192 in Kissimmee), 6201, 8959 and 12650 I-Drive (among others, plus the one at the corner of I-Drive and Sand Lake Rd), are open 24 hours.

Gator safety

Alligators are found in many bodies of water in Florida but they rarely approach humans and are rarely a threat. However, they should NEVER be approached or fed (which is illegal). They usually avoid people but swimming in lakes in the evening is not advised and small children should never be allowed in or near open water on their own.

Travel insurance

Don't travel without insurance, but there's no need to pay over the top or to buy travel agent policies. Any policy should cover these options, and if you are *personally* affected by COVID-19:

- Medical cover of at least £2m.

- Personal liability up to £2m (but you still need Supplementary Liability with your car hire firm).

- Cancellation or curtailment cover up to £5,000.

- Personal property cover up to £1,500 (but check as most policies limit single articles to £250).

- Cash and document cover, including your passport and tickets. 24hr emergency helpline.

- Cancellation in case of a new government travel ban or lockdown (if available).

BRITTIP

Look up Battleface for a new (in late 2022) insurance option for US travel that offers an unbundled approach depending on your holiday activities. Find it at **battleface.com**.

- Shop around at reputable dealers like:
- **AllClear Travel Insurance** (**allcleartravel.co.uk**)
- **Allianz Assistance** (**allianz-assistance.co.uk**)
- **American Express** (**americanexpress. com/en-gb/insurance/**)
- **Aviva** (**aviva.co.uk**)
- **AXA** (**www.axa.co.uk/travel-insurance**)
- **Columbus Direct** (**columbusdirect. com**)
- **Direct Travel** (**direct-travel.co.uk**)
- **Money Supermarket** compares travel insurers online at **moneysupermarket.com/travel-insurance**.

BRITTIP

To avoid costly overseas roaming charges on your mobile in the US, switch off data roaming and use free WiFi or buy a pre-paid data Sim before you go. To call the US from the UK, dial 001, then the number; from the US to the UK, dial 011 44 and omit the first 0 of the area code.

Florida with children

There is no 'right' age to take children to Orlando. Some toddlers take to it instantly, while some 6–7-year-olds are overwhelmed. Often, the best attractions are the hotel swimming pool or the tram ride to a park gates! Some love the Disney characters instantly, while others find them frightening. At 4½, Simon's oldest boy loved just about every second of his first experience (apart from the fireworks!) and still talks about it. A 3-year-old may not remember much, but will have fun and provide you with great memories, photos and videos. Here are our top tips.

The flight: Pack a bag with lots of little treats and activities (comics, sweets, colouring books, small surprise toys, etc.) and keep vital extras like Calpol (in sachets, if possible), a change of clothes, a small first-aid kit, plasters, antiseptic cream, baby wipes, sunglasses, a hat and sunscreen in your hand luggage.

Once you're there: Take things slowly and let your children dictate the pace to a large extent. In hot, humid summer, only the most placid children (and few under-5s, in our experience) will happily queue for an hour or more, so use Disney Genie (p85) judiciously. The heat, in particular, can quickly result in grizzly kids, so take breaks for drinks and splash zones or head for attractions with air-conditioning. Keep your 'extras' kit from the flight with you. Go back to the hotel for an afternoon snooze to dodge the worst of the heat and crowds.

In the sun: Always carry sun cream and sun block and use it often, in queues, on buses, etc. Use a children's after-sun lotion and make sure they drink a lot of water or non-fizzy drinks; tiredness and irritability are often the signs of mild dehydration.

Dining out: Look for Kids-eat-free deals as they can apply to children up to 12, and take advantage of the many buffet options (see Chapter 11) to fill up the family or for picky eaters. Many restaurants do Meals To Go if you want a quiet meal in your own accommodation. And try to let your children get used to the characters (especially their size) before you go to one of the many wonderful character meals.

BRITTIP

Need to buy children's clothes? Orlando is THE place to go shopping, with a huge array of discount stores in the malls (see Chapter 12).

Having fun: Let your children do some of the decision-making and be prepared to go with the flow if they find something unexpected – such as the many squirt fountains and splash zones in the parks (bring swimsuits and/or a change of clothes!). The Orlando rule of 'You Can't Do It All' applies especially with kids. Be aware some youngsters find the evening

Wheelchair users are well catered for in the Magic Kingdom

Merchandise from the flagship City Walk store

fireworks too loud, but the hotels around the Magic Kingdom offer a view from a distance.

Baby centres: All the parks have facilities for nursing mothers (locations are on the park map) and can provide baby food, nappies and even spare children's underpants for those little accidents. All Disney hotel gift shops stock baby food and nappies. Expectant mothers are strongly advised not to ride some of the more dynamic attractions, and there are clear warnings on park maps and at the rides.

Pushchairs: 'Strollers' are essential, even if your children are a year or so out of them. The walking wears kids out quickly. You can take your own, hire them at the parks or buy one for as little as $25 at a local shop like Walmart. Babysitting is available through many Disney resorts and some of the bigger hotels elsewhere.

Travellers with disabilities

The parks pay close attention to the needs of visitors with disabilities and Florida is extremely disabled-friendly. (Note: Americans use the word 'handicapped' as we use 'disabled'.)

Access: Wheelchair availability and access is usually good (though there are a few rides that cannot cater for them) and all hotels have disabled-accessible rooms. For hearing-impaired guests, there are assistive listening devices and reflective captioning where a commentary is part of a show. Braille guidebooks are available, plus rest areas for guide dogs, and there are Audio Descriptions for blind guests. Disney, Universal and SeaWorld offer Accessibility Guides for disabled guests in all their main parks (and online). Life-jackets are always on hand at water parks. For Disney disability assistance, call 407 560 2547; for Universal, call 407 224 4233.

Guest Assistance: If you or someone in your party has special needs, register for a Disability Access Service card (DAS) via virtual chat, from 2 to 30 days in advance. Then, select return times for up to 2 attractions for the day of your visit. Or visit Guest Services in any Disney theme park. Once both return times have been used, DAS guests can receive another using My Disney Experience app. This can be used in addition to Disney's Genie+ service (p85). Universal, SeaWorld and Busch Gardens provide similar help through their Guest Services.

Parking permits: To use any of the plentiful designated disabled parking areas in all public areas (including the parks), UK drivers must obtain a **Temporary Disabled Parking Permit**, which costs $15 and is valid for 90 days (although you may renew a permit within 12 months for no fee). Apply in advance via the Orange County Tax Collectors office at **octaxcol.com/contact/** as follows:

1. Visit the <u>Contact Us</u> page, enter your name, email, choose 'Parking Placards', provide a brief note of where you are travelling from, and Submit.

2. A customer service specialist will reply with a list of documents.

3. Reply, attaching your completed <u>HSMV 83039</u> form, copy of driver's licence/state ID or passport and both sides of your UK Blue Badge.

4. After verification, you will be contacted for payment processing.

5. The temporary placard will be mailed to your home address.

There is a $2 processing fee and you should allow two weeks for it to arrive. Alternatively, you can visit any Tax Collectors office in central Florida (most open 8.30am–5pm Mon–Fri only, but you can request an appointment in advance). For tax offices in Orange County (for the Orlando area), call 407 845 6200 or visit **octaxcol.com** and click Locations; in Osceola County (for Kissimmee), call 407 742 4000 (**osceolataxcollector. com**). The main tax office in Kissimmee is located at 2501 E. Irlo Bronson Highway.

- **Walker Mobility:** Electric scooters and wheelchair rentals, with free delivery and pick-up, even from holiday villas (407 518 6000, **walkermobility.com**).

- **Mobility Works:** Specially equipped vans for hire for wheelchair users (1877 275 4915, **mobilityworks.com**).

- **Orlando Medical Rentals:** Wide range of medical equipment for hire, including powered scooters and wheelchairs (1877 356 9943, **orlandomedicalrentals.com**).

Orlando for grown-ups

You don't need to have kids to enjoy Orlando. There is so much clever detail and imagination, adults usually get the most out of the experience.

In fact, as many couples and singles visit the parks as do families with children and you can see the attraction. There's great entertainment, a brilliant range of bars and fine restaurants, a friendly, sociable atmosphere that's ideal for singles and late opening at the parks and clubs. The downtown area of Orlando is coming back as a happening night-time venue, and the Craft Beer scene is booming, with plenty of ways to sample it (p273).

BRITTIP

Freeze drink cartons in your hotel fridge overnight and they will be cool for much of the next day. Also freeze some water bottles in a cheap coolbag and leave it in the car for the end of the day.

City Works Eatery and Pour House at Disney Springs

© Disney

Repeat visitors

Here are some of the things popular with the many returners. See also Chapters 8 and 9.

1   Behind-the-scenes tours at the Disney parks
2   Dolphin watch cruise from Dolphin Landings at St Pete Beach
3   Wildlife eco-tour with Island Boat Lines at Cocoa Beach
4   The scenic boat ride and Morse Museum in Winter Park
5   Bok Tower Gardens
6   St John's River Eco Tour Cruise in Debary
7   St John's Rivership cruises
8   Orlando Tree Trek
9   Lake Apopka Wildlife Drive
10 Kayaking at Kissimmee Paddling Center

Orlando for seniors

Mature travellers are likely to have just as much fun, just within slightly different parameters. Seniors can also take advantage of numerous discounts and special deals at many attractions, restaurants and hotels.

Hotels: For the older person, staying in a Disney hotel is recommended as it removes the stress of driving. The extra cost is offset by the convenience and relaxation factor.

Parks: Even if the thrill rides are not a draw, just watching can be fun! Both EPCOT and Disney's Animal Kingdom have plenty for seniors while the shows of Disney's Hollywood Studios are also popular and the Magic Kingdom, while a bit hectic, is still an essential experience.

There's plenty for senior guests to enjoy

© Disney

Evenings: Disney Springs can feel a bit frenetic for the senior crowd, but the Boardwalk Resort is popular and the whole EPCOT resort area offers much in the way of fine dining and relaxation. It is often a prime area for seniors, notably the quieter Disney's Yacht and Beach Club Resorts, and Swan-Dolphin complex.

Weather: Mar and late Oct/Nov are ideal times to visit, but the summer months are hard going for older folks. Good coats (and gloves) may still be necessary at times in winter.

Attractions: Highlights for seniors.

- **Animal Kingdom:** Kilimanjaro Safaris, the Maharajah Jungle Trek, Gorilla Falls Forest Trail, Finding Nemo show, Festival of the Lion King and Na'vi River Journey.

- **Disney's Hollywood Studios:** Muppet Vision 3-D, Indiana Jones Stunt Show, Beauty and the Beast, Stars Wars: Galaxy's Edge area and Fantasmic!.

- **EPCOT:** Spaceship Earth, Soarin', all of World Showcase and the live entertainment (plus the superb gardens and architecture).

- **Magic Kingdom:** The Haunted Mansion, Jungle Cruise, Pirates of the Caribbean, Mickey's PhilharMagic, Under the Sea – Journey of the Little Mermaid and Festival of Fantasy Parade.

- **Universal Studios and Islands of Adventure:** The amazing Wizarding Worlds of Harry Potter.

- **Others:** Watching the children at the many parades and character greetings; dinner at the California Grill in Disney's Contemporary Resort (and other fine dining locations); shopping at the Mall at Millenia and Altamonte Mall.

- **More options:** SeaWorld remains popular for seniors and even Busch Gardens, despite its many roller-coasters, has plenty to offer. Places such as Mount Dora, DeLand, Winter Garden and Winter Park (see Chapter 8) are also slower-paced.

You've got mail

You won't find many post boxes and some post offices don't seem to know the fees for postage to the UK. All the parks have post boxes and you can get stamp books from most stamp machines and City Hall at the Magic Kingdom. A standard postcard or greetings card in an envelope to the UK both need a $1.30 stamp; standard postage within the US is 58c.

The main post offices are:

- **Disney area:** 10450 Turkey Lake Road (just north of the junction of Palm Parkway and Central Florida Parkway; 8am–7pm Mon–Fri, 9am–5pm Sat).

- **Kissimmee:** 1415 W Oak Street (8.30am–5pm Mon–Fri, 9am–2pm Sat).

- There is also a small post office inside the **Mall at Millenia**, off the lower level of the Grand Court.

Spaceship Earth at Epcot

© Disney

Wedding bells

Florida is a popular choice for couples wanting to tie the knot. Its almost guaranteed sunshine and lush, natural landscape make it a huge hit as a wedding backdrop. Orlando also has terrific services, co-ordinators and venues like Wild Florida, Cypress Grove Estate House, Winter Park wedding chapel, Casa Feliz, Leu Gardens, Imperial Design Banquet Hall and hotels like Rosen Shingle Creek, Walt Disney World Swan and Dolphin and the Omni Orlando Champions Gate. Even scenic golf courses such as Celebration Golf Club and Mission Inn can stage grand occasions extremely well. More unusual ones include the Hard Rock Café, a hot-air balloon or helicopter, Danville B&B (**danvillebnb. com**), on the beach, a luxury yacht, or even the Wheel at ICON Park. All tour operators feature wedding options, or you can pick a local specialist like Get Married In Florida (p30). Prices vary from £300/couple (for a basic civil ceremony) to more than £6,000.

BRITTIP

Looking for essential travel accessories and useful knick-knacks, like TSA-approved locks, plug adapters and waterproof accessories? Type in 'essentials for travel' on Amazon. Asda supermarkets also sell a good travel range.

Walt Disney World's Wedding Pavilion: True fairytale romance, with the backdrop of Cinderella Castle, you can opt for traditional elegance in this Victorian setting with up to 260 guests or the full Disney experience, arriving in Cinderella's coach with Mickey and Minnie as guests. Disney's wedding planners can tailor-make the occasion for you (407 828 3400) but at a price – venue rates START at $3,500 for the basic ceremony and can top $50,000!

Licence: To obtain a marriage licence, visit a local courthouse: Osceola County Courthouse, Courthouse Square, Suite 2000, Kissimmee (just off Bryan Street in downtown Kissimmee) 8am–4pm Mon–Fri (407 343 3500); Orange County Courthouse, 425 N Orange Avenue (downtown Orlando) 7.30am–4pm

Fairytale wedding

© Disney

Top things to do for FREE!

Disney's Boardwalk Resort: Free nightly entertainment includes jugglers, comedians and live music. Time your visit to coincide with the 9pm EPCOT fireworks show at nearby EPCOT.

Downtown Orlando Historic Tour: From the Visitor Center on Orange Avenue, local historian Richard Forbes leads a free tour of downtown at 9.30am on the first Fri of every month from Oct–May. Must call in advance to check availability on 407 246 3789 (**www.downtownorlando.com/Fun/Things-to-Do/Tours**).

Lake Eola Park: Take a walk on the mild side in downtown Orlando. The kids can play or feed the swans and summer sees live music and films at the Walt Disney Amphitheater (**bit.ly/brit-eola**).

Lake Tibet-Butler Preserve: Just 5mins from Disney but a world away from the theme park bustle (on local highway 535, Winter Garden-Vineland Road) is this local nature preserve, with quiet trails, lake overlook and interpretive centre. Open 9am–dusk (not public holidays), it is on the Great Florida Birding Trail and is a minor gem of native wildlife (**www.sfwmd.gov/recreation-site/tibet-butler-preserve-vera-carter-environmental-center**).

Lakeridge Winery and Vineyards: Join one of its fun, free wine-tasting tours and you'll know why Lakeridge (in nearby Clermont) has won more than 700 awards. Designate a driver as sample sizes are generous! 10am–5pm Mon–Sat, 11am–5pm Sun (**lakeridgewinery.com**).

Old Town, Kissimmee: The biggest vintage car parade in the US every Sat, with cars on display from 1pm and the Classic Car Cruise at 8.30pm, plus Wednesday Night Themed Car Show from 5pm and a Muscle Car Cruise 8.30pm each Fri, and live music 7–10pm (**myoldtownusa.com**).

Osceola County History Museum: Part of the Welcome Center on Highway 192 in Kissimmee (by Marker 15), this offers a great insight into the region's back-story and heritage (**osceolahistory.org**; see also p243; daily 10am–4pm, Tues–Sun, closed on public hols).

PLUS: Watching the participants at iFLY Orlando on I-Drive (p227); and the hiking trails of Ocala National Forest, north of Orlando (**stateparks.com/Ocala.html**).

Mon–Fri (407 836 2067); or Clermont Courthouse at Minneola City Hall, 800 North Highway 27, Minneola, 8.30am–4.30pm (closed noon–1pm; 352 394 2018). All are closed on US bank holidays. Both parties must be

Epcot's nightly Harmonious show

© Disney

present to apply for a licence, which costs $93.50 (in cash, travellers' cheques or by credit card) and is valid for 60 days, while a ceremony (equivalent to a British register office) can be performed at the same time by the clerk for an extra $30. You'll need passports, birth certificates and, if you have been married before, your decree absolute. After acquiring a licence, a couple can marry anywhere in Florida. It is also possible to obtain a licence BEFORE arriving in Florida (see **floridamarriagelicensebymail.com**). For flowers and floral design, be sure to look up Flourish on 407 644 7474 or **flourishproductions.com**).

Get Married in Florida: This local business has been dedicated to organising weddings for UK couples since 2002. Ideally placed to deliver great personal service, it offers the complete package for the perfect wedding (**getmarriedinflorida.com**).

Disney special occasions

Birthday badges: Get free badges from City Hall in the Magic Kingdom and Guest Services at EPCOT, Disney's Hollywood Studios and Disney's Animal Kingdom. Cast Members make a fuss over children (and adults!) wearing a birthday badge.

Birthday cakes: Contact room service at your resort or Guest Services at one of the parks. All Disney restaurants can offer ready-made 15cm/6in cakes ($39 at each restaurant) or something larger ($50–225) if ordered 48 hours in advance on 407 827 2253. If someone in your group has a birthday, tell the Cast Member at check-in (or when you make your reservation), as well as hosts and/or servers in restaurants. While not guaranteed, Disney staff often go out of their way to make the day special. If characters know it's a birthday when they sign a child's autograph book, they may add a special birthday wish.

Birthday cruise: Celebrate a special occasion with a 90-minute pontoon boat trip from one of five Disney resorts, complete with snacks, drinks, streamers and balloons for a 90min tour for up to 10 from $399, plus tax (407 939 7529).

Disney's Pirate Adventure: This two-hour activity for kids 4–12 sails (on pontoon boats) from two of the resorts (the Yacht/Beach Club and Caribbean Beach at 9.30am) to find pirate 'booty' at different ports of call, with a final stop for snacks; $39–49 per child (407 939 7529, up to 180 days in advance).

The Bourne Stuntacular

Money matters

You'll need to carry ID for both cheques and some credit card purchases (take your UK driving licence card).

Cash: It is worth separating larger notes from smaller ones in your wallet to avoid flashing all your money in view. Losing £300 of travellers' cheques shouldn't ruin your holiday – but losing $600 in cash might. All the theme parks have ATMs (cash machines).

FairFX card: Perhaps the best option is this convenient card, which you preload to a chosen amount (**fairfx. com**). The exchange rate is fixed at loading and you can save 5–10% on High Street currency rates.

Safety and security

While crime is not a serious issue in Florida, this is still big-city America. Tourism is such a vital part of the economy, the authorities have a highly safety-conscious attitude. Just don't ignore the usual safety guidelines for travelling abroad.

BRITTIP

Use a business rather than your home address on your luggage. It is less conspicuous and safer should any item be lost or stolen.

Disney's Typhoon Lagoon

© Disney

Simon and Susan

Apart from the *Brit Guide to Orlando*, we contribute to a wide range of media on many travel subjects. Find out more about our work on **venesstravelmedia.net**, our Facebook page, YouTube (Veness Travel Media), or Twitter (@VenessTravelMe1), including *Walt Disney World Hacks* and *The Hidden Magic of Walt Disney World, Third Edition*.

Common-sense tips: A bumbag (or 'fanny pack') is better than a handbag or shoulder bag in the parks. Make sure bags are always firmly zipped up when not in use. Don't leave camera equipment on view in the car (the heat could damage it anyway).

Dealing with assault: The VERY strong police advice in the unlikely event of being confronted by an assailant is: DO NOT resist or 'have a go', because this can often make a bad situation worse. But it is comforting to know Orlando does not have any no-go areas in the main tourist parts. The nearest is the portion of the Orange Blossom Trail south of downtown Orlando (a selection of strip clubs and 'adult bars').

Hotel security: Always use door peepholes and security chains when someone knocks at the door. DON'T open the door to strangers without asking for ID, and check with the hotel desk if you are not sure. Keep doors and windows locked and always use deadlocks and security chains. Take all valuables when you go out (or put them in the room safe), and don't leave the door open, even if you pop down the corridor to the ice machine.

Most hotels now have electronic card-locks and can offer deposit boxes as well as in-room mini-safes. Ask reception staff for safety advice for surrounding areas or if you are travelling somewhere you are not sure about. Safety is a major issue for the Central Florida Hotel & Lodging Association (**cfhla.org**) and hotel staff are well briefed to be helpful.

BRITTIP

If your room has been cleaned before you go out for the day, put the 'Do Not Disturb' sign on the door. Always keep valuables out of sight whether in the hotel or car.

Car safety: Make the basic safety checks of your hire car straight away and familiarise yourself with the car's controls BEFORE driving away. Try to memorise your route in advance, even if you just remember the road numbers. Most hire firms now give good directions to all the hotels, so check them before you set off (or, better still, hire a GPS system if you don't have one on your phone). Make sure the fuel tank is well filled and never let it get near empty so you risk running out of 'gas' in an unfamiliar area. If you do stray off your pre-determined route, stick to well-lit areas and ask for directions only from official businesses like hotels and petrol stations. Try to park close to your destination where there are plenty of lights and DO NOT get out if there are suspicious characters

around. Always lock the car when you leave it – note that not all rental cars have central locking.

More info: For more info on safety, contact the Orange County Police (**ocso.com**) or the I-Drive police team office (407 351 9368). If you are the victim of theft in Orange County, call 407 836 4357.

Emergencies

Emergency services: For police, fire department or ambulance, dial 911 (9-**911** from your hotel room). Make sure your children know this number.

General: For smaller-scale crises (e.g. mislaid tickets, lost passports or rescheduled flights), your holiday company should have an emergency number in the hotel reception.

You'll find masses of info on all things Orlando on the discussion forums at **attractiontickets.com** and, as we are both Moderators on the site, you can come and 'talk' to us and pass on your own ideas and experiences. It's a fun, friendly community and we're always happy to see new faces.

Weasley's Wizard Wheezes at Universal

© Universal Orlando Resort

© Universal Orlando Resort

© Disney

Christmas decorations at the Magic Kingdom

Enjoying some refreshment

© Disney

Know before you go

Here are the best sources for additional info before you go.

Kissimmee: More useful online info and a monthly e-newsletter at, **experiencekissimmee.com**.

Fan websites: Check out **thedibb. co.uk** ('Disney with a British accent', including busy forums, villa pages and more); the huge **wdwinfo.com**; and specialist UK Universal podcast **uuopodcast.blogspot.com**.

Attractions Magazine: (which we also write for) offers a feature-packed site, **attractionsmagazine.com**, plus all the latest theme park news and a terrific selection of videos.

Orlando Sentinel: The online local paper (**orlandosentinel.com**) is packed with info, especially for shopping, dining and nightlife, while the Orlando Weekly is also handy (**orlandoweekly.com**).

Visit Orlando: The official tourism bureau has a wealth of online resources, including trip-planning ideas and guides, as well as a handy App for info, news and tools to help you get the most out of your holiday (**visitorlando.com**).

And don't forget to check our website, **britguideorlando.net**, for valuable extra content and insider info that we can't squeeze into the book!

Seeing the real Florida

Central Florida is an amazing place (it's one of the reasons we live here) but it's not all about the theme parks. Venture beyond the main tourist areas and you'll discover the *real* Florida, which is bursting with great scenery and wildlife. It's not hard to see alligators, deer, raccoons, armadillos and even bobcats in the wild. There are also panthers, bears, wild pigs and foxes. The exotic birdlife includes eagles, ospreys, herons, cranes and egrets, and the waterways boast manatees, dolphins, rays and dozens of types of fish. Chapters 8 and 9 highlight how to discover these great opportunities and we urge readers to try at least one to experience what truly makes Florida special. There are many state parks and wildlife reserves and, increasingly, nature tours and trails to enjoy them. There is also more overt history – dating back to the 16th century – than you'd imagine, plus fabulous museums and other cultural aspects. Florida had cowboys (or 'crackers') before the Wild West and is still a huge cattle-producing state. Cute towns and suburbs like Gulfport, Mount Dora, Winter Park, Stuart, DeLand, Dunedin, Winter Garden and Tarpon Springs abound, while the beaches are simply superb – everywhere. The varied tropical terrain boasts lakes, marshes, cypress forests, sandhills, flatwoods and prairies, and is about as different to most European landscapes as it's possible to get. There are also two official **All American Road** routes to discover, through the Florida Keys (**scenichighwayflkeys.com**) and A1A Scenic Byway (**scenica1a.org**), along the historic north-east coast. It all adds up to way more than you thought when you decided Orlando was the place for you – just make sure you see some of it!

Now, on to the next step of the holiday, your transport….

Sunset on the pier at Hillstone restaurant in Winter Park

Christmas cheer

The festive season is our favourite time of year here, from late Nov–early Jan. Every park adds a fab Christmas overlay and there is more to enjoy everywhere, even at the smaller attractions and places like Disney Springs and the town of Celebration. It can get seriously crowded 17 Dec–10 Jan, but visit in early Dec and you get all the festivities with fewer crowds.

Walt Disney World: Every park has its own extensive decorations and magnificent Christmas tree, with a daily lighting ceremony at the **Magic Kingdom**, plus Mickey's Once Upon A Christmastime Parade, the Castle Dream Lights (a stunning effect on Cinderella Castle) and the chance to meet Santa, as well as the extra-ticket event of Mickey's Very Merry Christmas Party (p106). At **EPCOT**, the standout feature is the Candlelight Processional, a choral retelling of the Nativity story with a guest narrator, as well as Holidays Around The World, with traditional storytellers at each World Showcase pavilion. Mr and Mrs Claus visit the American Adventure pavilion, where vocal group Voices of Liberty become carollers for the season. **Disney Springs** features the Spirit of the Season, with Santa's chalet, school choirs and more lavish decorations, including the character-filled Christmas Tree Trail. Each resort also boasts plenty of Christmas cheer, with the best being Disney's Grand Floridian, offering a life-size Gingerbread House.

Universal Orlando: Miles more garland, lights and tinsel are on offer here, plus three daily features. At **Universal Studios**, Universal's Holiday Parade is a fabulous cavalcade of floats, giant balloons, Father Christmas and a tree-lighting ceremony at dusk each day, as well as carollers, hot cocoa kiosks and a Christmas Village of traditional fare and gifts. The Wizarding World of Harry Potter: Diagon Alley adds its own festive overlay, buskers in Kings Cross Station and a special Celestina Warbeck show. **Islands of Adventure** offers Christmas both Harry Potter and Dr Seuss style. Grinchmas can be found in Seuss Landing, including the family-friendly stage show *The Grinch Who Stole Christmas*. The Wizarding World of Harry Potter: Hogsmeade features the stunning projection show *The Magic of Christmas at Hogwarts Castle* multiple times each evening.

SeaWorld: Arguably the biggest Christmas celebration, with magnificent shows, special effects and extravagant theming. It starts with the Sea of Trees, a fabulous musical sequence spread over the main lagoon, and continues with the Christmas Marketplace and Rudolph's Christmastown at one end of the park. Two unmissable seasonal shows are Winter Wonderland On Ice and a Sounds of the Season live performance series, while nightly 'snowfalls', dancers, musicians and the Holiday Reflections fireworks round out a glittering seasonal occasion.

Busch Gardens: The centrepiece is Christmas Town, another after-dark spectacular throughout the park, with themed areas, shows and decorations (each Fri, Sat and Sun from late Nov/early Dec, and nightly from mid-Dec). Highlights include the Carol of the Bells, an Ice Show, the Three Kings Journey and a lavish array of seasonal dining and shopping, plus Santa's 'North Pole' home and some more superb lighting effects.

Gaylord Palms Resort: The hotel's annual ICE! Exhibition is a mind-boggling presentation of 2 MILLION pounds of ice in marvellous tableaux, hand-carved by Chinese artisans in the 'Florida Freezer,' including huge ice slides. There are festive presentations, a headline Cirque show, trees, snow-tubing, kids' activities and the chance to meet Santa, making for an astounding Christmas offering. Book in advance at **christmasatgaylordpalms.marriott.com/**.

Celebration: This pretty Disney-inspired town offers nightly 'snow-falls' 6–9pm on Market Street in Dec and also features ice-skating for kids, horse-drawn carriage rides, carollers and other festive touches.

And more: Downtown Orlando is well worth a visit for its many festive touches, notably around **Lake Eola**, which has Christmas trees, ice-skating and the nightly Holiday Lights show. The child-sized fun of **LEGOLAND Florida** boasts superb decorations and daily Tree Lighting, while the dinner shows add extra festive theming. One final event is at the **Central Florida Zoo**, where their new tradition of the Asian Lantern Festival has become a major hit. It features a series of clever set-piece LED lantern creations by Chinese artisans and runs on select evenings from Nov-Jan (**centralfloridazoo.org/lanterns/**).

3 Getting Around

Or, The Secret of Driving on the Wrong Side of the Road!

Arriving and driving in Orlando are among the biggest concerns for visitors, especially first-timers, but there's no need to worry. Although most people begin their holiday by leaving the airport in a newly acquired, automatic, left-hand-drive hire car on roads that can appear bewildering, driving here is a lot easier and more enjoyable than in the UK. Anyone familiar with the M25 should find Florida FAR less stressful.

Before you get to your hire car, though, you need to be aware of the arrival process at the two airports.

BRITTIP

Don't forget you must have filled in your ESTA form and immigration details online before you travel (p12). For country of residence put UNITED KINGDOM; for Passport Issuing Country, put UK – BRITISH CITIZEN. You must give a valid US address for your accommodation.

Orlando International

This is an efficient, modern airport, with its dazzling new Terminal C, where BA, Aer Lingus and others now arrive. Terminals A and B – still used by Virgin and most US domestic airlines – have four satellite arms, linked by a shuttle tram.

Terminal C is self-contained, from landing to ground transportation, with new baggage handling and then Customs and Immigration. Car hire and taxis, etc, are down on Level 1, while there is also a shuttle tram to the bigger Terminals A and B if you need anything there. The Immigration kiosks use a modern biometric scan system, with facial recognition, to help speed up the process. See more about the new Terminal on p310, including the fabulous array of food and beverage options.

Virgin Atlantic flights still arrive at Terminal B, satellite arm 4, where you go through Immigration *before* collecting your luggage. You then have the choice of putting it on another conveyor belt to the main building or taking it up the escalator yourself onto the shuttle tram. If you do the former, you need to cross the main hall to Terminal A and go down to Level 1 for the baggage reclaim, where there is also a Virgin Holidays tour desk. Car hire is also on Level 1. Allow at least an hour from landing to ground transportation. US domestic airlines use Terminal A, satellite arms 1 (gates 1–29) and 2 (100–129) as well as Terminal B, satellite arms 3 (gates 30–59) and 4 (70–99). Domestic arrivals don't have the double baggage conveyor for international flights at Terminals A and B. Passengers just take the tram to the main building and go down to Level 2.

Transfers: Kerbside pick-up – including for taxis, Uber and Lyft – is outside the doors on Level 2, at the bottom of the escalators or by your baggage reclaim. Some tour operators have help desks here, while Virgin has a reception desk on Level 1, side A.

The public bus system, Lynx (p40), operates ONLY from the A side of Level 1 (5am–10/11pm; 5am–8.20/10.30pm on Suns and public holidays), in spaces 38–41. Links 11 and 51 depart every hour or half-hour for Orlando city centre, while Links 42 and 111 serve I-Drive, and they take 40–60mins.

Car hire: All the main hire companies are on site (with 28 off-airport). The main 10 to choose from include *Brit Guide* partner **Alamo** (with new automated self-service kiosks), **Dollar, National, Thrifty, Hertz** and **Avis**, and all offer a full service. Complete your paperwork, then walk out of Level 1 across the road to the multi-storey car park.

BRITTIP

Car hire rates went through the roof in 2021/22 as a result of major shortages in inventory. Things should even out in 2023 but it pays to book as early as possible.

Leaving the airport: When you drive out of the airport, DON'T follow signs to 'Orlando'. The main tourist areas are south and west of the city, so follow the signs for your accommodation.

The Martin Andersen Beachline Expressway (528) and Greeneway (417) are both toll roads, so make sure you have some US currency before leaving the airport. Toll booths hate to change notes above $20, while some auto-tolls take ONLY coins.

- **For International Drive:** (I-Drive), take the north exit and the Beachline Expressway (Route 528) west until it crosses I-Drive just north of SeaWorld at exit 1 (it costs $2.75 in toll fees). Most hotels on I-Drive are to the north, so keep

Arriving at Melbourne Orlando International Airport

Florida Rail

Considering Florida was originally opened up by railways in the late 1800s by railroad barons Henry Flagler and Henry Plant, modern rail travel has been a poor option, until recently. Central Florida's commuter rail system **Sunrail** arrived in 2014 and offers a few tourist possibilities as it runs over a 49ml/78km, 16-station stretch from Poinciana, south of Kissimmee, to the city of DeBary north of Orlando. The best stretch for visitors to know about is from Sand Lake Rd station, at the junction with S. Orange Ave, to Church Street in downtown Orlando (2 stops) and Winter Park (5 stops). However, it ONLY operates Mon–Fri (and not public holidays), every 30mins in peak periods and every 2hrs otherwise, 5.30am–10pm. Fares are modest ($3.75/adult for a round-trip from Sand Lake Rd to Winter Park while an unlimited weekly SunCard is $42.50) and tickets can be bought in machines at each station using cash or credit card. Just tap your ticket on the validator machine on the platform before you board and at your destination. There are bus connections at every station, including Link 111 from SeaWorld and 42 from I-Drive to the Sand Lake Rd station (**sunrail.com**).

Florida's first high-speed rail, **Brightline**, opened in 2018, from West Palm Beach to Miami, with an extension to Orlando due to open in 2023. Orlando International Airport to downtown Miami will take 3hrs and feature the latest trains, two classes of travel and on-board comforts (including dining and free WiFi). Once complete, it will make the journey to Miami far more enticing, with multiple departures each way every day. Check out **gobrightline.com** for the latest info.

right at the exit. NB: there is now only one toll kiosk on this route but the fee is still $2.75.

- **For Kissimmee, Disney and villas in Clermont/Davenport:** Take the south exit for 3ml/5km and pick up the Central Florida Greeneway (Highway 417) west.

- **For most Disney resorts:** Take exit 6 and follow the signs ($3.50 in tolls).

- **For Animal Kingdom resorts:** Use exit 3 and take Osceola Parkway west ($4).

- **For eastern Kissimmee:** Come off Highway 417 at exit 11, the Orange Blossom Trail (Highway 17/92), and go south ($2.50 in tolls).

- **For west Kissimmee and Clermont/Davenport (Highway 27):** Take exit 2, turn right on Celebration Avenue and left (west) on Highway 192 all the way to Highway 27 (you will need $4 in toll fees).

━━━━━BRITTIP ⚡

For traffic news and reports, tune to 107.3FM (WDBO) or **wdbo.com**. Call 511 on a mobile phone for motorway traffic info or **fl511.com**.

Melbourne Orlando International Airport

New in 2022 was this regional gateway for **TUI**, having moved from Orlando Sanford Airport. The first thing to know is that it is further away from Orlando than Sanford (71 miles to International Drive rather than 42) and it could take 90mins to make the drive. If you're staying in a villa on Highway 27, it could take up to 2hrs. The good news is TUI get express treatment at the airport, straight from plane to Immigration and baggage reclaim, then off to Orlando via pre-arranged shuttle or hire car. The arrival process could be even quicker than Orlando International, while baggage screening will use the latest computer scanning technology to speed things even further.

Ground transport: As you exit the Customs building, you will see TUI's dedicated Welcome Center, with a desk for villa clients and another for Alamo, National and Enterprise (TUI's car hire partners). Five more rental companies, including Dollar, Budget and Hertz, are in the main terminal while TUI's bus transport is to one side. The airport aims to have people deplaned and into the Welcome

Center in 45 minutes or less via their new baggage hall and expanded Customs hall, and the whole complex is compact and user-friendly. See more at **mlbair.com** (and Chapter 13 for departure details).

Leaving the airport: It is 93mls from Melbourne to the villa epicentre of Highway 27, and, while it is slightly quicker to use I-95 and 528 than the more direct 192 and Central Florida Greeneway, it is actually a longer drive with more tolls. Happily, both routes are pretty basic and easy to drive, although the 528 will cost $5.50 in tolls and the Greeneway $4.50. You can join motorway I-95 right outside the airport and go north for 23mls to pick up the 528. You can stay on 192 for the full drive west to Kissimmee, I-4 and

Highway 27, but it will usually be 15–20 minutes slower, with more traffic. Either way, be ready for a longish drive before you can relax at your hotel or villa.

WITHOUT A CAR

Although being mobile is advisable, you can survive without a car. However, few attractions are within walking distance of hotels, and taxis can be expensive. You also need to plan in extra travelling time (and with children, taking buses can be tiring). For non-drivers, your best base is either Walt Disney World itself (free transport throughout, but harder to get to the rest of Orlando) or I-Drive for its location, 'walkability' and the great I-Ride Trolley. Many hotels have free shuttles to some of the parks or a cheap, regular mini-bus service. The main options are: public transport; shuttle services; taxis/ride-shares.

Public transport

Lynx bus system: Reliable and cheap but slightly plodding, it covers much of metro Orlando. Its online system map shows all its routes (or 'links') and main attractions (407 841 5969, **golynx.com**).

- **Link 18:** Kissimmee to downtown Orlando (from Osceola Square Mall, east on Highway 192 north on Boggy Creek Road, Buenaventura and Orange Ave).

- **Link 38:** I-Drive to downtown Orlando (from the Convention Center via Kirkman Road and I-4).

- **Link 42:** Orlando International Airport to I-Drive.

- **Link 55:** Kissimmee to Four Corners (from Osceola Square Mall west via Highway 192 and Summer Bay Resort).

Disney's Skyliner

© Disney

- **Link 56:** Kissimmee to Disney's Magic Kingdom (from Osceola Square Mall, along Highway 192 via Old Town and Celebration to TTC).

- **Link 300:** Disney Springs to downtown Orlando (via I-4).

- **Link 304:** Top of I-Drive to Disney Springs (from Oak Ridge Road via Sand Lake Road).

- **Link 350:** Downtown Orlando to Disney Springs via SeaWorld/I-Drive.

BRITTIP

Lynx buses use the Disney Springs West Side Transfer Center as their Disney hub, with Link 300 going to the Transportation and Ticket Center, Disney's bus hub.

Lynx fares are $2/ride (free transfers) or $16 for a weekly pass (children six and under free with a full-fare passenger). The service is every 30mins in the main areas, every 15mins 6–9am and 3.30–6.30pm, but you must have the right change. All buses are wheelchair accessible and stop at the pink paw-print Lynx stops.

There can be *long* bus queues at park closing. Taking a taxi can save a lot of hassle to return to I-Drive – about $30–45 from EPCOT and the Studios park; about $40–45 from Magic Kingdom and Animal Kingdom. Uber or Lyft can often be a third less than that.

- **I-Ride Trolley:** Great-value, two-route service along a 14ml/23km stretch of this tourist corridor.

Jurassic World VelociCoaster at Universal's Islands of Adventure

© Universal Orlando Resort

Park maps

Each of the park maps contains a QR code that you can scan with your smartphone or tablet to take you to a high-res online map. Download a QR reader from iTunes or Play Store.

- **The Main/Red Line:** 38 stops from Orlando International Premium Outlets at the top of I-Drive to SeaWorld and Aquatica via Westwood Boulevard and Sea Harbor Drive, then Orlando Vineland Premium Outlets.

- **The Green Line:** 29 stops from the Universal resort (Windhover Drive and Major Boulevard) south to Vineland Premium Outlets via Universal Boulevard, the Convention Center and SeaWorld.

Every day, 8am–10.30pm roughly every 25–40mins, it costs $2/trip ($1/kids 3–9, 25c/seniors) – have the right change – or you can buy Unlimited Ride Passes for 1, 3, 5, 7 or 14 days at $5, $7, $9, $12, $18. If you need to transfer between routes, ask for a transfer coupon when you board (not needed with Unlimited Ride Passes). All trolleys have hydraulic wheelchair lifts. Buy a pass at 100+ locations in the I-Drive area and at most hotel desks, plus online, but NOT on the trolleys themselves (**iridetrolley.com**).

Busch Shuttle Express: Six departure points in this regular daily service, 8.15–9.40am, from SeaWorld to Busch Gardens. This is FREE with any advance ticket for Busch (notably the 3-Park Ticket with SeaWorld and Aquatica). See **buschgardens.mears.com** for the latest info.

BRITTIP

The cheapest way to get from I-Drive to Disney is the $2 Lynx bus Link 350 from SeaWorld – 6600 Sea Harbor Drive – to the TTC next to the Magic Kingdom. All Disney transport then operates from there. Use the I-Ride Trolley to get to SeaWorld.

Shuttle services

Several dozen firms offer alternatives to public transport, with set-fee shuttles from hotels to attractions.

FL Tours: A popular company specialising in shuttles from Orlando International Airport to Disney, Universal and the Kissimmee area, plus Port Canaveral transfers. One-way trips from $95 and round trips from $180, plus tip; also a free 15min grocery stop and kids' booster and car seats; 24-hour online reservation; no extra charge for late pick-ups (**fltours.com**).

Lake Buena Vista Factory Stores: Shuttle collects guests free each day from 60 hotels in the Orlando and Kissimmee areas (**lbvfs.com/free-hotel-shuttles**).

Maingate Transportation: with scheduled services from the airport to all the main tourist areas, and most hotels to the attractions (**maingate.net**).

Mears: The most comprehensive service, with a 1,000-vehicle fleet from limousines to coaches. Typical round-trip shuttle fares: Airport to I-Drive, $35 and $27 ($23 and $18 one way); Airport to Highway 192 in Kissimmee, $42 and $33 ($30 and $24 one way); Disney to Universal Orlando or I-Drive, $23 round trip.

You can book a shuttle on arrival at the Mears' desks in the luggage halls, but it can be a longish trip if it has a full van stopping at several hotels before yours (**mearstransportation.com**). **Mears Connect** replaced Disney's Magical Express in 2022 for direct service from Orlando Airport to all Disney hotels. See **mearsconnect.com** for details and pricing.

Quick Transportation: Another reliable operator for round-trip airport service – which can include a grocery stop – and transport to the theme parks and other attractions, including Kennedy Space Center, with competitive rates (**quicktransportation.com**).

Sunshine Flyer: New in 2022, this direct Orlando Airport-Disney hotel service aims to make up for the cancellation of Disney's Magical Express in 2021, with specific service to every Disney resort.

Their modern coaches are designed like vintage 1920s transport and they aim to make the journey (which can take up to an hour with various drop-offs) a fun experience. It costs $17/adult and $12.50 per child one way ($34 and $25 round-trip; **sunshineflyer.com**).

Excursions: There are also tours offered by *Brit Guide* partners Gray Line Orlando (**graylineorlando.com**), Real Florida Adventures and City Sightseeing Orlando (see more on p248).

> **BRITTIP**
>
> Be firm with the car hire check-in clerk if they push you for extras, like car upgrades you won't need.

Taxis

For groups of four or five, taxis can be more cost-effective than shuttles. Orlando International to I-Drive would be around $45 (plus tip); $45–75 for the Kissimmee area; $55–68 to Disney resorts; $15–20 I-Drive to Universal Orlando; and $20–30 I-Drive to Disney Springs. You'll find plenty of taxis in ranks at parks, hotels and shopping centres, but they don't cruise for fares. Elsewhere, you should pre-book. Reliable companies will show a driver's ID, insurance and rates. It's illegal for drivers to look for fares in the airport baggage hall. All taxis will be on Level 1. Most are metered but you can ask what the fare is likely to be. Some hotels have Town Cars at their ranks which don't have meters.

Steakhouse 71 at Disney's Contemporary Resort

© Disney

Reliable firms: Mears operate Checker Cabs, Yellow Cabs and City Cabs (407 422 2222); or try **Quick Cab** (407 447 1444) or **Diamond Cab** (407 523 3333).

App-based ride-sharing services **Uber** and **Lyft** are both popular, with the usual caveat about prices varying with demand (**uber.com/global/en/cities/orlando, lyft.com/rider/cities/orlando-fl**).

WITH A CAR

Having a car is the key to being in charge of your holiday. There are dozens of hire companies and rates can be as low as $200/week for the smallest car. Orlando is also the world's largest car-hire market so you should never be short of choice.

BRITTIP

Your first call for car hire should be to *Brit Guide* partner Alamo. See inside the front cover for our special offer or visit **alamo.co.uk/brits**.

The cars will be mainly American – Chevrolet, Dodge, Buick, plus international makes like Kia, Hyundai, Honda and Nissan.

- **Economy or Subcompact:** Usually a Vauxhall Corsa-sized hatchback.

- **Compact:** Small family saloon like a Nissan Versa.

- **Midsize or Intermediate:** 4-door, 5-seater like a Toyota Corolla.

- **Fullsize:** Larger-style executive car like a Ford Mondeo.

- **Premium, Luxury, Convertible, SUV and Minivan:** Upmarket options, while the Minivan is a Ford Galaxy or Renault Espace type.

Most holiday companies offer 'free car hire', but it is only the rental cost that is free. You must still pay the insurance and taxes (which makes all-inclusive packages more attractive).

Also beware low starting rates. Essential insurances and surcharges can practically double the weekly rate. However, most companies now offer all-inclusive rates that work out cheaper if booked in advance.

Car rental companies: Alamo is our *Brit Guide* partner and offers excellent rates and service (see inside front cover). You also benefit from choosing your own car in each range, where most other companies assign a specific car. Or try Dollar (**dollar.co.uk**), Avis (**avis.co.uk**), Budget (**budget.co.uk**), or Thrifty (**thrifty.co.uk**), or comparison website **carrentals.co.uk**.

Insurance: You must have a credit card. There are two main kinds of insurance: Loss or Collision Damage Waiver (LDW or CDW) costs $29–32/day and covers any damage to the car. You can do without it, but you'll pay a hefty deposit on your credit card, and you are liable for ANY damage. Liability Insurance Supplement (LIS) or Extended Protection costs $13–16/day. It is not essential but covers most damage you might cause.

BRITTIP

The Central Florida Expressway Authority has a handy money-saving option for all automated tolls in the area as an alternative to the pricey rates charged by the hire companies. Called **Visitor Toll Pass**, it works via an App and guarantees the lowest toll rates at all times. See more at **visitortollpass.com**.

Another option is Underinsured Motorists Protection (in case someone with minimal cover runs into you) at around $9 a day.

Specialist insurance: You can cut costs by taking specialist insurance like Insurance4CarHire (0844 892 1770, **insurance4carhire.com**), offering an annual policy, including CDW/LDW and LIS, from £125. **iCarHire Insurance** also features independent insurance, including CDW/LDW from £8/day (**icarhireinsurance.com**).

Other costs: Drivers must be at least 21, and those under 25 pay an extra $25 a day. Other costs include local and state taxes, plus Airport Access and 'Facility' fees, which can

The satnav solution

The best way to navigate is by a GPS, especially if you don't trust your phone to work consistently in Florida. All car hire companies offer this as an extra (at $90–105/week) or you can bring your own. If your system has only the base-level (i.e. UK) maps loaded, download the maps for the USA for around £35. If you are thinking of buying a GPS system, the likes of Wal-Mart offer new systems, fully loaded for the US, for as little as $50.

add more than $40 a week. Many companies also offer a Roadside Plus (around $5/day), which covers flat tyres, running out of fuel or locking your keys in the car, but this is optional.

Fuel: 'Gas' is still cheaper than in the UK. You can either pre-pay for a full tank (so you bring it back empty; the charge is usually slightly under the local rate/gallon for this); fill it up yourself so you have a full tank on return; or pay a fuel surcharge at the end for the company to refill the tank (the most expensive option).

Pre-pay tolls: You can also opt for the SunPass auto-pay system, so you just drive through; all your tolls are auto-recorded for payment when you return the car. It is called PlatePass or TollPass and there is a flat-rate fee ($5–11/day, depending on the company, up to a maximum of $20–53/month). But the new Visitor Toll Pass option (p43) is much cheaper.

Universal Orlando

© Universal Orlando Resort

You must stop at the toll booths marked 'Change Given' (in green) or 'Exact Change Only' (in blue) unless you have accepted the SunPass pre-pay auto-toll from the car rental firm, or the Expressway's Toll Pass, in which case, use 'Sunpass' or 'E-Pass'.

Getting used to your car

Most people find driving in the US is a pleasure, because almost all hire cars are automatics and nearly new. Speed limits are lower (and rigidly enforced), so you are rarely rushed into taking a wrong turn.

- All cars have air-conditioning, which is essential for most of the year. Turn on the fan as well as the A/C button or it won't work! A small pool of liquid will form under the car from condensation.

- Power steering is universal.

- Larger cars have cruise control, so you can set the desired speed and take your foot off the accelerator. There will be two buttons on the steering wheel, one to switch on cruise control, the other to set the speed. To cancel, either press the first button or touch the brake.

- Keep your foot on the brake when you are stationary as automatics tend to creep forward. Always put the gear lever in 'P' (Park) when switching off.

- To start, put the gear in 'P' and depress the brake, then put in 'D' to drive. D1 and D2 are extra gears for hills (none in Florida)!

- Not all cars have central locking, so make sure you lock ALL the doors before leaving it. With an automatic, put on the handbrake and put the gear lever in 'park' or the keys will lock in the ignition.

Fuel: All local gas stations are self-service and you pay before filling up. However, the pumps should allow you to pay by credit card without having to visit the cashier (some stations ask for a local zip code with a credit card swipe, which means you DO need to go inside). To activate the petrol pump, you may need first to lift the lever underneath the pump nozzle.

BRITTIP

RaceTrac and the three Speedway stations in Walt Disney World are among the cheapest, while the Wal-Mart on Vineland Road is also a cheaper option. Petrol stations just *outside* Disney and the airport are the most expensive.

Finding your way

Your car hire company should provide you with a basic map of Orlando, plus directions to your hotel, but these days most people get their info online.

BRITTIP

Be organised – get your directions in advance off the internet at sites like **mapquest.com** or use Google Earth to source maps, directions and even check out the lie of the land in advance. Download it free from its website at **google.com/earth**.

Signposting: Leaving the theme parks can be harder than getting to them in the first place as the exit route may be different. Familiarise yourself with the main roads in advance and learn to navigate by road numbers (given on the signposts), exit numbers off the main roads, and directions around the attractions (i.e. if you want I-4 east or west or 192 as you exit Walt Disney World).

Lanes and exits: Exits off motorways can be on EITHER side of the carriageway, not just on the right, and you don't get much notice. You can overtake in ANY lane on multi-lane highways, and it's OK to sit in the middle lane until you see your exit.

Road names: Around town, road names are displayed at every junction suspended ABOVE the road underneath the traffic lights. This road name is NOT the road you are on, but the one you are CROSSING.

There is little advance notice of each junction and road names can be hard to read, especially at night, so keep your speed down if you think you are close to your turn-off to allow time to get into the correct lane. If you do miss a turning, most roads are on a grid system, so it's easy to work back.

Occasionally you will meet a crossroads where no right of way is obvious. This is a Four-Way Stop, and the priority goes in order of arrival. So, when it's your turn, just indicate and pull out slowly (America doesn't have many roundabouts, so this may be the closest you get to one).

Mars Rover Concept vehicle at Kennedy Space Center

© Kennedy Space Center

Rules and regulations

As well as driving on the opposite side of the road, there are several differences in procedure.

Tolls: For toll roads, have some change handy in amounts from 25c to $3. Most give change (in the GREEN lanes), but you will get through quicker if you have the correct money (in the BLUE lanes). On minor exits of Osceola Parkway and the Greeneway, there are auto-toll machines *only*, so keep some loose change to hand. Several exits of the Florida Turnpike will now take SunPass **only**, not cash, hence PlatePass or Visitor Toll Pass is valuable if you plan to travel widely (p43–44). Look up the main Toll Calculator site for central Florida on **cfxway.com/for-travelers/#**.

Traffic lights: The most frequent British errors occur at traffic lights (which are hung above the road). At a red light, you can still turn RIGHT providing there is no traffic coming from the left. Stop, check there are no pedestrians crossing and make your turn – unless there is a sign indicating 'No turn on red'. Turning left at the lights, you have the right of way with a green ARROW but must give way to traffic from the other direction on a SOLID green. A YELLOW flashing arrow means it is OK to turn left providing the way is clear.

Left turns: The majority of accidents involving overseas visitors take place on left turns, so take extra care. There is also no amber light from red to green, but there IS from green to red. A flashing amber light at a junction means proceed but watch for traffic joining the carriageway, while a flashing red light indicates it is okay to turn if the carriageway is clear.

BRITTIP

On nearly all toll roads, for the manned toll booths you have to pull in to a slip road on the right to pay. It is SunPass/E-Pass only on the main carriageway. This can catch you out when you have just left the airport.

BRITTIP

The Osceola Parkway toll road (522) that runs parallel to Highway 192 is a better route to Walt Disney World from east Kissimmee and costs only $2.50. Use Sherberth Road for Disney access from west 192 or the Western Beltway (Highway 429).

Speed limits: Speed limits are well marked with black numbering on white signs and the police are hot on speeding, with steep fines. There are varying limits of 55–70mph/88–113kph on the Interstates, where there is also a 40mph/64kph minimum speed limit. It can be just 15–25mph/24–40kph in built-up areas.

BRITTIP

Parents, to make sure of a professionally trained driver for your taxi or transfer, download the KidMoto App to ensure the right car seats, etc, at **kidmoto.taxi**.

Seat belts: These are compulsory for all passengers, while child seats must be used for under-4s and can be hired from the car companies at $10–15 a day (so bring your own or buy one locally for $70–80). Also 4 and 5-year-olds *must* use either a car or booster seat, depending on the child's size.

Parking: It is illegal to park within 10ft/3m of a fire hydrant or a lowered kerb, or in front of a yellow-painted kerb (they are stopping points for emergency vehicles and you will be towed away), while you should never park ON a kerb. Park bonnet first – reverse parking is frowned upon because number plates are only on the rear of cars and police then can't see them. If you park parallel to the kerb, you must point in the direction of traffic.

Other traffic laws: Flashing orange lights over the road indicate a school zone, with reduced speed limit, while school buses must NOT be overtaken in either direction when they are unloading and have their hazard lights on. U-turns are forbidden in built-up areas and where there is a solid line down the middle of the road. You must pull to the side of the road to allow emergency vehicles to pass, in either direction, when the lights and/or sirens are on. Also, on multi-lane highways in Florida, the Move Over law means you must pull into an adjacent lane if you see a police car on the hard shoulder, or slow right down if you can't move over. And you must put on your lights in the rain.

Finally, DON'T drink and drive. Florida has strict laws, with penalties of up to 6 months in prison for first-time offenders. The blood-alcohol limit is lower than in Britain, so it is safer not to drink at all if you are driving. It is also illegal to carry open containers of alcohol in the car.

Bonus for AA members:
Produce your AA card where you see the AAA 'Show & Save' signs to enjoy some handy discounts. Visit **autoclubsouth.aaa.com** and click Discounts & Rewards for the full range, which includes shopping and dining, like 10% off at Hard Rock Café and Dennys restaurants (use the zip code 32819). You can also get maps and books from their office in Lake Mary in Seminole County (near Sanford).

Accidents
In the unlikely event of an accident, no matter how minor, you must contact the police before moving the cars (except on the busy I-4). Car hire firms will insist on a full police report for the insurance. If you break down, there should be an emergency number for the hire company in its literature or, if you are on a main highway, raise the bonnet and wait for one of the frequent police patrol cars to stop (or dial *FHP on your mobile). *Always* carry your driving licence and car hire forms when driving, in case you are stopped.

Key routes
All main motorways are prefixed I, the even numbers going east–west and odd numbers north–south. Federal Highways are the next grade down, with black numerals on white shields, while state roads are prefixed SR (black numbers on white circular or rectangular signs).

All American motorways have their junctions numbered in mileage terms, which makes it easy to calculate journey distances. I-4 starts at exit 1 in Tampa and goes to exit 132 at Daytona, 132ml/211km away. In Orlando, the main junctions run from exit 55, at Highway 27, to exit 87 (Winter Park) and exit 101 for the town of Sanford. Downtown Orlando can be found off exits 82B to 85.

BRITTIP
The big I-4 junction for Disney Springs and Lake Buena Vista (Exit 68) is likely to see extra congestion for the next two years as the western side is completely rebuilt, including on the site of the old Crossroads Plaza.

Interstate 4: I-4 is the main route through Orlando, a four, six or eight-lane motorway linking the coasts. Interstates are always indicated on blue shield-shaped signs. It also now features express (toll) lanes from Sand Lake Rd (Exit 74) to Longwood (Exit 94), so beware using these if you don't have PlatePass or Toll Pass. All the attractions of Walt Disney World, Universal Orlando and SeaWorld are well signposted from I-4. LEGOLAND Florida in Winter Haven, Lake Wales and Bok Tower Gardens are a 45min drive from Orlando west on I-4 and

Peppa Pig Theme Park

© Legoland

south on Highway 27, while Busch Gardens is 90mins down I-4 to Tampa. I-4 can be packed in the morning and evening rush hours; check for traffic on **fl511.com** or Google maps on your phone.

International Drive: I-Drive is the second key local road, linking 14½ml/24km of hotels, shops, restaurants and attractions like ICON Park, Pointe Orlando and Orlando Premium Outlets. From I-4, take exits 71, 72, 74A or 75A going east, or 75A, 74A or 72 going west. I-Drive is also bisected by Sand Lake Road and runs into World Center Drive (536) to the south, also convenient for Disney. I-Drive is a huge tourist centre and makes an excellent base, especially around Sand Lake Road, as it's pedestrian-friendly. It's a 20min drive to Disney and 10mins from Universal. However, at peak times, heavy traffic means it's best to avoid the stretch from the Convention Center north. Use Universal Boulevard instead. Try to bypass I-4 from exits 60–68 in the daily rush-hours, too, as traffic can be severe.

Kissimmee: The other main tourist area, south of Orlando and south-east of Disney, its features are grouped along a 20ml/32km stretch of the Irlo Bronson Memorial Highway (192), which intersects I-4 at junction

SheiKra at Busch Gardens

64B, and is close to Walt Disney World (though a good 25mins from SeaWorld and Universal). Downtown Kissimmee is off Main Street, Broadway and Emmett Street, and is ideal for walking.

The unique Disney-created town of Celebration is also here (just south of Walt Disney World).

Highway 27: At the west end of Highway 192, running north to Clermont and south to Davenport (and Haines City) is a major area of holiday villas, convenient for Disney – although some owners claim to be 'only 5mins from Disney' when they are 20–30mins away! The area features shops and restaurants, notably at Cagan Crossings just north of where 192 meets 27.

Western Beltway: Highway 429 provides a west Orlando bypass, avoiding I-4 to link with the Florida Turnpike and Apopka. It offers Disney entry at exit 8 (Western Way), which is handy for the Davenport/ Clermont areas. This junction also features Flamingo Crossings, with a fast-developing area of hotels, restaurants and a big Target store.

ChampionsGate: Right on I-4 at exit 58 is this mushrooming area of hotels, shops, apartments and restaurants, which makes for a handy self-contained destination as an alternative to Highway 192. Dining includes Red Robin, Chili's, Miller's Ale House, First Watch Café, 4 Corners Tavern and the British-owned Fish & Chip Shop, among a growing array of choice (**championsgate.com/restaurants**).

BRITTIP

Sadly, the morning traffic on I-4 east can be almost solid from Exit 55 to 68. You're often better off staying on 27 to go north, then east on 192; getting on the (toll) 429 to get to Disney via the Western Way; or getting off at ChampionsGate to take Osceola Polk Line Rd east to Old Lake Wilson Rd and north to Highway 192.

Now, let's go on to the next vital step – your holiday accommodation….

4 Accommodation

Or, Making Sense of American Hotels, Motels and Villas

Choosing your accommodation is the first major decision in store and, as with everything in Orlando, there is a massive array of options. There are more than 500 hotels, 26,000 villas and additional possibilities with Airbnb. Finding the right place for you will be the key to a memorable holiday.

The main choice is between a traditional hotel and one of the many self-catering villas/vacation homes or condos. Do you want the extra space, style and amenity of a villa, or do you prefer having your room made up every day? Prefer to save money by doing your own cooking and laundry or do you want resort facilities on tap? Those are the main differences between villa and hotel, along with the all-important question of location. Most vacation homes are some distance from the parks and, with traffic to deal with as well, you could be a 30 or 45-minute drive from Disney or Universal each day. But hotels close to Disney all come at a premium, so you can save money if you don't mind a longer journey.

BRITTIP

As much as we like Disney's hotels, there were big price increases in 2022, with even the Value hotels topping $200/night, so it pays to shop around for good deals.

Endless Summer Resort at Universal

© Universal Orlando Resort

© Disney

The reopening of the All-Star Sports Resort

The right location

Being on-site at Disney or Universal is obviously the ideal way to enjoy the parks, but their hotels are among the most expensive. The closest areas to Disney are Lake Buena Vista and West Highway 192 in Kissimmee, which allow you to avoid busy motorway I-4 for the most part. There is a good range of budget-priced hotels on the 192 in particular. International Drive is ideal for Universal and SeaWorld, and not too far from Disney, and has the highest concentration of hotels as well as good public transport (p40–43). There is an increasingly sophisticated choice, too, with upmarket brands like Four Seasons, Ritz-Carlton and Waldorf Astoria on offer. We therefore break down the hotel choice by area, starting with Disney and Universal, then I-Drive, Lake Buena Vista and Kissimmee.

Go south of Highway 192 and you find all the main villa developments (in purpose-built sub-divisions), especially on Highway 27, which runs north–south on the western edge of the Kissimmee area. There are some beautiful properties to choose from, nearly all with their own private pools, and some positively mansion-esque, but there are far fewer restaurant choices nearby and you *will* need a hire car, and longer drives to the attractions. Some villa developments are now as far south as Haines City on Highway 27, which is 27ml/43km from the Magic Kingdom and 31ml/49km from Universal.

Prices

Hotel and villa rates are cheaper out of main holiday periods. Ask for rates if you book direct and check for special rates (don't be afraid to request their 'best rate' at off-peak times, which can be lower than published or 'rack' rates). There may be an extra charge for more than two adults sharing a room ($5–15 per person), plus there is state tax and, sometimes, a sneaky Resort Fee that can add $15–35/day. Once you move away from Walt Disney World, the hotel choice becomes more diverse. Budget types are common, and *where* you stay affects the price. East on Highway 192, hotels and motels are cheaper (and more basic). On I-Drive, hotels south of Sand Lake Road are more expensive than the northern stretch. Shop around, and feel free to ask to see a room before you book.

Bookings: Compare prices on sites like **Priceline** (priceline.com), **Kayak** (kayak.co.uk) and **Expedia** (expedia.co.uk) but also check on hotel websites as they often have special rates for booking direct.

Rosen at Pointe Orlando

© Rosen

HOTELS

Orlando is chain-hotel territory. All the big brand names are here, plus independents like the Rosen hotels. The general standard is consistently good, with rooms often much larger than in Europe. Many feature two queen-sized beds but couples without children can request a king room for extra space. All US hotels charge per room, and not per person, and a family of four (with younger children) can usually fit in one room. Meals are rarely included, but many budget choices provide a simple buffet breakfast.

Most hotels are big, clean, efficient and great value. You'll find plenty of soft-drink and ice machines (though it's cheaper to buy drinks from a supermarket), with ice buckets in all rooms. Rooms are air-conditioned, so you have to get used to the drone of the A/C unit. If you need more space, look for an all-suites hotel, which has living rooms and mini-kitchens, as well as 1–3 bedrooms. Happily, all Orlando hotels have brought in advanced cleaning and sanitising procedures in the wake of the pandemic.

Budget hotels

The big hotel groups have multiple brands in this range, all with pools but not restaurants or bars. Some provide a free breakfast and offer fridges, microwaves and free wi-fi.

- Choice Hotels offer the **EconoLodge** and **Rodeway Inn** brands (1877 424 6423, **choicehotels.com**).

- **Motel 6** (1800 899 9841, **motel6.com**).

- Red Lion Hotels have two brands, **America's Best Value Inn** and **Knights Inn** (1877 737 9275, **redlion.com**).

- **Red Roof Inn** (1877 843 7663, **redroof.com**).

- Wyndham Hotels have four brands, **Days Inn, Super 8, Howard Johnson** and **Travelodge** (1800 407 9832, **wyndhamhotels.com**).

BRITTIP

Hotels designated Maingate East or Maingate West should be close to Disney's main entrance on Highway 192, though it is wise to check.

Gran Destino Tower at Coronado Springs

SS

Value choices

In the bigger chains, you find better facilities, not all with a restaurant, but many provide a breakfast option.

- **Best Western** (1800 780 7234 in US, **bestwestern.com**).

- **Choice Hotels** feature the **Comfort, Clarion,** and **Quality** hotels (1877 424 6423, **choicehotels.com**).

- **Country Inn & Suites** (1800 830 5222, **countryinns.com**).

- **Extended Stay America** (1800 804 3724, **extendedstayamerica.com**).

- Hilton brands here include **Doubletree, Hampton Inn & Suites, Home2 Suites, Homewood Suites** and **Tru by Hilton** (1800 445 8667, **hilton.com**).

- InterContinental Hotels (IHG) offer **Candlewood Suites, Holiday Inn, Holiday Inn Express** and **Staybridge Suites** (1877 424 2449, **ihg.com**).

- Marriott Hotels feature **Aloft, Fairfield Inn, Residence Inn, TownePlace Suites** and **Springhill Suites** (1888 236 2427, **marriott.com**).

- Wyndham Hotels have another six brands, **Baymont Inn & Suites, Hawthorn Suites, La Quinta Inn & Suites, Ramada, TRYP** and **Wingate Inn** (1800 407 9832, **wyndhamhotels.com**).

Kidsuites = happy families

Orlando has pioneered a great family accommodation style, worth seeking out if you have kids who enjoy bunk beds. Basically, a kidsuite is a separate area within the hotel room that gives the kids their own 'bedroom' (with bunks), usually also with their own TV and games consoles.

Moderate hotels

If you're looking for more amenities, including the guarantee of a restaurant and bar, this range of big-brand hotels is worth considering. All provide a good pool (often with extras like a waterslide, kids' pool and/or playground), a gym and at least one restaurant, bar and café, plus extra in-room comforts.

- **Crowne Plaza Hotels** (1877 227 6963, **ihg.com/crowneplaza**).

- Hilton hotels offer **Embassy Suites** and **Hilton Garden Inn** (1800 445 8667, **hilton.com**).

- **Hyatt Place** (1800 233 1234, **hyatt.com/brands/hyatt-place**).

- Marriott hotels feature **AC Hotels, Courtyard by Marriott, Element, Delta** and **Sheraton brands** (1888 236 2427, **marriott.com**).

- **Wyndham Hotels** (1877 999 3223; **wyndhamhotels.com/wyndham**).

La Quinta Inn by Wyndham, I-Drive

© Wyndham Hotels

Disney Dining Plans

This perk of staying onsite allows guests to pre-pay for most meals, but it is an *expensive* option: from $55–120 per adult per DAY ($26–48 per child 3–9). There are 4 tiers and all include a mug (usually $20) for free refills of sodas, etc, at the resort.

Quick Service Dining Plan: Two counter-service meals and two snacks a day. Counter-service meals are an entrée or combo meal, plus dessert and drink (alcoholic for guests 21+) for lunch/dinner; an entrée or combo meal and drink for breakfast. Snacks can be items like ice-cream, popcorn, pastry, fruit, crisps, bottled drink, soda, tea/coffee.

Disney Dining Plan: One table-service meal, one counter-service and two snacks per day. Table-service meals are an entrée, dessert and drink (alcoholic for guests 21+).

Disney Dining Plan Plus: Adds a second table-service meal in place of a counter-service option.

Deluxe Dining Plan: Three meals (table or counter) and two snacks a day.

All meals do NOT have to be used per day and can be spread over your stay, so you can miss one day, then use two credits another day. Gratuities are NOT included. Dining Plans CAN be used for Character Meals, when one table-service meal is required per person (two at ultra-popular Cinderella's Royal Table in Magic Kingdom), and for the 14 'signature' restaurants in WDW, which all require two table-service meals. They can also be used at the Hoop-Dee-Doo dinner shows (p267), at two table-service credits per person.

However, ALL members of the group must book a Plan for the full duration of the stay and inclusive of park tickets. It is also advisable to pre-book full-service meals well in advance. See more at **bit.ly/brit-disney** where you can book table service restaurants online. *NB: Disney suspended Dining Plans in 2020 but their return is expected in 2023.*

Deluxe hotels

Then there are the Deluxe brands like Autograph Collection, Four Seasons, Hyatt Regency, Loews, Marriott, Omni and Ritz-Carlton. We highlight some of the best choices and personal favourites area by area, but always be sure to check the latest reviews on TripAdvisor and other review websites.

Disney's Skyliner

© Disney

DISNEY HOTELS & RESORTS

Our review of Orlando's hotels starts with Walt Disney World. Situated conveniently for all its attractions – and linked by an excellent free transport system of monorail, buses, boats and new Skyliner (p55) – Disney's hotels, villas and campsites are all magnificently appointed and maintained. Their categories are:

BRITTIP

It is usual to tip hotel housekeeping staff by leaving $1/adult each day before your room is made up.

- **Value:** Pop Century, All Star and Art of Animation Resorts.
- **Moderate:** Port Orleans, Caribbean Beach and Coronado Springs Resorts.

- **Deluxe:** Contemporary, Polynesian Village, Boardwalk Inn, Wilderness Lodge, Grand Floridian, Yacht and Beach Club, Swan and Dolphin, Animal Kingdom Lodge and new Galactic Starcruiser resorts.

- **Deluxe Villas:** (Disney's timeshare properties, or Disney Vacation Club) – Old Key West, Saratoga Springs, Bay Lake Tower, Animal Kingdom Villas, Beach Club Villas, Boardwalk Villas, Polynesian Village Villas, Grand Floridian Villas, Wilderness Lodge Villas and new Riviera Resort.

- **Campground:** Fort Wilderness (cabins, campsites and RV sites).

- They range from $135/night (All Star Sports resort) to over $4,000 (Grand Floridian), and dining at Disney resorts isn't cheap. However, staying with the world-famous Mouse is one of the great thrills, for the style, service and extras.

The 25 resorts, with 36,000 rooms, offer superb facilities that children especially love. Benefits include the chance to book the **Disney Genie+** Individual Lightning Lane attractions (p85) at 7am daily instead of at park opening; **dining priority** 180 days in advance; **Early Park Entry**, with all 4 parks open 30min early for Disney hotel guests; **Package Delivery** from the parks to your hotel; and the **Disney Dining Plan** (p53). New in 2022 were the **MagicBand+**, with more interactive features (at an additional cost), and the in-room **Hey Disney!** gadget that performs like Amazon's Alexa, with fun character interactions, resort info and even meal advice. Need a wake-up message from your favourite Disney character? That's in Hey Disney! too.

> **BRITTIP**
> Disney changed its Extra Magic Hours perk for hotel guests in 2021 from one park, one hour early to ALL parks for an early-entry 30 minutes each morning.

Value resorts

There is no full-service dining at this group, and rooms are more basic, but they still feature plenty of Disney style.

Disney's All-Star Resorts: Choose from Sports, Music or Movies in this playfully-themed – and extensive – complex of pools, bars, food courts, shops, laundries and games rooms. Standard rooms are a bit small for families with older children, but well designed for those who want the Disney convenience but not the price. The All-Star Music Resort also has 192 two-room Family Suites that sleep six, each with two bathrooms, kitchenette, lounge and master bedroom. Resort transport is by an efficient bus service.

> **BRITTIP**
> The best new perk for Disney's Deluxe resort guests is **Extended Evening Theme Park Hours** at one park each evening (see p57).

Disney's All Star Music Resort

© Disney

Disney's Pop Century Resort: Themed to the decades from 1950s–90s are five blocks with giant icons – yo-yos, Rubik's cubes and juke-boxes – and a riot of visual gags. Blocks are grouped around the main building with check-in area, food court, lounge (with quick-breakfast bar), Disney store and games arcade. The 177acre/72ha complex also features a central lake and lots of bright landscaping, plus bus service to the parks, and the Skyliner system to EPCOT and Hollywood Studios (see p55).

Disney's Art of Animation Resort:
This suites-style hotel builds on the popularity of the Family Suites at the All-Star Music Resort and is a four-part, 1,984-room complex based on *The Lion King*, *The Little Mermaid*, *Finding Nemo* and *Cars*. It has a themed main pool and play areas, two 'quiet' pools, an excellent food court, huge games arcade and gift shop. All park transport is by bus or Skyliner.

Moderate resorts

Rooms are still relatively plain (except where specially themed) but each resort offers at least one main restaurant, plus a food court and extensive pool and recreation areas.

Disney's Caribbean Beach Resort:
Spread over five Caribbean 'islands', the heart of the resort is Old Port Royale, with the main lobby, food court, gift shop, and excellent full-service Latin and Caribbean menu of Sebastian's Bistro. Main pool Fuentes del Morro features water slides and cannons, and there's a separate kiddie pool. Pirate-themed rooms (request at booking) feature ship-shaped beds and other clever décor touches. There are bike and boat rentals, and each 'island' has its own pool. Transport is by bus, plus the Skyliner to EPCOT and Hollywood Studios.

Disney Skyliner

This imaginative new transport system opened in late 2019. A glorified cable-car service, it starts at Pop Century and Art of Animation, runs to a hub at Caribbean Beach, then splits to either Hollywood Studios (helping to ease traffic congestion from the new Star Wars area) or EPCOT, via the Riviera Resort. Be aware, its operation may be affected by stormy weather.

BRITTIP

Try to visit a Disney resort restaurant even if you aren't staying there. Advance book at any of the parks (407 939 1947 or 0800 16 60 748 in the UK; **bit.ly/brit-disney**).

Disney's Coronado Springs Resort:
Possibly the best value of this trio, it has more facilities and the smart new (in 2019) Gran Destino tower, with a more upscale style, including fab rooftop restaurant Toledo – Tapas, Steak & Seafood. It is spread over 125acres/50ha with Mexican-Spanish theming, and features four pools (including huge Lost City of

Lobby of Disney's Caribbean Beach Resort

© Disney

© Disney

Disney's Boardwalk Inn and Villas

Cibola activity pool and waterslide), games arcades, food court, two more restaurants, convenience store/café, sports bar, gift shop, beauty salon, health club, business centre and two launderettes. Theme park transport is all by bus.

Disney's Port Orleans Resort: Split into Riverside and French Quarter sections, it also features Royal Guest Rooms, themed for princes and princesses right down to headboards that perform fibre-optic fireworks! Dining is imaginative (look out for Boatwright's restaurant with its Cajun-Creole menu), as are the flamboyant pool areas, and the clever design elements vary from rustic Bayou backwoods to 1900-era New Orleans. Transport is by bus to the parks and bus or boat to Disney Springs.

Deluxe resorts

Disney specialises in deluxe hotels in grand style, and now adds a perk with Extended Evening Theme Park Hours, an extra 2hrs at one of the parks after regular closing each day.

Disney's Animal Kingdom Lodge: This stunning 'private game lodge' is set on a 33acre/13ha animal-filled savannah, which many rooms overlook. The full African theme is lavish and detailed, and the effect of opening your curtains to see giraffes and zebras is immense. There are two restaurants, a café, bar, elaborately themed 'watering-hole' main pool (with waterslide) and

kids' pool, Spa and fitness centre, large gift shop, children's play area and awesome four-storey atrium. Main restaurant, Jiko, is spectacular, but there is also superb buffet-style Boma, a 'marketplace' restaurant featuring African-tinged dishes from a wood-burning grill and rotisserie for breakfast and dinner. Transport is by bus (5mins to Animal Kingdom).

BRITTIP

Jiko at Disney's Animal Kingdom Lodge offers an array of South African wines in a wonderful, romantic setting.

Disney's Boardwalk Inn and Villas: Next to EPCOT is this extravagant inn and entertainment 'district', featuring a 512-room hotel, 383 villas, four themed restaurants, sports bar and two nightclubs, plus shops and huge, freeform pool with waterslide, all on a semi-circular boardwalk around the lake. The Big River Grille is a super gastropub; the Flying Fish is an upmarket seafood choice

Disney's Contemporary Resort

© Disney

Victoria and Albert's

with magic-themed lounge, the AbracadaBar; Trattoria al Forno offers Italian cuisine (notably for pizza and risottos); and there are tempting treats at Boardwalk Ice Cream and the new Cake Bake Shop, with its dreamy desserts. Transport is by boat to EPCOT and Hollywood Studios and bus to the other parks.

Disney's Contemporary Resort: On the monorail next to the Magic Kingdom, this 15-storey resort boasts five shops, four restaurants, four lounges, a marina, two pools (one with waterslide), tennis courts, a games centre and health club – and fab views, especially from the superb, hotel-top California Grill (one of the most romantic settings in Orlando; aim to go to coincide with the park's fireworks). Chef Mickey's offers breakfast or dinner with your favourite characters, while the monorail runs *through* the hotel. Within walking distance of the Magic Kingdom, transport to other parks is by bus.

Disney's Grand Floridian Resort & Spa: This five-star hotel is like an elaborate Victorian mansion, with a huge domed foyer and staff in period costume. On the monorail to the Magic Kingdom, it commands a high price tag, though it's worth a look if you're not staying. Restaurants include top-of-the-range Victoria and Albert's, seafood-based Narcoossee's, with its excellent water view, and Mary Poppins-themed Citricos. The 1900 Park Fare restaurant is ideal for character meals, while the Beauty and the Beast lounge evokes the romance of the classic animated film. Other impressive features are the fab Senses Spa, relaxing main pool and second pool with zero-depth entry and water-slide. Also here is an outlet of the Bibbidi Bobbidi Boutique for kids 3–12 to enjoy a Princess makeover ($70–$450).

The Garden View Lounge serves a variety of traditional afternoon teas 2–5pm daily, $35–150/person ($24 for 3–9s). Transport to the Magic Kingdom is by boat and monorail; by bus to the other parks.

> **BRITTIP**
>
> For all the details of the Extended Evening Theme Park Hours, see disneyworld.co.uk/guest-services/extended-evening/.

Disney's Polynesian Village Resort: This is a South Seas tropical fantasy, with modern sophistication and comfort. Also on the monorail opposite the Magic Kingdom, it boasts a lovely landscaped atrium featuring an iconic Tiki god, and the dining is excellent, with stylish 'Ohana featuring lively character dining and Kona Café offering a more subdued alternative. Interactive tropical lounge Trader Sam's Grog Grotto (4pm–midnight) is a must-see for its fun style and exotic cocktails. A beautiful 'Volcano' pool area features a waterslide and bar. Take a monorail or boat to the Magic Kingdom and buses to the other parks. New in 2021 was a *Moana*-themed makeover for the guest rooms. There are also 20 gorgeous two-bed lakefront bungalows on stilts over Seven Seas Lagoon, boasting full kitchens, living and dining rooms, outdoor deck with plunge pool and a grandstand view of the fireworks.

Whispering Canyon Café at Wilderness Lodge

© Disney

© Disney

But beware the price – from \$3,126/night! A new Disney Vacation Club tower is under construction here, due to open in late 2024.

Disney's Wilderness Lodge: A picturesque and romantic resort, this is a re-creation of a National Park lodge, from the stream running through the massive wooden balcony-lined atrium to a geyser that erupts every hour. Offering backwoods charm with luxury, it has the stylish Artist's Point restaurant (lunch and dinner) and Whispering Canyon Café (lively breakfast and all-you-can-eat family meals), plus a snack bar, pool bar and Geyser Point Bar & Grill, with views over Bay Lake. There is a quiet pool, hot-tub and Health Club, with fitness centre, sauna, and massage and facial treatments. The resort is linked to the Magic Kingdom by boat and bus, with buses to the other parks.

Disney's Yacht and Beach Club Resorts: There is more refined quality here, featuring nautical-themed décor set around Crescent Lake next to EPCOT. For dinner, the Yachtsman Steakhouse offers elegant dining, Cape May Café serves lovely character breakfasts and a nightly New England-style clambake buffet, and Beaches & Cream is a classic 1950s-style diner for burgers, shakes and sundaes. Both are set along a white-sand beach like a tropical island and share Stormalong Bay, an extensive lagoon-style pool. Catch a water-shuttle to EPCOT and Disney's Hollywood Studios; other park transport is by bus.

BRITTIP

The Crew's Cup Lounge in the Yacht Club Resort is a true hidden gem, ideal for a cocktail before dinner, or to unwind after a day in the parks.

Star Wars: Galactic Starcruiser: This dramatic new development in 2022 raised the bar for hotel style, allowing guests to enjoy a Star Wars adventure in space! The *Halcyon* starcruiser is a two-day experience with a simulated launch into space and series of events, including meals,

activities and cabaret, like being on a cruise ship. There is a day-trip to Batuu (a clever shuttle to the Star Wars land at Disney's Hollywood Studios); a chance to join the Resistance on a mission against The First Order; a visit to the ship's bridge to work the controls (and laser canons); and lightsaber training, among a variety of cleverly themed options. The character interaction is superb (be sure to be in role-playing mood) and the food is excellent, but alcoholic drinks are extra and not cheap. And, while rooms all boast a space view, the out-of-this-world experience comes at a high price – around \$2,400/person. **disneyworld.co.uk/ star-wars-galactic-starcruiser.**

BRITTIP

Most Disney hotel rooms will sleep four, except Port Orleans Riverside (which can take an extra child on a trundle bed). For larger groups, consider Old Key West, Saratoga Springs, the Boardwalk Villas, the villas at Animal Kingdom Lodge, Wilderness Lodge Villas, Fort Wilderness cabins or two-room suites at the All-Star Music and Art of Animation Resorts.

Walt Disney World Swan, Dolphin and Swan Reserve: These high-quality hotels are not owned by Disney but conform to the same high standards, with some of the best facilities, locations, restaurants and night-time views, while usually slightly cheaper than most Deluxe resorts. They're within walking distance of EPCOT and Hollywood Studios, the Boardwalk Resort and Fantasia Gardens mini-golf, but also have a boat service to both parks (and bus to the others). The Dolphin offers the Balinese-inspired Mandara Spa, with a tea garden and Meru Temple. The full resort has 20 restaurants and lounges, six pools (one an amazing grotto pool

Galactic Starcruiser

© Disney

with hidden alcoves and waterslide), a kids' pool and white-sand beach, two health clubs, a range of shops, video arcade and Camp Dolphin centre for 4–12s (5pm–12am, $12/hour/child).

Shula's Steak House and Todd English's Bluezoo are especially worth seeking out, along with the fun soda-shop style of The Fountain for ice creams, sundaes, milkshakes and other speciality desserts and Il Mulino Trattoria, copying New York's top Italian restaurant. The lovely Garden Grove Café features Disney character dining, while intimate Kimonos offers sushi and a karaoke bar. The new (in late 2021) 14-storey tower expansion of **The Swan Reserve** added an elegant elevated pool deck, rooftop event space and four restaurants and lounges, including the Mediterranean style of Amare and Stir lobby cocktail bar (407 934 1609, **swandolphin.com**).

Four Seasons Resort: Tucked within the exclusive private home enclave of Disney's Golden Oak is this fabulous five-star brand, an oasis of tranquillity within the Disney confines. Built in luxurious Spanish Revival style, it has an amazing array of amenities, including five restaurants, three pools, lazy river and water-play area, tennis courts, extensive spa, fitness centre and golf course. It has terrific children's facilities and activities, too, making it a superb family choice. Rooftop steakhouse restaurant Capa is one of Orlando's most spectacular while Italian-styled Ravello, with its show kitchen, is another show-stopper. Golf clubhouse diner Plancha features Cuban–American cuisine in a lakeside setting. The whole ambience is magnificent, but room rates *start* at $655/night. Park transport is by bus (1800 267 3046, **fourseasons.com/orlando**).

BRITTIP

Book dinner at the Four Seasons' superb rooftop restaurant, Capa, and you can enjoy a high-level view of the Magic Kingdom fireworks.

Disney's Yacht & Beach Club Resorts

© Disney

Campground & cabins

Disney's Fort Wilderness Resort & Campground: Possibly the best value of all the Disney properties, on Bay Lake opposite the Magic Kingdom, this offers impressive camping facilities and chalet-style cabins housing up to six in a rural setting. Two 'trading posts' supply groceries and there is a lounge/bar and full-service restaurant. Facilities include two swimming pools, the thrice-nightly Hoop-Dee-Doo Musical Revue, (a traditional hoedown-style song-and-dance dinner show, p267), campfire programme, open-air films, sports, games and a prime spot for the nightly Electrical Water Pageant. You can rent bikes or boats, take horse rides around the country trails or even try a Segway Tour (the great two-wheeled personal transports), providing a two-hour trundle around the many trails ($90/person, over-15s only; 8.30 and 11.30am Tues–Sat; call 407 939 8687 to book).

The Trail's End restaurant offers a good-value family-style breakfast and dinner, while Crockett's Tavern serves appetisers (dinner only). Boats link the resort to the Magic Kingdom and buses serve the other parks.

Disney Vacation Club resorts

Disney's smart timeshare resorts are open to non-timeshare guests periodically, and several also feature some fine dining opportunities as well as stylish, spacious rooms, most with full kitchens for self-catering.

Disney's Old Key West Resort: Choose from one, two or three-bed studios in a Key West setting. Facilities include four pools, tennis courts, a games room, shops and a fitness centre, plus the lovely Olivia's restaurant. Transport to all parks is by bus, plus boat to Disney Springs.

BRITTIP

Looking for a diversion from Disney Springs? Take the boat from The Landing to Old Key West and try a meal at Olivia's for a laid-back vibe.

Disney's Saratoga Springs Resort & Spa: The largest DVC resort is opposite Disney Springs and goes from standard two-bed hotel-style studio rooms to massive two-storey, three-bed apartments sleeping 12. The theme is the 1880s' New York resort of the same name, with a gracious look and great facilities, including the freeform main pool (with waterslide and squirt-fountains), smaller quiet pool and varied dining, like the upscale Turf Club Bar & Grill, with its cocktail lounge, for dinner. Also here are 60 three-bed **Treehouse Villas**, beautiful chalets among a wooded area next to Sassagoula River that sleep up to nine and feature superb furnishings, two full bathrooms,

Fort Wilderness Campground cabin

© Disney

Samawati Springs at Kidani Village

outdoor barbecue grills and their own leisure pool. All transport by bus.

Bay Lake Tower at Disney's Contemporary Resort: Linked to the Contemporary Resort by a bridge, this boasts its own pool, waterslide and whirlpool spa, kids' water-play area, shuffleboard and bocce courts. Studios (sleeping up to four) have small fridges, microwaves and coffee-makers, while the villas (up to 12) have full kitchens and laundry facilities. The Tower affords wonderful views over the Magic Kingdom and nightly fireworks from its exclusive rooftop lounge.

Disney's Animal Kingdom Lodge – Kidani Village: An addition to Animal Kingdom Lodge, this features hotel-room studios (sleeping four) and one, two and three-bed villas (sleeping five, nine or 12), offering full kitchens and laundry facilities. There is a separate wildlife preserve, fab pool and kids' play area, and another restaurant, Sanaa, which continues the Lodge's reputation for fine dining. Other amenities include a video arcade, basketball court, fitness centre, gift shop and animal programmes, from flamingo-feeding to campfire story-telling. Transport to all parks is by bus.

Grand Floridian Villas: This elegant resort consists of stylish one and two-bed villas sleeping 5–9, plus 'grand villas' that sleep 12 and include a media room with home theatre system. The elegant building, with subtle Mary Poppins theming, has a reception, laundry room and lovely private gardens.

Riviera Resort: New in 2019, and on the Skyliner route to EPCOT and Hollywood Studios, this nine-storey homage to classic Mediterranean Riviera hotels offers one, two and three-bed villa-style rooms with a grand Cote d'Azur feel, including elaborate gardens, fountains and rooftop restaurant, Topolino's Terrace, offering classic Riviera cuisine with views of the fireworks at the two nearby parks. Breakfast features a Character Dining experience.

Bay Lake Tower

Disney Hotel Plaza

If Disney's hotel prices are out of your range, consider the seven on-site 'guest' hotels that offer lower rates on Hotel Plaza Boulevard next to Disney Springs. There's a free bus service to the parks, Early Theme Park Entry, and you can make show and restaurant reservations before the general public.

- **B Resort & Spa:** Chic, high-tech contemporary hotel with a lot of built-in style and fab dining.

- **DoubleTree Suites by Hilton:** Well-priced and versatile option, with extra-large rooms.

- **Hilton Orlando Buena Vista Palace:** Extensive, recently refurbished with a lot packed in.

- **Hilton Orlando Lake Buena Vista:** Ultra-smart executive resort with many mod cons.

- **Holiday Inn:** One of our faves, a surprisingly fresh and modern style, with excellent dining.

- **Wyndham Garden:** Wonderfully stylish resort opposite Disney Springs with impressive amenities.

- **Drury Plaza:** New in 2022, with lots of value-added extras, large pool and novel dining/bar concept.

- For more info on these, go to **disneyspringshotels.com**.

UNIVERSAL ORLANDO

Disney hasn't cornered the market in smart, creative hotel design, and Universal has seven that are equally attractive. They offer benefits like free bus service to SeaWorld and Aquatica; early entry to the Wizarding Worlds of Harry Potter and select attractions at Volcano Bay water park; FREE

Universal Express access (for guests at Portofino Bay, Royal Pacific and Hard Rock Hotel); and unlimited club-to-club access to select CityWalk venues. They come in three tiers, Value, Prime Value and Premier.

Endless Summer Resort: The huge Value resort is split into two sections on the site of the old Wet 'n Wild water park on International Drive. The Surfside Inn & Suites is suitably surf-themed while the newer and larger Dockside Inn & Suites offers bright coastal styling. They both feature standard rooms and two-bed suites sleeping up to six, resort-style pools and splash pads, games room, fitness centre and food court. For this location, they are superb value. Park transport is by shuttle bus.

Cabana Bay Beach Resort: Moving up to Prime Value, Cabana Bay is an extensive, feature-packed resort with classic 1950s styling. Again, dining is food court style, although there are also a retro Starbucks coffee shop, lobby bar, two elaborate pool bars and the Hideaway Bar & Grille for lunch and dinner. Guests can even have pizza delivered to rooms that feature all mod cons, with flatscreen TVs, mini fridge, wi-fi and a clever bathroom that features two wash-basins and separate bathtub-shower. Amenities include a 10-lane bowling alley with its own bar and restaurant, and two feature-packed resort pools, with sandy beaches, waterslide and a lazy river. It has its own shuttle bus to Universal's CityWalk hub, or it's a 15min walk.

Aventura Hotel: This 16-storey tower features a dramatic roof-top bar and great views over the whole Universal resort, as well as rooms, including kids suites, boasting floor-to-ceiling windows. An elaborate pool area contains a kids' splash pad and hot-tubs, there is a high-tech fitness centre, innovative food court and a Starbucks. It has a 10min walking route to the parks, plus a shuttle, but is still at the more modest end of Universal hotel pricing.

Sapphire Falls Resort: This Caribbean-themed tropical oasis falls between the Value Plus and Premier

Dockside Inn and Suites

© Universal Orlando Resort

tiers as it has many of the facilities of the best hotels – including excellent dining – but doesn't include the Universal Express bonus. A resort-style pool features a water-slide, children's play area, sandy beach, hot-tub, private cabañas and fire pit, while full-service Caribbean restaurant Amatista offers scenic views and outdoor dining. There's also a quick-service marketplace, lobby lounge and fancy poolside bar, Drhum Club Kantine, plus state-of-the-art fitness centre with saunas. There is water taxi and shuttle access to CityWalk and it is one of Universal's most picturesque hotels.

BRITTIP

Don't miss the superb Strong Water Tavern at Sapphire Falls with its unique array of vintage rums, plus a fabulous small-plate Caribbean menu.

Hard Rock Hotel: The first of the Premier, this icon of rock chic is themed as a rock star's home, with high ceilings, wooden beams, marble floors and eclectic artwork, plus black-suited staff and fairly constant music.

It has three bars (including the ultra-cool Velvet Bar), three dining options (including five-star, dinner-only Palm Restaurant), plus a fitness centre, gift shop and games room. The huge pool deck boasts an underwater sound system, water-slide, two hot-tubs, volleyball, shuffleboard and oversized chess. Rooms, including 12 kidsuites and 10 king suites, are beautifully furnished and comfy.

Royal Pacific Resort: Welcome to the exotic 1930s South Seas, where you feel you've stepped into another world as you cross the bamboo bridge into the opulent lobby. Standard rooms feature hand-carved Balinese furniture among many refined touches, and there is also a Club level, with separate lounge and extended facilities, and 51 superb suites – including eight Jurassic Park-themed kidsuites. The Islands Dining Room offers breakfast, lunch and dinner in an oriental setting (children have their own buffet area with TV screen), while the Bula Bar & Grille is the ideal poolside dining venue. The luau garden area features the Wantilan Luau Saturday nights, featuring a Polynesian feast and dinner show.

Loews Royal Pacific Resort Hotel

© Disney

The huge freeform pool is ideal for kids, with zero-depth entry and a boat-shaped interactive play area of squirting fountains. Other amenities include a health club, kids' club, video arcade and two shops. It is within a short walk of the parks but also offers boat service to CityWalk.

Portofino Bay Hotel: The jewel in Universal's crown is a splendid re-creation of the famous Italian port. Elaborate porticos, *trompe l'oeil* painting and harbourside piazza make it a five-star setting. Even standard rooms are sumptuous while Club Rooms offer concierge service with private lounge, extra room amenities and free entry to the Mandara Spa fitness centre. 18 *Despicable Me* themed kidsuites have separate bedrooms – with missile beds! Facilities are equally smart – a Roman aqueduct-style pool with waterslide, kids' play area and wading pool, separate quiet pool, hot tubs, Mandara Spa, array of gift shops and video games room. The hotel has eight restaurants and lounges, including superb Bice Ristorante (p282), boisterous Trattoria del Porto, family dining at Mama Della's, an aromatic deli and

Hard Rock Hotel

© Universal Orlando Resort

swanky Bar American. Park transport is by boat and bus.

For all Universal hotels, visit **universalorlando.com/web/en/us/ places-to-stay/hotels/at-a-glance/hotels-overview** or call 1888 273 1311.

INTERNATIONAL DRIVE
Away from the theme park hotel style, this more traditional area of hotels and attractions remains a go-to choice for many. We'll use Disney's three hotel categories – Value, Moderate and Deluxe – and add a Budget range.

Budget hotels
Avanti Resort: An ideal location is boosted by a fab resort pool and free shuttles to Universal, SeaWorld, EPCOT and Aquatica (407 313 0100, **avantiresort.com**).

Drury Inn & Suites: A smart choice with a LOT included for your money (407 354 1101, **druryhotels.com/ locations/orlando-fl**).

Tru by Hilton: Modern, large hotel just off I-Drive close to SeaWorld, with free breakfast, wi-fi and parking (407 351 4091, **hilton.com/en/tru/**).

Ramada Plaza Resort & Suites: Great value choice in a good I-Drive location with free wi-fi, breakfast and Disney transport (407 345 5340, **ramadaorlando.com**).

Rosen Inn at Pointe Orlando: One of I-Drive's 'old faithfuls', this continues to be a reliable and sound choice, with plenty of amenities (407 996 8585, **roseninn9000.com**).

Rosen Inn International: Another long-serving hotel still providing great value in budget territory (407 996 1600, **roseninn7600.com**).

Rosen Inn I-Drive: Completing a trio of clean-and-cheerful value-conscious hotels, this is another well-designed but well-priced option (407 996 4444, **roseninn6327.com**).

StaySky Suites I-Drive Orlando: This Brit-friendly resort just off the main drag of I-Drive features over-large one and two-bed suites (407 956 6101, **stayskysuitesidriveorlando.com**).

International Drive Accommodation

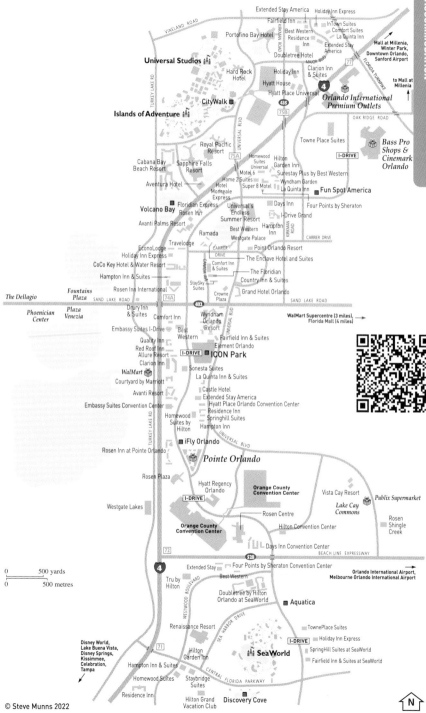

© Steve Munns 2022

Value hotels

CoCo Key Water Resort: This action-packed hotel offers excellent amenities with its extensive water park, chic lobby and smart rooms, (407 351 2626, **cocokeyorlando.com**).

Four Points Orlando International Drive: A 21-storey icon close to Universal Orlando, it features a heated tropical pool, games room and fitness room (407 351 2100, **fourpointsorlandointernationaldrive.com**).

Home2 Suites International Drive South: Excellent rooms with self-catering facilities and plenty of space make this ideal for long stays. Its location next to Orlando Premium Outlets is another bonus (407 944 1705, **hilton.com/en/home2**).

Sonesta ES Suites: This refreshing, spacious and Brit-friendly choice features full kitchens in one and two-bed suites sleeping 4–8 in three versatile layouts. It includes a quick-service breakfast cafe, and the pool area and hot tub provide a great end-of-day retreat (407 352 2400, **bit. ly/brit-sonesta**).

Staybridge Suites SeaWorld: A surprisingly chic big-brand choice, featuring an excellent free hot breakfast (407 917 9200, **ihg.com/staybridge/hotels/ us/en/orlando/mcoos/hoteldetail**).

The Point Hotel & Suites: Nicely tucked away just off I-Drive but close to all the action, this chic condo-hotel has wonderfully comfy rooms and a laid-back vibe (407 956 2000, **thepointorlando.com**).

Wyndham Orlando Resort: This well-equipped resort puts guests in the heart of I-Drive's entertainment district as well as benefitting from a recent multi-million dollar renovation (407 351 2420, **wyndhamorlandoresort.com**).

Moderate hotels

Castle Hotel: A boutique hotel with a luxury touch in the heart of I-Drive. Plush rooms, heated pool, fitness centre and creative dining provide individual style in mass market territory (407 345 1511, **castlehotelorlando.com**).

Doubletree by Hilton Orlando at SeaWorld: Just off I-Drive and set in tropical grounds, it offers two pools, two restaurants, fitness centre and extra-large suites (407 352 1100, **doubletree3.hilton.com**).

Embassy Suites International Drive Convention Center: An 'old faithful' in the heart of I-Drive, with spacious rooms, great outdoor pool deck and indoor pool, plus good dining options (407 352 1400, **embassysuitesorlando. com**).

Rosen Centre: This spectacular 24-storey property features a huge swimming grotto, tennis courts,

Castle Hotel

exercise centre and high-quality restaurants, including the must-try steak-and-seafood Everglades and 98Forty Tapas & Tequila bar (1800 204 7234, **rosencentre.com**).

Rosen Plaza: Another trademark I-Drive hotel, it offers an excellent pool deck, gym and a great array of dining, including the swish Jack's Place for great steaks and seafood, and its own nightclub, 3NINE. It is especially good for Kosher guests (407 996 9700, **rosenplaza.com**).

Deluxe hotels

Hilton Orlando: This impressive 1,400-room hotel boasts superb leisure facilities and fabulous dining, with a full-service spa, fitness centre, two pools, lazy river, tennis, volleyball and basketball (407 313 4300, **thehiltonorlando.com**).

Hyatt Regency Orlando: Another resort that appeals to convention business but is well stocked for holiday fun, with a series of pools, tennis courts, huge fitness centre and spa, and seven restaurants, bars and lounges. Rooms are equally gorgeous, but conference business can make it hectic at times (407 284 1234, **bit.ly/brit-hyattregency**).

Renaissance Orlando Resort: This superb hotel opposite SeaWorld features a fab children's water park and gorgeous resort amenities. It has a 10-storey atrium lobby and huge rooms and suites, a lavish spa and fitness centre and video arcade, plus terrific dining options (407 351 5555, **bit.ly/brit-renaissance**).

Rosen Shingle Creek Hotel: This resort ranks among the grandest, set amid Shingle Creek Golf Club on lower Universal Boulevard. Rooms are suitably sumptuous, as is the full-service spa and fitness centre, while there are five restaurants, four bars, a lounge, coffee house, deli and ice-creamery. Three outdoor pools, tennis, basketball, nature trails and chic shopping gallery complete a hugely attractive picture (407 996 6338, **rosenshinglecreek.com**).

BRITTIP

Nearly all hotels provide hair-dryers but, if you bring your own, you will need a US plug adaptor (with two flat pins). The voltage is 110–120AC (ours is 220) so UK appliances will be sluggish.

Hilton Orlando's lazy river feature

© The Hilton Orlando

Walt Disney World and Lake Buena Vista Accommodation

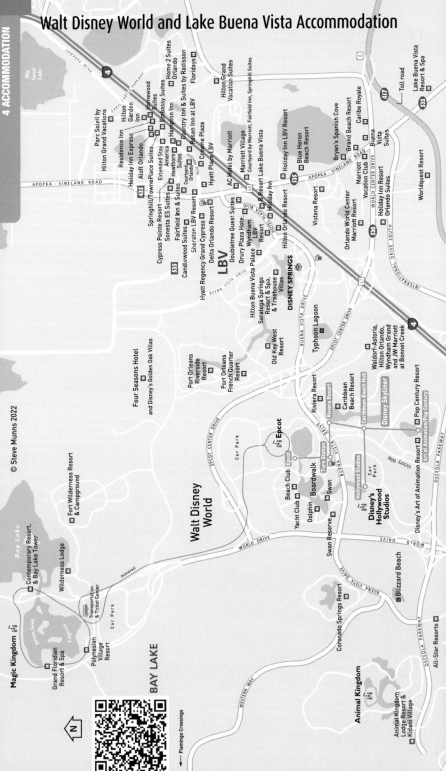

© Steve Munns 2022

LAKE BUENA VISTA

This area either side of I-4 features a number of fairly smart alternatives that are a bit cheaper than Disney but live up to the standard of the area, and are all close to some good restaurants.

Value hotels

A/C Hotel Lake Buena Vista: This contemporary brand has taken over and rebuilt the old Radisson, with stylish rooms, lobby bar and lounge. It includes a full-service restaurant, fitness centre and elegant outdoor pool (407 597 3400, **marriott.com/en-us/hotels/mcoab-ac-hotel-orlando-lake-buena-vista**).

Aloft Lake Buena Vista: Brand new on Palm Parkway away from the hustle-bustle, this boutique brand offers super-smart rooms and an eclectic, offbeat style (407 778 7600, **marriott.com/hotels/travel/mcoav-aloft-orlando-lake-buena-vista**).

Buena Vista Suites: This extensive resort offers terrific value for money just a bit further away from the parks, with spacious rooms and quality amenities, right next to sister (upmarket) resort Caribe Royale (407 239 8588, **buenavistasuites.com**).

Extended Stay America Lake Buena Vista: A good choice in a quieter area but still convenient for Disney and delivering top value (407 239 4300, **bit.ly/brit-extended**).

Holiday Inn Express & Suites: Just around the corner from the busy Crossroads area and entrance to Disney Springs is this smart and well-appointed hotel featuring a great free breakfast (407 230 1508, **bit.ly/brit-holidayinnexpress**).

Hyatt Place Lake Buena Vista: In an ideal location, close to the Disney hustle-bustle but just out of the way, it is a great example of this contemporary brand, as everything looks and feels like new (407 778 5500, **bit.ly/brit-hyattlbv**).

Sheraton Lake Buena Vista Resort: A popular choice with Brits, with spacious, well-furnished rooms, spectacular pool complex and fitness centre, and impressive restaurant and lounge (407 239 0444, **sheratonlakebuenavistaresort.com**).

40 years of innovation at Epcot

Moderate hotels

Caribe Royale Resort: A huge, quality-conscious suites hotel boasting dazzling amenities (including tropical pool with water-slide, tennis courts and fitness centre), plus great dining, notably at the award-winning Venetian Chop House, which offers gourmet fare, and the new Rum Bar for cocktails and Cuban cuisine (1800 823 8300, **cariberoyale.com**).

Candlewood Suites Lake Buena Vista: Super value new hotel featuring most rooms with full kitchens. Facilities include a neat pool deck, gym, free wi-fi and outdoor barbecue grills. Close to Disney and with a good variety of restaurants within easy walking distance (407 477 4433, **ihg.com/candlewood/hotels/us/en/lake-buena-vista/orllb/hoteldetail**).

Delta Orlando: Close to Disney Springs, the Delta offers chic dining, excellent family pool and super-comfy rooms. Organic breakfast choices, low-energy features and patio with fire-fountain feature highlight this as above average (407 387 9999, **bit.ly/brit-deltaorlando**).

Embassy Suites Lake Buena Vista South: This well-kept example of the brand is an oasis of calm and modernity, close to Disney and with smart features and a free breakfast (407 597 4000, **embassysuites3.hilton.com**).

Holiday Inn Resort Orlando Suites: This vast resort boasts its own water park, video arcade, mini-golf, laser tag and a quiet pool, plus a fine array of shops and dining, with a bar, pizzeria, Deli and Lakeside Café. Rooms come in one-bed kitchen suites and two and three-bed kidsuites (407 387 5437, **bit.ly/brit-holidayinnresort**).

Orlando World Center Marriott

© Orlando World Center

BRITTIP

La Luce at the Hilton at Bonnet Creek is a wonderfully chic and individual dinner venue, featuring modern Mediterranean cuisine with a Napa Valley flair.

Deluxe hotels

Hilton at Bonnet Creek Resort: Extensive privately owned development inside Walt Disney World, part of a 482acre/194ha resort with the Waldorf-Astoria and sharing some facilities. It features four restaurants, a lagoon pool complex with lazy river and waterslide, golf course, tennis courts and adjoining full-service Spa and fitness centre, plus excellent kids' activities (407 597 3600, **hiltonbonnetcreek.com**).

Hyatt Regency Grand Cypress: The area's first genuine deluxe hotel in 1984, this is still one of the best. It includes a golf academy, boating lake and superb pool complex with a kids' water park, rock-climbing wall and bar. Rooms have a modern, amenity-laden finish and the dining is superb, notably at the new Four Flamingos and stylish LakeHouse, with its two-storey atrium and lake views (407 239 1234, **bit.ly/brit-hrgrandcypress**).

BRITTIP

If you're looking for a special occasion restaurant with bags of style and a modern seafood menu, don't miss the new **Four Flamingos** at the Hyatt Regency Grand Cypress, created by celebrity chef Richard Blais.

Orlando World Center Marriott: This iconic resort on Disney's outskirts is set in 200 landscaped acres, surrounded by a beautiful golf course. With eight restaurants and a food court, and a series of pools and water-slides, it is a colossal prospect boosted by a Jack Nicklaus Golf Academy, tennis courts, volleyball, basketball, Spa and fitness centre. Highlights are Mikado Japanese Steakhouse, Hawk's Landing Steakhouse, Siro Urban Italian Kitchen and High Velocity Sports Bar. The pool complex offers true relaxation and the spacious rooms are equally impressive (407 239 4200, **bit.ly/brit-wcmarriott**).

JW Marriott Bonnet Creek Resort & Spa: New in 2021, this eye-catching development near the Hilton and Waldorf-Astoria complex features an extensive resort pool, elegant rooms and swish rooftop bar with views of the Disney fireworks, plus lobby bar, Market Café and two full-service restaurants. Families love the kids' activity centre, while couples are well catered for at the Spa by JW (1888 236 2427, **bit.ly/brit-marriottbc**).

Waldorf-Astoria: Sister resort to the Hilton, this famous-name hotel features gorgeous standard rooms, plus grand suites with butler service. The zero-entry pool has cabañas and waiter service, while the dining is superb, from the poolside grill and classic Bull & Bear Steakhouse to small-plate cuisine of Peacock Alley, gourmet style of Oscar's brasserie and private club vibe of Sir Harry's Lounge. The renowned WA Kids Club provides active, creative fun for 5–12s (407 597 5500, **waldorfastoriaorlando.com**).

Wyndham Grand: Another high-quality resort inside Bonnet Creek, with Mediterranean flair. Beautifully fitted rooms are matched by excellent dining, notably Deep Blu Seafood Grille, Tesoro Cove (for an extensive buffet breakfast) and Back Bay Bar and Grill overlooking the lake. An excellent fitness centre, lagoon-style pool and spa complete an extremely pretty picture (407 390 2300, **wyndhamgrandorlando.com**).

BRITTIP

From early November, Gaylord Palms features a superb Christmas programme of traditional scenes and entertainment, including an Alpine Village and snow tubing, among a dazzling array of festive attractions. See details at **christmasatgaylordpalms.marriott.com**.

Christmas at Gaylord Palms

© Gaylord Palms

KISSIMMEE/HIGHWAY 192

On this extensive stretch of busy highway, there is an enormous choice.

Budget–Value hotels

These are mostly of the chain variety, but a few individuals also stand out.

Destiny Palms Hotel: Well located for Disney, this pleasant hotel also offers free wi-fi and a continental breakfast (407 396 1600, **destinypalmsmaingate. com**)

Wyndham Kissimmee: Close to Disney, this well-equipped value-for-money resort boasts spacious rooms and a good dining choice (407 396 1400, **wyndhamneardisney. com**).

Staybridge Royale Parc Suites: Spacious one and two-bed suites, free Disney shuttle, buffet breakfast and fun poolside bar make for great value in this hotel, next to Old Town on Highway 192 (407 396 8040, **royaleparcsuitesorlando.com**).

Moderate hotels

Delta Orlando Celebration: New in June 2022, this converted former Grand Orlando Resort offers 20 acres/8 hectares of tropical garden setting for its newly renovated rooms and lobby, two pools and smart dining (407 396 7000, **marriott.com/ hotels/hotel-information/restaurant/ mcodk-delta-hotels-orlando-celebration**).

Galleria Palms Hotel: Just off Highway 192, this has a smart, modern look, ultra-comfy rooms, ideal location close to Disney, plus free breakfast, wi-fi and shuttle to the parks (407 396 6300, **gphkissimmee.com**).

Holiday Inn Orlando SW: Nicely situated for Disney, with well-maintained rooms (including kid-suites) in two high-rise towers and a great range of amenities, plus Kids-eat-free programme and varied dining (407 396 4222, **ihg.com/ holidayinn/hotels/us/en/kissimmee/mcoib/ hoteldetail**).

Kissimmee Accommodation

Club Cortile
Econo Lodge
Knights Inn Kissimmee
Villas at Seven Dwarfs Resort
Howard Johnson by Wyndham
WalMart
Medieval Times
Sevilla Inn

Palm Lakefront Hostel
Howard Johnson
Golden Link Motel
Sam's Club
Super Target
Publix
Lake Cecile

Hampton Inn & Suites
Springhill Suites
Embassy Suites
Holiday Inn Express
Toll road
Lake Buena Vista Factory Stores

Magic Castle Inn, Fantasy World
Quality Inn
Comfort Inn
Palazzo Lakeside
GreenPoint Hotel

Blue Heron Beach Resort
Lake Bryan
Grand Beach Resort
Caribe Royale
Buena Vista Suites

Lake Buena Vista Resort & Spa
Holiday Inn Express LBV East
WalMart

APOPKA - VINELAND ROAD

Vistana Resort
Marriott J/C
Holiday Inn Resort Orlando Suites
Worldquest Resort

Orlando World Center Marriott Resort

WORLD CENTER DRIVE
EPCOT CENTER DRIVE
BUENA VISTA DRIVE

LBV
DISNEY SPRINGS

Epcot
Boardwalk
Disney's Hollywood Studios

Walt Disney World

Animal Kingdom

Magic Moment Resort
Seralago Hotel
Comfort Suites Maingate East
Holiday Inn Orlando SW
Studio 6, Motel 6
OLD TOWN KISSIMMEE
Regal Oaks
Staybridge Suites Orlando

Gaylord Palms
Rodeway Inn Maingate
Parkway International
Fairfield Inn & Suites
Publix
Delta by Marriott
Melia Orlando Celebration
Bohemian Hotel
CELEBRATION

OSCEOLA PARKWAY

Pop Century Resort
Disney's Art of Animation Resort

Parkway Palms Resort Maingate

All-Star Sports Resort
All-Star Music Resort
All-Star Movies Resort

Silver Lake
Magic Village Yards
Magic Village Views
Wyndham Orlando Resort
Knights Inn Maingate
Ramada Gateway
WalMart
Magic Tree Resort
Oakwater

Coronado Springs Resort
Animal Kingdom Lodge Resort
Quality Inn & Suites by the Lake
Kidani Village
Island H2O Live
Margaritaville Resort
Formosa Gardens Village
Garden Inn
Maingate Lakeside Resort
Galleria Palms
Grand Lakes Resort
Quality Inn & Suites By The Parks
Westgate Towers

Town Center at Orange Lakes, Publix
Highway 27

Formosa Gardens
Windsor Hills
Mystic Dunes
Indian Ridge
Indian Creek
Rolling Hills
Tempus Palms
Windsor Palms
Oak Island

WESTERN WAY
WORLD DRIVE
BUENA VISTA DRIVE
OSCEOLA PARKWAY
POINCIANA BOULEVARD
OLD LAKE WILSON ROAD
WESTERN BELTWAY (TOLL)

N

© Steve Munns 2022

Deluxe hotels

Bohemian Hotel: In the Disney-inspired town of Celebration just off Highway 192, this boutique hotel offers small-town America style a long way from the usual tourist frenzy. It has a classy ambience and a wealth of high-quality touches, notably in the ultra-comfy rooms and Lakeside Bar & Grill. It is just a short stroll to the town's shops, restaurants and lakeside walks and makes a great romantic choice (407 566 6000, **celebrationhotel.com**).

ette hotel

© ette hotel

ette Hotel: This new brand (in summer 2022) brings a luxury boutique touch to Kissimmee, with distinctive touches like a herb-garden terrace, rooftop lounge and Michelin-starred cuisine, along with organic design and sleek, minimalist rooms. Artsy but laid back, it still offers impeccable service and five-star amenities, with a strong emphasis on cocktails and mixology (407 288 1901, **ettehotels.com**).

Gaylord Palms Resort: One of the most dramatic hotels, it features 4½acres/2ha of indoor themed gardens, fountains and landscaped waters under a glass dome in three Florida-themed sections for the Everglades, Key West and St Augustine. The restaurants and bars include spectacular Wreckers sports bar and fine steakhouse dining at Old Hickory. Cypress Springs Family Fun Water Park is a huge zero-entry pool featuring water-slides, surf simulator, massive water-play structure, lagoon and toddler splash area. Then there is the signature Relâche Spa, one of the area's largest, and unique shopping along the indoor 'retail street', plus the Cocoa Bean coffee shop, seafood dining at MOOR and Cuban-inspired bar, Socio (407 586 0000, **bit.ly/brit-gaylordpalms**).

Meliã Orlando Celebration: This luxury resort is located just off Highway 192 at the entrance to the town of Celebration. Set around a fabulous 'vanishing edge' swimming pool, it boasts upmarket dining at the new The Wilson Cocktails & Seafood restaurant and beautifully furnished one and two-bed suites with full kitchens. Balconies overlook the infinity pool or lush landscaping. There is also privileged use of the AdventHealth Celebration Wellness Center & Spa (407 964 7000, **bit.ly/brit-melia**).

BRITTIP

If you're like many travellers who have trouble falling asleep with a whirring air conditioner in your room, pick up a pack of soft foam earplugs from Wal-Mart, Walgreens or CVS – effective enough to filter out the drone without making you deaf to 'important' noises.

Melia Orlando

FURTHER AFIELD

There are a few more deluxe hotels that are not in the main areas but still have exceptional appeal.

Alfond Inn: In a quiet part of Winter Park, but handy for the shops, restaurants and museums, this gorgeous boutique hotel is run with great style. Rooms are opulent, service is gracious and dining is some of the best in the area. There is also a terrific roof-top pool, gym and outdoor patio, plus a popular cocktail bar and library lounge (407 998 8090, thealfondinn.com).

BRITTIP

Even if you don't stay at the Alfond Inn, it is worth a visit if you are in Winter Park, especially for Hamilton's Kitchen, an award-winning restaurant that serves modern Southern cuisine with panache for lunch and dinner (p295).

Grande Lakes Orlando: This combo of Ritz-Carlton and JW Marriott hotels offers extensive luxury, including a grand spa, 18-hole Greg Norman golf course, tennis centre

Omni Orlando at Champions Gate

and upscale shops and dining. On a forestry preserve, it feels secluded and remote and is slightly off the beaten track, at the junction of John Young and Central Florida Parkway, yet only 10mls/16km from Disney and Orlando Airport. It also features eco-tours, like kayaking, fishing, bird-watching and nature walks. The **JW Marriott** has Spanish-Moorish design and splendid dining at organic-inspired Whisper Creek Farm: The Kitchen and classic Italian at Primo. It also features a great mini-water park, kids' pool and splash fountain. The **Ritz-Carlton** offers lush gardens and streams with its Venetian architecture, plus a huge sloped-entry pool and kids' pool. Dining includes Southern-tinged Highball & Harvest and newly Michelin-starred Knife & Spoon (p297), plus Fairways pub and Bleu pool bar and grill. Rooms are sumptuous, with marbled bathrooms, plasma-screen TVs, mini-bar, slippers and robes (407 206 2300/2400, grandelakes.com).

Omni Orlando Resort at Champions Gate: This imposing hotel offers elegant rooms, décor and dining to go with its impressive facilities, which include the David Leadbetter golf academy, two Greg Norman-designed courses, activity pool (including a lazy river, fountains and water-slide), four restaurants (notably the superb Asian cuisine of Zen and chic David's Club bar-grill), coffee bar, deli, three lounge bars, state-of-the-art health club and full-service spa (407 390 6664, bit.ly/brit-omni).

The Wave: In the smart – and growing – residential district of Lake Nona, this new (in 2022) luxury lifestyle hotel features a mix of high-tech amenities and stylish dining and recreational facilities. It has a distinctly eclectic and one-off vibe, but is decidedly chic and welcoming. Dinner at the eye-catching Bacan restaurant, with its dramatic open theatre kitchen, is highly recommended even if you don't stay here (407 675 2000, lakenonawavehotel.com).

SELF-CATERING

This is now a big choice for British visitors who prefer the space and convenience (and social distancing) of villa communities, town homes, studios and condo resorts, all of which are essentially self-catering (although some offer restaurants and other amenities). They tend to be further from the parks but represent a flexible option, especially for large groups. They usually have fewer amenities than a hotel but can be more comfortable for longer stays, and you can save money on not having to dine out each day.

Bahama Bay Resort: A wonderful lakeside location south of Highway 192, this offers 498 two and three-bed condos sleeping up to eight in 38 two and three-storey buildings. It is woven with tropical landscaping and water features, a recreation centre and clubhouse, excellent dining, Cenote Day Spa, fitness centre, tennis, basketball and volleyball, and four heated pools. You can go fishing, walk the nature trails or play billiards. Shuttle transport to the parks is available for a small charge. Condos all have a full kitchen, living room, dining area and laundry room. The Grand Bahama 3-bed unit is as large as some villas (1877 299 4481, **bit.ly/brit-bahama**).

BRITTIP

If you prefer a tranquil Lake View room at the Blue Heron Beach Resort, you can still get a view of Disney's fireworks at night from the outdoor corridor/terrace on each floor.

Balmoral Resort: A smart lakeside development of 160 villas – made up of three-bed town-homes sleeping six, and three, four, five and six-bed pool-homes sleeping 6–14 – in Haines City, 10 miles south of I-4 on Highway 27, it's maintained by builders Feltrim with every home decorated and furnished alike, which makes for hotel-level quality. The high standard of fixtures and fittings is impressive, along with the well-equipped Clubhouse, featuring a games arcade,

Bar & Grill, fitness centre and extensive pool-deck, with firepits, cabañas and movie nights, plus a child-friendly water park and mini-golf. There is also a wedding pavilion and lake fishing. It is just 13mls/21km from LEGOLAND Florida and 25/40 from the Magic Kingdom, and makes for a blissful retreat after the frenzy of the theme parks (1866 584 5527, **feltrimresorts.com/balmoral-resort**).

Blue Heron Beach Resort: A superb complex of two high-rise towers on Highway 535 in Lake Buena Vista, this features one and two-bed condos, with two bathrooms, a balcony and fully equipped kitchen. There are bunk beds in the spacious units, which sleep 6–8. All have balconies overlooking Lake Bryan while the Deluxe suites have a second balcony with a Disney fireworks view. There is a superb lido deck, with a large pool, kids' pool and hot tub, plus lake frontage and watersports (jet-skis and water-skiing, for an extra charge), with the Hawaiian Rumble mini-golf next door, plus two fitness centres, but no restaurant (although there are plenty nearby). Housekeeping is available for a charge, and there's a free daily shuttle to Disney and SeaWorld (407 387 2200, **blueheronbeachresort.com**).

Balmoral Resort

© Balmoral Resort

Encantada Resort: A lovely development of two and three-bed town-homes, this offers a lot of facilities at the central clubhouse and a great location south of west Highway 192 but still close to Disney. Each home has two bathrooms, kitchen, dining area and living room with big-screen LCD TV and home cinema, a private terrace, sunbeds and Jacuzzi. The clubhouse has a heated zero-entry pool with a Jacuzzi, children's play area and private lake surrounded by a walking trail. It also has a restaurant and pool bar, games arcade, gym and fishing pier (407 997 9478, **clcworldflorida.com/encantada**).

Encore Resort: Adjacent to the huge Reunion Resort (p78), this is a complex of upscale villas surrounding a well-appointed clubhouse. Homes vary from four beds (all with en suite) to massive 12-bed mansions, all with private pools, designer kitchens and many including Jacuzzis, games rooms and home theatres. Some even have themed bedrooms. The clubhouse includes a full water park, as well as a resort pool, fitness centre, kids' club, Grab & Go market, full-service restaurant (the excellent Finns) and bar/lounge. The concierge can arrange tickets and transport to the parks, plus services like baby-sitting, personal chefs and grocery deliveries (407 396 9000, **encorereunion.com**).

Floridays Resort: One of the smartest condo-hotels, this is situated in a quieter part of I-Drive, but close to Orlando Premium Outlets and with a free shuttle to the parks. The tropical layout features two pools (including the main zero-depth entry pool and water-play area), pool bar and grill, fitness centre, Welcome Center, kids' activity centre and games room, plus concierge services and business centre. The spacious two and three-bed suites are beautifully furnished, sleep 6–10, and have either a balcony or patio, plus flatscreen TV, wi-fi, and two bathrooms, one with a Jacuzzi tub. The nearby Publix supermarket offers delivery service and the Palm Café and Marketplace (serving Starbucks coffee) is open

from 7am–10pm daily, with room service 11am–10pm. All rooms are wheelchair-accessible and some have roll-in showers (1866 994 6321, **floridaysresortorlando.com**).

The Grove Resort & Water Park: This complex is a wonderful mix of full-scale hotel and self-catering suites. Just off Highway 192 in Kissimmee (on Avalon Road), it is set in a landscaped 106acres/43ha, with seven-storey accommodation blocks grouped around the pools, bars, luxury Spa and dining options, plus its own water park and feature-packed Family Activity Center, with arcade games and glow-in-the-dark mini-golf. The hugely spacious one, two and three-bed units are fully equipped with kitchen and laundry facilities, all with balconies. There are two indoor bars, the smart Alfresco Market for snacks, coffees and grab-and-go items, Springs pool bar and the swish full-service Valencia restaurant. The pool complex is geared for children and couples (with separate sections, and private cabañas), and there is a private lake with boating and fishing (407 545 7500, **groveresortorlando.com**).

Lake Buena Vista Resort Village & Spa: Another stylish condo-hotel, it features five tower blocks of two, three and four-bed suites, next to Lake Buena Vista Factory Stores on Highway 535. Impressive facilities include a superb freeform pool, with pirate play-ship, a quiet pool, fitness centre, video games room and kids' club. There is a convenience store and gift shop, Pizza Hut Express, Frankie Farrell's Irish Pub & Grille and poolside bar and grill, as well as a shuttle to the parks. Suites (all with full kitchens and Jacuzzi-tubs) are wonderfully spacious, and housekeeping is available either daily or weekly for a charge, while the $20/day resort fee covers parking, wi-fi, theme park shuttle, pool towels and fitness room use. The Reflections Spa & Salon offers some wonderful relaxation (407 597 0214, **lbvorlandoresort.com**).

— **BRITTIP**

Visiting Lake Buena Vista Factory Stores? Relieve aching limbs by popping next door to the Reflections Spa in the Resort Village for a soothing pedicure, massage or other treatment (407 597 1695).

Magic Village Yards and **Magic Village Views:** Two beautiful sister resorts of three and four-bed town-homes, close to Disney but in a quiet location, and with sharp, modern design. Central clubhouses offer a gorgeous main pool, kids' play-room, gym and excellent restaurant (at Magic Village Yards), Villaggio, which features Italian cuisine and gourmet pizza. There is a daily shuttle to the parks (on request, for a fee), 24hr reception and a concierge desk that can arrange in-home private parties, chefs and grocery delivery. Homes boast stylish kitchens, bathrooms with each bedroom and a first-floor balcony with sun-loungers. Some have outdoor barbecue grills or Jacuzzis, and all have washer-dryers and flatscreen TVs (407 507 5900, **magicvillagevacationhomes.com**).

Margaritaville Resort Orlando: This immense, feature-packed resort on Highway 192 in Kissimmee is based on the 'Floribbean' style of musician Jimmy Buffett, and features a hotel, vacation homes, timeshare units *and* condos. It includes a fully-fledged water park, wedding pavilion, kids' club, signature St Somewhere Spa, and an extensive lagoon-style pool, along with waterfalls and other water features that evoke a Key West feel. The hotel features three restaurants – notably the fine dining and open-air kitchen of Euphoria – while the Sunset Walk district of shops and restaurants includes Rock & Brews (a brew-pub by rock band KISS), classic 1920s burger bar Ford's Garage, mega candy store It'Sugar, Capone's Coal-Fired Pizza, Cuban concept Estefan Kitchen and Yeoman's Cask & Lion pub. Hotel rooms are gorgeously fresh and inviting, while the cottage-style vacation homes range from one to eight bedrooms. There is even a grocery delivery service to make this one of the most eye-catching resorts in Florida (407 479 0950, **margaritavilleresortorlando.com**).

Mystic Dunes Resort & Golf Club: This action-packed timeshare resort is tucked away in a quiet corner of Kissimmee and offers hotel-type rentals, often at terrific rates. It offers four pools, waterslide and water-play area, plus one, two and three-bed condos sleeping up to 12, a championship-quality golf course, mini-golf and great dining (1877 747 4747, **mystic-dunes-resort.com**).

Magic Village Yards living room

© Magic Village

Holiday Inn Club Vacations at Orange Lake Resort: This vast resort on west Highway 192 offers a mix of one, two and three-bed condo-style villas and studios that sleep 4–12, plus wonderful family-friendly amenities, from world-class golf to multiple pools. Villas all have full kitchens, TVs in each room, DVD players, hot-tubs, living and dining areas and a patio or balcony. Central River Island water park boasts a lazy river style pool, two zero-depth entry pools and pool-bars, mini-golf, hot-tubs and a clubhouse with arcade and fitness centre, as well as three restaurants and a coffee/ice cream café. There are more pools, dining choices, arcades and four golf courses spread over the three Villages that make up this immense complex (1866 892 5890, **bit.ly/brit-orangelake**).

BRITTIP

When staying in self-catering accommodation, ask in advance about any precautions or requirements for the virus. Rigorous disinfecting should take place between *every* group rental.

Regal Oaks at Old Town: This mix of three and four-bed town-homes follows the successful blueprint of homes set around an elaborate clubhouse, with great water features (zero-entry pool, waterslide and whirlpool), restaurant, bar, tennis courts, fitness centre and kids club for 4–12s. All the homes feature an enclosed patio with a hot tub. Next to all the fun and shopping of Old Town in Kissimmee, it offers terrific value (407 997 1000, **regaloaksorlando.com**).

Reunion Resort

Sheraton Vistana Villages

Regal Palms Resort & Spa: Next to Highlands Reserve villa community on Highway 27 is this mix of three and four-bed town-homes and four and five-bed villas set around a beautiful clubhouse that includes a mini water park (with lazy river and waterslides), pools, Jacuzzis, extensive sun terraces and free wi-fi. The sister resort to Regal Oaks, it also boasts a tiki bar, arcade, gym and spa, plus a volleyball court (407 965 3887, **regalpalms.com**).

Reunion Resort & Club: One of the most extensive resorts, this will interest golfers who appreciate the chance to stay where they play and lovers of the high life. On Highway 532 in Kissimmee (just off I-4 south of Disney), it boasts a vast line-up of condos, town-homes and luxury villas set around three superb golf courses. Choose from one, two and three-bed condos (many with stunning golf-course views); modest three-bed villas to 15-bed mansions; and the high-rise Grande Tower with superb dining and rooftop pool. There are 11 pools sprinkled through the resort, including the scenic Seven Eagles pool, complete with The Cove bar and grill, and an amazing water park consisting of lazy river, slides, pools, waterfalls and interactive kids' area. Add in tennis courts, mini-golf, walking trails, fitness centre and concierge service, and you have one of Florida's most upmarket resorts (407 662 1000, **reunionresort.com**).

BRITTIP

At both Sheraton Vistana properties, for a nominal fee, you can arrange to have your condo pre-stocked with food and laundry products.

Sheraton Vistana Resort: This huge family-friendly complex close to Disney is a mature development of modern, roomy one and two-bed/two-bath condos, sleeping four to eight, with full kitchens, plus magnificent resort facilities. Multiple TVs, DVD player and a screened-in private patio or balcony, plus large washer-dryers, serve to underline the self-catering value, and there is a wide variety of dining, from Castaways Bar & Grill to a food court, full-service restaurant and pool bars. Massages are available by appointment and there are mini-golf, volleyball, tennis, bike rentals and a sauna, plus lots of family-orientated activities. Scheduled transport to Disney parks costs $10/person, round-trip (bookings required), and there is no resort fee (407 239 3100, **bit.ly/brit-sheraton**).

Sheraton Vistana Villages: The sister property, on I-Drive south of SeaWorld, this upmarket resort offers spacious one and two-bed/two-bath condos with fully equipped kitchen or kitchenette in five and six-storey blocks set around scenic landscaping and pools. For those who don't want to cook, there's the smart Breeze Restaurant & Bar for breakfast, lunch and dinner and a mini-market/deli. There is regular transport to Disney parks ($10/person, bookings required), daily activities, three pool areas (some with slides and water-play areas), a fitness centre, games room, tennis and basketball courts and a grocery store. A Publix supermarket and Premium Outlets shops are nearby (407 238 5000, **sheratonvistanavillages.com**).

Solterra Resort: Another of Davenport's new – and growing – luxury villa collections, with a fantastic clubhouse and resort pool, plus the bonus of the super-deluxe subdivision of **Villatel Village**, with its sumptuous mansion-esque villas and additional services like in-home yoga, personal training and kids entertainment (407 456 8943, **solterraresortvacationhomes.com**, and 407 307 2794, **villatel.com**).

Tuscana: This Mediterranean-inspired condo-resort bordering the Champions Gate golf courses offers 288 large, elegant two and three-bed condos, each with two baths, balcony, fully equipped kitchen, washer and dryer. Resort amenities include a superb clubhouse and pool, kiddie pool, fitness centre, 30-seat cinema and picnic area with barbecue grills (407 787 4800, **aquaaston.com/hotels/tuscana-resort-orlando-by-aston**).

Vista Cay: This resort offers some of the most extensive facilities in the I-Drive/Universal Boulevard area. Handy for the attractions but away from the main bustle, it has lovely three-bed townhomes and deluxe two and three-bed condos, plus a large clubhouse and pool, whirlpool spa, kids' pool, games room and fitness centre. Spacious suites offer full kitchens, large HD TVs with DVD players, dining rooms, master bedrooms with separate tubs and showers, and balconies (407 996 4647, **vistacayholidays.com**).

Windsor Palms Resort: Just off west Highway 192 in Kissimmee, this popular resort offers two-bed condos, two and three-bed townhomes, and three to six-bed villas. Amenities include a large clubhouse and fitness centre, tennis courts, a huge main pool, kiddie pool, billiard room, basketball, volleyball court, video arcade, playground and a 58-seat cinema. Sister resort **Windsor Hills** on Old Lake Wilson Road offers the same amenities, like its lagoon-style pool with waterslide and state-of-the-art fitness centre and is even closer to the parks. **Windsor at Westside** in Davenport features four and five-bed town-homes and gorgeous six to nine-bed private pool villas. The clubhouse facilities are equally impressive, with huge resort pool, lazy river, waterslide, tiki bar, fitness centre, video arcade and sports courts. New **Windsor Island**, just off Highway 27 in Davenport, offers townhomes and luxury villas from five to a massive 10 bedrooms, as well as the impressive Aloha Club, with extensive recreation and water facilities (407 396 0642, **globalresorthomes.com**).

Rental Accommodation

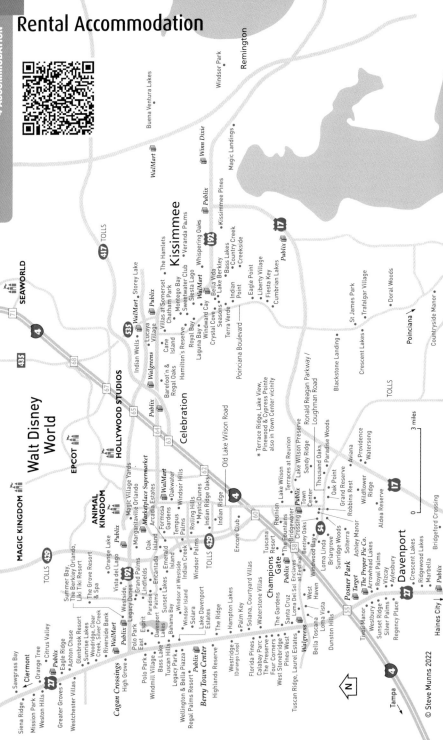

© Steve Munns 2022

HOLIDAY HOMES

This is in many ways the biggest area of accommodation for UK visitors as it is a cost-effective way for large families and groups to stay together. Since the pandemic, it also provides a more socially distanced option with plenty of personal space.

The homes, many in purpose-built, gated communities, usually have a private pool, and some offer extra communal facilities and recreation areas. They always have full kitchens, laundry facilities and multiple TVs. Some are classed as 'executive', which means more facilities (games rooms, barbecues, Jacuzzis, etc.) rather than larger size. A hire car is usually essential, but savings (compared to a hotel) can be significant. Prices can be as low as $700/week off-peak, but expect to pay at least $1,800/week for a five or six-bed villa in high season. But once you've experienced villa life, you may never go back to a hotel!

If you book independently, there are several vital questions. Do you need to collect keys from an office or is there a combination lockbox at the house? Is there a local contact if anything goes wrong, and is the property maintained by a local company? Does it offer a secure bonding for your booking? Is it a member of a reputable organisation, such as the Better Business Bureau? In winter, is the pool heated, and what is the charge? Is it actually 'just minutes from Disney', as it says, or half an hour away?

There are more than 26,000 villas across Osceola, Polk and Lake Counties to the west and south-west of Disney, most in well-established developments. Homes within a community can still vary in quality depending on the care and attention of owners/managers, hence just being in, say, Cumbrian Lakes, is not a guarantee of executive quality. You can rent direct from the owners or a property management company that will look after multiple villas. For direct rentals, check sites like **vrbo. com**, **vr360homes.com** and **thedibb.co.uk/ forums/villa-search.php**. **Owner Direct** also have a well-vetted Orlando selection of 800+ properties, often good for late deals at **bit.ly/brit-late**.

There are increasing numbers of terrace-style town-homes, so, for a 'detached' house, ask for a 'single family home'. You must do your homework and shop around for recent reviews. The following all pass the *Brit Guide* credibility test, and have added CDC-required measures for cleaning and disinfecting.

Advantage Vacation Homes: In the villa business since 1989 and one of the largest companies, it keeps its 3–8 bed homes (the majority on west Highway 192 and Highway 27 in Clermont and Davenport) fresh while also managing a range of condos (notably in the Bahama Bay Resort) and town-homes. It offers 24hr management, with courteous and efficient staff at its office just off Highway 192 (9am–10pm daily). Its holiday homes are rated Silver, Gold or Platinum, with the difference measured in extras rather than size (flatscreen TVs, tiled floors rather than carpeting, a Jacuzzi or games room, etc.), though some of the more exclusive villas might be in a golf community or have tennis courts (407 396 2262, **advantagevacationhomes.com**).

Alexander Holiday Homes: Family-owned Alexander manages more than 200 properties in Kissimmee, from standard condos to luxury seven-bed executive homes sleeping 14, all with pools and immaculately furnished, within 20mins of Disney. It was only the third company to earn the AAA (American Automobile Association) Three Diamond rating, as well as being fully accredited with the official Walt Disney World Vacation Rental Home Connection (where homes are inspected quarterly). It shows prices in UK and US currency and offers a free concierge service to ensure you get to your home, plus arrival grocery packages, barbecue rentals and wheelchair hire (407 932 3683, **floridasunshine.com**).

Debbie's Villas: Based in Kent but with an excellent team in Orlando, this is a fully British-owned company that offers a high standard of care and attention specifically with UK visitors in mind. They have been specialists for more than 20 years, managing a wide range of high-quality homes, from 3-bed villas to huge 11-bed properties. All come with a free Welcome Pack, and full ABTA/ATOL bonding, as well as a Covid-19 refund guarantee for all bookings (01892 836822, **debbiesvillas.co.uk**).

Elite Vacation Homes: This is another company with a long and solid track record of villa management in the Kissimmee area, with the majority of their 3–7-bed villas just a 10–15min drive from Disney. With a lot to choose from, including the latest executive-style homes with hot-tubs, large-screen TVs and games rooms, there is something for all budgets here (407 397 0850, **elitevacationhomes.com**).

Florida Leisure Vacation Homes: Another reliable company that has been around for more than 30 years, with an upscale approach that sets it apart from many operators. With 100 Kissimmee area homes (3–10 beds), it prides itself on a personal touch (even down to providing personal chef, massage and concierge services) and offers some of the biggest and newest properties. Many are Executive in style, with the fullest array of amenities, and often in gated communities. All villas have lockboxes, so you don't need to visit the office to check in (407 870 1600, **floridaleisurevacationhomes.com**).

Jeeves Florida Rentals: For the deluxe touch, British-owned Jeeves is one of the best in the business, specialising in high-end properties, including some of the most lavish mansions in Reunion Resort, where they are a preferred partner, allowing guests staying in properties with membership full access to all resort amenities. They also have a boutique approach, offering bespoke services. Need an in-villa private chef, spa treatment or butler? Ask Jeeves! Some of their most eye-catching properties feature themed bedrooms that wouldn't be out of place in the theme parks. They offer welcome packs, special-occasion services and a 'Car on the Drive' option

for those who don't want to pick up their hire car straight away. Their knowledge of the area is first class and they feature villas in gorgeous Encore Resort and exclusive Villatel Village, a gated section within Solterra Resort featuring six, 11 and 12-bed villas and exclusive concierge services (407 704 8986, **jeevesfloridarentals.com**).

Top Villas: For a one-stop shop, UK-owned booking agent Top Villas takes some beating. A specialist in villa rentals worldwide – but especially in Orlando – they work with local management companies to offer hundreds of properties, from one-bed condos to 15-bed villas, including luxurious resorts like Reunion and Encore. They also feature extras like car hire, private catering and housekeeping (407 495 2595 in the US, 01227 647042 in the UK; **thetopvillas.com**).

BRITTIP

For home delights, British-owned **The Proper Pie Company** – in its new location in Haines City Mall (just off Highway 17–92) offers fab home-made pies, pasties, scones and British groceries, plus fresh fish and chips, and proper afternoon tea (863 438 2705, **theproperpiecompany.com**). Groceries like Marmite, Ribena and McVities can also be found in the International aisle of supermarkets in the tourist areas.

Air BnB

While all the main villa developments are in Osceola, Lake and Polk counties, the advent of Airbnb has opened up a lot more possibilities for Orlando/Orange County, which traditionally has not allowed short-term rentals. You will still find plenty of typical vacation villas on offer but also a mix of downtown apartments and even homes and condos closer to the parks. If you are comfortable with the unique Airbnb style (where you are renting a room in someone's home), it can work out cheaper than hotels or villas (**airbnb.com/orlando-fl/stays**).

OK, that's enough accommodation advice. Now it's on to the parks….

5 The Theme Parks: Disney's Fab Four

Or, 50 years of Mickey Magic

The heart of Orlando's magical holiday experience is undoubtedly Walt Disney World, and its four major theme parks. With the vast resort's 50th anniversary still under way (until March 2023), there has never been a better time to dive into the intoxicating world that Walt imagined way back in the early 1960s.

The recent additions of the Pandora section of Disney's Animal Kingdom, Toy Story Land and Star Wars: Galaxy's Edge at Disney's Hollywood Studios, plus the ongoing transformation of the EPCOT park, have added immensely to this astounding portfolio of imagination and creativity, and the anniversary celebrations – which began on 1 October 2021 – provide the icing on the cake.

But, before we outline all the fun and excitement in store, let's consider the basics.

BRITTIP
Before you leave home, photocopy the back of your park passes and your passport info page, then you'll have the info you need should you lose them.

Buying your tickets in advance saves time and is often better value, but work out your requirements first – you won't get full value for the 14-day Disney, Universal AND SeaWorld tickets in just a fortnight. Try to use your credit card for all purchases for the built-in extra security (for our list of recommended ticket outlets; p10).

Discount options: You will find a welter of discount coupons for many of the smaller attractions in tourist publications distributed in Orlando (or from your hotel Guest Services desk – it's often worth asking). What you won't find is discounted Disney tickets (unless it is a timeshare lure). Disney never discount, apart from occasional '5th Day Free' offers through the official outlets.

BRITTIP
Walt Disney World's live entertainment and character meals were modified or curtailed during the pandemic, but they are all due to be back to normal in 2023.

It IS possible to bag free tickets by attending timeshare presentations but they can easily take half a day of hard-sell out of your precious holiday.

Timeshare: If you DO want to look at timeshare options, look first at Disney Vacation Club for the guarantee of memorable holidays. A tour (for which you will be picked up) will take about 3hrs and you'll receive a small parting gift (dining coupon, etc). Visit **disneyvacationclub.disney.go.com**.

BRITTIP
Smoking is not permitted in the restaurants or in the parks, apart from in a designated area outside each park's gates.

Character dining

Having a meal with Mickey and Co is one of the great Disney experiences – even without children – and is often the best way to meet your favourite characters without a wait. Make reservations up to 180 days in advance (180 plus your length of stay if you are booked at a Disney hotel) by phoning 407 WDW DINE (939 3463), calling at any Guest Services desk in a hotel, or on **disneyworld.com**.

Some meals are difficult to get. Breakfast at Cinderella's Royal Table or Be Our Guest at the Magic Kingdom usually sell out within minutes of the 180-day window being open. Chef Mickey's and the Princess meals also go quickly. If you cannot book in advance, try calling the day you'd like to dine or, as a last resort, show up to see if there have been any cancellations. You must check in at the podium 10mins before your time and you will be given the next available table. Some characters don't enter the restaurant so, if they are in the lobby, meet them before you are seated. Dining is all-you-can-eat, served buffet, pre-plated or family-style. Inside the restaurant, characters circulate among the tables, giving attention to each group (particularly when children are holding the camera!).

Character interaction is top-notch, especially if you dine off-hours when the restaurant is quieter. Bring your autograph book, a fat pen or marker (easier for the characters to hold) and a large capacity digital card. Some characters are huge, and children may be put off by them. If you aren't sure how they'll react, see how they are with the characters in the park before booking. Price range: breakfast $42–52 adults, $27–34 children; lunch $55–63 and $36–41; dinner $55–63 and $36–41 (NB: beware peak season price rises – Disney raises its rates in high season and even weekends, and some of those children's prices are outrageous, in our opinion).

Ratings

Our unique rating system splits attractions into thrill rides and scenic rides, earning T or A ratings out of 5.

- TTTTT is as exciting as they get and, along with AAAAA is unmissable. These will have the longest queues, so you should plan your visit around them.

- TTTT or AAAA should be high on your 'must do' list.

- TTT or AAA should be seen if you have time.

- TT is worth seeing only if there is no queue, AA is likely to be twee and missable.

Some rides have height restrictions and are not advisable for people with back, neck or heart problems or for expectant mothers. Where this is the case we say, for example, '**R:** 3ft 6in/106cm'. Height restrictions (strictly enforced) are based on the average five-year-old being 3ft 6in/106cm tall, those aged six being 3ft 9in/114cm and nines being 4ft 4in/132cm.

My Disney Experience

This online system of guest interaction is devised to enhance your park visit. It allows guests to create their own profile, input ticket details, add family and other groups, and plug in to an array of features that include the option to book dining and other extra opportunities, plus add park photos to your account through Memory Maker (p88), and more besides. It includes the new **Disney Genie** service (see p85) that opens up more ways to enjoy the parks and use the new paid-for Disney Genie+ option that replaces the old FastPass+ system. You don't have to sign up for My Disney Experience, but you won't be able to access all the perks if you choose not to. It builds into a wide-ranging digital platform, notably with an App that links everything together. Originally, it was created to work with the unique MagicBand that acted as your ticket, payment card, PhotoPass card and hotel key (for those staying at a Disney hotel), but it has been expanded to work with the Disney MagicMobile Pass app and

Disney Genie. Create your account at **https://disneyworld.disney.go.com/plan/my-disney-experience/**.

MagicBand+

In 2022, Disney introduced the enhanced MagicBand+ as part of their 50th Anniversary celebration. The band does everything MagicBands do, but adds interactive elements such as the 'Disney Fab 5 Quest' scavenger hunt and 'Star Wars: Batuu Bounty Hunters' missions in Star Wars: Galaxy's Edge, plus colour-changing lighting effects during night-time shows, and gesture recognition that allows guests to interact with things like the Fab 50 Character Collection (p93).

Disney has an App for that

Get essential Park info on your Mobile device with the **My Disney Experience App**, from park hours and wait times to menus, ride info and Genie+ reminders, all free for iPhone and Android, from **bit.ly/disney-app**. The **app** also allows you to order food and drinks. Go to Mobile Food Orders, choose the restaurant you'd like to order from and press Order Food. Make your selections, and pay via credit card, debit card or Disney Dining Plan. When you arrive at the restaurant, tap 'I'm Here, Prepare My Order', and your food will be made while you wait. Pick it up at a special Mobile Order Pickup Window.

The **Disney MagicMobile Pass** app debuted in 2021, moving the benefits of a MagicBand to your mobile phone for a fully contactless experience. You can find it on the app above.

For added fun, download the **Play Disney Parks app**, which unlocks superb interactive elements within Star Wars: Galaxy's Edge, among many neat additions: **disneyworld.disney.go.com/guest-services/play-app**.

BRITTIP

Free wi-fi is available throughout Walt Disney World to ensure you can access the online facilities, including all the benefits of MyMagic+.

Disney Genie

Perhaps the most dramatic – and controversial – development in recent Disney history is the advent of this service in late 2021. The next level of My Disney Experience, it offers ways to maximise your park time by creating personal itineraries, offering a virtual queue for key attractions, order food, and, contentiously, paying for shorter-wait ride access via **Genie+**. You start by creating a personalised itinerary for your day, inputting preferences for rides, shows, food and other experiences. Genie collates your selections and turns them into a programme to follow all day. It updates as you go, showing current and forecast wait times at the attractions on your list so you can decide the ideal time for each one. It also suggests meal options, if you haven't made reservations, and answers any questions you may have via a 'virtual assistant.'

Disney Genie+

This is where things become more complex, as there is now the *option* to pay a set fee per day to bypass the main queue for a variety of attractions. For **$15-22/day** (low to high season), select Genie+ and receive the next available time for rides and shows like *Millennium Falcon: Smugglers Run* at Disney's Hollywood Studios and classics like *Haunted Mansion* at Magic Kingdom. There are more than 40 attractions through the four parks, accessed via the new Lightning Lane (the old FastPass+) entrance. Pick one at a time throughout the day, until availability is used up (and there is a finite amount each day). Like the old FastPass system, this cuts out a LOT of queuing, but it will cost a family of four $60/day. You don't have to pay for it to benefit from the main Disney Genie service. Genie+ also offers a range of **audio experiences** featuring fun facts and insights about the parks from Disney Imagineers and special guests, plus exclusive **photo effects** using augmented reality lenses that add beloved Disney characters or magical effects to each

Character Dining: the meals

MAGIC KINGDOM: Crystal Palace for breakfast, lunch or dinner with Winnie the Pooh and Co – especially good for smaller children; and **Cinderella's Royal Table** for the (expensive) Once Upon A Breakfast, with Cinderella and her Princess Friends; Lunch (Cinderella and Friends); and Dinner (Fairy Godmother only). Breakfast (off-peak) is $42 adults, $27 children; lunch and dinner $62 and $37. Credit card payment in full is required to book and you WILL be charged the full price if you cancel less than 24hrs in advance (photo package and gratuity included, additional photos for a fee).

EPCOT: Garden Grill for lunch or dinner with Farmer Mickey, Pluto, Chip and Dale; Princess Storybook **Dining at Restaurant** Akershus (Norway) for breakfast, lunch and dinner; an alternative to Cinderella's, with some of Belle, Jasmine, Snow White, Mulan, Aurora (Sleeping Beauty) and Mary Poppins. Breakfast $53 adults, $34 children; lunch and dinner $63 and $41. Credit card needed to book; full charge applied for cancelling less than 24hrs in advance.

DISNEY'S HOLLYWOOD STUDIOS: Hollywood & Vine for breakfast or lunch with the Play 'n Dine pals, including Doc McStuffins, Sophia the First, Vampirina and Goofy ($42/$27). At peak times, Minnie's Seasonal Dining (with Goofy, Donald and Daisy) features lunch and dinner ($55/$36).

DISNEY'S ANIMAL KINGDOM: Donald's Dining Safari Breakfast and Lunch at **Tusker House** with Donald, Goofy, Pluto and sometimes Daisy and Mickey.

DISNEY RESORTS

Beach Club Resort: At **Cape May Café**, breakfast with Goofy, Minnie and Donald.

Contemporary Resort: At **Chef Mickey's**, breakfast or dinner with Mickey, Minnie, Goofy, Pluto, Donald Duck – peak times book up quickly.

Four Seasons Hotel: At **Ravello**, Thurs and Sat (plus Tues during peak seasons) breakfast with Goofy and pals, $48/adults and $28 3–9s.

Grand Floridian: At **1900 Park Fare**, breakfast with Alice, Mary Poppins, Tigger, Pooh Bear and Mad Hatter; dinner with Cinderella, Anastasia, Drizella, Lady Tremaine and, sometimes, Prince Charming – book early. Wonderland Tea Party 2–3pm Mon–Fri, 4–12s only, $49, meal, activities and storytelling with Alice and friends.

Polynesian Resort: At **'Ohana**, breakfast with Lilo, Stitch, Pluto and Mickey.

Walt Disney World Swan: At **Garden Grove**, Mon–Fri, dinner and Sat and Sun breakfast, both with Goofy and Pluto.

photo. Genie+ can *only* be purchased on the day of your visit to a park, and ride selections can only be made starting at 7am on the day of your visit.

Individual Selections

Additionally, ALL guests can use Genie to pay for the **Individual Lightning Lane** (ILL) selections, one or two key rides that usually draw the biggest queues in each park (and are NOT on the Genie+ list), like *Seven Dwarfs Mine Train* at Magic Kingdom, *Guardians of the Galaxy:* *Cosmic Rewind* at Epcot and *Rise of the Resistance* at Disney's Hollywood Studios. Once selected, guests will get a specific time to ride via the Lightning Lane entrance. Pricing runs from $15–$22, depending on the attraction, and pricing will vary by date, costing more at peak times. Disney hotel guests can make ILL choices from 7am, while other guests can only do so from park opening time, and availability may run out early in the day. Genie+ and ILL attractions are listed as G+ or ILL in the text for each ride or show description. *For summer 2022, Disney also changed some* ILL *rides, like Space Mountain at the Magic Kingdom and Expedition Everest at Magic Kingdom, to the* **Genie+** *list, so be sure to check for the latest list at:* **https://disneyworld.disney.go.com/genie/lightning-lane**.

---BRITTIP---

If you prefer a MagicBand to the MagicMobile app in the parks, they cost $19.99 (basic model; $10 off if pre-booked with a Disney hotel stay), $30 (with Disney characters) or $35 to $58 (special editions). The new MagicBand+ bands are $35 to $45.

All Disney parks offer pushchair ('stroller') hire, and you can save money by buying a multi-day rental at your first park. Children of ALL ages seem to get a big thrill from collecting autographs from the various Disney characters, and most shops sell autograph books ($9.99). Parents wanting healthier dining options for kids in Disney parks and resorts should look on the menu for Mickey Check, a standard for more nutritious meals. You should find at least one choice at every counter-service and full-service restaurant (**disneymickeycheck.com**).

Theme Park Reservations

Along with a valid admission ticket, guests ages 3 and up must make a Park Pass reservation for each day they would like to visit a Disney theme park. Purchase your admission ticket, link it to your My Disney Experience account, check availability and make a booking for each theme park and each day you would like to visit. We believe this requirement will stay in place for the foreseeable future.

PhotoPass

This worthwhile scheme is available in all Disney's parks and in Disney Springs. Disney photographers take photos of guests that are linked to an online account via a card you receive with your first photo or via Memory Maker (see below). There is no charge for a card or for viewing them online, but there is if you want to download and print them. Photos can be enhanced with Disney characters and special effects, while there are 'magical' photos where photographers ask guests to pose in a fun way and Tinker Bell (or Stitch, or Simba or Mickey) will appear in the frame.

Harmonious at Epcot

© Disney

Guests have 30 days after the photos are taken to decide if they want to buy at **mydisneyphotopass.com.**

Memory Maker: This package links to a My Disney Experience account (p84), collecting each PhotoPass, on-ride and character dining photo for $199 ($169 in advance) for the full duration of your visit or $69 for one day of photos. Images can be put on mugs, mouse pads and more. Just swipe your card or Magic Band with every photo (ride photos add automatically with a Band). UK Disney Magic tickets include Memory Maker.

Cast Members

Disney employees are called Cast Members or CMs (never 'staff') and they're renowned for their helpful, cheerful style, always willing to assist, advise or chat. If you've had exceptional service, let Disney know (at Guest Relations, City Hall or on the My Disney Exerience app via the 'compliment' section) as it values feedback and CMs get credit.

Seven Dwarfs Mine Train

Rider Switch

If you have small children or one person who does not wish to ride but cannot be left alone, tell the operator at the entrance you want to do a Rider Switch. While riders enjoy the ride, non-riders wait in a quiet area, then the other riders swap. You will be given a Rider Switch ticket.

Park security

Visitors must go through a security check at the Transportation and Ticket Center for Magic Kingdom or at park entry for EPCOT, Hollywood Studios and Animal Kingdom. There is a separate lane for those without bags, but all visitors must go through a metal detector screening.

There is NO smoking inside any theme park (smoking sections are located outside each park's entrance).

Pushchair size is limited to 31 x 52in/79 x 132cm.

Selfie sticks, stroller wagons, loose ice and dry ice are banned.

© Disney

MAGIC KINGDOM PARK

The starting point for any visit, the Magic Kingdom is Celebration Central for the big 50th anniversary, from October 2021 to March 2023, and best embodies the genuine sense of enchantment Disney bestows on its visitors. A few rides are the same as those in Disneyland Paris or Disneyland in LA, but there are key differences, notably on Pirates of the Caribbean, Big Thunder Mountain Railroad, Haunted Mansion and especially Space Mountain. And, even if a couple of attractions are closed for refurbishment, you won't be short of things to do! Here's our guide to a typical day, including the rides, shows and places to eat; how to park, how to avoid the worst of the crowds – and how much you should expect to pay.

Magic Kingdom Park at a glance

Location	Off World Drive, Walt Disney World
Size	107 acres/43ha in 6 'lands'
Hours	9am–7pm off peak; 9am–10pm President's Day (see Brit Tip, p18), spring school holidays; 8am–11pm or midnight high season (Easter, summer holidays, Thanksgiving and Christmas)
Admission	Under-3s free; 3–9 $104–154 (1-day base ticket, priced seasonally), $437–595 (5-day Standard Theme Park Ticket), £469 (14-day Magic, includes Memory Maker); adult (10+) $109–159, $455–610, £489. US prices do not include tax.
Parking	$25, $45-$50 premium
Lockers	To the right of the main entrance $10 small, $12 large, and $15 jumbo
Pushchairs	$15 and $31 (underneath Main Street Train Station; $13 and $27 per day for multiple days)
Wheelchairs	$12 or $70 ($20 deposit refunded) underneath Main Street Train Station
Top attractions	Splash Mountain, Space Mountain, Seven Dwarfs' Mine Train, Big Thunder Mountain Railroad, TRON Lightcycle/Run, Pirates of the Caribbean, Haunted Mansion, most rides in Fantasyland
Don't miss	Festival of Fantasy Parade and Disney Enchantment fireworks (most nights)

Hidden costs	Meals	Burger, chips and coke $15, 3-course dinner (Tony's Town Square) $30–$59 Kids' counter service meal $6.79–7.99
	T-shirts	$27–42 Kids $18–40
	Souvenirs	$1.99–35,500
	Sundries	Magic Bands $20–$35

MagicBand+

© Disney

The Magic Kingdom takes up just 107acres/43ha of Disney's near 31,000acres/12,555ha but attracts almost as many as the rest put together. It has six 'lands', like slices of a cake, centred on Florida's most famous landmark, Cinderella Castle. More than 40 attractions are packed into the park, plus shops and restaurants. It's easy to get overwhelmed, especially as it gets so busy (even the fast-food restaurants have long queues in high season), so plan around what most takes your fancy, but do look out for the interactive queues at some rides, including Big Thunder Mountain Railroad, Haunted Mansion, Peter Pan's Flight, Space Mountain, Little Mermaid, Winnie the Pooh and Seven Dwarfs Mine Train.

50th Anniversary Frenzy

Walt Disney World's official 50th anniversary began on 1 October 2021 and concludes 18 months later. Mickey and Minnie Mouse are decked out in celebratory costumes, Remy's Ratatouille Adventure debuted at Epcot, and spectacular **Beacons of Magic** night-time projections light up Cinderella Castle, Spaceship Earth, Tower of Terror and the Tree of Life.

© Disney

Mirabel from Encanto *appears in the Celebration Cavalcade*

The Magic Kingdom features new fireworks and special effects show Disney Enchantment, and Mickey's Celebration Cavalcade runs several times a day. See all the details at **https://disneyworld.disney.go.com/50th-anniversary**.

Disney's 50th anniversary Cinderella Castle

© Disney

ADVENTURELAND

1 Swiss Family Treehouse
2 Jungle Cruise
3 Magic Carpets of Aladdin
4 The Enchanted Tiki Room
5 Pirates of the Caribbean

FRONTIERLAND

6 Splash Mountain
7 Big Thunder Mountain Railroad
8 Country Bear Jamboree
9 Raft to Tom Sawyer Island

LIBERTY SQUARE

10 Liberty Tree Tavern
11 Liberty Square Riverboat
12 The Haunted Mansion
13 The Hall of Presidents

FANTASYLAND

14 'It's a Small World'
15 Prince Charming Regal Carrousel
16 Mad Tec Party
17 The Many Adventures of Winnie The Pooh
18 Princess Fairytale Hall
19 Dumbo The Flying Elephant
20 Mickey's PhilharMagic
21 The Barnstormer starring The Great Goofini
22 Casey Jr Splash 'n' Soak Station

23 Peter Pan's Flight
24 Castle Forecourt Stage
25 Cinderella's Royal Table
26 Brave – Meet Merida
27 Enchanted Tales with Belle
28 Be Our Guest Restaurant
29 Under The Sea – Journey of the Little Mermaid
30 Ariel's Grotto
31 Seven Dwarfs Mine Train

TOMORROWLAND

32 Space Mountain
33 Tron Lightcycle/Run (2023)
34 Tomorrowland Indy Speedway
35 Walt Disney's Carousel of Progress
36 Astro Orbiter
37 Tomorrowland Transit Authority
38 Buzz Lightyear's Space Ranger Spin
39 Monsters Inc. Laugh Floor

TRANSPORT

40 Walt Disney World Railroad Stations
41 Boat Dock
42 Monorail Station
43 Bus Station

Location

The Magic Kingdom is situated at the innermost end of Walt Disney World, with its entrance Toll Plaza three-quarters of the way along World Drive, the main entrance off Highway 192. World Drive runs north–south, while the Interstate 4 (I-4) entrance, EPCOT Drive, runs east–west. Unless you are staying at a Disney resort or are an Annual Pass holder, you must pay the $25–50 parking fee at the Toll Plaza to bring you into the massive car park (we really don't believe the Premium Parking is worth it, by the way).

The car parks are busiest from 9.30–11.30am, so it's vital to get here EARLY. If you can't arrive by 9am at peak times, wait until after 1pm, or later when the park is open late. Remember to note where you park: there are Heroes (Woody, Simba, Rapunzel, Aladdin, Peter Pan and Mulan) and Villains (Ursula, Jafar, Zurg, Hook, Scar and Cruella) sections of the 'parking lot'. Note the side, section and number you're in (e.g. Ursula row 94) as many hire cars look the same!

© Disney

Meet and Greet returns to the Town Square Theater

A tram takes you to the Transportation and Ticket Center, where you go through a security check. Unless you already have tickets (which saves valuable time), you visit the ticket booths here. Then, to get to the Magic Kingdom itself, the monorail is quicker if there isn't a queue, otherwise take a ferryboat. For Disney hotel guests, the resort buses drop you almost at the front door. Uber and Lyft drop off at the Transportation and Ticket Center.

BRITTIP

Take a photo of the Section and Row number on your camera or phone so you know where you've parked.

A rainbow adds to the magic of the Magic Kingdom

© Disney

Golden statues for the 50th anniversary

© Disney

Main Street USA

Hopefully, you've arrived early and are among the first to swarm through the entrance. The opening time may say 9am but the gates can open up to 45mins earlier, bringing you into the first of the 'lands'. On your right is **Town Square Theater**, the place to meet Mickey Mouse and Tinker Bell. On the left is **City Hall** for any queries, problems and restaurant bookings (highly advisable). Main Street also has the park's best shopping (notably the massive **Emporium**) and **Walt Disney World Railroad** (AAA), a Western-themed steam train that circles the park and is a good choice when queues are long elsewhere (though Town Square station is often the busiest). The Railroad will begin running again once the construction of the new TRON ride is complete.

Dining: Italian-style **Tony's Town Square Restaurant** serves lunch and dinner; **The Plaza Restaurant** offers breakfast platters (7.45–10.30am) and a lunch/dinner menu of salads, sandwiches and classic American dishes like Meatloaf, with beer and wine. **The Crystal Palace** (lunch and dinner $39/adult and $23 ages 3–9) is classic food with Winnie the Pooh and Co. Quick bites can be bought from **Casey's Corner** (hot dogs, chips and soft drinks); **Main Street Bakery** (a Starbucks coffee shop, also serving great pastries); **Main Street Confectionery** (chocolate and sweets); and the **Plaza Ice Cream Parlor**. Disney characters also appear periodically in the Square.

Info: Check the **Guest Information Board** at the top of Main Street (on the left) for waiting times for all the attractions. The **Baby Center** (for nursing mums) and the **First Aid Station** are at the top of Main Street, to the left next to Crystal Palace.

BRITTIP

Don't miss the golden Mickey and Minnie 50th Anniversary statues in the plaza in front of the castle, among the **Fab 50 Character Collection** throughout all four parks, many of which react to the new MagicBand+.

Beating the queues: Unless you are late, skip Main Street and head for the end of the street to the real entrance to the park, where you await official opening hour. Adopt one of three tactics, to do some of the most popular rides before the queues build up (like 2hrs for Splash Mountain at times). 1: If you fancy the five-star, log-flume Splash Mountain, keep left in front of the Crystal Palace with the majority. 2: If you have young children who can't

Mickey and Minnie at Town Square Theater

© Disney

wait to try the Fantasyland rides (especially the Seven Dwarfs Mine Train, which draws l-o-n-g queues), stay in the middle and pass around the Castle. 3: If the thrills of indoor roller-coasters Space Mountain and TRON Lightcycle/Run appeal, move right by The Plaza Restaurant for Tomorrowland. Now you're in pole position for the initial rush (and it will be a rush; take care with kids).

Other entertainment: The day starts with **Let The Magic Begin**, a five-minute welcome show on the Castle Forecourt stage, with a royal herald and a few well-known Disney faces appearing to mark the official opening of the park. The **Main Street Trolley Show** happens 3–4 times a day, with a horse-drawn trolley arriving for a 20min song-and-dance interlude. Fun barbershop quartet the **Dapper Dans** and brass band **Main Street Philharmonic** (who also play in Storybook Circus) add lively musical interludes, as does **Casey's Corner Pianist**, and don't miss the **Glass Blowing Demonstrations** at Crystal Arts Shop. There is a daily **Flag Retreat** at 5pm, with a military veteran helping the Security Colour Guard to bring down the national flag. Need a haircut? Try the traditional style of **Harmony Barber Shop** for a truly old-fashioned experience.

Adventureland

Head left (going round clockwise) to enter Adventureland. If you're going to Splash Mountain first, pass the Swiss Family Treehouse on your left and bear right through an archway (with toilets) into Frontierland, where you turn left and Splash Mountain is ahead. Stopping in Adventureland, these are the attractions.

Swiss Family Treehouse: This imitation banyan tree is a clever replica of the treehouse from Disney's 1960 film *Swiss Family Robinson*. It's a walk-through attraction where the queues (rarely long) move steadily if not quickly, providing a neat glimpse of the ultimate tree house. AA

> ►**BRITTIP**
>
> Most character meet-and-greets have returned, but some may still be reduced to 'character cavalcades' because of the ongoing pandemic.

Jungle Cruise: It's not so much the scenic, geographically suspect boat ride (where the Nile suddenly becomes the Amazon) that is so amusing as the non-stop yarn about your adventure from the boat's captain. Long queues, so visit early morning (opens 10am) or late afternoon (evening queues are shortest, but you'll miss some of the detail in the dark). AAAA G+

Jungle Cruise

© Disney

Pirates of the Caribbean: One of Disney's most impressive attractions that involves Walt's pioneering work in audio-animatronics, life-size figures that move, talk and, in this instance, lay siege to a Caribbean island! Your 8min underground boat ride visits a typical pirate adventure and the world of Captain Jack Sparrow and nemesis Captain Barbossa as they search for buried treasure. It's terrific family fun (though perhaps a bit spooky for young children, with one small drop in the dark). Queues are longest from late morning to mid-afternoon. AAAAA (TTTT under-10s) G+

The Enchanted Tiki Room: A classic bird-laden, South Seas audio-animatronic show starring various parrots, macaws and other tropical feathered friends – plus the angry Tiki Gods! Queues are rare and it is air-conditioned. AA

Magic Carpets of Aladdin: In an Agrabah-themed area, this ride spins you up, down and around as you try to dodge the spitting camel! Your 'flying carpet' tilts as well as levitates, simple stuff geared for younger children (like the Magic Carpets of Agrabah ride in Disneyland Paris). T (TTTT under-5s), G+.

A Pirate's Adventure: Treasure of the Seven Seas: Join this clever scavenger hunt disguised as an interactive card game to help Captain Jack Sparrow see off his foes and locate secret treasure around Adventureland, using a map and magic talisman. Visit the kiosk through the archway past the Pirates ride to get started (noon–6pm). AAA

Disney characters from the movie Aladdin also turn up next to the Magic Carpets ride.

Shopping: The best shopping is in **Pirates Bazaar**, with all manner of pirate-themed gifts and toys.

Dining: Skipper Canteen is casual full service 'adventure dining' themed like the Jungle Cruise and in three different dining rooms. It features 'World Famous Jungle Cuisine', served by Jungle Cruise skippers, and is an excellent choice for lunch or dinner, offering surprisingly upscale food for a theme park. **Aloha Isle** adds signature Dole Whips and **Sunshine Tree Terrace** has ice cream, Dole Whips and drinks, and **Tortuga Tavern** (open seasonally) features chicken strips, burgers and hot dogs.

Magic Carpets of Aladdin

© Disney

Frontierland

This Western-themed area is one of the busiest and is best avoided from late morning to late afternoon.

Splash Mountain: Based on classic Disney cartoon *Song of the South*, this is a watery journey with Brer Rabbit, Brer Fox and Brer Bear. It features jolly cartoon scenery and fun with the main characters and several minor swoops in your log boat, followed by a five-storey plummet into a mist-shrouded pool! **R**: 3ft 4in/101cm. TTTT G+ In 2020, Disney announced that this ride will close for re-theming to the *Princess and the Frog,* but it looks like this won't happen now until 2024. The story will pick up after the final kiss in the movie as guests join Princess Tiana and Louis on a musical adventure "featuring some of the powerful music from the film – as they prepare for their first-ever Mardi Gras performance." There is also a (usually less busy) station for the Walt Disney World Railroad right next to Splash Mountain.

Big Thunder Mountain Railroad: When Disney does a roller-coaster it will be one of the classiest, and here it is – a runaway mine train that swoops, tilts and plunges through a mock mine filled with clever scenery. You have to ride it at least twice to appreciate all the detail, but again queues are heavy, so go early

(after Splash Mountain) or late in the day. **R**: 3ft 4in/101cm. TTTT G+

Country Bear Jamboree: Here's a novelty: a 16min musical revue by audio-animatronic bears! It's great family fun with plenty of novel touches (watch for the talking moose head). Crowds are rare, so it's a good one when it's busy elsewhere. AAA

Frontierland Shootin' Arcade: The park's single attraction that costs extra ($1 for 35 shots), as you take aim at a series of animated targets. T

Tom Sawyer Island: Take a raft to a playground of caves, grottos, mazes and rope bridges, plus Fort Sam Clemens, where you can fire air guns at passing boats (opens 11am). A good choice in early afternoon when queues are long elsewhere. TT

Other entertainment: The **Hoedown Happening** with the Country Bears provides musical interludes.

Shopping: Frontierland shops sell cowboy hats and badges, as well as Native American and Mexican crafts. Look out for the themed **Briar Patch** and **Prairie Outpost** for interesting gifts.

Dining: Try **Pecos Bill Tall Tale Inn & Café** (burgers, Tex-Mex, Fajitas), **Golden Oak Outpost** (fish sandwich, chicken strips, chili cheese fries, cookies and drinks) or **Westward Ho!** (breakfast sandwich, corn dog nuggets, drinks).

Big Thunder Mountain Railroad

© Disney

it's a small world

Liberty Square

The clockwise tour brings you to a homage to post-independence America. Much of the history will be unfamiliar to the Brits but it still has some great attractions.

Liberty Belle Riverboat: Cruise America's 'rivers' on an authentic paddle steamer, be menaced by river pirates and thrill to the stories of How the West Was Won (9.30am–7 or 8pm). This is also good at busier times of the day, especially early afternoon. AAA

The Haunted Mansion: A clever delve into the world of Master Gracey's ghostly bride that is neither too scary for most kids nor too twee for adults. Not so much a thrill ride as a scenic adventure. Watch out for the 'hitch-hiking ghosts' dropping in at the end! Longish queues for much of the day, so try to visit late on. AAAA (TTTT under-6s), G+

Hall of Presidents: See all 46 US Presidents in this 25min show of animatronic wizardry. AAA

Shopping: Look for **Ye Olde Christmas Shoppe** and the fabulous Haunted Mansion-themed **Memento Mori**.

Dining: Eating options are the full-service **Liberty Tree Tavern** (hearty soups, salads, and traditional dishes like roast turkey, roast pork and pot roast), **Columbia Harbour House** (counter-service platters, good salads and sandwiches, notably for vegetarians), **Diamond Horseshoe** (lunch and dinner buffet of turkey, pot roast, pork, mac & cheese and sides), **Liberty Square Market** (turkey legs, fresh fruit, snacks and drinks) and **Sleepy Hollow** (a picnic area serving breakfasts, corn dogs, turkey legs, sweet and savoury waffles, snacks and drinks).

Fantasyland

Leaving Liberty Square, you come to the park's spiritual heart, the area that most enchants young children. The attractions, in three areas, are designed with kids in mind, but the shops are sophisticated and the Tangled 'village' (basically a courtyard with restrooms) is wonderfully scenic.

'it's a small world': This could almost be Disney's theme ride, a family boat trip around the world, each continent represented by hundreds of dancing, singing audio-animatronic dolls in delightful set-piece pageants. If it sounds twee, it actually creates a surprisingly striking effect, accompanied by an annoyingly catchy theme song that young children adore. Crowds peak in early afternoon. AAAA G+

BRITTIP

Watch for enhanced allergy-friendly menus in the parks. If you're still not sure, a chef is always happy to speak to you directly. Just ask!

Main Street at Christmas

Peter Pan's Flight: This may seem a rather tame ride but is another Walt classic and a big hit with kids. Its novel effect of flying with Peter Pan is good fun and there's a lot of clever detail as your ship sails to Neverland. An interactive queue helps pass the time in air-conditioned comfort. AAA (AAAAA under-6s) G+

Mickey's PhilharMagic: This special-effect laden 3-D film show features Donald's hapless attempts to conduct the Enchanted Orchestra, immersing guests in the world of *Beauty and the Beast*, *The Little Mermaid*, *The Lion King*, *Peter Pan* and *Aladdin* before Mickey saves the day. The lavish theatre, animation and special effects (you can 'smell' the food!) make for a hugely enjoyable family attraction. AAAA G+

Prince Charming Regal Carrousel: The Fantasyland centrepiece shouldn't need any more explanation other than it is a vintage carousel that kids love. Long queues for much of the day, though. T (TTT under-5s)

The Many Adventures of Winnie the Pooh: Building on the timeless popularity of Pooh, Piglet and Co, this family ride offers a musical jaunt through Hundred Acre Wood with some clever effects (get ready to 'bounce' with Tigger!) and an original soundtrack. Wait times are made easier by hands-on elements throughout the queue. AAA (AAAAA under-5s) G+

Mad Tea Party: The kids will insist you take them in these spinning, oversized tea cups that have their own 'steering wheel' to add to the whirling effect. Actually, they're just a heavily disguised fairground ride. Again, go early or expect crowds. TT (TTTT under-5s) G+

Princess Fairytale Hall: This elaborate 'royal' residence features a dramatic castle gallery area where visitors gather before being summoned for an audience with some of the Disney princesses (meet Princess Tiana and her princess friends; characters alternate) AAA (AAAAA under 13 girls!)

Enchanted Tales with Belle: A wonderfully clever Beauty and the Beast character show, here you visit Maurice's Workshop, nestled in the shadow of the Beast's Castle, and guests are transported via a magic mirror to the Castle Library for a memorable interactive story-time with Belle and Lumière. AAAA

New scenes from Mickey's Philharmagic include the movie Coco

© Disney

Under the Sea – Journey of the Little Mermaid: Be a part of her world as you journey under the sea with Ariel in this gentle ride aboard stylised clamshells, past colourful scenes from the movie. Ariel, Prince Eric, Flounder, Scuttle, Sebastian, King Triton and evil sea witch Ursula all make appearances, while favourite songs add to this charming adventure (with some surprising special effects!) that is sure to have a happy ending. AAAA. G+

Ariel's Grotto: Next door is the elaborate setting for a meeting with the Little Mermaid.

The Seven Dwarfs Mine Train: It's 'off to work we go' in this charming ride through a gem-laden mine. Your trip begins as a family-friendly coaster, enters the mine for a gentle journey past the Dwarfs as they dig, dig, dig, then plunges back outside again for the grand finale. The mine cars have the swaying motion of a real mine train, all the charm of the fairytale and the sense of being 'in the film'. TTT (TTTTT under 10s) ILL

Storybook Circus

Themed for the classic film *Dumbo*, this colourful circus-inspired land features more family-friendly fun.

Dumbo the Flying Elephant: Young children cannot pass this one by and, with a clever interactive, air-conditioned queue, parents can survive a long-ish wait. It's a 2min ride on the back of a circling flying elephant, and its charm is undeniable. TT (TTTT under-5s) G+

The Barnstormer: Get ready for a junior-sized coaster in the company of classic stunt pilot The Great Goofini as this surprisingly whizzy (but very short) ride takes some sharp twists and turns in best circus style. **R**: 2ft 11in/89cm. TTT (TTTTT 4–8s) G+

Casey Jr Splash 'n' Soak Station: The Circus Train has pulled into a siding – and sprung a leak! In fact, it is a cleverly disguised water-play area, with all manner of squirting fountains, pop-jets and dumping buckets guaranteed to get the kids good and wet – so don't forget swimsuits OR a change of clothes. AAAA (under 10s).

Dumbo the Flying Elephant

© Disney

Pete's Silly Sideshow: More themed fun under the Big Top as Minnie, Goofy, Donald and Daisy (in fancy circus outfits) line up for a clever meet-and-greet. AAA

Other entertainment: The Castle Stage hosts **Mickey's Royal Friendship Faire,** featuring Mickey, Goofy, Donald and Daisy with guests Princess Tiana and Prince Naveen, Rapunzel and Flynn Rider, and Olaf, Anna and Elsa in a festival of music, dance and the celebration of friendship. AAA The Fantasyland station for the Walt Disney World Railroad will also return once the TRON ride is complete.

Other **character experiences** include Meet Merida from the 2012 film *Brave* in the Fairytale Garden, Pooh and friends next to the Winnie the Pooh ride, Gaston outside Gaston's Tavern, Peter Pan and Co outside Peter Pan's flight, and *Alice in Wonderland* characters next to the Mad Tea Party. Look out also for more of the **Fab 50 Character Collection**, including the golden statues of the Cheshire Cat, Winnie the Pooh and Piglet.

Shopping: Shop at the excellent **Sir Mickey's**, **Fantasy Faire**, **Hundred Acre Goods**, **Big Top Souvenirs** and **Bonjour! Village Gifts**. There is also an outlet of the **Bibbidi Bobbidi Boutique** here (the others are at Disney Springs and the Grand Floridian Resort), where 'little princesses' three and older can choose from eight makeover styles ($75–450), including the Crown, Carriage, Courtyard and Castle packages, plus deluxe versions and Frozen themed packages. Two Knight Packages for young dragon-slayers are also available ($20–80) from 8am–7pm (reservations highly recommended on 407 939 7895).

Dining: Eating opportunities are at **Pinocchio Village Haus** (flatbreads, salad, chicken strips and plant-based pizza), **Storybook Treats** (ice-cream) and **Friar's Nook** (breakfast sandwich, mac and cheese, hot dogs, brats, tots and drinks). **Cinderella's Royal Table** is a fine setting for the popular character breakfast, lunch and dinner with various Disney princesses (Cinderella greets guests in the foyer only). The majestic hall, waitresses in costume and well-presented food – salads, beef, fish, pork tenderloin and chicken – provide a memorable experience. Be aware you pay in FULL by credit card when you book, and, if you cancel less than 24hrs in advance, there is NO refund. More fun (and better value) is the spectacular **Be Our Guest** restaurant inside the Beast's Castle, a truly unique setting that offers the choice of a full-service lunch or dinner from a prix fixe menu, with beer and wine (reservations). Set in three themed sections – the Ballroom (complete with snow on the terrace!), Rose Gallery and dark and moody West Wing – it's one of the most ornate

Cinderella's Royal Table

© Disney

dining options. Lunch ($62 adults, $37 ages 3–9; 10.30am–2.30pm) offers a choice of one starter, one main (pork tenderloin, fish, chicken, spiced vegetables or filet mignon), and dessert; and prix fixe dinner ($62/$37; 4pm–10pm or park closing) offers French-influenced chicken, sustainable fish, pork tenderloin, spiced vegetables or filet mignon. Dinner books up FAST, so try to get a reservation at the 180-day mark (407 939 3463 or online at **disneyworld. com**; credit card deposit required, $10/person charge if you don't turn up).

Gaston's Tavern is a counter-service cafe featuring sandwiches, snacks and drinks, again with some great *Beauty and the Beast* theming.

BRITTIP

Many Walt Disney World dining outlets, including quick-service spots, now carry plant-based options. Look for the 'green leaf' icon on restaurant menus.

Tomorrowland

This area's cartoon-like space-age styling, novel shops and varied rides provide guaranteed all-round appeal.

TRON Lightcycle/Run: The Magic Kingdom's headline new ride for the 50th anniversary is due to open in the spring of 2023. A dramatic coaster whirl into the cyber-world of the TRON films, it features a train of the signature two-wheeled Lightcycles for a high-speed journey alongside Kevin and Sam Flynn and their computer-generated battles with The Grid, which include dazzling lighting effects and fast-launch start, hitting speeds up to 59mph – the fastest in the Magic Kingdom. TTTTT ILL (expected).

Space Mountain: One of the three most popular attractions, its reputation is deserved. Launching from Starport 75, this is a high-thrills, tight-turning roller-coaster, completely in the dark save for occasional flashes as you whiz through the galaxy. Don't do this on

TRON Lightcycle/Run installation

a full stomach! The only way to beat the crowds is to go either first thing, late in the day or during one of the parades (or use Genie+). Ride photos are available for $17–27 (included with Memory Maker, p88). **R**: 3ft 8in/111cm. TTTTT ILL (sometimes on G+)

Tomorrowland Speedway: Despite the long queues, this is a rather tame ride on supposed race tracks that just putt-putts along on rails with little real steering required (children must be 4ft 4in/132cm to drive alone). T (TTTT under-6s) G+

Astro Orbiter: A jazzed up version of Dumbo in Fantasyland, this ride is a bit faster and higher and features rockets. Long, slow-moving queues are a reason to give this a miss unless you have young children. TT (TTTT under-10s).

Walt Disney's Carousel of Progress: This overlooked gem will surprise, entertain and amuse. It is a journey through 20th-century technology with audio-animatronics in a revolving theatre that reveals different periods in history. Its 22min duration is rarely threatened by crowds. AAA

Tomorrowland Transit Authority: A neat 'future transport system', this offers an elevated view of the area, including a glimpse inside Space Mountain, in electro-magnetic cars. Short queues. AAA (TTT under-8s)

Buzz Lightyear's Space Ranger Spin: Ride into action against evil Emperor Zurg and the robot army – and shoot them with laser cannons! A sure-fire family winner, especially as you keep score. TTT (TTTTT under-8s) G+

Monsters Inc Laugh Floor: With 'live' animation, special effects and voice links, guests can match wits with Mike, Sulley and Roz from *Monsters Inc* and be entertained by their patter. Billy Boil introduces comedians like two-headed jokester Sam-n-Ella in order to capture the audience's laughter. Watch the screen – you may be featured! AAA G+

Other entertainment: Disney characters are often on hand by the Carousel of Progress, notably Buzz Lightyear. The **Rockettower Plaza Stage** features live entertainment and greetings with the likes of Buzz Lightyear and Stitch.

Tomorrowland

© Disney

Shopping: Highlights are provided by **Mickey's Star Traders** and **Tomorrowland Light & Power Co**.

Dining: For food, try **Cosmic Ray's Starlight Café** (good burgers, chicken strips, hot dogs, plant-based burgers, and salads); **Auntie Gravity's Galactic Goodies** (ice-cream, smoothies); the **Lunching Pad** (hot dogs, chicken strips, snacks and frozen drinks) or **Tomorrowland Terrace** (open seasonally and for dessert parties).

Having come full circle you're now back at Main Street USA and it's best to return here in the afternoon to avoid the crowds and enjoy the impressive shops.

—BRITTIP

To watch a parade, sit on the left side of Main Street USA (facing the Castle) to stay in the shade if it's hot, or grab a spot in the Hub or Frontierland. People start staking out the best places an HOUR in advance.

Disney parades

Disney really knows how to do a parade. Coupled with its range of special seasonal events, there is always much more to look forward to than just the rides.

Festival of Fantasy Parade: A dazzling and unmissable pageant of creative floats, costumes, dancers and music. The seven featured floats include The Little Mermaid, Disney Princes and Princesses (including *Frozen*'s Anna and Elsa), Maleficent (with a magnificent fire-breathing steampunk style dragon!), Tangled and Peter Pan and friends, plus a special balloon-like vehicle for Mickey and Minnie. The energetic dancers, stiltwalkers and rather menacing outfits of the 'Raven' men combine for dramatic effect. AAAAA for special viewing area.

New for the 50th Anniversary is **Mickey's Celebration Cavalcade**, a musical parade through the park up to 5 times a day featuring the gang in all their special finery.

Festival of Fantasy Parade

© Disney

MAGIC KINGDOM PARK with children

Here is a rough guide to the attractions that appeal to different age groups (height restrictions have been taken into account):

Under-5s

Country Bear Jamboree, Mickey's Royal Friendship Faire, Dumbo the Flying Elephant, Enchanted Tales With Belle, The Enchanted Tiki Room, Festival of Fantasy Parade, Magic Carpets of Aladdin, 'It's a Small World', Journey of the Little Mermaid, Jungle Cruise, Liberty Square Riverboat, Many Adventures of Winnie the Pooh, Mickey's PhilharMagic, Monsters Inc Laugh Floor, Peter Pan's Flight, Prince Charming Regal Carousel, Tomorrowland Speedway (with a parent), Tomorrowland Transit Authority, Walt Disney World Railroad.

5–8s

All of above, plus Astro Orbiter, The Barnstormer, Big Thunder Mountain Railroad, Buzz Lightyear's Space Ranger Spin, Haunted Mansion, Mad Tea Party, Pirates of the Caribbean, Seven Dwarfs Mine Train Ride, Space Mountain (with parental discretion), Splash Mountain, Swiss Family Treehouse, Tom Sawyer Island, Walt Disney's Carousel of Progress, Disney Enchantment fireworks.

9–12s

Astro Orbiter, Big Thunder Mountain Railroad, Buzz Lightyear's Space Ranger Spin, Country Bear Jamboree, Festival of Fantasy Parade, The Haunted Mansion, Journey of the Little Mermaid, Mad Tea Party, Mickey's PhilharMagic, Monsters Inc. Laugh Floor, Pirates of the Caribbean, Seven Dwarfs Mine Train Ride, Space Mountain, Splash Mountain, Tomorrowland Speedway (without a parent), Disney Enchantment fireworks, TRON Lightcycle/Run (if tall enough).

Over-12s

Astro Orbiter, Big Thunder Mountain Railroad, Buzz Lightyear's Space Ranger Spin, Festival of Fantasy parade, Haunted Mansion, Mad Tea Party, Mickey's PhilharMagic, Pirates of the Caribbean, Seven Dwarfs Mine Train, Space Mountain, Splash Mountain, TRON Lightcycle/Run, Disney Enchantment fireworks.

Once Upon A Time: This stunning nightly state-of-the-art projection show uses the Cinderella Castle as its backdrop, incorporating animated special effects and video that make the castle seem to come alive, transforming again and again with a sequence of Disney characters and films in dynamic colour. Watch as a magical montage brings to life favourite scenes from classic Disney films, with the imagery weaving visual trick after trick to leave your eyeballs breathless! AAAA

Disney Enchantment: Bringing down the curtain most nights is this all-new extravaganza of pyrotechnics, lighting and projection mapping. It invites guests to believe in magic through an awe–inspiring mix of fireworks and special effects that include the first immersive use of the buildings along Main Street USA and a memorable musical medley of all your Disney favourites. Definitely not to be missed to conclude a memorable day. AAAAA

BRITTIP

After the fireworks crowd exits, you are allowed to take the Resort Only monorail back to the Transportation & Ticket Center, rather than queue for the main Express monorail.

Fireworks Cruises: If you prefer not to fight the crowds for a fab look at the fireworks show, book one of three speciality cruises to view the fireworks from Seven Seas Lagoon. The cruise holds up to 10 on a

25ft/7.6m pontoon boat (for $399) And includes water, soft drinks, snacks and an audio feed to the fireworks music (plus banners and balloons upon request). Or, splash out for the **Ferrytale Fireworks: A Sparkling Dessert Cruise** onboard a Magic Kingdom ferryboat, complete with specialty drinks, treats, and a scavenger hunt (select Wed and Sat nights; $99 per adult, $69 ages 3–9). Each can be booked 90 days in advance.

BRITTIP

For a final bit of typical Disney entertainment head outside the Magic Kingdom at 10.25pm and catch the Electrical Water Pageant passing by on Seven Seas Lagoon in front of the park.

Leaving the park

When it comes to leaving, the monorail is quicker than the ferry but it can still take up to an hour to get back to your car. Also, if the crowds get too heavy during the day, you can escape by leaving in the early afternoon (your car park ticket is valid all day) and returning to your hotel for a few hours' rest or a dip in the pool. Alternatively, catch a boat to one of the Disney resorts. Fort Wilderness is especially fun for kids and boasts the good value Trails End restaurant for dinner.

Halloween and Christmas

Two additional annual events in the Magic Kingdom provide a separate, party-style ticketed event 7pm–midnight, with most of the rides open and extra themed fun and games.

Mickey's Not So Scary Halloween Party: Aug–Oct sees many visitors dress up for the American trick-or-treat fun, with plenty of treats for all. With special features, shows, Mickey's Boo To You Halloween Parade and a brand new projection, laser and fireworks night-time

spectacular that tells a Trick-or-Treating story, tickets ($109–199 adults, $99–189 for children 3–9) go on sale about five months in advance and sell quickly.

Mickey's Very Merry Christmas Party: The Christmas party (Nov–Dec; variously from $109–199 adults, $99–189 ages 3–9) sees 'snow' on Main Street and magnificent festive decorations and theming. There is free hot chocolate and cookies, a parade and more fireworks. The atmosphere is enchanting, though the evening can be prone to unfriendly weather.

BRITTIP

Not all of Disney's backstage tours had returned in 2022. Check Disney's website to be sure any tours you are interested in are running again.

Park tours

Keys to the Kingdom: One of the park's little-known secrets is this 5hr tour of many backstage areas, including the service tunnel under the park and production buildings. It costs $114 (including lunch; ages 16 and over only) but is a superb journey into the park's creation. **Disney's Family Magic:** This 2hr guided adventure takes you on a search for clues throughout the park at $39/person. Mon, Tues, Fri and Sat. **Magic Behind Our Steam Trains Tour:** A 3hr tour ($54/ person; no under-10s) that joins the crew preparing the park's trains each day. Sun–Thurs. **Walt Disney: Marceline to Magic Kingdom:** A 3hr tour on how Walt's early years in Marceline, Missouri, inspired the creation of the Magic Kingdom ($49/person; no under-12s). Wed–Sun. **Disney Private VIP Tour:** Create your own tour (minimum 7hrs) for up to 10 guests ($425–850 per hour) with a Disney VIP guide and private transportation. Park admission and theme park reservation required but not included.

EPCOT

EPCOT originally stood for 'Experimental Prototype Community of Tomorrow', but it might be more accurate to say Every Person Comes Out Tired. For this is a BIG park, with a lot to see and do, and much legwork required to cover its 300acre/122ha extent. Because construction was delayed during 2020, Epcot is still undergoing a transformation from its original two-part adventure (Future World and World Showcase) to a four-area wonderland so there is likely to be ongoing construction into 2023.

While World Showcase remains intact, Future World will be completely redeveloped, and our tour will be based on the new version.

At almost three times the size of the Magic Kingdom Park, it is more likely to require a two-day visit (though under-5s might find it less entertaining) and your feet will notice the difference! Remember, ILL means you can buy these high-demand rides individually, and G+ is the paid-for Genie+ add-on.

EPCOT at a glance

Location	Off Epcot Drive, Walt Disney World
Size	300 acres/122ha in four sections
Hours	9am–9pm (11am–9pm in World Showcase)
Admission	Under-3s free; 3–9 $104–154 (1-day base ticket, priced seasonally), $437–595 (5-day Standard Theme Park Ticket); £459 (14-day Magic, includes Memory Maker); adult (10+) $109–159, $455–610, £479. US prices do not include tax.
Parking	$25, $45-$50 premium
Lockers	Through the main entrance to the right hand side and at International Gateway $10, $12, $15
Pushchairs	$15 and $31 to the left after the main entrance and at International Gateway; $13 and $27 per day for multiple days
Wheelchairs	$12 or $70 ($20 deposit refunded) with pushchairs
Top attractions	Mission: SPACE, Test Track, Spaceship Earth, Soarin' Around The World, American Adventure, Remy's Ratatouille Adventure, Guardians of the Galaxy: Cosmic Rewind
Don't miss	Harmonious, Space 220 restaurant, Turtle Talk With Crush, live entertainment (including JAMMitors and Voices of Liberty in America), and dinner at any of the World Showcase pavilions
Hidden costs	**Meals** Burger, chips and coke $20.50 3-course dinner $42–85 (La Hacienda, Mexico) Kids' meal $7.50–8
	T-shirts $25–37 Kids' T-shirts $20–37
	Souvenirs $1.99–1,500
	Sundries Souvenir popcorn bucket $20

The queue for Remy's Ratatouille Adventure is full of clever detail

© Disney

World Nature

16 Journey of Water inspired by Moana
17 The Land
18 The Seas with Nemo and Friends

World Showcase

19 Mexico
20 Norway
21 China
22 The Outpost
23 Germany
24 Italy
25 The American Adventure
26 America Gardens Theatre
27 Japan
28 Morocco
29 France
30 Remy's Ratatouille Adventure
31 United Kingdom
32 Canada
33 Harmonious
34 Disney Skyliner Station

World Celebration

1 Spaceship Earth
2 Dreamers Point
3 Communicore Plaza & Hall
4 EPCOT Gardens
5 Club Cool
6 Imagination!
7 Disney & Pixar Short Film Festival
8 Odyssey Events Pavilion
9 Creations Shop
10 Connections Eatery & Cafe

World Discovery

11 Guardians of the Galaxy: Cosmic Rewind
12 Play! Pavilion (2023/24)
13 Mission: Space
14 Test Track
15 Space 220

EPCOT

The American Adventure

Japan

Italy

Germany

Morocco

France

WORLD SHOWCASE

Harmonious
See My Disney Experience for show times.

Outpost

China

Norway

Mexico

International Gateway

PARK ENTRANCE & EXIT
Access to *Disney's Hollywood Studios*, *EPCOT* Resorts and Disney Skyliner

United Kingdom

Canada

WORLD DISCOVERY

Future Home of PLAY!

WORLD CELEBRATION

WORLD NATURE

TRANSPORTATION
▲ Resort Bus Service
▲ Rideshare Pick-Up Area
   Hosted by Lyft
◀ Monorail Transportation
▼ Guest Parking

Main Entrance

The France pavilion in World Showcase

Location

EPCOT opened in October 1982 and its giant car park can hold 9,000 vehicles, so a tram takes you to the main entrance (or go by monorail, boat or bus service to the gates from a Disney hotel; International Gateway is a separate entrance for guests at the EPCOT resort hotels). Don't forget to note where you have parked (e.g. Create, row 49). If you have your ticket, MagicBand or MagicMobile app, you pass through the gate area and wait in front of the huge Spaceship Earth (the park's 'giant golfball') for the official opening time.

Beating the queues: EPCOT will consist of four areas once the big makeover is complete, with the global expo of World Showcase staying the same but Future World being reimagined as three separate 'worlds.' This new trio will open up from the main entrance, with World Showcase at the back of the park (and also accessible via the entry of International Gateway). From the front (**World Celebration**), you need to decide whether to head right (**World Nature**), for the fab Soarin' Around The World ride; left (**World Discovery**) for Test Track, Mission: Space and the new Guardians of the Galaxy ride; or straight through to **World Showcase** for Remy's Ratatouille Adventure in the France pavilion.

Planning your visit

The best way to tackle EPCOT is with a two-day plan, arriving early on Day One and heading for one of the Big Four rides (Soarin', Remy, Guardians and Test Track), which have the longest queues all day. Guardians will be THE big draw through 2023, with Remy also popular, so head for one of these FIRST, then make the other one your main target on Day Two (unless you are going to pay for them individually on ILL, in which case, focus on Soarin' and Test Track). Then slow down and enjoy EPCOT more leisurely.

You CAN do EPCOT in a day – if you arrive early, put in speedy legwork and give most of the detail a miss. But it is a shame to hurry this park. Browse in the 60-plus shops when the rides are busiest.

Kidcot Fun Stops: At 11 activity centres around EPCOT (each country in World Showcase), children can decorate a cardboard character and get a stamp from each country on the handle attached to the character.

Guardians of the Galaxy: Cosmic Rewind

Creations at Epcot

© Disney

World Celebration

The park's new entrance section includes a signature ride and a dedicated Festival area.

Spaceship Earth: Spiralling up 18 storeys, this attraction is a convincing time-travel story into the history of a variety of technologies, all narrated by Dame Judi Dench. From cave painting to the Internet, and including a superb depiction of Michaelangelo's Sistine Chapel, the gentle ride unfolds in imaginative historical stages, culminating in an interactive finale that invites riders to 'predict' the future. AAAA G+ Once the World Celebration area is complete, riders will exit Spaceship Earth into **Dreamers Point**, with a dramatic view of the rest of the park and a special statue dedicated to Walt Disney himself. Other new areas will be **CommuniCore Plaza**, for live performances, and **CommuniCore Hall,** with seasonal exhibits,

galleries, a demonstration kitchen and mixology bar, while the **EPCOT Gardens** will add a hub area of lush nature and night-time lighting that change periodically with each of the park's Festivals.

Club Cool: Sept 2021 saw the return of this special tasting centre hosted by Coca–Cola, offering free samples of Coke products worldwide in a fun setting. Just beware the Beverly from Italy!

Imagination!: This two-part attraction starts with **Journey into Imagination with Figment**, a quirky ride into experiments with imagination, with Eric Idle (as Dr Nigel Channing of the Imagination Institute) and cartoon dragon Figment. It's gentle fun and rarely draws a crowd. AA G+ You exit into **Image Works – The 'What If' Labs**, an interactive playground of sight and sound, which usually amuses kids more than adults.

Disney & Pixar Short Film Festival: Next door to Imagination is the Magic Eye Theater, featuring three classic short films with in-theatre special effects. Until CommuniCore Hall is complete, this is also the place to **Meet Mickey** in a film-themed setting. AAA G+

Connections Café and Eatery

© Disney

Odyssey Events Pavilion: Find the baby-care centre, first aid and restrooms here.

Other entertainment: Live fun is provided periodically by the zany JAMMitors percussion group. New character meetings will be available at **Mickey & Friends** as part of CommuniCore Hall.

Shopping: Creations Shop features a massive variety of speciality EPCOT and Disney merchandise.

Dining: Connections Eatery features burgers, pizza, plant-based pizza and salads, plus shakes, beer, wine, and cocktails while **Connections Café** is the place for Starbucks coffees and pastries.

World Discovery

This new area will incorporate several existing attractions, and one blockbuster new arrival.

Guardians of the Galaxy: Cosmic Rewind: Get ready for a pulse-pounding journey into the film world of Star Lord and Co as this dramatic new indoor coaster launches riders into an adventure of galactic proportions based on the Xandarian realm of the Marvel movies. It starts as a visit to the Wonders of Xandar intergalactic pavilion, along a dazzling queue area, but quickly becomes a rollicking adventure with those dare-devil Guardians to thwart the worst intentions of Eson the Celestial. The ride features novel rotating cars that go forwards, backwards *and* sideways, with a fast-launch section and a focus on story-telling right through (i.e. it's not just another coaster), which involves a series of special effects and giant screens that envelop riders in this elaborate sci-fi realm. TTTT/ AAAAA. ILL **R**: 3ft 8in/112cm. In 2022, this ride was available *only* by ILL selection or the 'virtual queue' on the My Disney Experience app, which allows guests to apply twice a day for a "boarding group," at 7am and 1pm, but you need to be online at *exactly* the right time to apply for a group, and they get snapped up *fast*.

Play! Pavilion: This reimagined venue (the former Wonders of Life pavilion), featuring interactive exhibits and play areas aimed at children, was originally due to be part of the park's transformation, but has been put on the back-burner with no word of when it will open.

Mission: SPACE: This is a high-tech journey into a mission with the International Space Training Center. Guests get to be Pilot, Navigator, Engineer or Commander – each with different duties to perform – for a blast off to Mars (on the dynamic Orange version) or a full orbit of Earth (on the

Journey of Water

© Disney

milder Green version). The ride vehicle has capsules that close down tightly with shoulder restraints and screens that move forward to just in front of your face (not ideal for those prone to claustrophobia or motion sickness, or for expectant mothers), but the sense of realism is magnificent. For those on the full version, the blast-off simulates genuine launch forces (thanks to its huge centrifuge, which is part-ride, part-simulator), and you should heed the advice to keep your head still and look at the screen or you may feel sick (not a worry with the tamer Green version, where the capsules just tilt and turn). **R**: 3ft 8in/112cm. **TTTTT** G+

There are post-ride activities and games, plus a play area for children, **Space Base**, with a chance to climb, slide and crawl through a series of obstacles.

Test Track: This large-scale ride travels into the realm of car design. It starts with an interactive queue inviting riders to design a prototype vehicle, then it's off through a digital world of hair-pin bends, rough surfaces, temperature extremes and a high-speed finale. Each guest's design is computer tested and scored alongside the ride vehicle while the

lighting and special effects of this unique, high-tech world feel like you're inside a computer (like the film *Tron*). This does draw big queues, though, so aim for this early on or use the Single Rider option if you're riding solo or don't mind your group being split up. **R**: 3ft 4in/101cm. **TTTT** (**TTT** teens). G+

Dining: Take an elevator to 'outer space' and view Earth from 'an international space station' at the **Space 220** table service restaurant. This novel locale is EPCOT's most immersive dining experience, featuring international cuisine and special wine and craft beer selections. **Space 220 Lounge** has the same brilliant atmosphere if you're just looking for drinks (reservations required).

World Nature
This section introduces EPCOT's gentle side, with another new attraction, plus one of the most popular.

Journey of Water inspired by Moana: Take a relaxing stroll along this novel walk-through feature based on the 2016 film *Moana*, offering a

Soarin' Around the World

maze-like path through a series of interactive water elements, from pop-jet fountains to leaping streams. A lovely family-friendly attraction, it highlights the importance of water in nature via the message of goddess Te Fiti in a beautifully forested landscape of tropical trees and foliage. AAA (expected in late 2023).

The Land: This three-part pavilion features positive environmental messages and two huge rides. **Living with the Land** is an informative 14min boat journey through food production, which may sound dull but is revealing and enjoyable, with plenty to make children sit up and take notice of its three different communities, especially the greenhouse finale. AAAA G+ Film-show **Awesome Planet** is a fabulous large-screen presentation on the beauty – and urgent ecological challenges – of our planet. AAAA.

Soarin' Around the World™: One of Disney's most imaginative attractions, this 'flight simulator' offers an exhilarating global journey for all ages, visiting the Great Wall of China, Sydney Harbour Bridge, the Matterhorn and other world icons. An interactive game for mobile devices leads to a 'departure lounge', with passengers embarking on rows of seats that are hoisted over a giant screen. A bit like a hang-glider ride, the sounds and scents become all-encompassing as you soar up, over and around great sights such as the Pyramids and Eiffel Tower, with the projection system, special effects, magnificent music and superb technology ensuring a five-star experience. Queues build up fast, so visit early, use Genie+, or save it for the last 2hrs of the day. **R**: 3ft 4in/101cm. AAAAA G+

Dining: The **Sunshine Seasons Food Court** offers the chance to eat some of Disney's home-grown produce, while the **Garden Grill** restaurant is a slowly revolving platform that offers Harvest Feasts (beef, turkey, mac & cheese, sides, and dessert at lunch and dinner), all in the company of Mickey, Goofy, Pluto and Chip 'n' Dale.

BRITTIP

Queues for Soarin' and Test Track are notably shorter in the last hour of the day, and you're guaranteed to get on provided you are in the queue before 9pm.

The Seas with Nemo & Friends: This pavilion does for the oceans what The Land does for terra firma, starring the characters from *Finding Nemo*. You start with the ride, which takes you underwater to meet Nemo and Co (brilliantly interwoven into the huge aquarium). Nemo has gone missing (again), hence it becomes a quest to reunite him with the rest of the class in a rousing musical finale. AAAA G+ You exit into **Sea Base**, a massive, two-level aquarium featuring stories of undersea exploration and marine life, including a research centre for the endangered manatee. Crowds are steady, but queues rarely get too long – except for **Turtle Talk with Crush**, a brilliantly interactive meet-and-greet with the surfer dude turtle, plus Dory and other characters from *Finding Nemo* and *Finding Dory*. Crush is the star, though, as he engages children with some fun live banter. AAAA G+ Next door, **Bruce's Shark World** is an interactive walk-through area (TTT under-6s). A self-guided scavenger hunt provides more fun for kids.

Dining: The pavilion includes the highly recommended **Coral Reef Restaurant** that serves great seafood with a grandstand view of the massive aquarium. A 3-course dinner will be $44–62, depending on your choices, which isn't cheap, but the food is first class (kids' menu $11–13).

Shopping: SeaBase Gift Shop offers Nemo and Friends toys and apparel, while you can also donate to Disney's Conservation Fund.

Seas with Nemo and Friends

World Showcase

If you found the first three 'Worlds' amazing, prepare to be astounded by the imaginative pavilions around the World Showcase Lagoon, each featuring a glimpse of a different country in dramatic settings. Several have rides or films to showcase their main features, while the restaurants offer some outstanding fare and many character greeting spots can be found here (check the daily Times Guide for locations and timings).

BRITTIP

World Showcase is the last part of EPCOT to get busy, hence it's an ideal area to visit from 11am–3pm. Both Norway (for the *Frozen* ride) and France (for the new Remy ride) draw crowds quickly, but the other pavilions stay relatively crowd-free for quite a while. It will be busy from mid-afternoon to closing, though.

Mexico: Starting at the bottom left of the circular tour of the lagoon and moving clockwise, your first encounter is inside the spectacular pyramid. Here you have the amusing boat ride **Gran Fiesta Tour Starring The Three Caballeros**, a 9min journey through the people and history of the country guided by Donald, Panchito and José Carioca. Queues build up in mid-afternoon but are usually light otherwise. AAA

Other entertainment: As in all of the World Showcase pavilions, there is live entertainment, with periodic 25min music shows from **Mariachi Cobre**, including their *Story of Coco* with folkloric dancers, while Donald Duck puts in character appearances.

Shopping: Much of the pavilion comprises market-style gift shops.

Dining: The San Angel Inn is a romantic Mexican restaurant (lunch from noon–4pm, dinner 4.30–10pm), and **La Cava del Tequila** has tempting cocktails, light bites and tequilas. Outside, choose from the counter service **Cantina de San Angel** (open-air, serving tacos, nachos and empanadas) and full-service

La Hacienda de San Angel (dinner from 3pm) serving authentic Mexican fare with a superb lagoon view and grandstand seat for the nightly fireworks show. This gets our thumbs-up as a stand-out choice.

Norway: A reproduction of Oslo's splendid Akershus Fortress is the exterior façade, while the interior is given over to headline attraction, **Frozen Ever After**. This delightful boat ride through the realm of Arendelle features a 'Winter in Summer' celebration that visits Queen Elsa in her Ice Palace, as well as Troll Valley and the Bay of Arendelle to share in some of *Frozen*'s iconic moments. Clever animatronics, projection screens and animated scenes bring the journey to life in classic Disney style, while *Frozen* fans can then visit Elsa and Princess Anna in their **Sommerhus**, a themed location for character meet-and-greets; AAA ILL for the ride (or G+ at peak periods); AAAAA for the meet-and-greet.

Other entertainment: Look for historical exhibits in the **Stave Church Gallery**.

Shopping: Gift shop **Wandering Reindeer** features all things *Frozen*, while **The Fjording** stocks Norwegian clothes, toys, perfume, camera needs, food and spirits.

Dining: The **Akershus Royal Banquet Hall** offers the Princess Storybook dining for breakfast, lunch and dinner, complete with a host of Disney Princesses, while the counter-service **Kringla Bakeri og Kafe** serves desserts, pretzels, pastries and drinks, including the signature Viking Coffee (with Bailey's Irish Cream!).

BRITTIP

If you can't get a booking for Cinderella's Royal Table in the Magic Kingdom, the Akershus Royal Banquet (8am–8.45pm; breakfast $53 for adults, and $34 kids 3–9; dinner $63/$41) is the next best thing and should keep most young 'princesses' happy! Call 407 939 3463 up to 180 days in advance or book online at **disneyworld.com**.

China: The spectacular vistas and landmarks of China are all depicted beautifully in the 360° film **Reflections of China** in the circular Temple of Heaven. Queues are rare and it is fully air-conditioned. A new film, Wondrous China, is expected to replace Reflections of China, but has been delayed, with no opening date yet announced. AAAA

Other entertainment: Disney characters from *Mulan* appear throughout the day.

Shopping: Yong Feng Shangdian Dept Store is a warehouse of Chinese gifts and artefacts.

Dining: Two restaurants, the **Nine Dragons** and the counter-service **Lotus Blossom Café** offer tastes of the Orient.

The Outpost: Between China and Germany, this features hut-style shops and snacks, with crafts from Africa and the Caribbean.

Germany: There is more in the way of shopping and eating than

Temple of Heaven in China

entertainment, though you still find a magnificent re-creation of a **Bavarian Biergarten**, with regular, lively Oktoberfest shows featuring the resident Musikanten brass band. It also offers hearty portions of German sausage, sauerkraut and rotisserie chicken. The **Sommerfest** is fast food German-style (bratwurst and pretzels), while there are eight shops,

Norway paviion

© Disney

more than anywhere else in EPCOT, including chocolates, wines, crystal, porcelain, toys and cuckoo clocks.

BRITTIP

With seating for 400, Biergarten often takes walk-ups even when Disney's reservations system indicates the restaurant is full.

Other entertainment: An elaborate outdoor **model railway** is popular with children, while an outdoor stage adds periodic live musical shows. Look out for **character appearances** from Snow White.

Italy: Similarly, Italy has pretty, authentic architecture, including a superb reproduction of Venice's St Mark's Square, three gift shops with wine, chocolates, Armani gifts, crystal, porcelain and Venetian masks, and two full-service restaurants. **Tutto Italia** is the fine-dining option, designed like the Medici Palace, with a gluten-free menu and a splendid cellar-style wine bar, **Tutto Gusto**, that offers small plates and light bites (reservations not needed), while the superb **Via Napoli** is a delightful pizzeria, featuring wood-burning ovens and genuine Neapolitan style, as well as an outdoor terrace. **Gelateria Toscana** kiosk serves up classic gelatos and sorbets, plus sweet treats, beer and wine.

The American Adventure: At the top of the lagoon and dominating World Showcase is this huge edifice, not so much a pavilion as a celebration of the country's history and Constitution. It boasts a wonderful singing group that adds authentic sounds to the 18th-century setting, overlooked by a reproduction of Philadelphia's Liberty Hall. Inside, you have the **American Adventure** show, a magnificent half-hour film and audio-animatronic production that details the country's founding, its struggles and triumphs, presidents, statesmen and heroes. It's a glossy, patriotic display, featuring some outstanding technology and, while

some of it will be unfamiliar to foreign visitors, it's difficult not to be impressed. A good choice at most times of the day – and it's all in the cool! AAAA Also here is the new *Creating Tradition* exhibit featuring Native American art and artefacts.

Other entertainment: Superb *à capella* group **Voices of Liberty** appear in the pavilion's rotunda several times a day, while the **America Gardens Theater**, next to the lagoon, presents concerts with well-known performers during the International Art, Flower & Garden and Food & Wine Festivals.

Shopping: Antiques and handcarts provide touches of nostalgia, along with the **Heritage Manor Gifts** store.

Dining: Regal Eagle Smokehouse is the newest counter-service dining option, featuring succulent barbecue platters, burgers, side dishes and craft beers, while the **Block & Hans** kiosk has craft beers and pretzels, and the **Funnel Cake Stand** offers sweet treats.

Japan: Next up on the clockwise tour, you are introduced to typical Japanese style and architecture, including a five-storey 8th-century Pagoda, some magnificent art exhibits, notably in the **Bijutsu-kan Gallery**, featuring art and insights into Japanese history and culture, a tranquil **Bonsai garden** (complete with carp pond) and landmark Torii gate.

Tutto Italia

© Disney

BRITTIP

Need a chill-out zone in World Showcase? Head to one side of the Bonsai garden in the Japan pavilion and there is a tranquil seating area where you can sit with a drink or snack and enjoy the view.

Shopping: The huge **Mitsukoshi** store adds fascinating shopping, from traditional calligraphy, tea kettles and wind chimes to Hello Kitty souvenirs.

Dining: Great food is a real highlight, and the restaurant line-up consists of the wonderful fine dining of **Teppan Edo** (with its traditional chefs at each table) and **Tokyo Dining**, featuring Japanese cuisine and ingredients, showcasing sushi and innovative presentation. **Katsura Grill** is its fast-food equivalent, with great noodle dishes, teriyaki and sushi dishes while the **Kabuki Café** serves sake, beer, plum wine, tea and soft drinks. New in 2019 was **Takumi-Tei**, a traditional fine-dining experience, drawing inspiration from nature and art, and with a menu of authentic Japanese dishes, including sushi, seafood and Wagyu beef, as well as a superb Omakase tasting menu ($150/person).

Morocco: A shopping experience, with bazaars, alleyways and stalls selling a well-priced array of carpets, leather goods, pottery, brass ornaments, clothing and antiques.

All the building materials were imported for the pavilion, which was hand-built to give Morocco a greater degree of authenticity, even by World Showcase's high standards. The **Gallery of Arts and History** offers more historical and cultural insights, while the **Fez House** depicts a typical Moroccan home.

Other entertainment: *Aladdin* characters appear from time to time.

Dining: Full-service **Restaurant Marrakesh** has been closed since the start of the pandemic but there are signs this could make a comeback in 2023, with its traditional Moroccan menu and style. **Tangierine Café** offers roast lamb, hummus, tabbouleh, couscous, lentil salad and Moroccan breads ($11–18; kids' meals $9–10). **Spice Road Table**, a clever

Katsura Grill

© Disney

indoor/outdoor restaurant, offers tasty Mediterranean-style small plates as well as beer, wine and cocktails, all with a Lagoon view, and select tables can see the nightly fireworks.

France: Predictably overlooked by a replica Eiffel Tower, this is a clean and cheerful pre-World War I Paris, with the new Ratatouille area adding to the rather dreamy atmosphere and pleasant gardens, plus stylish shopping and dining. Don't miss **Impressions de France**, a big-film production that serves up all the grandest sights of the country to the music of Offenbach, Debussy, Saint-Saëns and Satie. Crowds are rarely heavy, and it's air-conditioned. AAAA A **Beauty and the Beast Sing-Along** show alternates with Impressions de France.

Rémy's Ratatouille Adventure: Like its counterpart in Disneyland Paris, this 4D dark ride is a delight of storytelling. Big-screen technology, trackless vehicles and special effects combine for a grand adventure in best animated style. Riders shrink to rat-size as they enter Gusteau's restaurant and follow Chef Rémy in a mad chase through the kitchen, dining room and even the duct work before arriving safely into Bistrot Chez Rémy. Cue popping champagne corks! AAAAA ILL (G+ at peak periods)

Other entertainment: Princess Aurora (Sleeping Beauty) makes regular appearances, along with Belle from *Beauty and the Beast.*

Shopping: Suitably chic, there's an authentic **Wine Shop** and elegant **La Signature** perfumery.

Dining: This is THE pavilion for a gastronomic experience provided by four restaurants, of which **Les Chefs de France** and **Monsieur Paul** are major discoveries. The former is a classic, full-service establishment featuring top-quality French cuisine for lunch and dinner, while the latter, upstairs, is named (and themed) for late, great chef Paul Bocuse, with his staff still overseeing both restaurants. Monsieur Paul is a touch more formal and upscale, with a 4-course prix fixe menu ($89/person), and, while an expensive meal (dinner only; appetisers from $16–29 and main courses $39–47), it is a fabulous choice. Also here is the **Les Halles Boulangerie Patisserie**, a genuine French patisserie featuring freshly made baguettes, croissants, salads, quiches and fab pastries, and **L'Artisan des Glaces**, an artisan ice-cream and sorbet shop, with everything made fresh in-house every day (and with liqueur treats for grown-ups!). The all-new **La Crêperie**, next to the Ratatouille ride, features table-service dining with the culinary accent of Brittany and a counter-service option with savoury galettes ($16.95) and sweet crepes ($7–$9.59), plus a price fixe option of soup or salad, one galette one crepe and cider or soft drink ($35).

United Kingdom: The least inspiring of all the pavilions, and certainly with little to entertain those who have ever visited a pub or shopped for Royal Doulton or Burberry goods, it is partly offset by some good live entertainment and pleasant gardens, but that is about it.

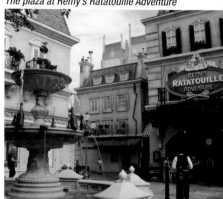

The plaza at Rémy's Ratatouille Adventure

EPCOT with children

Here is our rough guide to the attractions that appeal to different age groups:

Under-5s
Frozen Ever After, Gran Fiesta Tour Starring The Three Caballeros, Journey into Imagination with Figment, Kidcot stops, Living with the Land, The Seas with Nemo and Friends, Soarin Around the World'™ (if tall enough), Spaceship Earth, Turtle Talk with Crush.

5–8s
All the above, plus The American Adventure, Image Works, JAMMitors, Test Track, Rémy's Ratatouille Adventure, Awesome Planet.

9–12s
All tho above, plus Guardians of the Galaxy, Impressions de France, Mission: SPACE, Canada Far and Wide, Reflections of China.

Over-12s
The American Adventure, Bijutsu-kan Gallery, JAMMitors, Impressions de France, Living with the Land, Mission: SPACE, The Seas with Nemo and Friends, Canada Far and Wide, Reflections of China, Soarin' Around the World™, Spaceship Earth, Test Track, Guardians of the Galaxy, Rémy's Ratatouille Adventure, Awesome Planet.

Other entertainment: Mary Poppins and Alice in Wonderland make daily appearances, while British rock tribute band **The Hooligans** play five days a week (not Wed–Thurs).

Shopping: The best shops are the **Tea Caddy**, the **Queen's Table**, **Crown and Crest** (perfumes and heraldry), **Sportsman Shoppe** (sweaters, kilts, football shirts) and **Toy Soldier** (traditional games and toys), but prices are WAY above what you'd pay at home.

Dining: The Rose and Crown Pub is antiseptically authentic but you can get better elsewhere at these prices (shepherd's pie $25, chicken masala curry $24, Impossible Hot Pot $22 or fish and chips $26, and a pint of Bass for a whopping $10). **Yorkshire County** offers takeaway fish and chips.

Canada: Completing World Showcase, the main features here are **Victoria Gardens**, based on world-famous Butchart Gardens on Vancouver Island, Rocky Mountain scenery, and 360° film, *Canada Far and Wide*. As with China and France, this highlights the epic sights and traditions in a terrific national showcase, led by actors Eugene Levy and Catherine O'Hara. AAA

Shopping: The Trading Post and **Northwest Mercantile** provide a range of Canadian clothing and souvenirs, notably wonderful glass ornaments and Deauville perfume.

BRITTIP
Best way to tour World Showcase? Start in Canada and continue anticlockwise or jump on a Friendship Boat and go straight to Italy or Morocco.

Dining and shopping: Le Cellier Steakhouse is an excellent dining room, offering great steaks, prime rib, seafood, chicken, fish and poutine for lunch and dinner.

Spaceship Earth all lit up at night

© Disney

Harmonious

After the end of the classic IllumiNations in 2019, **Harmonious**, a celebration of night-time effects with a new interpretation of Disney music, lights up the evening skies over World Showcase lagoon. With huge, purpose-created platforms rising up to 6 storeys above the water and equipped with a mix of LED panels, fountains and lasers, they combine in an extravagant carnival of storytelling, featuring Disney animated characters, pyrotechnics, special effects and a stirring musical score in a global celebration of the stories and songs that unite people across the world. AAAAA

Harmonious will, in its turn, be discontinued later in 2023 to make way for an all-new evening show that celebrates the Walt Disney Company's 100th anniversary. Few details were available as we went to press but Disney promises "it will continue the park's legacy of inspiring night-time entertainment".

50th Anniversary: Be sure to stay after dark to see the 'stardust' celebration lighting effects on Spaceship Earth as one of the four Beacons of Magic in the parks, while Epcot's 'Fab 50 sculptures' include Dante from the film *Coco* and iconic dragon, Figment.

Behind-the-scenes tours

EPCOT also has a range of tours that can be booked on 407 939 8687 (although most tours remained temporarily unavailable through 2022).

Dolphins in Depth: This is a 3hr dip into the research areas of The Seas pavilion, with a chance to meet the dolphins ($199, with refreshments, photo and T-shirt; 13–17s must be with an adult; take your cossie!).

Undiscovered Future World: A 4½hr journey into the creation of EPCOT, Walt's vision and backstage areas like Test Track ($69).

Behind the Seeds: 1hr tour, every 45mins from 9.45am–4.30pm at The Land pavilion, looks at Disney's innovative gardening practices ($25 adults, $20 3–9s).

Dive Quest: A 3hr experience, with a 40min dive into The Seas aquarium, plus a backstage look at the facility at 4.30 and 5.30pm daily. Must have scuba certification; park admission not required ($179/person, 10 and over, includes T-shirt and certificate).

Seas Aqua Tour: A similar tour without the scuba diving, daily at 12.30pm ($145/person, 8 and over; under-18s with an adult).

Backstage Magic: The most comprehensive tour goes behind the scenes of EPCOT, Magic Kingdom and Hollywood Studios on a 7hr foray into little-seen aspects, like the backstage areas of the Studios and tunnels below Magic Kingdom ($275, 16+).

Annual festivals

There are also three annual EPCOT events (plus the Christmas season – p36) to watch out for.

International Festival of the Arts: Showcasing a wide variety of arts Jan to Feb, from painting and printing to performance art and concerts (including a Disney on Broadway series at the America Gardens Theater), there are also seminars and workshops, delicious food offerings and a hands-on wall mural to try out.

International Flower and Garden Festival: This puts the whole park in full bloom with an amazing series of set-pieces, topiaries and live entertainment from Mar to July. All exhibits and concerts at the America Gardens Theater are free, and they add a beautiful aspect to an already scenic park, along with food kiosks around World Showcase that offer regional tastes and drinks.

Food and Wine Festival: From July to late Nov, this features national and regional cuisines, wines and beers, and you can sample more than 30 food booths dotted around World Showcase. Each Festival offers free concerts three times a day at the America Gardens Theater.

DISNEY'S HOLLYWOOD STUDIOS

Walt Disney World's biggest adventure in more than 20 years arrived in August 2019, and is still a HUGE hit with all concerned. This park has always been a journey into the movies, but it raised the bar in 2018 with Toy Story Land and then blew the doors off with **Star Wars: Galaxy's Edge** in 2019, redefining theme park design and raising the level of Disney's superb immersive storytelling. Mickey and Minnie's Runaway Railway opened in 2020 and the Star Wars: Galactic Starcruiser hotel launched in 2022, with links to the park. The Disney Skyliner is also a memorable way to arrive, and it all makes for a hugely compelling park experience.

Disney's Hollywood Studios at a glance

Location	Off Osceola Parkway and Victory Way
Size	154 acres/62ha
Hours	8 or 9am to 8 or 9pm.
Admission	Under-3s free; 3–9 $104–154 (1-day base ticket, priced seasonally), $437–595 (5-day Standard Theme Park Ticket), £459 (14-day Magic, includes Memory Maker); adult (10+) $109–159, $455–610, £479. US prices do not include tax.
Parking	$25, $45–$50 premium
Lockers	From the Crossroads kiosk through the main entrance; $10, $12, and $15
Pushchairs	$15 and $31 Oscar's Super Service Station; $13 and $27 per day for multiple days
Wheelchairs	$12 or $70 ($20 deposit refunded), from Oscar's
Top attractions	Star Wars: Rise of the Resistance, Millennium Falcon: Smugglers Run, Mickey & Minnie's Runaway Railway, Toy Story Mania, Twilight Zone™ Tower of Terror, Rock 'n' Roller Coaster Starring Aerosmith, Slinky Dog Dash, Star Tours
Don't miss	Indiana Jones™ Epic Stunt Spectacular, Beauty and the Beast – Live on Stage, Fantasmic!, Stars Wars: A Galactic Spectacular
Hidden costs	Meals	Burger, chips and coke $15 3-course dinner $36–59, child's $13–14 (Mama Melrose) Beer $7.50–10.25 Kids' meal $6.79–7.99, Kids' Mickey Check Meal $6.49
	T-shirts	$25–37 Kids' T-shirts $20–37
	Souvenirs	$3.99–2,000
	Sundries	Baby Yoda ears $30

Rise of the Resistance

© Disney

Location

The entrance is on S. Studio Drive, between Victory Way and Osceola Parkway, and once again you catch a tram to the main gates, where you wait for the official opening time. If queues build up quickly (quite likely with Galaxy's Edge so popular), the gates will open early, so be ready for a running start. Once through, you are in Hollywood Boulevard, a street of shops, then you must decide which attraction to head for first, as these are where the queues will be heavy most of the day. Try to ignore the shops as it is better to browse in the afternoon when the attractions are at their busiest.

BRITTIP

With the advent of Disney Genie+, Hollywood Studios, with its l-o-n-g queues for at least eight attractions, becomes a leading contender, along with the Magic Kingdom, for using the new paid-for system, if it fits your budget.

The main attractions

The park is laid out in a more confusing fashion than its counterparts, with their neatly packaged 'lands', so have your map handy to keep your bearings.

Beating the queues: The opening crowds will surge in one of three directions. By far the biggest will be towards **Star Wars: Galaxy's Edge**, with LONG waits for its two main attractions, so head here first if you arrive for park opening. If Toy Story Land is more important, and you're not using Genie+ for **Slinky Dog Dash** or **Toy Story Mania**, make this your first target of the day. The other major crowd-pullers are **Twilight Zone™ Tower of Terror**, a magnificent haunted hotel ride that ends in a 13-storey drop in a lift, where queues hit 2hrs at peak periods, **Rock 'n' Roller Coaster**, and the newer **Mickey & Minnie's Runaway Railway**. Head straight up Hollywood Boulevard for the latter, or turn right into Sunset Boulevard for the other two and you'll see them at the end of the street. Most are available on Genie+ (p85), while Rise of the Resistance and Mickey and Minnie's Runaway Railway are the ILL selections (and the latter was added to the G+ selection for summer 2022).

Star Tours, the Star Wars simulator Ride, is not a part of the new Galaxy's Edge development but is another of the park's serious queue-builders, hence it is also a Genie+ attraction. If you are not up for the really big thrills (or the really big waits!), head straight for Star Tours (across the main square past the Indiana Jones™ show), and then continue on to another of the more gentle experiences with the hilarious Muppet*Vision 3-D show, which rarely gets so crowded that it generates long waits.

Slinky Dog Dash in Toy Story Land

© Disney122

Hollywood Boulevard

Move clockwise around the park, starting along this street of shops and services that are best visited in early afternoon when it's busier elsewhere.

Immediately to the left through the turnstiles are the Guest Relations and First Aid offices, plus the Baby Care centre. An up-to-the-minute check on queue times at the attractions is kept on a Guest Information Board on Hollywood Boulevard, just past its junction with Sunset Boulevard, where you can also book restaurants. To the right is Oscar's Station for pushchair and wheelchair hire, while locker hire is obtained at the Crossroads kiosk in front of you.

Mickey & Minnie's Runaway Railway: Located inside the Chinese Theatre (replacing the former Great Movie Ride), this zany train ride with Goofy starts as a visit to the movie premier of the new Mickey cartoon *Perfect Picnic*, but takes a turn for the wacky as guests go 'through the screen' (the special effects here are superb) for a wildly unpredictable journey into the world of Mickey and Minnie. The trackless vehicles are a real marvel and the scenery is 24-carat animated craziness, with all types of visual gags and tricks. Our cartoon pals do save

the day, though, and you'll struggle to get the soundtrack out of your head for the rest of the day! AAAA ILL (likely G+ at peak periods)

Other entertainment: A series of **Citizens of Hollywood** acts enliven Hollywood Boulevard throughout the day, staging impromptu movie shoots, casting calls or even detective investigations. Have fun with them and you might end up in the show! **Disney characters** usually appear in the morning (NB: Neither had returned in summer 2022, but we do expect to see them again in 2023).

Shopping: Hollywood Boulevard has the best of the park's shopping (nine of the 21 stores), including **Keystone Clothiers** (some of the best clothing), **Mickey's of Hollywood** (souvenirs and gift items) and **Celebrity 5&10** (apparel and home goods).

Dining: The Brown Derby is the park's signature restaurant, offering fine dining in best vintage Hollywood style (reservations usually necessary) while the **Brown Derby Lounge** offers outdoor dining with a full bar (beer $8–12, wine $11–17, cocktails $14–17) and terrific people-watching (11am–7 or 8pm). **Trolley Car Café** quick-service offers breakfast all day, plus cakes and Starbucks coffee.

Minnie greets guests at the Hollywood Studios

© Disney

Hollywood Boulevard

1 Mickey and Minnie's Runaway Railway
2 Hollywood Brown Derby
3 Brown Derby Lounge

Echo Lake

4 For the First Time in Forever
5 Indiana Jones™ Epic Stunt Spectacular
6 Star Tours
7 '50s Prime Time Café
8 Hollywood & Vine

Grand Avenue

9 Jim Henson's Muppet*Vision 3-D
10 Mama Melrose's
11 PizzeRizzo

Star Wars: Galaxy's Edge

12 Millennium Falcon: Smugglers' Run
13 Star Wars: Rise of the Resistance
14 Oga's Cantina
15 Docking Bay 7

Commissary Lane

16 Mickey and Minnie in Red Carpet Dreams
17 Sci-Fi Dine-in Theater Restaurant

Toy Story Land

18 Toy Story Mania
19 Slinky Dog Dash
20 Alien Swirling Saucers

Animation Courtyard

21 Voyage of the Little Mermaid
22 Disney Junior Dance Party
23 Walt Disney Presents
24 Star Wars Launch Bay

Sunset Boulevard

25 Rock 'n' Roller Coaster
26 The Twilight Zone™ Tower of Terror
27 Beauty and the Beast – Live on Stage
28 Fantasmic!
29 Lightning McQueen's Racing Academy

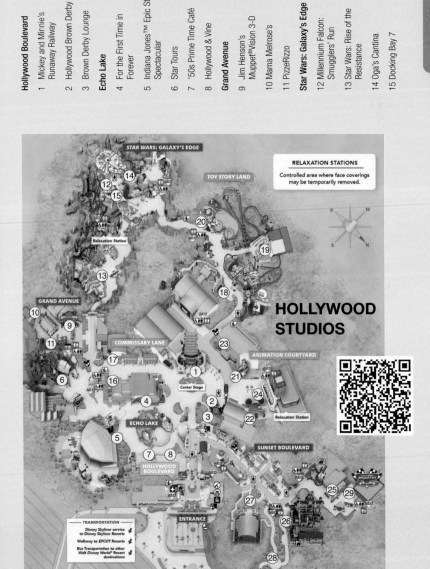

HOLLYWOOD STUDIOS

RELAXATION STATIONS
Controlled area where face coverings may be temporarily removed.

Echo Lake

Turn left out of Hollywood Boulevard to find another area that pays homage to the movies of the 1930s and 40s.

For The First Time in Forever: Join Anna and Elsa and the Royal Arendelle Historians for a *Frozen* Sing-Along Celebration, with music and clips from the movie. AAA G+ (AAAAA+ under 8s).

Indiana Jones™ Epic Stunt Spectacular: Consult your park Times Guide for show times as a special movie set creates three different backdrops for Indiana Jones'™ stunt people to put on a dazzling demonstration of scenes and special effects from the films. Audience participation is an element and there are some amusing sub-plots. Queues for the 30min show begin up to 30mins beforehand, but the auditorium holds more than 2,000 so everyone usually gets in. TTTT G+

Star Tours – the Adventures Continue: Climb into your StarSpeeder 1000 for a stunning high-speed journey through the worlds created by George Lucas, including Coruscant, Naboo, Kashyyyk, Jakku from *The Force Awakens*, Crait from *The Last Jedi* and Kef Bir from *The Rise of Skywalker*. Droids R2-D2 and C-3PO (with help from Lando Calrissian) must save your Speeder from disaster as you bid to evade the Empire or First Order. The ride has 96 different options from four key points, so you never quite know how it will turn out! The realism of the Star Wars™ world, from the queue to the post-ride gift shop, is immersive and lots of fun. **R**: 3ft 4in/101cm, no under-3s. TTTT AAAAA G+

Mickey Shorts Theater: Enjoy a cartoon romp in *Vacation Fun* with Mickey and the gang for 10 minutes of crazy animated adventures (and air-conditioned comfort), followed by a special post-show area with four photo opportunities from scenes in the film. AAA

Other entertainment: Kids should make a beeline for **Jedi Training: Trials of the Temple**, on stage outside Star Tours up to eight times a day. Here, young Jedi hopefuls try their light-sabre technique under the eyes of a Jedi master, before taking on Darth Vader, Kylo Ren or the Seventh Sister Inquisitor. Great fun just to watch. **Celebrity Spotlight** offers a chance to meet cuddlesome snowman Olaf from *Frozen* (TTTT for under-12s).

> **BRITTIP**
>
> Youngsters (ages 4–12) keen to try Jedi Training should sign up at the Indiana Jones Adventure Outpost first thing in the morning, as it is popular and availability is limited.

Shopping: Shop for Star Wars™ goods at **Tatooine Traders** (at the exit to Star Tours) and Indiana Jones souvenirs at the **Indy Truck and Adventure Outpost**.

Dining: There are also two good dining choices: the **'50s Prime Time Café** is fun as you sit in mock stage sets from 1950s American TV sitcoms and eat meals 'just like Mom used to make' (the waiters all claim to be your aunt, uncle or cousin and warn you to take your elbows off the table – good fun) while character meals are served at **Hollywood & Vine**, with the Play 'n Dine breakfast or lunch featuring the Disney Junior Pals (8–10.30am; $42 adults, $27 3–9s), while Minnie Mouse and friends take over on select dates in Spring and Summer, plus at Halloween and Christmas, with Minnie's Seasonal Dining ($55/$36).

Star Tours: the Adventure Continues

© Disney

Grand Avenue

This smaller area is home to the Muppets (and more dining).

Muppet*Vision 3-D: The 3-D is crossed out here and 4-D substituted, so be warned strange things are about to happen! A wonderful 10min holding-pen pre-show takes you into the Muppet Theater for a 20min experience with all the Muppets, 3-D special effects and more – when Fozzie Bear points his squirty flower at you, prepare to get wet! It's a gem, and the kids love it. Queues build up from late morning, but Disney's queuing expertise makes them seem shorter. AAAAA G+

Dining: Try **Mama Melrose's Ristorante Italiano,** for a fab table-service Italian option (one of our faves) or Muppet-themed **PizzeRizzo** for pizza, meatball subs, salads and drinks. Another great choice is **Baseline Tap House**, a Los Angeles 'neighbourhood pub' in keeping with the Grand Avenue style, serving craft beers, cocktails and a limited small-plate menu.

Star Wars: Galaxy's Edge

Welcome to the planet of Batuu, a remote outpost in the Outer Rim Territories (hence the Galaxy's Edge). This may very well be the most immersive, imaginative and downright exciting 'land' in any Disney park, as, from the second you walk through the entry tunnel to the heart-pounding moment you see the iconic Millennium Falcon, it all comes to vivid life around you. Black Spire Outpost is a relative backwater in the Star Wars universe, but is home to smugglers, rogues and renegades, as well as a Resistance base. That sets the scene for mysterious shops, cantinas and dining outlets, each hidden from view until you round *this* corner or take *that* turn in the pathway. At 14acres/5.6ha, it isn't huge, but the creative forced-perspective used to design this canyon outpost makes it feel enormous. With two main attractions, a Cantina lounge/bar, an epic counter-service diner, three food stalls, a 'marketplace' gift shop, and a whole array of character meet-and-greets, there is a LOT to see, and visitors who take the time to explore are richly rewarded. Batuu is not a well-known planet in the Star Wars realm, but you should notice many sights (and sounds) that are familiar. Just be aware this is THE big draw in Walt Disney World these days so you need a lot of patience to experience it.

Millennium Falcon at Star Wars: Galaxy's Edge

© Disney

Star Wars: Rise of the Resistance:
This immense experience puts
riders – travelling on unique
Intersystem Transports – at the
heart of a skirmish between the
First Order forces of Kylo Ren and
The Resistance, with stormtroopers
galore, droids, blaster-fire and many
of the trademark vehicles from the
films, including two full-size AT-ATs.
Guests are recruited by Resistance
hero Rey to help in a daring off-planet
mission that involves being drawn
into a Star Destroyer, escaping from a
jail cell and then being in the middle
of a pitched battle between the First
Order and Resistance fighters. Be
ready for the grandest, most involving
and multi-sensory ride in Disney
history – plus a total Star Wars geek-
out! AAAAA+/TTTT. ILL

Millennium Falcon: Smugglers Run:
Here's the one every fan has been
eagerly anticipating, the chance to
walk into the most famous spaceship
in movie history, become part of
its six-person crew – and pilot it
into action! The level of detail and
immersion is stunning, and each of
the six 'crew members' has specific
tasks to fulfil during the mission to
aid the Resistance, as Pilots, Gunners
or Engineers, including manning the
quad guns and prepping the navi-
computer for hyperspace. Be sure
to complete your tasks well, as your
skills will come under scrutiny in
the Spaceport after you have helped
Chewbacca and Hondo Ohnaka on
their quest. AAAAA/TTTTT G+.

BRITTIP

Arguably the best photo opportunity
in Walt Disney World is on the
Millennium Falcon ride as you get to hang
out in the ship's crew room – and sit at the
iconic 3-D chess table where Chewbacca
played C-3PO in *Star Wars: A New Hope*.

Other entertainment: The
interaction with the Batuu
'inhabitants' is outstanding, while
there are roaming meet-and-greets
for Chewbacca, Rey, Stormtroopers,
Kylo Ren and Resistance spy Vi
Morada, which adds a great element
of realism. Ask the locals about their
planet – they all have a story.

Shopping: Shopping (and dining)
here is as much a heavily themed

Star Wars: Rise of the Resistance

© Disney

experience as the land's two attractions. Visit **Black Spire Outfitters** for intergalactic clothing, **Creature Stall** for cuddly toys and **Dok-Ondar's Den of Antiquities** for unique 'artefacts' and rare lightsabres. You can create a personal lightsabre at **Savi's Workshop** (where there is a superb Jedi experience that goes with it) and build your own droid at **Droid Depot** (where you may also encounter R2-D2). **First Order Cargo** outfits those whose allegiance lies with the Dark Side, and **Toydarian Toymakers** is the shop for toys and collectibles. You may even see store owner Zabaka's silhouette through a window at the back of her shop. Of course, all this Star Wars merchandise magnificence comes at a price – creating your own R2 or BB unit costs $100, while a custom-made lightsabre is $220.

Dining: Oga's Cantina is a wildly run den by Black Spire Outpost's local crime boss (inspired by the Cantina in Mos Eisley from *Star Wars: A New Hope*), with a terrific array of themed drinks. It features 'DJ' Rex and a range of specially prepared cocktails, mocktails and ales (including a Beer Flight in a souvenir board with Rancor teeth for $85) in another wonderfully inventive setting. Counter-service **Docking Bay 7** is part of the spaceport's working area, themed as a food freighter and serving familiar dishes such as crispy chicken and ribs, made 'other-worldly' through unusual presentations. **Kat-Saka's Kettle** carries drinks and flavoured popcorns, **Milk Stand** offers the iconic Star Wars drink of Blue or Green Milk (a non-dairy, frozen treat) while **Ronto Roasters** features grilled meat wraps, snacks and themed drinks.

BRITTIP

For the best dining in Galaxy's Edge try the delicious roast pork Ronto Wrap at Ronto Roasters or Smoked Kaadu Pork Ribs and Felucian Garden Spread (vegetarian meatballs and hummus) at Docking Bay 7, which also offers a small selection of breakfast items.

It all adds up to an evocative experience inside an all-encompassing location of genuine star quality that has all the feel of the films, and even more of that close-up detail Disney does so well. The scenic splendour is a triumph of the Imagineers' art and well worth a AAAAA+ rating – before you even go on a ride!

Commissary Lane

This is another street of dining and character meetings. The **Sci-Fi Dine-In Theater Restaurant** is huge fun, a mock drive-in cinema, with cars as tables, and a big film screen showing old science-fiction movie clips. It offers burgers, salmon, pasta and sandwiches, as well as signature milkshakes and sodas ($36–49 for three-course lunch, $10–12 kids' meal). The counter-service **ABC Commissary** serves eclectic fare, including a buffalo chicken grilled cheese sandwich, pork or prawn tacos, salads and plant-based options.

Mickey and Minnie Starring in Red Carpet Dreams: Meet the main Mouse and his best girl at this themed meet-and-greet, with Mickey dressed for his role in The Sorcerer's Apprentice and Minnie in a dazzling show-stopper gown.

Docking Bay 7

© Disney

Toy Story Land

Get ready to shrink down to toy-size in this *Toy Story* themed land set in Andy's backyard and bedroom, including giant Tinker Toy sets, crayons, the Green Army Men and Woody's pals Rex, Wheezy and Jessie among the clever scene-setting.

Toy Story Mania: This family fun 3-D ride dives into a fantasy fairground of games with the *Toy Story* characters aboard carnival vehicles (with individual spring-action shooters) through Andy's Bedroom. There are five challenges, plus a practice round and, thanks to 3D glasses, riders can 'see' everything their shooter fires at the targets, while there are air-bursts and water effects – if you hit a water balloon, watch out! Throw virtual eggs at barnyard targets, launch darts at prehistoric balloon targets, break plates with baseballs, land rings on Buzz Lightyear's alien friends and finish up in Woody's Rootin' Tootin' Shootin' Gallery, before totting up your scores. It is a touch raucous and chaotic, but kids love the shooting element and the whole family can enjoy the amusing ride through the toys' world. (AAA TTTT G+). It's busy from mid-morning, so use Genie+ or get here *early*.

Slinky Dog Dash: This child-friendly coaster is the main element of the backyard area, a fast-turning whiz through the garden surrounded by many of Andy's other toys. It doesn't feature any big drops or high speed, though it does give riders delightful air time through its section of camelbacks. It's a "transitional" coaster that will seem quite big for youngsters (larger than The Barnstormer but not quite the size of Big Thunder Mountain Railroad at the Magic Kingdom). It is a fast-launch coaster (i.e. without a lift hill) and covers much of the expansion area in scenic style. TTTT (TTTTT under-12s) G+ This is busy from first thing, and the G+ option is well worthwhile here. Or wait until the last hour of the day.

Alien Swirling Saucers: The other eye-catching garden ride is primarily for kids, a hectic whirl in classic fairground fashion with the green aliens from the *Toy Story* films as they bid to escape the clutches of The Claw. It is designed as a toy set Andy got at Pizza Planet, but is basically a variation on the spinning tea cups ride at Magic Kingdom, but with special lighting, music and sound effects. TT (TTTT under-6s) G+ Another one that's popular for much of the day with the younger set.

Pixar Avenue: This is an area in its own right next to Toy Story Land and features *The Incredibles in Municiberg*, with special meet-and-greets for Edna Mode (also see her Super Suit Gallery) and the Incredible family, as well as a periodic street show. AAA. **Neighborhood Bakery** serves up themed drinks and pastries while **Municiberg Gifts** offers Incredibles toys and apparel.

Other entertainment: Look out for **Sarge and the Green Army Patrol** and the **Green Army Drum Corps** here, with the chance to take part in an army 'Boot Camp'. **Woody**, **Buzz** and **Jessie** also appear for regular meet-and-greets.

Shopping: Look out for the new **Jessie's Trading Post** and more themed gifts at **Toy Story Mania Shop**.

Dining: Woody's Lunch Box serves classic American fare, including breakfast bowls, BBQ brisket, sandwiches, plant-based items and ice cream floats, soft drinks, beer and cider for breakfast, lunch and dinner. **Roundup Rodeo BBQ** full-service restaurant was due to open in 2020, but was among several projects put on ice by the pandemic. Its theme is Andy's rodeo play set, with a menu heavy on succulent barbecue platters, grilled meats and traditional picnic dishes. Its delayed opening was due in late 2022.

BRITTIP

Look out for the signature drink of Toy Story Land, the Mystic Portal Punch (or Powerade Mountain Berry Blast), which is offered in a souvenir Alien Sipper Cup.

Animation Courtyard

Get ready for a series of wonderful family-friendly shows in this area of the park.

Voyage of the Little Mermaid: A 17min live performance that is primarily for children who have seen the Disney animated film. It brings together a mix of actors, animation and puppetry to re-create the film's highlights. Parents will still enjoy the special effects, but queues tend to be long, so go early or late. You may also get a little wet. AAA (AAAAA under-9s).

—BRITTIP

Try to sit at least halfway back in the Mermaid Theatre, especially if you are with young children, as the stage front is a bit high.

Disney Junior Play and Dance!: The latest incarnation of Disney Junior Live on Stage, with a lively musical presentation featuring popular Disney Junior TV shows like Mickey, Doc McStuffins, Timon and Vampirina. Hosted by Finn Fiesta and DJ Deejay, the interactive fun also has classic character appearances (AAAAA G+ under-5s).

Walt Disney Presents: Step into Walt's world for a multi-media look at the creativity behind his films and theme parks, including original concept art for Walt Disney World, forthcoming new attractions, and a short film highlighting his amazing catalogue of work. Forthcoming Disney-Pixar films may also be showcased periodically. AAA.

Star Wars Launch Bay: More Star Wars toys and collectibles are on offer here, along with dozens of prop replicas and exhibits, plus meet-and-greets for Chewbacca, BB-8 and Darth Vader. A 10min film in **Launch Bay Theater** gives a behind-the-scenes look at the making of the movies.

Other entertainment: Youngsters can meet all their favourite Disney Junior characters in **Animation Courtyard**, several times daily. Meet popular movie characters, such as Mike and Sulley from *Monsters Inc.* inside **Walt Disney Presents**.

Meet Dr Macstuffins

© Disney

DISNEY'S HOLLYWOOD STUDIOS with children

Here is our guide to the attractions that appeal to the different age groups in this park:

Under-5s

Beauty and the Beast – Live on Stage, Disney Junior Play and Dance!, Fantasmic!, For The First Time In Forever, Voyage of the Little Mermaid, Lightning McQueen's Racing Academy.

5–8s

All the above, plus Alien Swirling Saucers, Indiana Jones™ Epic Stunt Spectacular, Jedi Training: Trials of the Temple, Muppet*Vision 3-D, Slinky Dog Dash, Toy Story Mania, Star Wars: A Galactic Spectacular, Mickey and Minnie's Runaway Railway.

9–12s

As for 5-8s, plus Millennium Falcon: Smugglers Run, Star Wars: Rise of the Resistance, Rock 'n' Roller Coaster, Star Tours, Twilight Zone™ Tower of Terror.

Over-12s

Millennium Falcon: Smugglers Run, Star Wars: Rise of the Resistance, Fantasmic!, Indiana Jones™ Epic Stunt Spectacular, Muppet*Vision 3-D, Rock 'n' Roller Coaster Starring Aerosmith, Slinky Dog Dash, Star Tours, Toy Story Mania, Twilight Zone™ Tower of Terror, Star Wars: A Galactic Spectacular, Mickey and Minnie's Runaway Railway.

Sunset Boulevard

The final area contains the two high-thrill rides and big night-time finale.

Rock 'n' Roller Coaster: Disney's first inverted coaster is a big draw for thrill-ride addicts, with a great indoor setting and fast-launch ride. It features a clever holographic-style film show starring rock group Aerosmith, leading to their 'super-stretch' limos for a memorable whizz through 'Los Angeles' (including a close encounter with the Hollywood sign!). Go early or expect big queues. Ride photos cost $17–26 but are included with Memory Maker.
R: 4ft/124cm. TTTTT G+

━BRITTIP

If only one or two in your group want to ride Rock 'n' Roller Coaster, or you want to save time, opt for the Single Rider queue. You'll be split up, but the wait will be much shorter.

The Twilight Zone™ Tower of Terror: This 199ft/60m landmark invites you to experience another dimension in the Hollywood Tower Hotel that time forgot. The exterior is intriguing and the interior suitably spooky, and, just when you think you've reached the ride, there's another queue, so enjoy the superb detail. Eventually,

Hollywood Tower Hotel lit up for the 50ᵗʰ anniversary

© Disney

you board elevator cars for a journey into the 'Twilight Zone' and things take a quick turn for the quirky and bizarre, in a 13-storey lift shaft that seemingly has a mind of its own! **R**: 3ft 4in/101cm. TTTTT G+

Lightning McQueen's Racing Academy: Lightning McQueen, from the hit movie *Cars*, has opened his own racing academy, and is teaching rookie drivers the rules of the road – until his nemesis, Chick Hicks, challenges him to a definitive race. Lightning's friends pitch in to save the day in this cute stage and screen show, featuring one of Disney's most convincing audio-animatronics to date. AAA

Beauty and the Beast – Live on Stage: An enchanting live musical song and dance performance of the highlights of this Disney classic will entertain the whole family for 30min up to five times a day in the Theater of the Stars. Check the daily schedule for show times, usually starting at 11.45am. AAA

Fantasmic!: A not-to-be-missed special-effects spectacular. Staged nightly (twice nightly in peak periods) in a 6,900-seat amphitheatre, it features the dreams of Mickey, portrayed as the Sorcerer's Apprentice, which are hijacked by the Disney villains, leading to an epic battle, with Our Hero emerging triumphant. Dancing waters, shooting comets, animated fountains, swirling stars and balls of fire combine in a breathtaking presentation, especially the giant, fire-breathing dragon! The 25min show added characters from the movies *Mulan, Frozen, Aladdin* and *Moana* in 2022. It begins seating up to 2hrs in advance and it's best to head there at least 30min before (watch out for the splash zones!). AAAAA

Book the **Fantasmic Dining Package** at Mama Melrose's, Hollywood and Vine or Hollywood Brown Derby for special reserved show seating (starter, main, dessert, non-alcoholic drink from $45–70 adult, $20–45 child).

Disney Movie Magic: Stand in front of the Chinese Theater for this nightly 12min projection show featuring Disney classics like *Mary Poppins, Pirates of the Caribbean* and *Beauty and the Beast.* AAA.

Star Wars: A Galactic Spectacular: The evening's large-scale pyrotechnic extravaganza is a mix of projection screens, lasers, fire effects and fireworks as the Star Wars stories come to vivid life above the Chinese Theater, all set to John Williams' original film scores. AAAA.

50th Anniversary: Don't miss the dazzling night–time lighting projections on the Tower Of Terror, plus more Disney Fab 50 sculptures around the park, notably R2–D2, Woody and Bo Peep.

Other entertainment: Sunset Boulevard is also home to more of the park's **Citizens of Hollywood** characters.

BRITTIP

While the Galactic Spectacular fireworks show is genuinely breathtaking, the full effects can only be viewed from in front of the Chinese Theater.

Shopping: Legends of Hollywood, Beverly Sunset Boutique, Sunset Ranch Pins and Souvenirs and the **Once Upon A Time** shops (for limited edition watches, clothing and other collectibles) are the best.

Dining: Rosie's All-American Café (chicken, hot dogs, burgers, plant-based) **Sunshine Day Bar** (cocktails) and **Catalina Eddie's** (pizza, salads) market-style eateries.

Trolley Car Café

© Disney

DISNEY'S ANIMAL KINGDOM THEME PARK

This version of the Disney theme park represents a very different experience, emphasising conservation and nature instead of non-stop thrills. Its more relaxing pace still has Disney's seamless entertainment style – and several excellent rides. However, there are two elaborate wildlife trails, five shows (including two that are almost worth the entry fee alone), a huge adventure playground, conservation station and petting zoo. Pandora: The World of Avatar opened in 2017, adding even more to the park's appeal, plus huge crowds!

It is wonderfully scenic, notably with the huge Tree of Life, Kilimanjaro Safaris, Asian village of Serka Zong (home to the Expedition: Everest™ ride) and stunning Valley of Mo'ara, but it won't overwhelm you with Disney's usual grand fantasy. Rather, it is a chance to explore, experience and soak up the gentler, more natural ambience. It is not a zoo in the conventional sense, but it is home to 200-plus species of birds and animals. The educational tone is fairly strong, but children in particular may pick up easily on the conservation undertones of things like Kilimanjaro Safaris and Maharajah Jungle Trek. However, the park does get crowded, especially in Pandora, and there are fewer places to cool down. It is definitely advisable to be here on time, and make the first few hours count.

Disney's Animal Kingdom Theme Park at a glance

Location	Directly off Osceola Parkway, also via World Drive and Buena Vista Drive		
Size	500 acres/203ha divided into 6 'lands'		
Hours	7.30, 8 or 9am to 6, 7 or 8pm seasonally		
Admission	Under-3s free; 3–9 $104–154 (1-day base ticket, priced seasonally), $437–595 (5-day Standard Theme Park Ticket), £459 (14-day Magic, includes Memory Maker); adult (10+) $109–159, $455–610, £479. US prices do not include tax.		
Parking	$25, $45–$50 premium		
Lockers	Either side of Entrance Plaza; $10, $12, and $15		
Pushchairs	$15 and $31 at Garden Gate Gifts, through entrance on right; $13 and $27 per day for multiple days		
Wheelchairs	$12 or $70 ($20 deposit refunded) with pushchairs		
Top attractions	Avatar Flight of Passage, Na'Vi River Journey, DINOSAUR!, Kilimanjaro Safaris, It's Tough to Be a Bug!, Kali River Rapids, Festival of the Lion King, Finding Nemo – The Musical, Expedition: Everest™		
Don't miss	Gorilla Falls Exploration Trail, Maharajah Jungle Trek, Rafiki's Planet Watch, dining at Rainforest Café and Tree of Life Awakens at night.		
Hidden costs	Meals	Burger, chips and coke $16 3-course meal at Yak & Yeti $43.50–62 (kid's entrée and dessert $16) Beer $8.25–10 Kids' meal $10	
	T-shirts	$26–42 Kids' T-shirts $20–37	
	Souvenirs	$1.99–2,700	
	Sundries	Pressed Penny Holder $14.99	

Location

If you are staying in the Kissimmee area, Disney's Animal Kingdom is the easiest of the parks to find. Just get on the (toll) Osceola Parkway and follow it all the way west to the entry plaza. Alternatively, coming down I-4, take exit 65 on to Osceola Parkway. From West Highway 192, come in on Sherberth Road and turn right at the first traffic lights. If you arrive early, you can walk to the Entrance Plaza, otherwise the tram system takes you in. Again, note where you park (e.g. Unicorn, row 67). The entrance plaza is overlooked by the Rainforest Café, which is open for breakfast, lunch and dinner (but is busy 12.30–3.30pm and an hour before closing). With Orlando so hot in summer, the animals are more evident early in the day, especially on Kilimanjaro Safaris. If you don't arrive early, plan this attraction for its latest daytime excursion.

Beating the queues: If you arrive *before* opening time, head straight to **Avatar Flight of Passage** and **Na'vi River Journey** as they often have peak waits as early as 8.30, when park opening is 8am. If you're not *that* much of an early bird, save them for late afternoon as the worst of the crowds often tail off by 5pm. If you *have* taken an early Pandora excursion, follow up with **Kilimanjaro Safaris** and then the **Gorilla Falls Exploration Trail**, and you will have experienced the busiest ride and two of the park's best animal encounters before it gets too hot. Thrill seekers should head straight for Asia, where the **Expedition: Everest™** ride is the big draw. Then head to nearby **Kali River Rapids** raft ride, and then the scenic **Maharajah Jungle Trek**. The $15/person Genie+ service may not be especially good value here, as there are only a handful of Genie+ ride options, but the two Individual Lightning Lane selections should offer better value as they will have the longest queues throughout the day and could well save a lot of time. Here's the full rundown of this lovely park.

The Tree of Life Awakens at night

The Oasis

1 The Oasis Tropical Garden

Pandora – The World of Avatar

2 Na'vi River Journey

3 Avatar: Flight of Passage

4 Windtraders

5 Satu'li Canteen

6 Pongu Pongu

Discovery Island

7 The Tree of Life

8 It's Tough To Be A Bug

9 Discovery Island Trails

10 Flame Tree Barbecue

11 Pizzafari

12 Adventurers' Outpost

13 Tiffins

Dinoland USA

14 DINOSAUR!

15 The Boneyard

16 Finding Nemo: The Big Blue…And Beyond

17 Chester And Hester's Dino-Rama!

18 TriceraTOP Spin

19 Restaurantosaurus

Africa

20 Harambe

21 Kilimanjaro Safaris

22 Rafiki's Planet Watch

23 Gorilla Falls Trail

24 Tusker House Restaurant

25 Festival Of The Lion King

26 Harambe Market

Asia

27 UP! A Great Bird Adventure

28 Kali River Rapids

29 Maharajah Jungle Trek

30 Expedition: Everest

31 Yak & Yeti

Complimentary Wi-Fi
Wi-Fi is available in most areas. Some attractions and shows may have limited availability.

Rafiki's Planet Watch

Train to Rafiki's Planet Watch

AFRICA

Curiosity Animal Tours kiosk

ASIA

Discovery River

DISCOVERY ISLAND

DINOLAND U.S.A.

OASIS

ENTRANCE

Buses to *Disney* Resort hotels

Trams to Guest parking

PANDORA – THE WORLD OF AVATAR

DISNEY'S ANIMAL KINGDOM

The Oasis

Tropical Garden: A gentle, walk-through introduction to the park, this is a rocky, tree-covered area featuring animal habitats, streams, waterfalls and lush plant life. Here you meet miniature deer, exotic boars, waterfowl, a giant anteater and wallabies in an understated environment that leads you across a stone bridge to the main park area. AAA

Shopping: Stop at **Garden Gate Gifts** (on the right) for pushchair, wheelchair and locker hire, while Guest Relations is on the left.

Dining: The fun **Rainforest Café** also has an entrance inside the park here. If you haven't seen the one at Disney Springs, call in to view the amazing jungle interior with its audio-animatronic animals, waterfalls, thunderstorms and aquariums. A 3-course meal costs $44–65, but the setting alone is worth it and the food is above average. Try breakfast or an early dinner to avoid the crowds.

Discovery Island

This colourful village is the park hub, themed as a tropical artists' colony, with animal-inspired artwork, nature trails, four main shops and four eateries. You will also find the Baby Center and First Aid station here.

The Tree of Life: This arboreal edifice is the park centrepiece, an awesome creation that seems different from wherever you view it. It is covered in 325 carvings representing the Circle of Life, from the dolphin to the lion. Trails around the Tree are interspersed with fish and animal habitats. It has 103,000 leaves (all attached by hand) on more than 8,000 branches! AAAA

Discovery Island Trails: These pretty trails around the Tree of Life feature habitats for flamingoes, otters, vultures and more. AA

It's Tough To Be A Bug!: Winding down among the Tree's roots brings you 'underground' to a 430-seat theatre and another example of Disney's artistry in 3-D films and special effects. This hilarious 10min show, in the company of Flick from the Pixar film *A Bug's Life*, is a homage to 80 per cent of the animal world, featuring grasshoppers, beetles, spiders, stink bugs and termites (beware the 'acid' spray!) as well as several tricks we couldn't possibly reveal. Sit towards the back in the middle (allow a good number of people in first as the rows are filled up from the far side) to get the best of the 3-D effects. AAAAA G+

BRITTIP

The special effects and mock creepy-crawlies in It's Tough To Be A Bug can be VERY scary for young 'uns.

Other entertainment: The Island is home to the lively **Viva Gaia Street Band** and various **Disney characters**, notably Pocahontas along Discovery Island Trails, Russell and Dug from *UP!* opposite Discovery Trading Company, Kevin from *UP!* (wandering character) and Timon and Rafiki at Character Landing. **Adventurers Outpost** is the setting to meet Mickey and Minnie. Children can also sign up for the novel **Wilderness Explorers** programme here (also based on *UP!*), with the chance to visit kiosks around the park for interactive lessons and animal experiences, earning stickers on the way that act as a gentle educational story. **Winged Encounters – The Kingdom Takes Flight** free-flight macaw show takes place over Discovery Island several times daily.

Shopping: You will find a huge range of merchandise, souvenirs and gifts here, notably in **Discovery Trading Company** (clothes, accessories, gifts) and **Island Mercantile**.

Dining: Counter-service restaurants **Pizzafari** (pizza, salads, sandwiches, vegetarian options and cakes) and **Flame Tree Barbecue** (barbecued ribs, chicken and pork, mac & cheese, plant-based dishes and salads) are good choices. If it's not too hot, the Flame Tree is a picturesque option among the gardens and fountains alongside Discovery River, but air-conditioned Pizzafari is better in summer. Full-service **Tiffins** features an imaginative lunch and dinner menu in a creative, art-gallery style setting, with extensive artefacts from Disney Imagineers' travels. It features a 'global culinary expedition' menu, with the likes of Butter Chicken, Whole-Fried Sustainable Fish, Surf and Turf, North-African spiced tofu, vegetarian crispy cauliflower and Caramel Mousse, plus other creative dishes (three-course meals from $50–97). It includes the laid-back **Nomad Lounge** (our favourite haunt!) with a River view, great cocktails and small-plate dining. **Creature Comforts** carries Starbucks coffee and pastries, while **Isle of Java** has pastries, pretzels, Joffrey's coffees and soft drinks.

Pandora: The World of Avatar

One of Disney's most immersive and dazzling lands, especially at night, this delve into James Cameron's *Avatar* film is a full-on recreation of the Valley of Mo'ara on the planet Pandora, with masses of scenery, special effects and a totally convincing setting. Guests enter a pristine valley, where mystical 'Floating Mountains', bioluminescent plants, native totems and remnants of the planet's occupation by the predatory forces of the Research Development Administration (RDA) are among the host of stunning set-pieces and captivating place-making. It would be easy to spend a day just taking in the scenery, but there are two major attractions as well.

Na'vi River Journey: This pleasant river boat ride is a gentle journey into the mysteries and wonders of Pandora's bioluminescent forest and caves, where the only sounds you hear come from the world of nature that surrounds you. It is a large-scale diorama that gives visitors a close-up view of the native wildlife, the peaceful Na'vi and the astounding Shaman of Songs, who connects all living things through her mystical chants. AAAAA G+.

Avatar Flight of Passage: Swoop and soar over Pandora on the back of a Mountain Banshee in this 3-D simulator ride that is so realistic you'll believe you *have* taken part in an adventure like no other. Enter a cavern deep inside a mountain, pass through the former RDA facility hidden inside, and continue on to the Pandora Conservation Initiative's

Pandora, the World of Avatar

© Disney

research centre, where your DNA is 'scanned' for a match with an Avatar. Riders are then paired with a Banshee via 'linking chairs' (bike-style ride vehicles) and the journey of a lifetime begins. Fly with the Na'vi over forests and mountains, dive and twist through tangled treetops and along thundering waterfalls, catch your breath in a magnificent bioluminescent cave and experience up-close encounters with Pandora's wildlife – some of it friendly, some of it not (cue the fearsome Great Leonopteryx!). It is a traditional Na'vi 'rite of passage' so exhilarating it leaves you breathless, and we challenge you not to queue up immediately for a second go! (**R**: 44in/111cm; children under 7 must be accompanied by a 14 or up. No expectant mothers). TTTTT+ ILL Be aware wait times here can top 2hrs at peak times.

> **BRITTIP**
> As with the other parks, some of the Animal Kingdom's live entertainment may not return post-pandemic, but expect to see the most popular groups, possibly by a different name.

Other entertainment: Find Na'vi inspired face painting at **Colors of Mo'ara**. There is a **Wilderness Explorer** challenge in this area as well.

Shopping: Windtraders is an unusual shop, not only for its elaborate theming, but also because it sells Pandora-related merchandise *only*, from clothes and unique gifts to the must-have souvenir, a robotic mini Banshee that sits on your shoulder.

Dining: Counter service **Satu'li Canteen** offers an imaginative lunch and dinner (chicken, beef, shrimp and tofu bowls, and cheeseburger bao buns) plus desserts, soft drinks and an intriguing selection of cocktails, beer and wine. Kid-friendly choices include hot dogs and cheese quesadillas.

Pongu Pongu quick-serve counter has creative alcoholic and non-alcoholic cocktails, pineapple lumpia, pretzels and beer, plus an egg and sausage savoury scone and French toast at breakfast.

Mylo the baby rhino joins Animal Kingdom © Disney

Africa

The park's largest land recreates the forests, grasslands and rocky homelands of East Africa in a rich landscape that is part vintage port town and part savannah. Central Harambe Village is a superb Imagineer's eye-view of a Kenyan port town, with white coral walls and thatched roofs, and the starting point for adventure. The Arab-influenced Swahili culture is also depicted in the tribal costumes and architecture.

BRITTIP

It is difficult to take photographs during the Sunset Kilimanjaro Safari, so ride during the day when the animals are most visible.

Festival of the Lion King: This not-to-be-missed, high-powered 25min production (seven to 10 times a day) brings the film to life in spectacular fashion, with giant moving stages, huge animated figures, singers, dancers, acrobats and stilt-walkers, plus some fun audience participation. All the well-known songs are given an airing in a fiesta of colour and sound, with the usual Disney quality. Queuing often begins an hour in advance for the 1,000-seat theatre, but the first couple of shows of the day rarely hit peak capacity. AAAAA G+ Sign language shows are performed at 4.30pm each Tues and Sat; arrive at least 25mins early and ask a Cast Member if you can sit in the Warthog section.

Kilimanjaro Safaris: The queue alone earns high marks for authenticity, preparing you for the 110acre/45ha savannah beyond. You board a safari truck, with your driver describing the flora and fauna on view and a bush ranger-pilot overhead relaying facts and figures on the wildlife, including the dangers of poaching. Scores of animals are spread out in various habitats – with fences all cleverly concealed – as you splash through fords and cross rickety bridges for close-ups with lions, rhinos, elephants, giraffes, antelope, hippos and ostriches. The animals roam over a wide area, though, and can disappear from view. Not recommended for expectant mothers or those with back/neck problems. AAAAA G+

Kilimanjaro Safaris At Night: The route may be the same, but the night-time safari feels very different.

Festival of the Lion King

© Disney

Most of the Reserve is lit only by moonlight once the sun goes down, allowing guests to see the animals in a 'whole new light' – and a new level of activity. Other areas are softly illuminated as if by the rising moon, while a 'sunset' section creates stunning silhouettes as animals roam past.

Gorilla Falls Exploration Trail: As you leave the Safari, this nature trail showcases gorillas, hippos, okapi, zebras, meerkats and rare tropical birds. You wander at your own pace and visit 'research' stations to learn more about the animals, including the underwater view of the hippos and the savannah overlook, where giraffes and antelope graze and the meerkats frolic. There is a walk-through aviary, but the real centre-piece is the extensive gorilla habitat. Again, the natural aspect is fabulous and it provides many photo opportunities. AAAAA

Rafiki's Planet Watch: This subsection of Africa involves a (rather dull) rustic train ride, with a peek into some of the backstage areas, as a preamble to the park's educational exhibits (especially for children). The three-part journey starts with **Conservation Station**, offering exhibits and information about the environment and threats to its ecology, while the Veterinary Treatment Room and Science Center provide views into the park's working facilities. The **Animation Experience** adds the chance to draw your own Disney character using real-life animals in 25min classes G+. Finally, the **Affection Section** petting zoo consists of a collection of goats, sheep and a miniature donkey. AAA

Other entertainment: There's plenty more to enjoy here, with the pageantry and rhythms of **Tam Tam Drummers of Harambe**. The melodic harp sounds of **Kora Tinga Tinga** provide more live engagement, along with the **Harambe Village Acrobats**. One element resulting from the pandemic – and the need to stay socially distanced – that may stay in 2023 is the series of **Character Cruises** by boat around Discovery River between Africa and Asia, featuring the likes of Pocahontas and Meeko, Mickey and friends, and the Discovery Island Drummers.

Shopping: Harambe is home to **Mombasa Marketplace**, where you can suit up safari-style and buy African-inspired art, carvings and drums. **Mariya's Souvenirs** offers apparel, Vinylmation collectibles, housewares, camera accessories and toys.

Dining: Tusker House Restaurant (featuring Donald's Dining Safari for breakfast at $42 adults, $27 children, and lunch and dinner at $55 and $36; pricing is seasonal) is one of the best diners in the park, with a mouth-watering array of salads, rotisserie chicken, salmon, beef, pork, curry and vegetarian dishes. There are also four snack and drink bars, most notably the **Kusafiri Coffee Shop** (pastries, hand pies, flatbread and drinks), while **Tamu Tamu Refreshments** offers some ice cream and soft drinks, and the **Dawa Bar** is a great place to sit with a beer or cocktail and soak up the scenery. The **Harambe Market** has Kitamu Grill (chicken bowl), Famous Sausages (plant-based sausage), Wanjohi Refreshments (beer, wine, speciality drinks) and Chef Mwanga's (rib bowl).

Harambe Market

© Disney

DISNEY'S ANIMAL KINGDOM THEME PARK with children

Here is our guide to the attractions that appeal to the different age groups in this park:

Under-5s

Affection Section, The Boneyard, Discovery Island Trails, Festival of the Lion King, Finding Nemo – The Big Blue…And Beyond, Gorilla Falls Exploration Trail, Kilimanjaro Safaris, Maharajah Jungle Trek, Na'vi River Journey, TriceraTOP Spin.

5–8s

All the above, plus Avatar Flight of Passage (if tall enough), Conservation Station, DINOSAUR! (with parental discretion), UP! A Great Bird Adventure, Habitat Habit!, It's Tough To Be A Bug (with parental discretion) and Kali River Rapids.

9–12s

All the above, plus Expedition: Everest

Over-12s

Avatar Flight of Passage, DINOSAUR!, Expedition: Everest™, Festival of the Lion King, UP! A Great Bird Adventure, Gorilla Falls Exploration Trail, It's Tough To Be A Bug!, Kali River Rapids, Kilimanjaro Safaris, Maharajah Jungle Trek, Na'vi River Journey.

Asia

The next 'land' is elaborately themed as the gateway to the imaginary south-east Asian region of Anandapur, with temples, ruined forts, landscape and wildlife. The elaborate ruined temple exhibits for the gibbons and siamangs are worth looking out for – and you may well hear them wherever you are in the park!

UP! A Great Bird Adventure: This gentle show features Russell and Dug from the Pixar film *UP!* in a 25-minute presentation that showcases the world of exotic birds. It includes vultures, eagles, toucans and a singing parrot, and highlights many of the conservation issues facing their cousins in the wild. AAA

Kali River Rapids: Part thrill-ride, part scenic journey, this bouncy raft ride will get you pretty wet (not great for early morning in winter). It starts out in tropical forest territory before launching into a scene of logging devastation, warning of the dangers of clear-cut burning. Your raft then plunges down a waterfall (and one unlucky soul – usually the one with their back to the drop – gets seriously damp) before you finish more sedately. In the summer months, try to do this early before the crowds build up. **R**: 3ft 6in/106cm (a few rafts have adult-and-child seats allowing smaller children to ride). TTT AAAA G+

Maharajah Jungle Trek: Asia's version of the wildlife trail is another picturesque walk past decaying temple ruins and animal encounters. The first few exhibits – the water buffalo, Komodo dragon and a bat enclosure (including the flying fox bat, the world's largest) – lead to the main viewing area, the 5acre/2ha Tiger Range, whose pool and fountains are a popular playground early in the day for these magnificent big cats. An antelope enclosure and walk-through aviary complete this breathtaking trek. AAAAA

Expedition: Everest™: This clever roller-coaster takes you deep into the Himalayas for an encounter with the mythical Yeti. The queuing area alone will convince you of its authenticity (try to do the main queue at last once to appreciate all the detail) as you reach an abandoned tea plantation railway station to undertake a ride to the foothills of Mount Everest, trying not to disturb the hidden menace of the Yeti. Will the beast be in evidence? You bet! And the ride becomes a typically fast-paced whiz, forwards

AND backwards, as you attempt to escape the creature's domain. It is a memorable ride but draws big crowds, so try to head here first or take advantage of the Single Rider queue if you don't mind being split up. You can get ride photos here, too ($21–27; $17 digital download; included with Memory Maker, p88). **R**: 3ft 8in/115cm. TTTTT ILL (may be G+ at peak periods)

─────BRITTIP─────

While it's tempting to take the Single Rider short-cut at Expedition: Everest™, you'll miss most of the striking design and creativity in this particular queue.

Shopping and dining: The retail options are limited to two minor kiosks and **Serka Zong Bazaar** for Expedition Everest gifts, but it boasts the fab **Yak and Yeti** combination diner. Outside is counter-service **Local Foods Café** (breakfasts, honey chicken, sweet and sour tempura prawns, vegetable tikka masala and chicken salad), while inside is the full restaurant. Yak and Yeti offers imaginative cuisine, from a Korean Beef to Chicken Tikka Masala and Lobster Garlic Noodles, as well as Asian-fusion dishes like Soy-Herb Glazed Ribeye, Miso Salmon and Pork Pot Stickers. A good range of drinks and cocktails complement this tempting eatery. Extra incentive to visit: a full range of drinks to go, while you can just sit at the bar for a drink or full meal. The **Anandapur Ice Cream Truck** is also popular and **Caravan Road** features shaved ice treats and alcoholic beverages. **Thirsty River Bar and Trek Snacks** offers speciality cocktails, beer, wine, and soft drinks.

DinoLand USA
The final area of the park is somewhat at odds with the natural theme of the rest, a full-scale palaeontology exercise, with the accent on a 'university fossil dig'. Energetically tongue-in-cheek (the students who work the area have the motto 'Been there, dug that', while you enter under a mock brachiosaurus skeleton, the 'Oldengate Bridge' – groan!), it also features the character-filled Donald's Dino-Bash.

DINOSAUR!: This is a herky-jerky ride experience, rather dark and intense (and often too scary for young children). It is also a wonderfully realistic journey back to the end of the Cretaceous period, when a giant meteor put paid to dinosaur life. You enter the high-tech Dino Institute for a history show that leads to a briefing room for your 'mission' 65 million years in the past. However, one of the Institute's scientists hijacks your trip to capture a dinosaur, and you career back to a prehistoric jungle in a 12-passenger Time Rover. The threat of a carnotaurus (quite frightening for children; try to sit them on the inside of the car) and the impending doom of the meteor add up to a whirl through a menacing environment. You will need to ride at least twice to appreciate all the detail, but queues build up quickly, so go either first thing or late in the day. **R**: 3ft 4in/101cm. TTTT AAAA G+

The Boneyard: An imaginative adventure playground, offering kids the chance to slip, slide and climb through the 'fossilised' remains of triceratops and brontosaurs, explore caves, dig for bones and splash through a mini waterfall. TTTT

Finding Nemo – The Big Blue… And Beyond!: This show is a first for Disney, taking an animated film and turning it into a musical. It combines colourful puppets, dancers, acrobats and animation with innovative lighting, sound and animated backdrops. A big update in 2022 reimagined the story of the aquarium fish in Dr. P. Sherman's office crossing the ocean to reach the Marine Life Institute via larger-than-life puppetry, all designed by Michael Curry, who created the award-winning West End version of Disney's *The Lion King* show. It's a spectacular performance, and the 25min show is staged up to six times a day. AAAA

BRITTIP

Finding Nemo – The Big Blue... And Beyond! will have a long queue before showtime, but don't worry; the theatre is huge, and most will get in.

Chester & Hester's Dino-Rama!: This mini-land of fairground games and stalls is rather garish but is designed to have a quirky, tongue-in-cheek style from 1950s' American roadside attractions. It also features various character appearances and a fun children's ride. **TriceraTOP Spin:** Another version of the Dumbo/Aladdin rides in the Magic Kingdom, where a flying, twirling, spinning top bounces you up and down with a surprise at the top. AA (TTTT under-5s).

Donald's Dino-Bash: This character carnival creates a showcase for Donald, Daisy and friends around Dino-Rama, with each of Launchpad McQuack, Goofy, Pluto and Chip 'n' Dale having their own meet-and-greet areas, with colourful costuming and backdrops. AAA

Other entertainment: Dino-Rama also features the **Fossil Fun Games**, six fairground-type stalls (costing $5 per game) designed to tempt you to try to win a cuddly dinosaur.

Shopping: Chester and Hester's Dinosaur Treasures offers a wide range of dino-related souvenirs.

Dining: Restaurantosaurus serves burgers, hot dogs, sandwiches, chicken nuggets, plant-based burgers and salads while **Dino Bite Snacks** offers ice-cream and pastries.

Kali River Rapids

© Disney

Other entertainment

For a real Disney character extravaganza, **Donald's Dino Bash** takes place in the main Dinorama area several times a day (usually between 10am and 7pm), providing the chance to enjoy their 'Prehistoric Party' with Donald, Daisy, Goofy and Pluto, plus those scamps Chip 'N Dale. At night, the **Tree of Life** bursts into colourful new life as a 'Beacon of Magic,' all beautifully lit by enchanted fireflies. AAA

Tree of Life Awakenings: Projected onto the Tree of Life each night, this series of short shows tells stories as the carvings on the tree's trunk 'magically' awaken, and its branches glow with the light of thousands of fireflies. Through colour and imagery, the animals 'come to life' in 3min vignettes, transitioning into a procession of clips from classic Disney nature-inspired films. Viewing is from the entry to Discovery Island and is standing-room only. AAA

Tours: Join an animal specialist and a cultural representative for a fascinating insight into the park's African elephants with the 1hr **Caring for Giants** tour (several times daily; $30, no under 4s). **Savor the Savanna: Evening Safari Experience** takes guests on an evening safari, stopping to enjoy tapas, beer and wine, plus stories about the wildlife, in a secluded viewing area (5 and 6.15pm daily, $179, no under 8s; 21 and up only for alcoholic beverages). For something really different, try the **Wild Africa Trek**, a 3hr ride-and-trek into the savannah. From a precarious rope bridge crossing to a VIP safari in open-air vehicles and a visit to Harambe's private camp, this exclusive experience in groups of up to 12 is open to ages 8+ (minimum 4ft/122cm tall; under 18s with adult), six times daily. Closed-toe shoes required, dresses/skirts not advised; weight limit 310lb/141kg (407 939 8687, $199–249/person).

That's the full Disney theme park story, but there is still PLENTY more in store...!

6 Five More of the Best

Or, Wizards, Wildlife and Wonders

It's time to leave the wonderful world of Disney and explore the other theme parks. And there's still a LOT in store, as Universal Orlando and the SeaWorld parks have plenty of their own sizzling creativity and excitement on offer.

Universal is an increasingly dynamic proposition, and more centralised than Disney. For UK visitors, the 2 and 3-Park Tickets are extremely well priced, while they also offer their own paid-for front-of-queue system, **Universal Express**, which covers a one-time access to all of the main attractions. It is not cheap – it costs from $60–150 at one park, $75–160 at both, for one-time use at each attraction – but it can save a LOT of queueing at busy times. A limited number go on sale at park opening and are snapped up, but they can also be bought online for a specific day at **universalorlando.com**. The Park-to-Park Unlimited Express provides Express access to both parks for $90–190.

Universal hotel guests at Portofino Bay, Royal Pacific Resort and Hard Rock Hotel benefit from Express ride priority all day by showing their room key and all eight hotels enjoy the major perk of early access to The Wizarding Worlds of Harry Potter each day. In addition, some rides have Single Rider queues, which save time if you want to go by yourself or don't mind splitting up your group. Once again, height/health restrictions (R) are noted in ride descriptions. Universal is also home to some of the best (and most grisly!) Halloween celebrations on earth, with their Halloween Horror Nights programme (p153).

Watch out for Velociraptors in the queue for VelociCoaster

UNIVERSAL STUDIOS FLORIDA

Universal opened its first Florida park in 1990 and quickly became a serious rival to Disney. For the visitor, it means a consistently high standard and good value (though the choice can be bewildering), but there are few similarities to their Los Angeles park. Universal is also a different proposition to Disney, with a more edgy style that appeals especially to teens. Younger children are still well catered for, though. Universal parks can also need more than a full day in high season. Strategies are the same: arrive EARLY (up to 30mins before opening), do the big rides first, avoid main meal times and take an afternoon break (try shopping, dining or visiting the cinemas at CityWalk) if it gets too crowded.

Location

Universal Studios Florida® is divided into seven main areas, set around a lagoon, but there are no great distinguishing features. The main resort entrance is just off Interstate 4 (I-4 eastbound take exit 75A; westbound take exit 74B) or via Universal Boulevard from I-Drive. Parking is in its massive multi-storey car park and there is quite a walk (with moving walkways) to the front gates.

My Universal Photos

Universal's photo sharing system allows guests to collect all their ride photos in one source and is cheaper than buying them individually. Go online before your visit at **universalorlando.com/web/en/us/my-universal-photo** and buy the 1-day package for $70 (a $10 saving on buying it at the park) or 3 days for $90. Take your confirmation email to a My Universal Photo location in the park to activate. You will receive a themed lanyard for your Photo card, unlimited digital downloads of your photos, photo gift product discounts and two colour photos.

The Bourne Stuntacular

© Universal Orlando Resort

Universal Studios Florida® at a glance

Location	Off exits 75A and 74B from I-4; Universal Boulevard and Kirkman Road
Size	110 acres/45ha in 7 themed areas
Hours	9am–6 or 7pm off peak; 8am–9 or 10pm high season (Washington's birthday, Easter, summer holidays, Thanksgiving, Christmas)
Admission	Under-3s free; 3–9 $104–139 (1-day ticket), $210–258 (2-day Park-to-Park ticket), £299 (UK 3-Park Explorer ticket); adult (10+) $109–144, $218–266, £309. US prices do not include tax.
Parking	$27 (prime parking $50; valet parking $75)
Lockers	Immediately to left in Front Lot $15
Pushchairs	$20 and $35
Wheelchairs	$15, ECV $65, $85 with sun shade (with photo ID as deposit), with pushchairs
Top attractions	Harry Potter and The Escape From Gringotts, Hogwarts Express, Revenge of the Mummy, Men in Black, Despicable Me: Minion Mayhem, TRANSFORMERS: The Ride – 3-D, The Simpsons, Hollywood Rip Ride Rockit!
Don't miss	Universal's Cinematic Celebration, Curious George Playground (for kids), The Blues Brothers, Tales of Beedle the Bard, The Bourne Stuntacular
Hidden costs	**Meals** Burger, chips and coke $18.98; 2-course lunch $17–25 (Leaky Cauldron) Kids' counter service meal $7.49
	T-shirts $25-40, kids $20–35
	Souvenirs $2.99–$2,000
	Sundries Temporary tattoos $7–10

BRITTIP

A good way to enjoy the Universal Express perk is to book a night's stay at one of their three deluxe hotels. Check in early (they will store bags for you) and you get your hotel room key, with Express feature, for use that day AND the next day.

Beating the queues: With the opening of The Wizarding World of Harry Potter – Diagon Alley, this has become THE place to visit first, with heavy queues building up quickly and lasting all day. It is at the back of the park, so try to avoid all the other attractions if this is your top target. Turn right on Rodeo Drive, continue through Sunset Boulevard and the Springfield area of The Simpsons, and go left across the bridge straight to the Wizarding World. If you are not a Potter fan (although you should still give Diagon Alley a look at some stage) and want some of the big-time thrills, stop first at Hollywood Rip Ride Rockit (on your left in Production Central) and then take in TRANSFORMERS: The Ride – 3-D, and the nearby Revenge of the Mummy in New York. For interactive fun, take in Despicable Me first, then head back to the Springfield area and do The Simpsons and Men In Black. Many of the other attractions are now easier to do with the crowds flocking to Diagon Alley.

Here's a full guide to the Studios (for CityWalk, see Chapter 10).

BRITTIP

Watch out for the helpful mobile electronic Wait Times boards around both parks. Better still, get the free **Universal Orlando App** on Google Play or the App Store and have all the essential info at your fingertips, with free Wi-Fi throughout the parks.

UNIVERSAL STUDIOS FLORIDA

Production Central

Coming straight through the gates brings you into the administrative centre, with a couple of large gift stores plus Studio Sweets. Call at **Guest Services** for guides for disabled visitors, TDD and assisted listening devices, and to make restaurant bookings, which can also be made at a kiosk to the right after the turnstiles, next to the Today Café. **First aid** is available here (and on Canal Street between New York and San Francisco), while there are facilities for nursing mothers at **Family Services** by the bank through the gates on the right. Coming to the top of the Plaza of the Stars brings you to the business end of the park.

Despicable Me – Minion Mayhem: This outrageously funny 3-D simulator ride is based on the animated films starring Steve Carell. You enter the home of super-villain Gru and visit his lab where you are 'transformed' for Minion training. In the company of Gru's daughters,

Margo, Edith and Agnes, the zany scheme goes awry and his 'recruits' suffer some hair-raising adventures that need Gru's intervention to save the day. With dynamic, motion-based seats, things can get bumpy, so those with heart, neck, or back problems should ask for the stationary seats. TTT+ AAAA (TTTTT under-10s)

Hollywood Rip Ride Rockit!: This iconic ride is a high-tech colossus, with an onboard system that allows you to select your own ride music. It starts with a video intro while you queue that reveals five music choices (Rap/Hip Hop, Country, Classic Rock/Metal, Pop/Disco and Club Electronica), each with six tracks. You're then strapped into an open-sided car that goes straight up a 17-storey vertical lift-hill, then into a steep dive followed by the signature Double Take, the world's first non-inverted loop (you don't actually go upside-down but it feels like it!). You will soar over the heads of people in the queue, dive below ground level

Hollywood Rip Ride Rockit

© Universal Orlando Resort

and fly around a 150° banked turn, all in the course of the 1min 40sec ride. The innovative open cars make the experience feel even faster and more dynamic, while the mix of pounding music (from your headrest and speakers along the track) and concert-style lighting (flashy during the day, stunning at night) ensure this ride really rocks (ride photos $20–35). Ride early or leave it for the evening when queues tend to drop off. R: 4ft 3in/130cm. TTTTT+

BRITTIP

Universal Orlando has metal detectors at the bag check area that all guests must walk through. To help move crowds through faster, be sure to have your bags open and coins, mobile phones and keys removed from pockets.

TRANSFORMERS: The Ride – 3-D: The latest generation of Universal's dramatic 3-D technology allied with a dynamic ride vehicle, this puts guests at the heart of an explosive battle between the Autobots, led by Optimus Prime and the evil

Despicable Me, Minion Mayhem

© Universal Orlando Resort

Transformers: The Ride

© Universal Orlando Resort

Decepticons of Megatron. It feels like walking into a movie as the long, elaborate queuing area prepares riders for joining the planet-defending forces of NEST, and then a larger-than-life whirl through a Decepticon attack in a bid to defend the AllSpark – and the earth's existence! The combination of ultra-HD film, real scenery and dramatic special effects is breathtaking (if loud). Crowds build up quickly, hence you need to ride early on or late in the day. R: 3ft 4in/101cm. TTTT

Shrek no more: In January 2022, Universal closed its long-running Shrek 4-D show and began to convert it to…nothing they would confirm as we went to press. But, theme park rumours insist it will become a new, walk-through attraction based on those loveable yellow stars from the summer film *Minions: The Rise Of Gru*. Themed to a Villains convention, it aims to deliver an immersive, interactive experience, with the bonus of a Minions Café next door, where the old Monsters Café has been shut down ready for a transformation.

Character appearances: Optimus Prime, Bumblebee and Megatron can be found at the brilliant **Meet The Transformers** photo spot next to the ride, while you'll find **Minion photo ops** in the Super Silly Stuff shop.

Shopping: Great shops here, including **Supply Vault** for all things Transformers, **On Location** (cameras, hats, sunglasses and more), **Super Silly Stuff** (Despicable Me merchandise), the massive **Universal Studios Store** (with everything) and **It's A Wrap** (discounted items).

New York

Now head to New York with its impressive architecture, street scenes and park.

Race Through New York Starring Jimmy Fallon: Comedian and *Tonight Show* host Jimmy Fallon stars in this 3-D simulator ride experience through the streets of New York. Enter the famous NBC Studios at 30 Rockefeller Plaza, where Jimmy challenges his audience to a 'race through New York,' through subway tunnels, around the Empire State Building, into the Hudson River, and even to the moon! Popular *Tonight Show* characters The Ragtime Gals and Hashtag the Panda also appear in this special-effects filled, high-adrenalin laugh-fest that is part show, part character meet-and-greet, part ride, and all family-friendly fun. The best part? There is no queuing. Instead, visitors get a time to return to enjoy the pre-show areas with their TV exhibits, games and live entertainment. AAAA/TTT

BRITTIP

Don't miss the hilarious song routines of The Ragtime Gals before the Jimmy Fallon attraction. This is an amusing 'barbershop quartet'.

Race Through New York with Jimmy Fallon

© Universal Orlando Resort

Revenge of the Mummy: This superb offering is a high-thrill, high-fun journey into the Ancient Egypt of *The Mummy* film series, fusing coaster technology with special effects. It starts out as a slow, dark ride through curse-ridden Hamunaptra, but soon takes an ingenious launch into something more dynamic, with a host of special effects and audio animatronics as you brave the Mummy's realm. The high-speed whiz in the dark (backwards to start with) doesn't involve inversions but is still a thrill with its tight turns and dips, while there are several clever twists (the front row may get damp!). It is a hugely immersive experience but may be too scary for under-8s. Preview your ride photos ($20–35) as you enter the gift shop. **R**: 4ft/122cm. TTTT½

BRITTIP

For the best ride experience on Revenge of the Mummy, try to get a back row seat. You are not allowed to carry anything on the ride – loose items must be left in the (free) lockers provided.

Revenge of the Mummy

© Universal Orlando Resort

The Blues Brothers: Fans of the film will not want to miss this live show as Jake and Elwood Blues cruise up in their Bluesmobile and put on a stormin' performance of a series of the film's hits on New York's Delancey Street several times a day before heading off into the sunset, stopping only for autographs. AAAA

Other entertainment: New York also boasts an **amusement arcade**. Or just grab a drink at **Finnegan's bar** and listen to the **live music** from their fun singer-guitarist.

Shopping: Check out **Sahara Traders** for Mummy souvenirs, as well as jewellery and toys, and **Rosie's Irish Shop** for all things Irish. The **Tribute Store** changes seasonally for special events like Halloween and Mardi Gras, with spectacular theming, and **Park Plaza Holiday Shop** adds Christmas festivities and decorations.

Dining: Finnegan's Bar and Grill offers shepherd's pie, fish and chips, corned beef and cabbage, along with steak, burgers, fries and a good range of beers, plus Irish-tinged entertainment, while **Louie's Italian Restaurant** has counter-service pizza and pasta, ice-cream and tiramisu. There's also a **Ben and Jerry's** store for ice-cream and smoothies, and a **Starbucks** for coffee and pastries.

San Francisco

Cross Canal Street to get to this area that has undergone a major rebuild.

Fast & Furious – Supercharged: This slightly underwhelming ride experience is based on the underground street racing world from the films starring Vin Diesel, Paul Walker and Dwayne Johnson. It takes visitors on an all-new adventure using both motion and screen-based technology, with an immersive twist thanks to digital film and sound effects for a mix of simulation and real movement. It lacks real dynamism but boasts lots of visual fun, with plenty of humour mixed in, while guests can get up close with some of the super-charged cars from the films in an elaborate queue area. There's also an in-queue game you can play via the Universal App. AAA/TTT

Other entertainment: Although the **Jaws** ride is gone, you can still get a photo with the 'Great White' next to the **Chez Alcatraz** dockside bar, or try the **Amazing Pictures** kiosk and have your face added to a famous view, poster or magazine ($30–54). The **Beat Builders** add some fun live percussion entertainment using construction equipment. Yes, really!

Shopping: Custom Gear features *Fast & Furious* merchandise.

Dining: Lombard's Seafood Grille offers excellent seafood, steak, pasta and sandwiches (high season only; reservations accepted), while **San Francisco Pastry Co** serves up desserts and coffee, **Richter's Burger Co** has some tempting burgers and **Chez Alcatraz** is a neat dockside bar with appetisers.

The Blues Brothers

The Wizarding World of Harry Potter – Diagon Alley

This is where Universal really raises the bar for theme park entertainment. The second part of the hugely impressive Potter-verse not only repeats the immersive, film-like setting of Hogsmeade in Islands of Adventure (with a unique link between the two), it goes even deeper into JK Rowling's creation and leaves you in awe of the design and innovation.

Diagon Alley: Hidden behind a realistic setting of The Embankment lies the secret wizarding street and a full array of complex theming. The external design is modern London, right down to the ¼-scale King's Cross Station and Piccadilly's Eros Statue, where you will also find the iconic Knight Bus. Other elements include Grimmauld Place and the Wyndham Theatre but then visitors walk through the jumbled red-brick barrier next to the tube station and emerge in the jaw-dropping recreation of Diagon Alley, where the towering shop-fronts and mysterious businesses envelop visitors with the full visual effect of the films. Don't miss sinister Knockturn Alley, where it is always night, while Carkitt Market was created by JK Rowling just for Universal. AAAAA+

Harry Potter and The Escape From Gringotts: Prepare to be mesmerised as you enter the vaults – and dangers – of the wizarding world's bank. A fire-breathing dragon sits high atop the building and, if that doesn't take your breath away, the stunning entry hall will, with its amazing animatronic goblin staff. The queue twists and turns through the filing office and backrooms before reaching Bill Weasley's office, where you learn you have arrived during the famous episode when Harry, Ron and Hermione break into the

The Wizarding World of Harry Potter: Diagon Alley

vaults. Then you take the elevator deep underground and climb a flight of steel stairs into a vast cavern that only *feels* like it's miles below the bank. Here you board the ride to share in the perils of Harry and Co as they search for a crucial Horcrux. Half coaster and half 3-D simulator ride, it changes pace as riders brave the various guardians of the vaults, including the dangerous Bellatrix Lestrange, a fire-breathing dragon and, finally, an encounter with Lord Voldemort. Be aware it draws the park's longest queues, so head here straight away or expect a l-o-n-g wait. **R**: 3ft6in/106cm. TTTTT+

Hogwarts Express: This neat, realistic ride operates between the two parks, as guests journey to Hogsmeade from King's Cross Station. Again, the sense of realism is superb as you arrive at Platform 9¾ to board a replica of the famous Hogwarts train. While it runs on a special track backstage, the enclosed carriage 'windows' show highlights of the journey north to Scotland, including a close encounter with Hagrid on his flying motorcycle,

the flying Ford Anglia – and some dangerous Dementors. Oh, and look out for Harry, Hermione and Ron on the train! You will need a 2-park ticket to ride and the queue area is vast, with wait times typically above 30mins from 2–6pm. AAAAA+

Other entertainment: Look out for two original shows in Carkitt Market, where **Celestina Warbeck & The Banshees** take the stage several times a day to deliver a rollicking four-song performance. The 'Singing Sorceress' performs classics like 'You Stole My Cauldron But You Can't Have My Heart' and 'A Cauldron Full of Hot, Strong Love.' AAAA. Also on the Market stage is **Tales of Beedle the Bard**, a combination of live actor and puppetry show. It's especially engaging for children, and Potter fans. AAA. Other live entertainment is provided by the superbly atmospheric **Ollivander's** shop, where 'the wand chooses the wizard.' AAAA. Look out also for the **Knight Bus Conductor**, who engages visitors entering the Wizarding World, and don't miss the Talking Shrunken

Escape from Gringotts

Halloween Horror Nights

Universal's massively popular Halloween celebration occurs from early Sept to Oct 31 each year and is a wonderfully bloodthirsty – and thoroughly entertaining! – series of evening events. The Horror Nights have become a real trademark and add a suitably grisly touch to park proceedings. The park is transformed with imaginative set pieces from various horror movies, plus live shows and character interaction. The general mix is 10 indoor Scare Houses, each with its own macabre theme (such as Stranger Things and Walking Dead), plus open-air Scare Zones, with atmospheric dry ice and characters (zombies, chainsaw guys and various beasts!) lurking in dark corners, and two or three live presentations. The rides are all open (and often with fairly short queues), adding more novelty to the park experience, but this over-the-top (and occasionally downright gruesome) extravaganza is definitely not for kids, especially as the atmosphere can get a bit raucous late in the evening as alcohol is widely available. It goes down a treat with adults with the right sense of humour, though, and begins every evening at 6.30pm until 1 or 2am. It is a separate event costing $74–105/person, depending on the day, when purchased in advance online (it is more expensive on the night). Best value is the Frequent Fear Pass for multiple visits on select evenings (not Fri or Sat, when Scare House queues can top 2hrs). You can also get a HHN Express pass from $110–190, depending on dates. No costumes are allowed on any evening, though. Look up more at **universalorlando.com/hhn/en/us**.

Head. His wisecracks might be aimed at YOU!

Shopping: Another key experience, with eight immersive stores to please the eye and tease the wallet. **Weasley's Wizard Wheezes** is a multi-storey joke shop with all manner of gags, then there is **Wiseacre's Wizarding Equipment** (for all your essential school gear), **Quality Quidditch Supplies, Madam Malkin's Robes** (school uniforms and accessories), **Borgin & Burkes** (the Dark Arts store in Knockturn Alley), **Magical Menagerie** (a soft toy emporium – listen for the animals scurrying about in the upper levels!) and **Scribbulus**, for other Hogwarts mementoes. The shops also feature interactive windows that work with the special wands on sale at **Ollivander's** and **Wands By Gregorovitch** at $55–60 each. Look for the markers in the pavement, say the magic command and wave your wand for a host of surprises. You can even change dollars into wizarding notes at the **Money Exchange**, complete with a Goblin host.

Dining: The essential reality of the Wizarding World is continued into the main dining outlet of **The Leaky Cauldron**, a superb recreation of Diagon Alley's hallmark pub.

The food may seem standard pub fare, but the Cottage Pie is excellent, as is the Beef, Lamb and Guinness Stew, while their Ploughman's Platter is positively indulgent with its array of three cheeses, pickle, salad, scotch egg and fresh bread (prices from $12–22). There is also Toad in the Hole, Fish 'n Chips, two types of sandwich (sausage and chicken) and a Fisherman's Pie. Kids can choose from a mini-pie,

Halloween Horror Nights

© Universal Orlando Resort

mac and cheese and their own fish 'n chips ($7.49). There are then six tempting desserts, of which the Sticky Toffee Pudding is to die for. All this can be washed down with drinks such as Fishy Green Ale (a variation on bubble tea, and non-alcoholic), Otter's Fizzy Orange Juice, Tongue-Tying Lemon Squash and Gilly Water, as well as two outstanding beers – the IPA-like Dragon Scale Ale and porter-style Wizards Brew. There is a separate menu for breakfast. Still hungry? Head for **Florean Fortescue's Ice Cream Parlour** where Universal's culinary wizards have come up with a superb array of flavours that are all worth trying, including Earl Grey & Lavender, Apple Crumble, Chocolate Chilli and Clotted Cream. You can also grab a drink – alcoholic and otherwise – at the **Hopping Pot** and **Fountain of Fair Fortune**.

World Expo

Continuing around the park brings you to an extensive area that currently has just one major attraction.

Men in Black – Alien Attack: This combination thrill/dark ride takes up where the hit films, starring Will Smith, left off. Visitors are introduced to the MIB Institute in an inventive mock-futuristic setting and enrolled as trainees for a battle around the streets of New York with a horde of escaped aliens. Your six-person car is equipped with laser zappers for an interactive shoot-out, and only your collective marksmanship can save the day, with numerous ride variations according to your accuracy. Fast, frantic and a bit confusing, you'll want to come back until you can top 250,000 (for Defender status). **R**: 3ft 6in/106cm.

BRITTIP

For a big score in Men In Black, when you meet the Big Bug – push the big red button!

Shopping: Visit **MIB Gear** (at the exit to the ride) for Men In Black clothing and souvenirs, plus photo opps with the MIB themselves.

Diagon Alley

© Universal Orlando Resort

Springfield: Home of the Simpsons

The Simpsons Ride: The headline attraction here, this brings the TV characters to vibrant life in a colourful and amusing production, even if you're not a fan of The Simpsons. It is themed as Krustyland amusement park, brainchild of irascible Krusty the Clown, a bizarre funfair that is the setting for a hectic, breathtaking ride in the company of the Simpson clan. A wicked sound system and motion simulator technology ensure a frantic race through outlandish attractions, and the huge domed screen ensures an outrageously comical sensory experience. **R**: 3ft 4in/101cm. TTTTT

Kang and Kodos' Twirl 'n' Hurl: A standard fairground whirligig with some clever touches as the alien duo take 'foolish humans' into 'orbit' and provide a challenge as you twirl. TT (TTTTT under 6s).

Other entertainment: In Springfield, chance your hand at a series of fairground-type games that require $8 to play ($30 for five games). Look out for Simpsons **character meet-and-greets** and **photo ops** with icons like the Lard Lad Donuts statue, Founders statue and The Seven Little Duffs.

Shopping: To complete the immersive Springfield effect, visit the **Kwik-E-Mart** for Simpsons souvenirs (plus more gags).

Dining: Clever counter-service offerings of the **Fast Food Boulevard** food-court are found here, and you can dine in true Homer fashion (albeit with better quality) at **Krusty Burger, Luigi's Pizza, Frying Dutchmen, Cletus' Chicken Shack** and **Flaming**

The Simpsons Ride

Moe's (complete with the non-alcoholic Flaming Moe cocktail, $8.99). For a specially made brew, visit the **Duff Brewery & Shop** with a fab view of the Lagoon. **Bumblebee Man's Taco Truck** completes the picture.

Woody Woodpecker's KidZone

A great place to let the kids loose on their own, this is pure family fun territory.

Animal Actors On Location!: An amusing mix of video, animal performance and audience interaction, several children are invited to help present some unlikely feats and stunts featuring a range of wildlife, from parakeets to pigs. Many have been rescued from animal shelters and gone on to feature in films before finding a home at Universal. The theatre also provides an escape from the queues. AAAA

Fievel's Playland: Strictly for kids, this playground, based on the enlarged world of the cartoon mouse, offers the chance to bounce under a 1,000-gallon hat, crawl through a giant boot, climb a giant spider's web and shoot the rapids (a 200ft/61m waterslide) in Fievel's sardine can. TTTT (young 'uns only!)

Woody Woodpecker's Nuthouse Coaster: This junior-sized coaster is a whizzy little racer with plenty of kid-appeal. While its highest speed is just 22mph and its tallest hill is 28ft/8m, it does have a height restriction. **R**: 3ft/91cm TTTT (youngsters only).

Woody Woodpecker's KidZone

Trolls from Dreamworks Destination

DreamWorks Destination: Get ready for an interactive character experience with the likes of Kung Fu Panda, the Trolls and characters from *Madagascar* in this new, party-themed playground. AAA

ET Adventure: This glorious scenic ride comes with a grand queuing area and spectacular leap on flying bicycles to save ET's home planet. Steven Spielberg has added some new characters to the story, and queues rarely build up here. **R**: 3ft/91cm. AAAA

BRITTIP

If you want to let your youngsters loose in the Curious George playground, it is advisable to bring swimsuits or a change of clothing.

Curious George Goes To Town: Kids of all ages love this adventure playground with plenty of ways to get wet. It combines toddler play, water-based play stations and a huge interactive ball pool, and is a real bonus for harassed parents. It includes buildings to climb, hoses to spray water, a ball factory in which to shoot thousands of foam balls and – the tour de force – two huge water buckets that flood the street at regular intervals. TTTTT (under-12s)

Other entertainment: This is where you can **Meet Shrek and Donkey**, that humorous duo from the *Shrek* films, having been relocated from next to the old Shrek 4-D attraction. Princess Fiona makes regular appearances, too, while **Spongebob Squarepants and Friends** can also be found here.

Shopping and dining: Shop at the fun **Spongebob Storepants** for everything to do with Spongebob and friends in an immersive environment, complete with character photo opportunity, plus **ET's Toy Closet** and **Photo Spot**. For a quick bite, **Kidzone Pizza Company** offers pizza and chicken fingers.

Hollywood

Finally, your circular tour of Universal returns you to the main entrance via Hollywood (where else?).

The Bourne Stuntacular: Replacing the former Terminator 2: 3-D cinematic experience is this thrilling live-action theatre-and-cinema spectacular highlighting the Jason Bourne movies. Mixing stage work, film and special effects, it sees Bourne in action over three continents and a series of dangerous encounters that include fist-fights, shoot-outs and high-speed chases. The blend of technologies – including a motor-bike sequence – is astounding and really captures the movies' all-action vibe. TTTT.

Universal's Horror Make-Up Show: Not recommended for under-12s, this demonstrates some of the ways in which films have terrorised us, from classic black-and-white to modern horror movies. Using film clips and special effects 'experts', the audience is treated to a slapstick approach to horror make-up. Queues are rarely long and the spiel is highly amusing. AAA

Other entertainment: This is the place for the **Character Party Zone**, with appearances along Hollywood Boulevard from the likes of Scooby Doo and The Flintstones, plus the music and dance act of **Marilyn and the Diamond Bellas**.

Shopping: Some of the best shops are located here, including **The Brown Derby Hat Shop**, the fine apparel of **Studio Style**, **Five & Dime**, for Universal monsters and Jason Bourne merchandise, and themed stores for both **Hello Kitty** and **Betty Boop**.

Dining: Choose from **Mel's Drive-In**, a re-creation from the film *American Graffiti*, serving burgers and hot dogs, and the new **Today Cafe**, with breakfast fare, yummy pastries, some of the park's best sandwiches, plus salads and drinks.

The Bourne Stuntacular

© Universal Orlando Resort

UNIVERSAL STUDIOS with children

Our guide to the attractions that generally appeal to the different age groups:

Under-5s
Animal Actors On Location!, Curious George Goes To Town, ET Adventure, Fievel's Playland, Kang & Kodos' Twirl 'n' Hurl.

5–8s
All the above, plus Despicable Me, Hogwarts Express, Men In Black, The Simpsons, TRANSFORMERS: The Ride – 3-D (with parental discretion), Woody Woodpecker's Nuthouse Coaster.

9–12s
All the above, plus The Bourne Stuntacular, Hollywood Rip Ride Rockit, Fast & Furious, Harry Potter and The Escape From Gringotts, Revenge of the Mummy, TRANSFORMERS: The Ride – 3-D, Race Through New York Starring Jimmy Fallon.

Over-12s
The Blues Brothers, The Bourne Stuntacular, Despicable Me, ET Adventure, Fast & Furious, Race Through New York Starring Jimmy Fallon, Hollywood Rip Ride Rockit, Men In Black – Alien Attack, Revenge of the Mummy, The Simpsons, TRANSFORMERS: The Ride – 3-D, Universal's Horror Make-Up Show.

Night-time finale
Universal's Cinematic Celebration:
This special effects extravaganza brings down the curtain most nights, viewed from a three-tiered spectator area in the Central Park section for a grandstand view of the Lagoon, where a massive underwater platform provides all the razzamatazz. This special 'stage' is equipped with more than 120 fountains, pop-jets, fog effects, water-screens and more.

Jurassic World VelociCoaster

© Universal Orlando Resort

Combined with fireworks, lasers and projection equipment, it builds into a massive cinematic spectacular that goes through a repertoire of Universal films, including blockbusters like *Jurassic World, The Fast And The Furious, ET, Despicable Me, Transformers, Kung Fu Panda* and *Harry Potter.* ΛΛΛΛ.

The Universal Superstar Parade was discontinued in June 2022, with Universal only saying it will 'make way for new entertainment experiences in future'.

Special programmes
Universal Studios also features brilliant seasonal entertainment for **Mardi Gras**, with a massive, bead-throwing parade, plus music and authentic New Orleans food from Feb–April (and free with park admission). The spectacular Parade alone is worth coming to see, along with authentic music and a headline concert each weekend featuring international acts like LL Cool J, Diana Ross and Jason Derulo, but it does draw HUGE crowds. Universal also throws a party for **Fourth of July**, when the park presents a major firework spectacular. And don't miss the Studios at Christmas (p36).

ISLANDS OF ADVENTURE

Boasting the first Harry Potter 'land' and recent additions like Hagrid's Magical Creatures Motorbike Adventure and the fabulous VelociCoaster, the Studios' sister park is an exhilarating prospect in its own right.

The Islands of Adventure opened in 1999 under the supervision of creative consultant Steven Spielberg, and it provided one of the most complete and thrilling theme parks you could imagine, containing an upbeat collection of high-adrenalin rides, shows and entertainment, plus some fine dining. Then JK Rowling's boy wizard arrived and added a whole new 'world' of excitement.

The park has a full range of attractions, from out-and-out thrills to pure family entertainment. Seuss Landing will keep pre-schoolers amused, while Camp Jurassic is a clever adventure playground for 5–12s, but the rest of the park, with its nine 5-star thrill rides, is primarily geared to kids of 10 and over, their parents and especially teenagers. There are several elements that look alarming, but don't be put off – they all deliver immense fun as well as terrific spectator value! If any one ride sums up IoA, it is Harry Potter and the Forbidden Journey, which took theme park ride technology to a whole new level.

Private nursing facilities, an open area for feeding and resting (with high chairs) and nappy-changing stations, can be found at the **Family Service Facility** at Guest Services (to the right inside the main gates), while ALL restrooms throughout the park are equipped with nappy-changing facilities. First aid is provided in Sindbad's Village in the Lost Continent, and at Guest Services in Port of Entry.

Night-time lights at Hogwart's Castle

Port of Entry

You arrive for IoA as you do for Universal Studios, in the big multi-storey car parks off I-4 and Universal Boulevard and pass right through the CityWalk area, where you come to the main entrance plaza (head for the huge Pharos Lighthouse). As with Universal Studios, you can purchase the Universal Express pass (p143) for Islands of Adventure at various locations throughout the park and at Guest Services. Once through the gates, the lockers, pushchair and wheelchair hire are on your left as the Port of Entry opens up before you. This elaborate 'village' consists of shops and eateries, so push straight on to the main lagoon, but do take in the wonderful architecture throughout Port of Entry, which borrows from Middle East, Far East and African themes and uses bric-a-brac from all over the world.

Shopping: Later in the day, return to check out the extensive retail experience at places like **IoA Trading Company** and **Ocean Trader Market** for a full range of Islands of Adventure merchandise.

Dining: You can enjoy a coffee and pastry at the inevitable **Starbucks** or the **Croissant Moon Bakery** (also with croissants and sandwiches), or sample the huge cinnamon rolls and pastries of **Cinnabon**. Alternatively, try lunch or dinner at **Confisco Grille** with tastes from around the world including Italian, Mexican and Asian as well as American, and a range of dishes from sandwiches and burgers to salads, chicken, noodles and ribs. Or just grab a beverage and a snack at the **Backwater Bar**.

Islands of Adventure at a glance

Location	Off exits 75A and 74B from I-4; Universal Boulevard and Kirkman Road
Size	110 acres/45ha in 6 'islands'
Hours	9am–6, 7 or 8pm off peak; 8 or 9am–9 or 10pm high season (Washington's birthday, Easter, summer holidays, Thanksgiving, Christmas)
Admission	Under-3s free; 3–9 $104–139 (1-day ticket), $210–258 (2-day Park-to-Park ticket), £299 (UK 3-Park Explorer ticket); adult (10+) $109–144, $218–266, £309. US prices do not include tax.
Parking	$27 (prime parking $50; valet parking $75)
Lockers	Immediately to left in Front Lot $15
Pushchairs	$20 and $35
Wheelchairs	$15, ECV $65, $85 with sun shade (with photo ID as deposit), with pushchairs
Top attractions	Harry Potter and the Forbidden Journey, Hagrid's Magical Creatures Motorbike Adventure, Hogwarts Express, Amazing Adventures Of Spider-Man, Incredible Hulk Coaster, Jurassic Park River Adventure, Skull Island: Reign of Kong, VelociCoaster
Don't miss	Jurassic Park Discovery Centre, If I Ran The Zoo playground (for toddlers), Three Broomsticks restaurant and Ollivander's Wand Shop
Hidden costs	Meals	Burger, chips and soda $18.98
		3-course lunch $30-48 (Confisco Grill)
		Kids' meal $7.49
	T-shirts	$25–40, Kids $20-35
	Souvenirs	$1.50–$6,500
	Sundries	Butterbeer $7.99 regular or frozen

Port of Entry
1 Ocean Trader Market
2 Confisco Grille

Marvel Super-Hero Island
3 Incredible Hulk Coaster
4 Dr Doom's Fearfall
5 Café 4
6 Captain America Diner
7 The Amazing Adventures of Spider-Man
8 Storm Force Accelatron

Toon Lagoon
9 Popeye and Bluto's Bilge-Rat Barges
10 Dudley Do-Right's Ripsaw Falls
11 Me Ship, The Olive
12 Comic Strip Café
13 Toon Lagoon Amphitheater

Jurassic Park
14 Jurassic Park River Adventure
15 Pteranodon Flyers
16 Camp Jurassic
17 Discovery Center
18 Skull Island: Reign of Kong

19 Raptor Encounter
20 The VelociCoaster

The Wizarding World of Harry Potter
21 Harry Potter and the Forbidden Journey
22 Filch's Emporium
23 Flight of the Hippogriff
24 Olivander's
25 Dervish and Banges
26 Three Broomsticks
27 Zonko's
28 Hogwart's Express
29 Hagrid's Magical Creatures Motorbike Adventure

The Lost Continent
30 Mythos Restaurant
31 Mystic Fountain
32 Poseidon's Fury

Seuss Landing
33 Circus McGurkus Café Stoo-pendous
34 High in the Sky Seuss Trolley Train Ride
35 Caro Seuss-el
36 If I Ran the Zoo
37 The Cat in the Hat
38 One Fish, Two Fish, Red Fish, Blue Fish

Main Entrance

Beating the queues: At the end of the street, you will need to decide which way to head first as there are eight attractions where the queues build up quickly and remain that way. If you are among the majority lured by Harry Potter, turn right (through Seuss Landing and The Lost Continent). If you're after the big thrill rides, turn left into Marvel Super-Hero Island and head straight to Spider-Man, then do Dr Doom's Fearfall and the Incredible Hulk Coaster. The King Kong attraction (between Toon Lagoon and Jurassic Park) is a big draw, too, so you may want to head here first, and then visit Hogsmeade.

One Fish, Two Fish, Red Fish, Blue Fish

BRITTIP

There are two entrances to the Wizarding World of Harry Potter: from Jurassic Park and The Lost Continent. The latter is much more dramatic and offers the full Hogsmeade Village panorama.

Dinosaur fans should go left around the lagoon to Jurassic Park for the

thrilling new VelociCoaster and River Adventure before the masses arrive. Once you are wet, go back to Toon Lagoon for Ripsaw Falls and the Bilge-Rat Barges. Or those with younger children, turn right into Seuss Landing and enjoy The Cat in the Hat and High In The Sky Seuss Trolley Train Ride prior to the main crowd build-up.

Turning right, in an anti-clockwise direction, here's what you find.

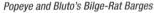

Popeye and Bluto's Bilge-Rat Barges

Seuss Landing

There is not a straight line to be seen in this vivid 3-D working of the Dr Seuss children's books. Even if the characters are unfamiliar, everyone can relate to the fun (though queues build up quickly).

Caro-Seuss-el: This intricate carousel ride on some of the Seuss characters – cowfish, elephant-birds and dog-a-lopes, for example – has rider-activated features that are a big hit with children. AA (AAAA under-5s).

One Fish, Two Fish, Red Fish, Blue Fish: A fairground ride with a twist as you pilot these Seussian fish up and down according to the rhyme that plays while you ride. Get it wrong and you get squirted! More fun for the younger set. TTT (TTTTT under-5s)

The Cat in the Hat: Prepare for a ride with a difference on these crazy six-passenger 'couches' to meet the adventurous cat and friends Thing One and Thing Two. The spinning element through this storybook world may be a bit much for very young children and queues move slowly, so try to get here early or leave it until later in the day. AAAA/TTT

If I Ran the Zoo: Interactive playgrounds don't get much better for the pre-school brigade than with these Seuss character scenarios, some of which can be pretty wet! Hugely imaginative and great fun to watch. TTTTT (under-5s)

The High in the Sky Seuss Trolley Train Ride: This fun family adventure high above Seuss Landing has terrific appeal to youngsters as you board a trolley to journey into the world of the Sneetches, visiting the Inking and Stamping Room, the Star Wash Room and a tour inside the Circus McGurkus Café Stoo-pendous. It is slow-paced and scenic, but it does draw slow-moving queues, so head here early with under-9s. AAAA

Character appearances: Look out for The Cat in the Hat, Thing One and Thing Two and The Grinch outside the Circus McGurkus, and the character-filled celebration of the Oh! The Stories You'll Hear street show.

Shopping: If the land has captivated you, you can buy the books at **Dr Seuss' All The Books You Can Read**, or a full variety of character merchandise at the **Mulberry Street Store**. **Snookers and Snookers Sweet Candy Cookers** is a super sweet shop.

Dining: Snacks and drinks can be had at **Hop On Pop Ice Cream Shop**, **Moose Juice Goose Juice** and **Green Eggs and Ham Café** (sandwiches and burgers). The **Circus McGurkus Café Stoo-pendous** is a mind-boggling eatery for fried chicken, burgers and pizza – with clowns and pipe organs.

Seuss Landing

The Lost Continent

This land underwent a rather drastic reduction to accommodate Harry Potter, but it still offers some eye-catching locations.

Poseidon's Fury: A walk-through show that puts its audience at the heart of the action as a journey in the company of a hapless young archaeologist takes a turn for the worse in the lost temple of Poseidon. You pass through an amazing water vortex before your expedition awakens an ancient demon. There is an element of suspense, but the special effects showdown between Poseidon and the demon is amazing. TTT

Other entertainment: Try a bit of mystic manipulation with **Star Souls - Psychic Reading**. But beware **The Mystic Fountain**; it can strike up a conversation – and then soak you! King Julien and Alex the Lion from the *Madagascar* films also pop up for appearances here.

Shopping: Find original souvenirs at **Treasures of Poseidon** (clothing, jewellery and handbags); unique coins and medallions from the mechanical hammer at **Mythical Metals**; and eclectic artwork and jewellery at **Shop of Wonders**.

Dining: Food options include **The Fire-Eater's Grill** (chicken fingers, hotdogs, salads, fries and drinks) and **Doc Sugrue's Desert Kebab House** (kebabs, hummus, salad and churros). The ornate **Mythos Restaurant** provides the best dining in IoA; the food (salads, beef, risotto, fish, pad thai and pasta) is first class, but the setting (inside a dormant volcano with fountains and clever lighting) is a real attraction (3-course meal $32–57.50, kids' meals $11–13).

Wizarding World of Harry Potter – Hogsmeade

This 'Island' has significantly boosted the park's attendance since it opened in 2010 and draws BIG crowds. The magnificent edifice of Hogwarts Castle looms large but the whole area is completely immersive as it uses the design genius behind the films. Here, you are drawn into an all-encompassing realm where chimneys smoke, icicles glitter, owls roost, visitors are warned to 'Observe the spell limits' and Butterbeer is real!

Hogsmeade Village: Walk through the grand archway into the Wizarding World and a powerful sense of realism envelops you. This is a shimmering, snow-covered version of the magical settlement Harry, Ron and Hermione inhabit. It is the shopping and dining heart of the Wizarding World, but is an attraction in itself. Here you will find a wonderful photo opportunity with the **Hogwarts Express**, while nearly all the shop windows feature 'wizardly' animatronic touches. The Owl Clock comes to life every 15mins; the wooden-raftered Owlery is a work of art; and you may just hear Moaning Myrtle in the loos! AAAAA+

> **BRITTIP**
> Don't forget your interactive wizard's wand in Hogsmeade. They were originally designed for the Diagon Alley area, but were added to the Islands of Adventure section in 9 different windows.

The Flight of The Hippogriff: This junior-sized coaster is aimed primarily at youngsters and features

Hagrid's Magical Creatures Motorbike Adventure

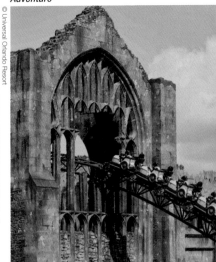

© Universal Orlando Resort

a journey into Hagrid's realm, where his love of outlandish creatures gives rise to this swooping ride. Hagrid offers instructions and warnings as you wind through the queue, and you may even hear Fang barking from inside his hut. There are no big drops, but it delivers a surprisingly fast-paced whirl. **R**: 3ft 4in/92cm. TTT (TTTT for 6–12s)

Harry Potter and the Forbidden Journey: This is the Big One: a trip inside the legendary halls of Hogwarts, and a breathtaking plunge on a state-of-the-art ride, Quidditch and all. The basic premise is that 'muggles' (non-wizarding types, i.e. you!) have been invited to tour the school. The immense queuing area is part discovery, part storytelling and part entertainment, so be ready for a LONG time on your feet as you traverse the corridors, traipse through the greenhouse, tiptoe along the Portrait Hall (where the paintings of the four founders of Hogwarts come to life in magical fashion) and tread the stone floors of the Gryffindor common room. Along the way, you'll be greeted by Professor Dumbledore in his study (complete with more talking portraits), be accosted by the Fat Lady (another painting-come-to-life) and enter the Defence Against the

Dark Arts classroom, where Harry, Ron and Hermione urge visitors to abandon their 'boring' tour and come to the Quidditch match (with the aid of a magic spell).

BRITTIP

Once again, this is an unpredictable, dynamic ride, with sudden twists, turns and tilts. You are strongly advised to leave all loose items in the free-to-use lockers just inside the castle.

Finally, you reach the Room of Requirement (past the Sorting Hat), where your mode of transport to the match is revealed – magical flying benches. With some pre-ride warnings, you are then strapped in to your 'bench' and are up, up and away. Only things don't go as planned and, before you can say 'Expecto Patronum' you're on a crazy dash through some of the young wizard's most dangerous adventures, through dramatic settings combining film technology and realistic scenery.

BRITTIP

Look for the Single Rider queue at Harry Potter and the Forbidden Journey – it can save a LOT of time

Harry Potter and the Forbidden Journey

There is a close encounter with a fire-breathing dragon, an army of giant spiders, a Death Eater and a narrow escape from the clutches of the Whomping Willow before the big finale in a spooky underground cavern where it's up to Harry, naturally, to try to save the day. It is an astounding theme park experience, but it WILL scare small children (and those with arachnophobia!), and it draws queues in excess of 2hrs, so head here early in the day. **R**: 4ft/122cm. TTTTT+ You exit through **Filch's Emporium of Confiscated Goods**, where you'll find a dazzling array of Hogwarts merchandise. You also pick up your ride photos here ($20–45).

> **BRITTIP**
>
> Look out for the Marauders Map in Filch's Emporium, plus other clever Hogwarts signature gadgets and gizmos among the merchandise.

Hagrid's Magical Creatures Motorbike Adventure: New in summer 2019 was this hugely elaborate and distinctly novel coaster that dives into the world of Hagrid and the magical creatures inhabiting the Forbidden Forest surrounding Hogwarts. Themed as a Care Of Magical Creatures class with Hagrid (beware his creation of the Blast-Ended Skrewts!), this roller-coaster hybrid – with pauses in the action to take in various set-pieces – hurtles riders on a manic journey, both inside and outside, with several surprises (including a sudden backwards section and a vertical drop). It has seven fast-launch moments but also a slow crawl through the Forest, featuring a meeting with Hagrid in his Hut, an encounter with a centaur, unicorns, Cornish pixies, Hagrid's three-headed dog Fluffy, and a scary moment in the clutches of the Devil's Snare, the deadly constricting plant from *Harry Potter and the Philosopher's Stone*. The queueing area is immense, and hugely detailed (look out for mysterious eggs – could they be dragons? – and Hagrid's magical creatures laboratory), while your coaster vehicle is also unique, a multiple-car version of Hagrid's motor-cycle and side-car. Riders need to choose which of the two seats to sit in before they ride, then it's off in suitably madcap fashion for a genuine Hogwarts adventure. **R**: 4ft/122cm. AAAAA+/TTTTT. Be aware the queues build up quickly here, as they do at Forbidden Journey.

Hogwart's Express: This is the 'northern' end of the famous train ride from King's Cross Station. With its own station (and queue area), it provides the full effect of arriving at or departing from this mythical

Hagrid's Magical Creatures Motorbike Adventure

© Universal Orlando Resort

Scottish village. The station is almost completely enclosed to allow the designers to build up the illusion, and then you pass through a small section of the Forbidden Forest to reach Hogsmeade itself and enjoy your first full view of the village with Hogwarts towering behind it. The ride from Hogsmeade to King's Cross is also different, screen-wise, from the one that brings you here, with more scenes of London and some of Harry's other exploits. AAAAA+

BRITTIP

Try all three sweet, non-alcoholic Butterbeers: 'regular', frozen (slushie style) or hot. It's usually easier to get served in the Hog's Head rather than at the busy street carts.

Other entertainment: The **TriWizard Spirit Rally** celebrates the upcoming tournament, with the Beauxbatons Academy ribbon dancers and staff-fighting wizards from Durmstrang Institute. Hogwarts is represented by the **Frog Choir** (four students and two huge frogs!), making for an entertaining show. The periodic **Nighttime Lights at Hogwarts Castle** each evening is a delightful 4min film show on the Castle, using state-of-the-art projectors, sound effects and a few pyrotechnics to provide more visual wizardry. The **Dark Arts at Hogwarts** show takes over for the Halloween season, featuring a suitably dark overlay that adds a deliciously threatening ambience to the area. It goes into overdrive for **The Magic of Christmas at Hogwarts** during the festive holiday season, with an even more dramatic 7min version that includes snow, ghosts and the Weasley's Wizard Whiz-Bangs. A whiz of a show!

BRITTIP

For the best view of the periodic Nighttime Lights at Hogwarts Castle show, try to grab a standing-room-only position in front of the stage used for the Tri Wizard Spirit Rally and Frog Choir.

Shopping: Be sure to check out the detailed shopping options, like **Honeydukes**, the place to buy Cauldron Cakes, Bertie Bott's Every Flavour Beans, Chocolate Frogs and more; **Dervish and Banges,** for Quidditch gear and school-related clothing, including the Nimbus 2001 broomstick; and **Ollivander's**, with 13 varieties of wand to choose from, and the same clever wizardly show as in Diagon Alley (albeit the one there has more capacity). AAAA

Dining: There is only one sit-down dining location here, but it's a corker. A 'Cathedral to Butterbeer', the **Three Broomsticks** menu features British favourites such as shepherd's pie, fish and chips and Cornish pasties, along with the Great Feast, a family-style meal of salad, ribs, chicken, roast potatoes and corn on the cob ($70 for 4; $18 per extra person). Entrées $11.50–19, with desserts $4–6, including strawberry and peanut-butter ice cream, found only in the Wizarding World. They also serve a different menu for breakfast ($18 for adults, $13 for children). Next door is the **Hog's Head Pub**, complete with animatronic boar's head, where you'll find Hog's Head Brew ($12 a pint).

The Three Broomsticks

© Universal Orlando Resort

BRITTIP

Of all the buildings, the Three Broomsticks is a must-see experience of dramatic interior design and special effects. Look in the rafters for owls, magical maids and the roaming House Elf!

All in all, it's an immense collection of dramatic and charming elements (witness the animated Prisoner of Azkaban poster in Hogsmeade) that add up to a vivid portrayal of JK Rowling's work. You don't need to be a fan to enjoy it and, like the Diagon Alley area in Universal Studios, the only snag is the seemingly permanent crowds it draws. Arriving early is highly advisable (the early entry perk with Universal hotels is so valuable here), but also try to see it magically lit after dark.

Jurassic Park

Now travel back to the Cretaceous age and the make-believe dinosaur film world where extravagant scenery will have you looking out for stray dinos.

Jurassic Park River Adventure:
From scenic splendour, the mood changes to hidden menace as your journey into this waterborne realm brings you up close and personal with some realistic dinosaurs. Inevitably, your passage is diverted to the hazardous, and the danger increases as the 16-person raft travels through the main building – with raptors loose everywhere. You are aware of something large lurking in the shadows – will you fall prey to the T-Rex, or will your boat take the 85ft/26m plunge to safety (plus a good soaking)? Queues usually

VelociCoaster

© Universal Orlando Resort

move briskly but will top an hour in mid-afternoon. **R:** 3ft 6in/106cm. The ride photo comes in various packages $19.95–39.90). **TTTT**

BRITTIP
Keep your valuables dry on the River Adventure by leaving them in the lockers at the start of the queue.

Pteranodon Flyers: The slow-moving queues are a major turn-off, especially for a fairly average ride, which glides gently over much of Jurassic Park (though it reaches a height of almost 30ft/9m). **R:** It is designed mainly for kids, and anyone OVER the height range of 3ft–4ft 8in/91–142cm (usually 11+) must be accompanied by a child of the right height. **TT** (**TTTT** under-9s). The Universal Express pass is not valid here.

Camp Jurassic: More excellent kids' fare with the mountainous jungle giving way to an 'active' volcano for youngsters to explore, climb and slide down. Squirt guns and spitter dinosaurs add to the fun (for kids, but parents can explore!). **TTTT**

Discovery Center: This indoor centre offers interactive games, like creating a dinosaur via DNA sequencing, mixing your own DNA with a dino on a touch-screen, playing Jurassic trivia game and handling 'dino eggs', plus other hands-on exhibits (10am–5pm; 7pm peak season). **AAA**

VelociCoaster: Hold tight for the most exciting new ride in town, as this Jurassic World-themed coaster added real high-speed thrills in 2021. You board the vehicles for a dash through the raptor paddock, soaring above both land and water to breathtaking effect, with Blue, Charlie, Echo and Delta giving chase. It catapults riders at up to 70mph/112kph through two fast-launch sequences and includes a 155ft/47m 'top hat' feature as well as a series of low-level twists and turns, a barrel roll over the water and a zero-gravity inversion, providing lots of 'air-time' for coaster fans. The high-tech queue and pre-show provide plenty of entertainment, and there are double-sided lockers to stow loose items in. It is an absolutely astounding ride that is also supremely smooth, plus it makes for great spectating! **TTTTT+**

Other entertainment: If you're not easily frightened, seek out the **Raptor Encounter**, where you can learn some interesting dino facts, then have your photo taken with the rather terrifying velociraptor, Blue (often to hilarious effect!). There are also fairground games at an extra $8 a time, or $30 for five games.

Shopping: Visit **Dinostore** and **Jurassic Outfitters** for the best shopping.

Dining: Try any of counter-service trio **Pizza Predatoria** (pizza, sandwiches and salads), **Thunder Falls Terrace** (rotisserie chicken, pork, turkey legs and salads, plus a great view of River Adventure) or the **Watering Hole** (cocktails and beer).

Pteranodon Flyers

© Universal Orlando Resort

Skull Island

There is only one attraction here, but it's good! Step back in time and meet the great ape himself.

Skull Island: Reign of Kong: In a world based on Peter Jackson's 2005 remake of *King Kong*, this is themed around a 1930s expedition to a mysterious isle where prehistoric predators are determined to eat your crew. Part ride, part 3-D film stunner, this large-scale truck ride encounters a variety of scary beasts, culminating in an up-close meeting with Kong that leaves riders convinced they face a terrible fate! High-def projection, film screens, superb sound and other effects make for a realistic environment, and the immense queue area (beware the lurking natives!) is worth seeing on its own. **R**: 36in/92cm, 36in–48in/123cm with adult. There are no age restrictions but this may be too intense for many youngsters. TTTT/ΛΛΛΛΛ.

Toon Lagoon

The thrills continue here with a watery theme and more comic-book elements.

Popeye and Bluto's Bilge-Rat Barges: Every park seems to have a variation on the white-water raft ride, but this is one of the wettest! Fast, bouncy and unpredictable, it has water coming at you from every direction, a couple of sizeable drops and a whirl through the Octo-plus Grotto that adds to the fun. If you don't want to get wet, don't ride, because there is no escaping the deluge here. **R**: 4ft/122cm. Look for the Water Blasters ($1 for 2 tokens; $5 for 12) on the bridge to give riders a wet start. TTTTT

BRITTIP

A change of clothes is often advisable after the Barges, unless it's mega hot. Bring a waterproof bag for your valuables or leave them in a locker.

Skull Island: Reign of Kong

© Universal Orlando Resort

ISLANDS OF ADVENTURE with children

Our guide to the attractions that generally appeal to the different age groups:

Under-5s
Caro-Seuss-el, The Cat in the Hat, High In The Sky Seuss Trolley Train Ride, If I Ran The Zoo, Jurassic Park Discovery Center, Me Ship, The Olive, One Fish, Two Fish, Red Fish, Blue Fish.

5–8s
All the above, plus Amazing Adventures Of Spider-Man, Camp Jurassic, Flight of the Hippogriff, Harry Potter and the Forbidden Journey (if tall enough), Hogwarts Express, Jurassic Park River Adventure (with parental discretion), Pteranodon Flyers, Storm Force Accelatron.

9–12s
All the above, plus Dr Doom's Fearfall, Dudley Do-Right's Ripsaw Falls, Hagrid's Magical Creatures Motorbike Adventure, Incredible Hulk Coaster, Popeye and Bluto's Bilge-Rat Barges, Skull Island: Reign of Kong, VelociCoaster (if tall enough).

Over-12s
Amazing Adventures Of Spider-Man, Dr Doom's Fearfall, Dudley Do-Right's Ripsaw Falls, Harry Potter and the Forbidden Journey, Hogwarts Express, Hagrid's Magical Creatures Motorbike Adventure, Incredible Hulk Coaster, Jurassic Park River Adventure, Popeye and Bluto's Bilge-Rat Barges, Skull Island: Reign of Kong, Storm Force Accelatron, VelociCoaster.

Dudley Do-Right's Ripsaw Falls: A flume ride that sends its passengers on a wild (and steep!) journey in the company of guileless Mountie Dudley Do-Right, bidding to save girlfriend Nell from the evil Snidely Whiplash. The action builds to an explosive finale at the top of a 75ft/27m abyss that drops you through the roof of a ramshackle dynamite shack to the lagoon below. Wet? You bet! **R:** 3ft 8in/111cm. TTTTT More Water Blasters on the bridge overlooking the final drop get riders even wetter.

Me Ship, The Olive: A kids' playland designed as a three-storey boat full of interactive fun, including water cannons, bells and slides (ideal for squirting riders on the Bilge-Rat Barges below), in best Popeye style. TTTT (for youngsters).

Other entertainment: Comic Strip Lane is the place to meet the Classic Comic Book Characters like Betty Boop, Popeye and Olive Oyl. Plus various **fairground stall games** for $8, or $30 for five.

Shopping: There is the usual array of character shops, like **Gasoline Alley**, **Betty Boop Store** and **Toon Extra**.

Dining: Grab a humongous sandwich at **Blondie's** (home of the Dagwood), a trademark burger at **Wimpy's**, sample the food court of **Comic Strip Café** (burgers, chicken, Chinese dishes, pizza and salad), or pick up something cool at **Cathy's Ice Cream**.

Dr Doom's Fearfall

© Universal Orlando Resort

Marvel Super-Hero Island

Finally, you arrive at total immersion in super-hero comic-book pages, with some of the best rides in the park.

The Incredible Hulk Coaster: Roller-coasters don't come much more dramatic than this giant green edifice that soars over the lagoon, blasting 0–40mph/64kph in 2secs, and reaching a top speed of 65mph/105kph. It looks awesome, sounds stunning and rides like a demon as you enter the gamma-ray world of Dr David Banner, aka the Incredible Hulk, and zoom into a weightless inversion 100ft/30m up.

BRITTIP

At the Hulk Coaster, keep left where the queue splits up and you will be in line for the front car for an even more extreme Hulk experience.

Deposit ANY loose articles in the lockers at the front of the building as the ride is guaranteed to shake anything out of your pockets. Crowds build up rapidly but queues move reasonably quickly. **R**: 4ft 6in/137cm. TTTTT Ride photos are available from $20–35, and also on My Universal Photos.

Dr Doom's Fearfall: Dr Doom's latest creation is a device for sucking fear out of his victims, and YOU are about to test it, strapped into chairs at the bottom of a 200ft/60m tower. The dry ice rolls, and whoosh! Up you go at breakneck speed, only to plummet back seemingly even faster, with a split second when you feel suspended in mid-air. Summon up the courage for this and enjoy an astonishing (if brief!) experience. **R**: 4ft 4in/132cm. TTTTT+

The Amazing Adventures Of Spider-Man: A visit to the Daily Bugle, home of ace reporter Peter Parker (aka Spider-Man) turns into a mission in a 'Scoop' vehicle – and an audio-visual extravaganza. This roving 3-D ride takes you into a battle with super-villains that includes a convincing 'drop' off a skyscraper. There are special effects aplenty and it is all loaded with the 'wow' factor. Go early or wait until late in the day – queues often top an hour by mid-morning. **R**: 3ft 4in/101cm. TTTTT+ PS: If this seems similar to the TRANSFORMERS ride at Universal Studios, it's because they use the same ride platform.

BRITTIP

You can beat some of the queues on the Spider-Man ride at busy times by opting for the Single Rider queue.

Storm Force Accelatron: This ride, primarily for kids, puts you in the middle of a battle between X-Men heroine Storm and arch-nemesis Magneto. It's basically an updated spinning-cup ride but with some neat twists (like a 3-way rotation where the cars look set to collide). TTT (TTTTT under-12s).

BRITTIP

For some of the park's best shopping bargains, visit Port Provisions right by the exit gates (to the left as you come through) where all the merchandise is 30–50% off.

Other entertainment: The **Marvel Super-Heroes** appear here periodically for photos and autographs, while **Spider-Man** has his own meet-and-greet booth at The Marvel Alterniverse Store. A high energy **video arcade** can be found at the exit to Dr Doom's Fearfall.

Shopping: Each ride has its own character merchandise, while the **Comic Book Shop** and **Marvel Alterniverse Shop** sell other souvenirs.

Dining: For a bite to eat, try the Italian buffeteria **Café 4** (pizza, pasta, sandwiches and salads) or a burger, chicken fingers or salad at the **Captain America Diner**.

And that, folks, is the full low-down on a truly immersive and exciting theme park. Miss it at your peril!

SEAWORLD

SeaWorld is firmly established as one of the most popular parks for its more peaceful and naturalistic aspect, the change of pace it offers and lack of substantial queues. It is large enough to handle big crowds well (though it still gets busy in peak season) and is a big hit with families in particular, but it has some fabulous rides and imaginative attractions too, including Antarctica: Empire of the Penguin, Turtle Trek, five superb coasters, the Infinity Falls raft ride and Sesame Street area for younger children.

Part of SeaWorld Parks & Entertainment with Discovery Cove, water-park Aquatica and Busch Gardens in Tampa, this makes for excellent multi-day adventures, notably with the UK Discovery Cove Ultimate Package, which includes all four. SeaWorld's recent additions and a brilliant Christmas overlay (p36) ensure this remains an exciting and meaningful place to visit. There are special offers for booking online at **seaworld.com**, where you can print your tickets to save waiting in the queue, plus a website for UK visitors – **seaworldparks.co.uk**. SeaWorld is also a **Certified Autism Center**, with a staff-wide autism training and awareness programme.

SeaWorld at a glance

Location	7007 SeaWorld Drive, off Central Florida Parkway (Junctions 71 and 72 off I-4)
Size	More than 200 acres/81ha, incorporating 26 attractions
Hours	9 or 10am–6pm off peak; 9am–7, 8 or 9pm some weekends; 9am–9 or 10pm high season (Easter, summer holidays, Thanksgiving, Christmas)
Admission	Under-3s free; $120/person (1-day ticket), $180 (2-Park ticket with Aquatica), 14 days with UK Discovery Cove ultimate tickets, from £253–313 pricing seasonal
Parking	$30-35 seasonally; preferred parking $35-60 (online discounts available)
Lockers	Inside Entrance Plaza (next to the Emporium shop), $15–25
Pushchairs	$40, to right of Guest Services
Wheelchairs	$40 manual, $100 ECV with canopy; with pushchairs
Top attractions	TurtleTrek, Antarctica: Empire Of The Penguin, Infinity Falls, Orca Encounter, Shark Encounter, Journey To Atlantis, Kraken, Manta, Mako, Dolphin Adventures, Ice Breaker, Surf Coaster (2023)
Don't miss	Manatee Rehabilitation, behind-the-scenes tours, Dolphin Nursery, dining at Sharks Underwater Grill, Sesame Street land and parade (with kids)
Hidden costs	**Meals** Burger, chips and coke $20.49 3-course lunch $47–65 (Sharks Underwater Grill) Kids' meals $8.50–15 **T-shirts** Adults $28–40, Kids $19–30 **Souvenirs** $1.99–600 **Sundries** Park-to-Planet Reusable bags $7.99

SeaWorld

Port of Entry
1 Entrance plaza

Key West
2 Dolphin Nursery
3 Stingray Lagoon
4 Flamingo Cove
5 Dolphin Cove
6 Dolphin Adventures
7 Dolphin Underwater Viewing
8 Manta
9 Turtle Trek & Manatee Rehabilitation

Thrill Ride Central
10 Journey to Atlantis
11 Kraken

Antarctica
12 Antarctica: Empire of the Penguin

Sea Lions & Shopping
13 Sea Lion and Otter Stadium
14 Pacific Point Preserve
15 Sky Tower
16 The Waterfront

17 Seafire Grill & Flamecraft Bar
18 Voyager's Smokehouse

Undersea Adventures
19 Shark Encounter
20 Nautilus Theater
21 Mako
22 Infinity Falls
23 Flamingo Paddle Boats
24 Sharks Underwater Grill
25 Mama's Pretzel Kitchen

Sesame Street at SeaWorld
26 Sesame Street Party Parade

Animals & Thrills
27 Orca Stadium
28 Orca Underwater Viewing
29 Wild Arctic
30 Ice Breaker
31 Bayside Stadium
32 Surf Coaster (2023)
33 Seaport Theater

Tours

Worth booking in advance are any of the many behind-the-scenes and animal up-close tours that take small groups of visitors backstage to see various aspects of the park's care and conservation efforts, notably with the dolphins, penguins, sea lions, killer whales and sharks. Prices vary from $20 to $179/person, and provide a fascinating insight into the day-to-day routines and ongoing research programmes. Book online at **seaworld. com/orlando/tours** or call 407 545 5550.

Location

SeaWorld is located off Central Florida Parkway, between I-4 (exit 71 going east or 72 heading west) and International Drive. It is still best to arrive before the opening time so you're in good position to book a backstage tour, dash to one of the attractions that draws a crowd, like Mako, Manta and Ice Breaker, or buy QuickQueue, the park's limited number of paid-for passes that provide front-of-line access to each of the main rides (priced seasonally, $15–70). There is also a Signature Show Seating option at $15–70/person.

The park covers more than 200acres/81ha, with four shows, nine major rides, 12 large-scale continuous viewing attractions and several smaller ones, plus a smart range of shops and restaurants. Try to eat before midday or after 2.30pm for a crowd-free lunch, and before 5.30pm if you want a leisurely dinner (better still, book Sharks Underwater Grill).

SeaWorld isn't arranged in neat 'lands', so keep the map (or App) handy as there is a fair bit of to-ing and fro-ing to catch all the shows. Going clockwise, here are the main areas you find (with our designations by area).

The new Surf-themed coaster coming in 2023

Port of Entry

Coming through the main entrance brings you to the park's functional area, including the Information & Reservations counter, Lost & Found, and lockers, pushchair and wheelchair hire. You will also find some good shopping and snack options here. Look for the **Emporium** for the full range of souvenirs; **Sea World Rescue** for gifts and clothing; and **Adventure Photos** for all park pictures taken by SeaWorld photographers. Grab a quick breakfast (pastries and coffee) at **Coaster Coffee Company** (serving Starbucks coffee and pastries) or something colder from **Edy's Ice Cream Shop** (heavenly sundaes, cones and shakes). This is also the place for a photo opportunity with a **cuddly Shamu**.

All Day Dining Deal: Also worth considering, a wristband gives unlimited visits to nine restaurants (including Lakeside Grill, Voyager's, Expedition Cafe and Seafire Grill), claiming an entrée, side dish or dessert and standard non-alcoholic drink each time (once per hour; seasonal pricing starts at $50 adults, $25 ages 3–9). It's good value if you eat at least twice in the park and can be booked at the Information & Reservations desk. Add the **Coke Freestyle** drinks package (with more than 100 Coke brand beverages to choose from) for $19.99 and get $1.99 refills throughout your stay.

Photokey: If you'd like to collect all your SeaWorld photos digitally, including ride photos and character meet-and-greets (but not backstage tours), sign up for this service, online or when you arrive at the park, for $70 (or $169 for the year) at **bit.ly/ brit-seaphotos**.

Other entertainment: The **Dolphin Nursery** provides wonderful close-ups of the park's younger dolphins, with different levels for viewing mothers and their babies, as well as digital displays that offer key conservation info.

Expedition Cafe

Key West

A whole collection of exhibits is grouped together here, as well as the eye-catching Dolphin Theater and one of the signature rides.

There is a clever Key West theme, starting with **Stingray Lagoon**, where you can feed ($6 per tray, 3 trays for $13) and touch fully grown rays, and there's a nursery for newborns. The centrepiece is the 2.1acre/0.8ha **Dolphin Cove**, a spectacular, naturalistic development that hosts a frisky community of Atlantic bottlenose dolphins, who make for great viewing, including from a special underwater window. The Key West area is designed in the eclectic, tropical flavour of America's most southerly city, but it also underlines the environmental message through interactive graphics and video displays to make it a fun, educational experience. AAA

Dolphin Adventures: This 'edutainment' show takes a literal dive into the world of bottlenose dolphins, replacing the former Dolphin Days presentation (which replaced the old Blue Horizons show). SeaWorld is increasingly in the business of showcasing marine life and its environmental issues, and Dolphin Adventures raises the bar by highlighting the role dolphins play in our planet's oceans, as well as the threats they face. The show explores their natural behaviours and provides inspiring insights into how we can all play a part in caring for our natural world. There's a lot of splashing, too! AAA

━━━━━━━━━━ **BRITTIP**

All the really dynamic rides feature lockers for your valuables while you ride at $2 for the first 2hrs or $8 for all day use.

Manta: This turns a coaster into a unique mixture of ride and animal encounter. The elaborate queuing area winds through rocky caverns, passing waterfalls and floor-to-ceiling windows showcasing some 300 rays and thousands of fish, which lead to the 'undersea world' of the manta ray. Themed like a giant ray, riders are swung face-down before being launched into an exhilarating series of four inversions, reaching nearly 60mph/96kph and 140ft/43m high as well as skimming the surface of the lagoon. The 'flying' nature of the coaster and smooth ride make this an original with great spectator appeal. There is a separate walk-through aquarium with its own entry while lockers next to the queue entry can be used during your ride. **R**: 54in/137cm. TTTTT. For the most powerful effects of the G-forces, opt for the back rows.

TurtleTrek: Right behind Dolphin Theater is this thrilling part exhibit and part show into the world of the sea turtle. A host introduces the story and doors open to reveal a domed cinema where you don 3-D glasses. Suddenly, you are in the world of the sea turtle, sharing the dangerous journey from beach to open ocean and back again, in an immersive 3-D environment with graphic encounters with a marauding crab and sharks. You exit to two open-air pools (the top of the lagoons you see below) where you learn more about sea turtle life and see them and manatees being fed. There is also a video game for kids, plus an exhibit showcasing Florida alligators. AAAAA NB: The menace of the crab in the early scene may be scary for young children.

Manatee Rehabilitation: Learn all about the fabulous work SeaWorld and their small army of volunteers does in rescuing and rehabbing endangered manatees, with information boards and animal keepers on hand. Well worth making time for. AAA

Shopping: There are three main gift shops here, the best being **Coconut Bay Traders** and **Trek Treasures** (apparel and soft toys), as well as **Manta Photo & Gifts**.

Dining: You can grab a hot dog, chili dog or fries at **Captain Pete's Hot Dogs** or ice cream at **Dippin' Dots**, plus drinks, snacks and refills and several cart-style kiosks.

Thrill Ride Central

Continue past Dolphin Theater and you come to the park's serious thrill quotient.

Journey to Atlantis: This terrific water-coaster is a combination of special effects and water-ride that becomes a runaway roller-coaster. The discovery of Atlantis in your eight-passenger 'fishing boat' starts gently through the lost city. But evil spirit Allura takes over and riders plunge into a dash through Atlantis, dodging gushing fountains and water cannons before a 60ft/18m drop and entry to the roller-coaster finale back in the candle-filled catacombs. Be ready to get soaked, which is fine in summer but not so clever on a winter morning. **R**: 3ft5in/106cm. **TTTTT**

Kraken: One of Florida's most breathtaking coasters, based on the mythical sea monster, this is an innovative ride that plunges an initial 144ft/44m at 65mph/105kph, diving underground, adding seven brain-scrambling inversions and a flat spin before riders escape the beast's lair. It's not for the faint of heart, but it is a mega-thrill of the highest order. **R**: 4ft 5in/137cm. **TTTTT+**

Shopping: Don't miss **Golden Seahorse Gifts** as you exit Journey to Atlantis, a combination gift shop and aquarium full of tropical fish (remember to look up), while there are coaster-orientated souvenirs in **Kraken Gifts**.

Dining: High Seas Market offers convenient grab-and-go snacks and drinks, and there is a **Dippin' Dots** for ice cream.

Journey to Atlantis

Antarctica

This section puts the focus back on the animals and is one of the most eye-catching. Both an extensive, themed area and an amazing ride, it features an epic journey into the ice-covered realm of the South Pole.

Antarctica: Empire of the Penguin: Walk between the towering snow-capped 'mountains' and the ride awaits, starting with a dramatic presentation about penguin life and then taking visitors on a unique expedition into the continent, following young Gentoo penguin, Puck. Guests choose either a 'Mild' or 'Wild' experience before setting off through a mix of film and ride elements that offer a stylistic taste of the polar region, moving seemingly at random and with no obvious track. The dangers – including a raging Polar storm – and beauty of life in this realm are graphically depicted as you track Puck's journey through this extreme landscape before arriving in a real penguin colony to experience more of their 'empire.' And it is *cold* (the temperature drops to -1C), so you may want to visit the gift shop for a scarf or gloves before you set off! The Wild version is quite fast-paced, with bumps, slides and spins, while 'Mild' is fine for all the family, with no height restriction. **R:** under 3ft 5in/106cm must be accompanied by an adult. AAAAA+ This can also draw long queues by mid-day.

Other entertainment: After the ride, there is a spectacular **underwater viewing area** where you can see the different species of penguin – Rockhopper, King, Adelie and Gentoo – at play. Back out in Antarctica you can marvel at this realistic environment, which includes a **Penguin Wall** for photo opportunities, and flatscreen TVs for more info about the region.

Shopping: Lone gift shop **Glacial Collections** has a huge selection of all things penguin-orientated and cuddly.

Dining: Expedition Café provides Italian, Asian and American food choices from their show kitchen which you can then enjoy in one of two clever 'Quonset Huts' that provide a South Pole setting.

BRITTIP

Be sure to see Antarctica at night as the brilliant blue lighting makes the setting even more impressive.

Antarctica: Empire of the Penguin

Sea lions & shopping

This extensive area features a live show plus some of the park's best dining and shopping.

Sea Lion and Otter Stadium: Get ready for marine wildlife fun and frolics, all loosely wrapped up in a presentation about the life, skills and characteristics of the park's sea lions, otters and walrus. *Sea Lion & Otter Spotlight* is a journey into the watery world of Californian sea lions and Asian otters, offering up an educational but entertaining view of their behaviours and issues. Inevitably, things get a little side-tracked by the cute otters, and there are some amusing audience participation moments with a neat twist. Oh, and don't miss the pre-show Mimes – they're worth coming in for on their own! AAAA

Pacific Point Preserve: A natural rocky habitat for the park's seals and sea lions with a hidden wave machine and lively talks from park attendants. You can also buy smelt ($6 per tray or three trays for $15) to feed the animals. AAA

Sky Tower: This 400ft/122m landmark offers slowly rotating rides for a bird's-eye view of the park for $5/person (free with an annual pass; closed when windy). AAA

Shopping: The linked series of **Waterfront** shops offer an extensive shopping plaza with a stylish range of souvenirs and other gift items, while the **Guy Harvey** shop features unique branded art and clothing from the eminent artist and conservationist, whose giant mural adorns the wall next to Mako. **Oyster's Secret** features the chance to select and open a real oyster and discover the pearl inside.

Dining: The excellent eateries are: **Seafire Grill** (chicken tenders, salads and wraps); **Voyagers Smokehouse** (barbecue chicken, brisket and ribs, plus salads, and a children's menu with chicken nuggets, hot dog, macaroni and cheese and smoked chicken); and the **Lakeside Grill** (burgers and kebabs with a Mediterranean flair). There are also two snack bars: **Café de Mar** for pastries, coffees, smoothies and soft drinks; and **Turkey Legs** for huge smoked turkey legs. The **Flamecraft Bar** is a water's edge hideaway, serving beer, wine and snacks – THE place to watch the sun go down each evening (craft beers at $10–11 for 20oz or $16 for a flight of four 7oz samples, cocktails at $13–15).

Surrounded by rays at SeaWorld's Manta

Undersea Adventures

Continuing the clockwise tour brings you towards the back of the park and this 'underwater' area with the showpiece Mako coaster.

Shark Encounter: Top of the bill, the world's largest collection of dangerous sea creatures can be found here, brought dramatically to life by the walk-through tubes that surround you with more than 50 prowling sharks (including sand tigers, black tips, nurse sharks and sandbars), sawfish, tropical fish and gigantic groupers. It's an eerie experience, but brilliantly presented and highly informative. AAAA TTTT

Shark Encounter

BRITTIP

For a tasty snack with a difference, call in at *Mama's Pretzel Kitchen* for a variety of delicious large salted pretzels, including the signature Jumbo Pretzel Dog – half pretzel, half hog-dog!

Nautilus Theater: This is home to weekend and special events throughout the year.

Mako: SeaWorld's dramatic steel rollercoaster – the tallest and fastest in Orlando – rises up between the Shark Encounter and Nautilus Theater, giving the park another iconic ride for its growing collection. It reaches 200ft high and 73mph and is named and themed for the world's fastest shark, hence it's sure to give adrenalin junkies a real blast.

Mako

Although there are no inversions, its big initial drop, tight twists and turns, fast pace and multiple 'air time' moments provide plenty of thrills, including a breathtaking U-shaped 'Hammerhead' turn and several camelbacks. TTTTT **R**: 54in/137cm.

Infinity Falls: The river raft ride will never be the same again after you experience this expedition-style adventure through Class IV rapids with a SERIOUS final splashdown! Your journey passes a flock of flamingos before reaching the tightly-winding rapids and a huge waterfall, where an outrageous vertical lift hints at what's to come. But there's no preparing for the final splashdown as your 8-person raft plunges 40ft/13m into a turmoil of white-water. Expect a good soaking! AAAA/TTTTT R: 3ft 5in/107cm.

Flamingo Paddle Boats

Other entertainment: The **flamingo pedal-boats** on the lagoon rent for $6 per 20min (for two). You can also feed the sharks and stingrays outside **Shark Encounter** ($6 per tray, $15 three trays).

Shopping: Check out **Fins Gifts** for toys, apparel and jewellery and **Reef's Treasures** for Mako souvenirs and all things shark-like, while **Whitewater Supply** has all manner of Infinity Falls souvenirs to complete your journey in style.

BRITTIP

If the day is cool but you still want to ride Infinity Falls, watch for the family-sized drying stations near the attraction. For a small fee, you can dry off quickly.

Infinity Falls

Dining: At the entrance to Shark Encounter is top dining choice, **Sharks Underwater Grill**, with an amazing backdrop for your meal in a subterranean environment (check out the mini-aquarium bar), and a high-quality menu featuring seafood, steak and chicken, as well as fab desserts, cocktails and kids' menu. Open from 11.30am to an hour before park closing, it's busy at lunch but quieter in late afternoon, so we advise booking (at the restaurant) as soon as you arrive. The **Panini Shore Café** (high season only) offers fresh-grilled panini sandwiches, salads and drinks. Grab a drink and an ice cream treat at **Soft Serve & Starbucks Coffee**, while you should try **Mama's Pretzel Kitchen** for freshly baked pretzels with a variety of dipping sauces. At Infinity Falls, **Waterway Grill** is a commissary-style restaurant serving Latin-inspired roasted and grilled meats, plus salads and side dishes, as well as a tempting selection of domestic and craft beers.

Sesame Street at SeaWorld

This section is primarily for kids, with a fabulous children's play area, water splash-pad, junior-sized rides, food trucks and meet-and-greets.

Sesame Street: Themed to the popular children's television programme, this is a nostalgic step back in time for parents and a chance to visit the most famous TV street for youngsters. Children can visit Mr Hooper's store, enjoy story time with Big Bird and meet their favourite characters at **Photos with Elmo and Friends**. It's all cleverly designed as an interactive 'community', with a playground and 11 hands-on stations where kids can ring Bert and Ernie's doorbell, transform their voice into a monster voice, peek into Elmo's window to watch him dance and sing, and more. Seven rides purely for the 2–5 age group are also sprinkled through the land.

Abby's Flower Tower: A fairground-style ride that raises riders to the top for a spin around the tower in cute flowerpots. **R**: 3ft 5in/107cm.

Cookie Drop!: Bounce up, then down again on this pre-schooler friendly samba tower themed to Cookie Monster. **R**: 3ft 5in/107cm.
Elmo's Choo-Choo Train: This classic train ride offers a gentle trundle through a garden setting. Watch for cleverly-placed bugs, including Elmo's friends the Twiddlebugs, hiding in the landscaping. **R**: 3ft/92cm **Super Grover's Box Car Derby**: Bigger thrills are found on this junior-sized coaster, a good introduction for youngsters with enough zip to be enjoyable for adults. **R**: 3ft 2in/97cm. **Big Bird's Twirl 'N' Whirl**: Hop into Big Bird's nest for a dizzying spin in this tea-cup style attraction. **R**: 3ft/92cm. **Slimey's Slider**: Big thrills for young 'uns can be found on this dynamic ride that rocks, spins and slides through Oscar's compost collection. **R**: 3ft 6in/107cm. **Sunny Day Carousel**: Enjoy a classic ride aboard this colourful merry-go-round (children under 3ft 6in/107cm must be accompanied). **Rubber Ducky Water Works**: Kids can cool off in this delightful water-playground splash area with pop jets, fountains and water wheels. Ideal for spontaneous play on a hot day!

Other entertainment: The superb **Sesame Street Party Parade** takes place here each day, with Elmo and friends leading a series of colourful floats. Children are encouraged to join in during stops in the parade when the characters lead youngsters in singing, dancing and child-friendly

Elmo's Choo Choo Train

games. AAAA Watch for **character meet-and-greets** that pop up periodically along Sesame Street.

Shopping: Pick up Sesame Street gifts and apparel at **Hooper's Store**.

Dining: Enjoy a meal or snack at **ABC Eats** or **Yummy Yummy Nom Noms** (chicken tenders, turkey and pulled pork sandwiches, plus grilled cheese sandwiches for kids at $10). **Sesame Sips** drinks stand carries 4 yummy smoothies (pineapple, strawberry, blueberry and raspberry) plus string cheese, salads, fruit and cookies.

Animals & thrills

The final main area of the park features the iconic Shamu Stadium, plus another engaging animal attraction, the high-season fireworks finale – and two fab new coasters.

BRITTIP

The first 14 rows at Shamu Stadium get VERY wet (watch out for your cameras). When a killer whale leaps into the air in front of you, it displaces a LOT of water on landing. In fact, the Splash Zones should be renamed Soak Zones!

Shamu Stadium: SeaWorld has effectively deconstructed the traditional killer whale 'show' here and replaced it with the **Orca Encounter**, an engaging presentation into the world of the ocean's biggest predator. Learn about these fantastic animals and their natural behaviours, as well as conservation and ecological concerns, while also being entertained by the genuine bond between the park's animal trainers and the whales themselves. AAAAA. The pathway outside Orca Encounter is also a good spot from which to watch the park's **Ignite 360** fireworks and special effects finale at the end of the summer's Electric Ocean extended evening hours (p186) if the Bayside Stadium is already packed.

All guests can then enjoy the **Shamu Underwater Viewing area**.

Wild Arctic: This frozen wonderland showcases the park's beluga whales, walruses and harbour seals in another major animal habitat. The ride part of the attraction (a simulated heli-jet journey into the Arctic) was suspended in 2021, but there is still a lot to enjoy on this extensive walk-through of the highly themed Base Station. AAAA.

Ice Breaker: SeaWorld's newest coaster is a total thrill machine, a multiple-launch ride that rockets backwards AND forwards, and features the steepest beyond-vertical drop in Florida – at 100 degrees from a height of 93ft/28m. It also includes an 84ft top-hat feature that guarantees a dramatic moment of 'air-time,' as well as a scintillating series of low-level twists and turns at up to 52mph to finish with. At just 1,900ft/500m, and barely 2mins, it is not a long ride, and there are no inversions, but it still feels pretty topsy-turvy and it is a guaranteed adrenalin buzz. It also highlights one of SeaWorld's worldwide conservation partners, the Alaska SeaLife Center, which rescues and rehabilitates marine mammals. TTTTT.

Surf Coaster: New in 2023 will be the park's first stand-up coaster, a high-thrill ride with a fast-launch sequence that mimics riding the big waves of high surf and adds a really novel riding style. TTTTT (expected).

Bayside Stadium: The final element is this large outdoor arena facing the central Lagoon. It's home to various seasonal entertainments, including the Seven Seas Food Festival concerts and an ice-skating show at Christmas.

Dining: At the new **Altitude Burgers,** take your pick from fresh-made pizza and succulent burgers, including a build-your-own burger option with 27 variations. The **Glacier Bar** adds craft beer, cocktails, Coca-Cola Freestyle and light bites (sliders, pizza and waffle fries) in cool surroundings.

Dine With Orcas: Get a close-up of SeaWorld's killer whales as you learn how the animal care specialists

SEAWORLD with children

The following gives a general idea of the appeal of the attractions to the different age groups:

Under-5s
Antarctica: Empire of the Penguin, Sea Lion and Otter Spotlight, Dolphin Cove, Dolphin Adventures, Orca Encounter, Pacific Point Preserve, Sesame Street, Wild Arctic.

5–8s
All the above, plus Infinity Falls, Shark Encounter, Turtle Trek.

9–12s
All the above (with the exception of Sesame Street), plus Journey to Atlantis, Kraken, Manta, Ice Breaker and Mako.

Over-12s
Antarctica: Empire of the Penguin, Sea Lion and Otter Spotlight, Dolphin Adventures, Infinity Falls, Journey To Atlantis, Kraken, Mako, Manta, Orca Encounter, Ice Breaker, Shark Encounter, Turtle Trek, Wild Arctic.

establish a special relationship at this fascinating dining experience ($31–59 adult seasonally, $22–29 children). The meal includes salad, grilled chicken, salmon, roast beef, vegetables, desserts and soft drinks (kids' choices are chicken nuggets, hot dogs and penne pasta). Book online or on 407 545 5550.

Shopping: Wild Arctic Gifts has a wide range of items, plus a year-round Christmas-themed section.

Ice Breaker

Summer extras

During the summer (weekends and some week-days late May to early Sep), SeaWorld has extended hours to 10 or 11pm and offers live entertainment as part of its **Electric Ocean** programme. The party atmosphere is generated by live DJs and other entertainers and features extra shows, like **Rescue Tails**, highlighting the park's animal rescue and rehab stories at the Seaport Theater (and Rescue Tails: Night Vision after dark), and **Elmo Rocks** for the Sesame Street crowd, while **Club Sea Glow** features a fun dance party, with more performers, sea-characters and dancing fountains. Finally, the big finale, **Ignite 360**, lights up the lagoon with a dazzling array of lasers, fireworks and other special effects, all set to a memorable soundtrack. It makes for the best summer show in town, so don't miss it! For the park's fab **Christmas Celebration** (late Nov–31 Dec each year) see p36.

And there's more

Other seasonal events (all FREE with park admission) include the superb **Seven Seas Food Festival**, each weekend from February to May, featuring more than 200 samplings of international street foods, craft brews and wine offerings ($7.99–$10.99/sample; sampling lanyards $65 for 10 samples, $80 for 15), plus unique cocktails at multiple kiosks around the park, along with free live concerts at weekends; and the ultra child-friendly **Halloween Spooktacular**, when there are fun activities for kids of all ages, including trick-or-treating, Penelope's Party Zone, sweet treat decorating and strolling entertainers. New in 2021 (and definitely not for children) was SeaWorld's own Halloween version of **Howl-O-Scream**, borrowing from sister park Busch Gardens. This separately ticketed night-time event of grisly ghouls and freaky frights features unique Scare Zones, Haunted Houses, entertainment shows, special food and drink, and the chance to ride the park's coasters in the dark (on select days Sept–Oct). The **Craft Beer Festival** (weekends Aug–Sept) offers the chance to try a huge variety of local, national and international craft brews, and more food tastes.

Kraken

DISCOVERY COVE

Fancy a day in a tropical paradise, swimming with dolphins, eyeballing sharks, snorkelling in a coral reef and diving through a waterfall into a tropical aviary? Discovery Cove is all that, and more. The only drawback is the price. This park comes at a premium because it admits just 1,300 guests a day, creating an exclusive experience that's reflected in the price. The weather can get distinctly cool in winter, but the water is always heated (apart from the dolphin lagoon, which remains at 72ºF/22ºC) and full wetsuits are available to keep out the chill. The attention to detail is superb, guest ratings are extremely high and it is hugely popular with British visitors. Discovery Cove is also a Certified Autism Center.

The costs

Ticket pricing varies ($224–549 for Resort & Dolphin Swim; plus $40 for 14 days at SeaWorld & Aquatica; plus $20 more for Busch Gardens, too), making UK Ultimate tickets good value (£253–313 for all four parks, plus free parking). Under 3s are free but 3–5s must pay the Day Resort price ($174–299). So, what do you get for your money? Well, it's a supremely personal park. You check in at the beautiful entrance lobby as you would for a hotel rather than a theme park. All your basic requirements – towel, mask, snorkel, wet-jacket, lockers, beach umbrellas, animal-safe suncream, food and drink – are included, and the level of service is excellent. Then there is a full breakfast, snacks, beverages (including beer and pre-mixed cocktails) and an excellent lunch at the Laguna Grill. But gift shop and photo prices reflect the entry fee – expensive. It is also an extra $199–599 (priced seasonally) to hire one of their swanky cabañas for the day (which include tables, chairs, loungers, towels and a fridge stocked with soft drinks, and must be booked in advance). Even a more humble (but ultra-relaxing) Day Bed costs $79–279 more.

Therefore, for all its style and dolphin appeal, Discovery Cove will take a BIG bite out of your holiday budget. A family of four,

Dolphin Swim

with children old enough to do the Dolphin Swim, could pay $2,196 in peak season. Even with a free SeaWorld and Aquatica pass, it's a big outlay. The charge for ages 3–5 is also pretty steep, in our opinion. Your sundries can add up, too, with photo packages from $99–$299, while there is a premium drinks package at $40/person (over 21s only) that adds a wider range of alcoholic beverages.

However, despite the fees, the feedback we get is almost unfailingly positive and most people are captivated by the experience.

BRITTIP

Try to pick up your Discovery Cove photos before 4pm or you might find everyone else trying to do the same!

Trainer for a Day: This programme is an exciting opportunity to go behind the scenes into the park's training, feeding and welfare. It includes an enhanced deep-water interaction with the dolphins; exclusive experiences with some of the animals and trainers; a private guided tour of the Aviary; fish-feeding in the Grand Reef; and a private session in the Otter Habitat. Participants must be

at least six and in good health, and it costs an extra $229–349/person. For all Discovery Cove bookings, call 1 877 577 or visit **discoverycove.com**.

Flamingo Mingle: Join the park's expert aviculturists to meet, mingle with, and help feed their famous Caribbean flamingos (£59–99/person).

Location

Situated on Central Florida Parkway, almost opposite the SeaWorld entrance (open year-round 7.30am–5pm; parking free), the whole 30acre/12ha park is magnificently landscaped, with thatched buildings, palm trees, lush vegetation, white-sand beaches, gurgling streams – even hammocks to chill out in. The overall effect is of being transported to a relaxing tropical paradise away from the hurly-burly. The 5-star resort feel is enhanced by a high staff-to-guest ratio, there are no queues (though the restaurant may get busy at lunchtime), and the highlight Dolphin Encounter is world class. Visitors with disabilities are well catered for, with special wheelchairs that can move in sand and shallow water, and an area of the Dolphin Lagoon that allows those who can't enter the water to touch a dolphin.

Freshwater Oasis

The main attractions

Freshwater Oasis: This combination of animal environment, walking trails and pools offers the chance to get a close-up of the park's otters and marmosets, where their habitats' incorporation into the tropical landscape is a real gem of clever design. AAAA

Wind-away River: This 800yd/732m circuit of gently flowing bath-warm water is a variation on the lazy river feature of many of the water parks, though with a far more naturalistic aspect and none of the inner tubes. It is primarily designed for snorkellers and features rocky lagoons, caves, a beach section, a tropical forest segment and sunken ruins. The lack of fish makes it a bit bland after the Grand Reef, but it is as much about relaxing as having fun. It is up to 8ft/2.4m deep, so non-swimmers should use a flotation vest. It finishes in the Serenity Bay pool, which provides more chill-out time. AAA

The Grand Reef

Explorer's Aviary: This three-part adventure is both an area in its own right and a 120ft/37m section of the Tropical River. You can walk in off the beach or swim in through the waterfall. Some 250 tropical birds fill the main enclosure and, if you stand still, they are likely to use you as a perch. There is a

small-bird sanctuary – full of finches, honeycreepers and hummingbirds – and a large-bird enclosure, featuring toucans and the red-legged seriema. Guides will introduce you to specific birds (which you can hand-feed) and tell you about their habitats and conservation issues. AAAA

Dolphin Swim: The headline attraction is the encounter with the park's Atlantic bottlenose dolphins. A 15min orientation programme in one of the beach cabañas, with a film and instruction from two trainers, sets you up for this thrilling experience. Groups of 6–8 go into the lagoon and, starting off standing in the waist-deep (slightly chilly) water as one of the dolphins comes over, you gradually become more adventurous until you are swimming with them. Timid swimmers are well catered for and there are flotation vests for those who need them. The lagoon is up to 12ft/3.6m deep so there is a real feeling of being in the dolphins' environment. You learn how trainers use hand signals and positive reinforcement to communicate, and get the chance to stroke, feed and even kiss your dolphin. The encounter concludes dramatically as you are towed ashore by one of these awesome animals (which weigh up to 600lb/272kg), though activities vary according to their attention span. You spend around 30mins in the water

Explorer's Aviary

and it is unforgettable. Under-6s are not allowed in the lagoon. **TTTTT+**

The Grand Reef: This area features a massive artificial reef with 125 species, including fish, rays, eels, sharks, urchins and lionfish (the dangerous ones are behind glass!). Beaches, meandering pathways and bridges lead to shallow wading areas, waist-deep paddling pools and deep-water snorkelling, while underwater canyons and inviting grottos combine with coloured artificial coral reefs for a convincing experience. **AAAAA**

> **BRITTIP**
> The Sea Venture area is not accessible to snorkellers during tours, but you can swim there when a tour is not running.

Sea Venture: One of the most innovative features of the Grand Reef is this underwater walking tour. Equipped with special dive helmets, guests make a 20min trek along the bottom of the reef, passing sharks and lionfish and interacting with schools of fish and gentle rays. This is a totally immersive experience and a sensation like no other (how often can you explore underwater while standing up straight?). There are handrails throughout the journey, which takes groups of 4–9 at a time. Total tour time is 1hr, including

preparation and underwater trek (for an extra $49–79 per person). Ages 10 and up only. **TTTT**

Discovery Cove 'extras'

This isn't a cheap day out, but the extra quality is everywhere. The Laguna Grill lunch is excellent and you can visit as often as you want (11am–3.30pm), while a Calypso band adds to the tropical paradise feel. Conservation Cabaña allows guests to meet a neat selection of the park's small mammals (like an anteater and tree sloth); parking is free and you also receive an 8x6in/15x20cm welcome photo.

Other extras are a 90min **Animal Trek** tour taking up to 12 guests behind the scenes, including a private aviary tour and meeting with one of the animal ambassadors ($79–129/person). **Ray Feeding** offers an early-morning (7–8.45am) encounter with the park's rays, including a chance to hand-feed these gentle creatures ($59–99). The **Shark Swim** offers a close-up with the other Reef denizens, including a shallow-water encounter and free swim among them ($149–199).

You are advised to book all packages at least two months in advance as they do sell out in peak periods and, in winter, the park is closed on some midweek days. There is also a 10% advance discount periodically for online bookings. See **discoverycove.com**.

Sea Venture

BUSCH GARDENS

While the Orlando parks may get more publicity, the 335acre/136ha Busch Gardens in Tampa offers just as much in terms of attractions and – especially – Brit appeal. In fact, the sister park to SeaWorld, which started as a mini-menagerie for the wildlife collection of the brewery-owning Busch family in 1959, is often one of the most popular of all Florida attractions with UK visitors for its nature appeal – and superb roller-coasters. It is a major, multi-faceted family park, the biggest outside Orlando and just an hour from International Drive. It is rated among the top four zoos in America, with more than 2,700 animals representing over 320 species of mammals, birds, reptiles, amphibians and spiders. But that's just the start. It boasts a safari-like section of Africa spread over 65acres/26ha of grassy veldt, with special tours to hand-feed some of the animals. Interspersed among the animals are more than 20 bona fide theme park rides, including the mind-numbing coasters Kumba, SheiKra, Montu, Cheetah Hunt, Cobra's Curse, Tigris and (new in 2022) Iron Gwazi, plus dramatic drop-tower ride, Falcon's Fury. Then there are animal exhibits, musicians and big-stage show productions.

The overall theme is Africa, hence the park is divided into areas like Nairobi and Morocco. It doesn't quite have the pizzazz of EPCOT or Universal, but it has guaranteed 5-star family appeal. It's like the big brother of Chessington World of Adventures in Surrey, though on a grander scale and in a better climate – albeit Busch Gardens can be more affected by bad weather than most, especially the threat of lightning, as so many of the attractions are outdoors.

Busch Gardens at a glance

Location	Busch Blvd, Tampa; 75–90mins' drive from Orlando
Size	335 acres/136ha in 11 themed areas
Hours	10am–6 or 8pm off peak; 10am—9 or 10pm at peak periods
Admission	Under-3s free; ages 3 and up $124.99 (1-day ticket), $194.99 (3-Park ticket, with any of SeaWorld, Aquatica and Adventure Island Gardens); UK 3-for-2 ticket (all 3 parks for 14 days with free parking) £157 adults, £152 children 3–9
Parking	$30; $35-45 preferred parking
Lockers	$15, $20, $25, in Morocco, Congo, Egypt and Stanleyville
Pushchairs	$30
Wheelchairs	$30; motorised $85; with pushchairs
Top attractions	Congo River Rapids, Kumba, Montu, Cheetah Hunt, SheiKra, Falcon's Fury, Cobra's Curse, Tigris, Iron Gwazi
Don't miss	Jungala, Edge of Africa, Animal Care Center, Myombe Reserve, Animal Care Experts
Hidden costs	**Meals** Burger, chips and coke $18.50 3-course meal $30–45 (Zambia Smokehouse) Kids meals: $9.99 **T-shirts** $24–40, Kids $21–35 **Souvenirs** $1.99–$2,000 **Sundries** Face Painting $11–20

Morocco
1 Moroccan Palace Theater
2 Myombe Reserve
3 Iron Gwazi

Bird Gardens
4 Festival Walkway
5 Lory Landing
6 Walkabout Way

Sesame Street Safari of Fun
7 Air Grover
8 Sunny Day Theater
9 Big Bird's 123-Smile With Me

Stanleyville
10 SheiKra
11 Stanley Falls Flume
12 Stanleyville Train Station
13 Stanleyville Theater
14 Skyride Station
15 Zambia Smokehouse
16 Tigris

Jungala
17 Jungle Flyers, The Wild Surge and Treetop Trails

18 Tiger Habitat
19 Orang Outpost

Congo
20 Kumba
21 Congo River Rapids
22 Ubanga-Banga Bumper Cars

Pantopia
23 Falcon's Fury
24 Sand Serpent
25 Grand Caravan Carousel
26 Pantopia Theater
27 Scorpion
28 Dragon Fire Grill

Nairobi
29 Animal Connections
30 Elephant Habitat
31 Animal Care Center

Edge of Africa
32 Cheetah Run
33 Cheetah Hunt and Skyride Station
34 Edge of Africa

Egypt
35 Cobra's Curse
36 Montu

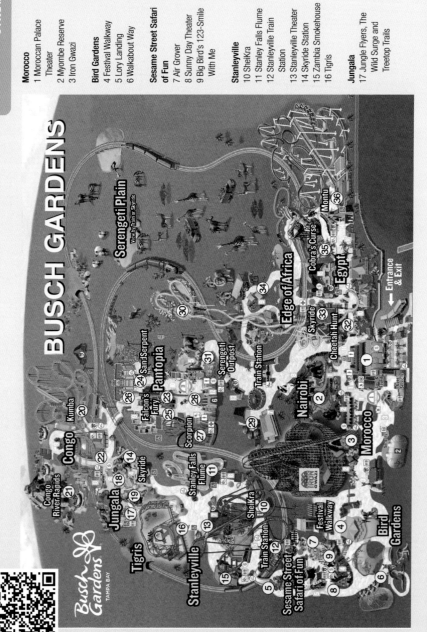

BUSCH GARDENS

BRITTIP

Like SeaWorld, Busch Gardens offers QuickQueue, the limited number front-of-the-line pass for all the park's main rides. Price varies (seasonally), $15–110 for use once at reach ride, $20–130 all-day use.

All Day Dining Deal: For just $50 ($25 3–9s) you can enjoy all-you-care-to-eat-and-drink privileges at four of the park's restaurants. Choose one entrée, one side dish or dessert and a soft drink or bottled water once per hour (child's price valid for kids' meal only).

Photokey: For all your ride photos and character meet-and-greets, sign up for this service, either online or when you arrive, for $49 (**photokeyonline.com**).

Location

Busch Gardens is easy to find from Orlando, just 55ml/88km west on I-4, then north on I-75 for 3½ml/5.5km to the exit for Fowler Avenue (Highway 582), then west for another 3½ml/5.5km, then, just past the University of South Florida on your right, turn LEFT onto McKinley Drive. One mile/1.6km down McKinley, the car park is on your *left*, while those with disabled badges should continue on and turn *right*.

Those without a car can use the free **Busch Gardens Shuttle**, which makes several round trips a day from Orlando; riders must have a Busch Gardens park ticket to board. There are six pick-up points in the I-Drive/Universal/Kissimmee area from 8.30–9.40am, returning at 6 or 7pm. Arrival time at the park is occasionally as late as 11.30am, with up to 3 stops en route (**buschgardens.mears.com**).

Beating the queues: You've not left the high-season Orlando crowds behind so it's still advisable to be here at opening time, if only to be first on the dazzling roller-coasters, which draw big queues (especially SheiKra, Cobra's Curse, Tigris, Iron Gwazi and Cheetah Hunt). Congo River Rapids and Stanley Falls Log Flume ride (if you want to get wet) are also prime draws in peak season. But queues take longer to build, so for the first few hours you can enjoy a relatively crowd-free experience.

Coaster fans flock to SheiKra and the new Iron Gwazi, and queues can top 1hr by noon. To ride these first, bear left through Morocco past the Zagora Café for Iron Gwazi, then carry on through Bird Gardens to Stanleyville for SheiKra. Tigris is also here. On through Stanleyville to Congo for Kumba, then retrace your steps to do Congo River Rapids and the other water rides. To start with the superb Cheetah Hunt coaster, veer right into

Cobra's Curse

Morocco and go past the Moroccan Palace Theater. After riding Cheetah Hunt, try Cobra's Curse and Montu in nearby Egypt, then take the SkyRide to Stanleyville and the big rides there. Here is the park layout going clockwise.

Morocco

Come through the main gates to the home of all the guest services and a lot of shops. EPCOT's Moroccan pavilion sets the scene better, but the architecture is still impressive and this version won't tax your wallet as much as Disney's! Turning the corner brings you to the first animal encounter, the alligator pen. Morocco is also home to one of the park's biggest shows.

Moroccan Palace Theater: The setting for the skilful 25min production **Turn It Up!**, a glittering cavalcade of super-slick ice dancing and stunts set to popular music in air-conditioned comfort. AAA

Myombe Reserve: One of the largest habitats for the threatened highland gorillas and chimpanzees of Central Africa, this 3acre/1.2ha walk-through has a convincing tropical setting with lush forest and landscaping. Take your time, as there are good, seated vantage points, and catch these magnificent creatures in their daily

routine. It is highly informative, with attendants ready to answer questions. AAAAA

Iron Gwazi: A hybrid wooden coaster on steel tracks, this is the steepest and fastest of its kind in the world. It uses elements of the old Gwazi coaster but the new steel track is much smoother and allows for inversions, loops and turns not possible with a standard wooden coaster. From a height of 206ft/63m, it dives spectacularly into a 91-degree first drop and hits a top speed of 76mph before flying through a series of fast, banked turns, three inversions and a dozen moments of serious 'air-time'! It lasts barely 2mins but it *seems* longer and is just terrific fun to ride, even if the first drop feels outrageously steep. **R**: 4ft/122cm. TTTTT

Other entertainment: Basketball fans can try the 3-Point Shootout (for $10), or tackle the Gwazi Climb ($3–10).

Shopping: The **Emporium** and **Marrakesh Market** are the best of the shops, along with a **Build-A-Bear** store.

Dining: For a quick meal, try **Zagora Café,** or the enticing **Sultan's Sweets,** serving Starbucks coffee, sandwiches and pastries.

Myombe Reserve

Bird Gardens

The most peaceful area – and starting point of the park in 1959 – you can unwind here from the usual hurly-burly among several attractive animal habitats.

BRITTIP

The Bird Gardens area is a good place to visit in mid-afternoon when most of the rides are busy.

Lory Landing: Walk through this tropical aviary featuring lorikeets, hornbills, parrots and more, with the chance to become a human perch and feed the friendly lorikeets. A cup of nectar costs $6–10 (seasonally), but makes for a great photo opp. AAA

Walkabout Way: This charming Australia-themed attraction offers the chance to meet free-roaming wallabies and wallaroo's, and visit Kangaloom to feed the kangaroos ($6, or 2 for $10, ages 5 and up only). It is a surprisingly captivating area, perfect for a relaxed stroll. AAA Other encounters include the lush, walk-through Kookaburra's Aviary and Flamingo Island.

Other entertainment: Festival Walkway is home to the seasonal live musical entertainment during summer and other special events, like the **Food & Wine Festival** (March–May).

Shopping: A real novelty here is the eye-catching **Xcursions** eco-friendly

One of the park's small animal encounters

gift shop, with all proceeds contributing to the Busch Gardens Conservation Fund.

Dining: Garden Gate Café offers small bites and snacks to go with its craft beers and frozen cocktails.

Sesame Street Safari of Fun

This impressive children's play area is the colourful 'home away from home' for Sesame Street characters and huge fun for pre-schoolers, with five junior-sized fairground-style rides, an entertaining stage show and wonderful water play and climb-and-slide areas. The extensive treehouse climb, ball pools and adventure play structures alone will keep most kids busy for hours!

Air Grover: A whizzy little dip-and-turn coaster packing plenty of thrills for young ones, piloted by everyone's favourite blue guy, Grover. **R**: 2ft 9in/97cm accompanied; 3ft 5in/104cm unaccompanied.

Sunny Day Theater: Sesame Street fun with Elmo, Zoe, Cookie Monster and Co. as they hit the stage for *Let's Play Together*, a kid-friendly story of friendship and diversity. The characters come out for a meet-and-greet afterwards, and also appear for the periodic *Storytime* readings.

BRITTIP

Arrive early and find a seat in the first five rows for an unobstructed view at the Sunny Day Theater. Seat children on the ends for the best character interaction.

1-2-3 Smile: Enjoy a special meet-and-greet with Big Bird and friends in their own themed, air-conditioned room, with photo packages from $18–30

Bert and Ernie's Watering Hole: Thoughtfully designed with even the smallest guests in mind, this gentle water-play area is filled with bubblers, water jets, dump buckets, geysers and splash tubs. Convenient

seating for parents surrounds the area. **TTTTT** (young 'uns only!)

Shopping: Look for **Abby Cadabby's Treasure Hut** for Sesame Street gifts and souvenirs.

Stanleyville

This brings you back into true ride territory, with two of the park's biggest coasters, and a water ride. You'll also find one of the two Train Stations here (next to SheiKra), for a gentle 35min journey round the park.

SheiKra: The park's outstanding big-thrill attraction is the giant steel structure of this monstrous coaster. At 200ft/62m tall and hitting 70mph/112kph, it puts Alton Towers' fearsome Oblivion in the shade. Higher, longer and faster, it features an initial drop at an angle as near vertical as makes no difference (with a delicious moment of stop-go balance as you teeter on the edge!), a second drop of 138ft/42m into an underground tunnel, an Immelman loop (an exhilarating rolling manoeuvre) and a water splashdown. The whole ride lasts less than 3min and is almost as much fun to watch

as to ride. It also draws big queues, so get here early or expect a long wait (or use the paid-for QuickQueue system). You can buy ride photos for $19–30. **R**: 4ft 6in/137cm. **TTTTT+**

Stanley Falls: Almost identical to Log Flume rides at Chessington, LEGOLAND, Thorpe Park and Alton Towers, this guarantees a good soaking at the final 40ft/12m drop. **R**: 3ft 10in/116cm. **TTT**

> **BRITTIP**
>
> Nervous about taking young children into such a big park? Stop by Guest Relations for a kid-friendly wristband with info that will help you reconnect quickly if you get separated.

Tigris: You can't miss this hugely imposing coaster, which reaches 150ft/46m at its highest point and features three launches, forward and backward movement, an inverted heartline roll, and a massive corkscrew drop that barrels into a final loop, just for good measure. It launches forward to the first hill's midpoint, barrels backwards,

Tigris track with SheiKra in the background

and then launches forward again as it gains full momentum and crests the first hill, straight into the iconic twisted top at more than 60mph/96kmh – and with enormous spectator value. Although the ride is silky-smooth, you may not want to do it just after eating! **R**: 4ft 6ins/137cm. TTTTT+

Skyride: The other end of the park's cable-car ride (from Cheetah Hunt), it offers spectacular views over the Serengeti Plain (with a thrilling moment as Cheetah Hunt races above!). However, it closes when it's windy and queues can build up here in late afternoon. AA

Other entertainment: Try **Bahati Hoops** and other fairground games (next to SheiKra) for an extra fee. The **Stanleyville Theater** hosts live entertainment in the summer.

Shopping: The **Kariba Marketplace** has the best of the shopping, and there is a small gift shop just outside Tigris.

Dining: For a hearty meal (and a great view of SheiKra), try **Zambia**

Smokehouse, where its wood-smoked ribs platter is a delight among a heavily barbecue-orientated menu (also with salads, sandwiches and kids' meals).

Jungala

This eclectic land contains some superb animal habitats and a hugely elaborate children's play area. It gets busy in the afternoon, so visit either early on or late in the day.

The Wild Surge: Get ready to 'surge' 4 storeys into the air on this tower ride from inside a giant waterfall, with a (brief!) glimpse over Jungala before bouncing back down again. Be aware queues are long and slow-moving as the ride takes just 14 at a time. **R**: 3ft 2in/96cm

Tiger Lodge: One of the park's most creative animal environments is this multi-level tiger exhibit (including its rare white tigers). It consists of an air-conditioned overlook and a walk-through section with close-up opportunities, including a unique pop-up turret (with a separate queue)

Stanleyville Falls Flume

in the main enclosure and a rope-pull for guests to 'test their strength' (periodically) against the big cats. Huge windows provide maximum viewing of the animals at play, especially in their plunge pool. AAAA

Orang Outpost: Another brilliant animal habitat, the orang-utans love to look in on guests, viewing them as much as vice versa. A series of close-up windows, including a glass floor over a hammock play area and a kids' tunnel, provide superb observation of the specially designed forest environment. AAAA

Shopping: Shop for gifts at **Tiger Treasures** (organic cotton T-shirts and conservation-related items).
Dining: Grab a chicken sandwich or other typical fast-food items from the new **Chick-fil-A** outlet.

Congo

Continue into this busy area that is geared around three stand-out rides.

Kumba: Another of the park's signature coasters, this unmistakable giant turquoise structure looms over the area. It's one of the largest in south-east USA and, at 60mph/97kph, features three high-thrill elements: a diving loop plunging a full 110ft/33m; a camel-back, with

© Busch Garens

Skyride at Busch Gardens

a 360º spiral; and a vertical loop. For good measure, it dives underground! It looks terrifying close up but is absolutely exhilarating, even for non-coaster fans. **R**: 4ft 6in/137cm. TTTTT

Congo River Rapids: These look pretty tame after Kumba, but don't be fooled. The giant rubber rafts will bounce you down some of the most convincing rapids outside of the Rockies, and you will end up with a fair soaking. **R**: 3ft 6in/106cm. TTTT

Ubanga-Banga Bumper Cars: Fairly typical fairground dodgems, you won't miss anything if you pass them by. **R**: 3ft 6in/106cm. TT

Tiger Habitat

Shopping and dining: There is just the **Congo River Outfitters** gift shop here, plus three refreshment kiosks.

Pantopia

This dramatic land boasts the park's tallest ride. There is also a full back-story, as Pantopia was created by a mystical Key-Master who arrived by hot air balloon to create a place where travellers could meet. The many doors tell a tale of the owners and travellers who passed this way and the land includes kinetic sculptures and re-purposed vehicles.

Falcon's Fury: The land's signature ride, this awe-inspiring tower lifts 32 riders at a time (slowly) up to its 300ft/91m height, tilts them forward so they are face down – then drops in best free-fall style. It is definitely for adrenalin addicts only as it really has that sky-dive feeling for several seconds before the brakes kick in and bring you more gently back to earth. It is aptly named (for the 160mph dive of a falcon) and provides an amazing view from the top – if you can keep your eyes open. We think it's as much a spectator opportunity as something you'll actually want to ride but it does provide an iconic look to the park. It's a relatively brief experience and queues move slowly, so you may want to try this early on – or chicken out completely! **R:** 3ft 6in/106cm. **TTTTT**

Sand Serpent: This family-orientated 'Crazy Mouse' coaster is surprisingly energetic, rising 46ft/14m and adding tight turns and swift drops. Top speed is 22mph/35kph, but it seems faster and thrills younger kids. **TTT** (**TTTTT** under-10s)

Scorpion: A vintage 1980 roller-coaster, this features a dramatic drop and 360° loop. It lasts just 120secs, but *seems* longer! Queues rarely top 30mins. **R:** 3ft 6in/106cm. **TTTT**.

Grand Caravan Carousel: Join this 'Bedouin caravan' in its layers of tapestries and tenting for a genuine carousel ride. **TT** (**TTTT** under 5s).

Pantopia Theater: In 2022, this was home to the Summer Celebration's *Celebrity Talent Showcase* (Wed-Sun), with some of the stars of the TV show *America's Got Talent*. They include a juggler, magician, dancers and stunt performers.

Other entertainment: The **Games Area** offers fairground-style games that require a few extra dollars, while the **Dragon Fire Grill & Pub** – a Moroccan-influenced nightclub that is Pantopia's gathering place for artists from around the world –

Scorpion

Dragon Fire Grill

offers a show while you dine (or just sit and watch). In summer 2022, it was live band Kings of Neon and *a capella* group Finish The Phrase (Tue–Fri).

Shopping: Painted Camel Bazaar offers a wide range of creative merchandise, some of it made from recycled materials from around the world, as well as Falcon's Fury and other souvenir items.

Dining: Headline restaurant the **Dragon Fire Grill** is an innovative food court-style offering including pizza, burgers, chicken, salads and Asian cuisine, as well as an extensive selection of local craft beers. **Twisted Tails Pretzels** is a delightful offering of fresh-rolled pretzels (don't miss the signature Bacon Pretzel Fury, along with the beer mustard sauce!), artisan sandwiches, pizza and pretzel dogs, as well as craft beers. **Lynx Frozen Treats** adds snowcones, smoothies and other icy delights and **Kettle Corn** is a haven for popcorn-lovers as well as serving turkey legs, potato twisters, chicken strips and drinks.

Nairobi

It's back to the animals as we enter this area, with five different habitats.

Serengeti Plain: A 49acre/20ha spread of African savannah, this is home to buffalo, antelope, zebras, giraffes, wildebeest, ostriches, hippos, rhinos and many exotic birds, and can be viewed for much of the journey on the Serengeti Express, a full-size, open-car steam train that chugs slowly from its main station in Nairobi to Stanleyville and back. AAA

BRITTIP

Take the Serengeti Express Railway from Nairobi or Stanleyville in mid-afternoon to give your feet a rest when it's busy elsewhere.

Animal Connections: The park's animal care hub makes for great close-up encounters with friendly flamingos, lemurs, sloths and more, with others on view through the large windows. The park's Animal Ambassadors also highlight education and conservation issues. AA

Animal Care Center: This is a peek into the way Busch Gardens cares for its residents, even down to performing live surgical procedures. The clever facility is in three parts, the Treatment Room, Nutrition Center and Pathology Lab. AAA

Serengeti Flyer: Due to debut in spring 2023 is this huge swing ride

Animal Care Center

that lifts 40 riders at a time over the Serengetic Plain, reaching 135ft high at speeds up to 68mph in back-and-forth style. **TTTTT** (expected)

Other entertainment: Look out for the **Elephant Interaction Wall** and periodic sessions with animal staff (notably the afternoon Elephant Wash), while you can see more park inhabitants at the **Reptile House, Penguin Point** (with its South African penguins) and **Tortoise Habitat**. The meeting area for park tours is also here, next to Kenya Kanteen.

Shopping and dining: Caravan Crossing (safari apparel and hats) has the best shopping here while **Kenya Kanteen** offers drinks and snacks.

Edge of Africa

This animal-rich area features the park's wonderful cheetah habitat – and signature ride.

Cheetah Hunt: This beast of a coaster re-creates the thrill of a cheetah pursuing its prey. With a fast-launch start from the loading station, the hunt is on. A second launch spirals you 10 storeys up the signature figure-of-eight tower before taking an exhilarating 130ft/40m drop into a subterranean gorge. Then you're off again, low and fast across the Serengeti. A final launch zips riders back across the grasslands (leaping over onlookers below and above the SkyRide!) and, just before you're completely out of breath, the hunt comes to an end after a sensational 2mins. The smooth ride, extensive theming and superb eye-appeal mark this out as one of Florida's finest rides, but it draws BIG queues, so try to do it early on. **R**: 4ft/120cm; **TTTTT+**

Skyride: Take to the air with this one-way cable car trip to Stanleyville, getting a fabulous aerial view of the park, including part of the Serengeti Plain. **TT**

Cheetah Run: Here you have the chance to see these magnificent cats up close, either chasing their favourite toy alongside Cheetah Hunt or just lounging around the splendid habitat designed especially for them. Sprints occur up to four times daily (check park map for times). Then, take time to learn more about the park's conservation efforts through touch-screen technology. AAA

Edge of Africa: This clever 15acre/6ha 'safari experience' guarantees a close-up almost like the real thing. The walk-through puts you in an authentic setting of native wilds and villages from which you can view

Cheetah Hunt

© Busch Gardens

giraffes, lions, baboons, meerkats, crocodiles, hyenas and vultures, and even an underwater hippo habitat. Wandering naturalists offer informal talks, and the attention to detail is superb. AAAA

Shopping and dining: Grab a souvenir at **Cheetah Gifts** or quick bite or drink from **Cheetah Snacks**.

For some of the best dining in the park, the Serengeti Overlook offers two choices, the **Giraffe Bar** for a wide selection of craft beers, wine, cocktails and light bites with panoramic indoor/outdoor views of the Serengeti; and fresh-made pizza, desserts and drinks at counter-service **Oasis Pizza**. Annual passholders also benefit from the stylish new **Pass Member Lounge** upstairs, with great views in air-conditioned comfort.

Egypt
The final area of Busch Gardens is somewhat tucked away, so it's best visited either first thing or late in the day. It sits in the park's bottom right corner and much of it is re-created pharaoh country, dominated by coasters Montu and Cobra's Curse.

Montu: You cannot miss the area's main attraction, another breathtaking

Falcon's Fury

© Busch Gardens

inverted coaster, covering nearly 4,000ft/1,219m of track at up to 60mph/97kph and peaking with a G-force of 3.85! Like Kumba, it looks terrifying but really is a 5-star thrill as it leaves your legs dangling and twists and dives (underground at two points) for almost 3min of brain-scrambling fun. **R:** 4ft 6in/137cm. TTTTT

Cobra's Curse: This novel coaster starts with an impressive vertical lift hill that brings riders face to fangs with a 70ft snake (well, an 'ancient cobra statue', at least!). From a height of 70ft/21.3m, it zips out into the African plain with multiple swoops and dips, twisting and turning as it snakes along more than 2,100ft/640m of track. It is a high-speed ride with a difference, as the cars will *reverse* and then spin at various points to provide a first-of-its-kind coaster experience. The clever theming, like an archaeological dig, plus live snake exhibits through the queuing area, ensure this is good family fun. TTTTT, **R:** 3ft 6/106cm.

> **BRITTIP**
> Edge of Africa offers some fantastic photo opportunities but, in the hot months, come here early in the day as many animals seek refuge from the heat later.

Shopping: Montu Gifts sells clothes, handbags and other merchandise, while **Cobra's Crypt Marketplace** offers clothes, plush toys and gifts.

> **BRITTIP**
> We find the Giraffe Bar a blissful lunch stop in the hotter months when its cool interior and views of the Serengeti Plain provide a welcome change of pace after all the rides.

Special tours
Busch Gardens features excellent behind-the-scenes tours and animal encounters that add an extra dimension to the park. For all tours, book at the Serengeti Outpost

in Nairobi or, better still, online at **buschgardens.com/tampa/tours**. By far the most popular is the **Serengeti Safari**, a 30min excursion (up to five times a day, taking 20 guests at a time) aboard flat-bed trucks to meet some of the Serengeti Plain's residents and feed the giraffes while learning about the park's environmental efforts ($40–70/ person seasonally, ages 5+, 5–15s must be accompanied by an adult). Other highlights include **Penguin** and **Elephant Insider** tours, a **Sloth Encounter**, **VIP Rhino Safari** and new **Keeper For A Day, Australia Insider** and **Orang-Utan Insider** experiences.

Special programmes

Food & Wine Festival: This imaginative event runs each weekend from Mar–May and is well worth sampling. Based in the Festival Walkway area, it consists of a series of themed food and beverage 'cabins' offering dozens of fresh dishes, with menus created especially by the park's culinary team. The festival runs from noon–9pm and starter-size samples range from $7–11, with wine, beer and cocktails from $9–14, plus bourbon and tequila tasting. It concludes each evening with a concert from the likes of Boyz II Men, Daughtry and Foreigner, all as part of regular park admission. There are food and wine sampler packages from $65–80 for 10 or 15 samples, while giant topiaries and food sculptors add extra colour.

Summer Celebration: From the end of May to early August, the park is open until 10pm in best party fashion, with live music, DJs, a special stage show and a big fireworks finale. The **Dragon Fire Grill** in Pantopia plays host to several live music acts, while the Gwazi Plaza in front of Iron Gwazi showcases the **Gwazi Beats** show, featuring drums, dancers and stilt-walkers. The acrobatic feats of **Cirque Electric** take to the stage of the Stanleyville Theatre, and **DJ party plazas** kick up the sounds next door to Iron Gwazi, SheiKra and Cheetah Hunt (with the latter aimed at children). Finally, the **Fireworks Spectacular** completes the celebration each Fri-Sun with a mix of pyrotechnics, fountains and special effects.

Howl-O-Scream: Don't miss the park's special Halloween presentation each Sept–Oct. A separately ticketed event ($105–120/ person; see online for early-booking discounts) offering grisly goings-on and themed houses, it also offers the chance to ride all the big coasters at night (7pm–midnight or 1am). It features some imaginative shows with all the shock-horror effects, plus a dance party, but it is definitely not advised for young children. It is similar to Universal's Halloween Horror Nights programme (p153), with elaborately themed haunted houses – like Witch of the Woods and Cell Block Zombies – plus a series of scare zones that change annually. The Busch Gardens version is more spread out and less frenetic than Universal's, but you may want to try both (**buschgardens.com/tampa/events/ howl-o-scream**).

Christmas: See p36.

Adventure Island: For a really full family day out, you can combine Busch Gardens with sister water park Adventure Island (on McKinley Drive), which is blissful when it's hot. The 25acres/10ha of watery fun, in a Key West theme, offer a full range of slides and rides, such as the **Colossal Curl,** a massive family raft ride, exciting four-lane mat slide **Riptide**, leisurely **Rambling Bayou** lazy river, spiralling tube ride **Calypso Coaster**, triple tube **Water Mocassin**, freefall drop-slide **Vanish Point,** dual tailspin waterslide **Solar Vortex** and new twin-raft slide **Rapids Racer**. Open mid-Mar to early Nov (weekends only from Sept) 10am–5pm (6 or 7pm in summer). Tickets are $80 (ages 3 and up), while a Busch Gardens–Adventure Island combo is $205 (but often with online discounts).

Well, that's the low-down on the main theme parks, but there's still a LOT to discover…

7 The Other Attractions

Or, One Giant Leap for Tourist Kind

If you think you can 'do' Orlando just by sticking to the main theme parks, think again! There is still a LOT more to discover, starting with Kennedy Space Center, which we rate as an essential place to spend a day.

Then there's LEGOLAND Florida – ideal for the 3–12 brigade – and Gatorland, another great-value experience. There are unique venues like WonderWorks, ICON Park and Ripley's Believe It Or Not and, for more individual tastes, the amazing 'skydive' experience of iFLY Orlando and helicopter rides, plus some great water parks. The choice is yours, but it's an immense selection. Let's start with One Giant Leap for Mankind.

BRITTIP
The Kennedy Space Center has more rocket launches than ever these days and you can get a great view from Jetty Park in Cape Canaveral or along Cocoa Beach, looking north.

Saturn V Rocket

© Kennedy Space Center

KENNEDY SPACE CENTER

Welcome to the past, present and future of NASA's space programme, and one of the most fascinating places in Florida. In addition to Space Shuttle *Atlantis*, there are a series of exhibits and shows (including two splendid IMAX films), a children's play area, Cosmic Quest Adventure interactive game, the daily Astronaut Encounter, poignant Astronaut Memorial, and the essential Space Center bus tours, which all add up to great value.

BRITTIP

Kennedy Space Center's handheld **SmartGuide** ($10) allows you to customise your touring through audio, photos and interesting facts, plus information on each exhibit and attraction you visit.

Once inside the Visitor Complex, the attractions are as follows. Start with Space Shuttle *Atlantis*, as this has proved THE big draw since it opened in June 2013. Late arrivals should do the Bus Tour first, though, then visit the Shuttle complex.

Atlantis: This dramatic $100m exhibit is the core experience of the new-look KSC, offering the 30-year history of the Shuttle programme through a mix of interactive media. Both hands-on and immersive, it features one of the three surviving orbiters and starts with a film pre-show into how the Shuttle programme was devised, then offers a vivid sense-surround presentation into the life and missions of *Atlantis* (stand about two-thirds of the way back for the full effect of the wrap-around screens). The specially written musical score reaches an emotional crescendo that is accompanied by a real 'wow' moment as...no, we won't reveal it! It is a breathtaking show that leads into the main exhibit hall, with the orbiter displayed with its payload bay doors open and robotic arm extended alongside an elevated viewing platform. The hall is subdivided into areas for the International Space Station, Hubble Space Telescope and Astronaut Training Simulation Gallery (complete with the chance to land a Shuttle and dock with the Space Station). In all, there are more than 60 interactive touch-screen experiences and simulators, Cosmic Quest Adventure game (p209) and climb-through Space Station, with its clear plastic tube suspended two storeys up. You can easily spend a couple of hours in here and we strongly advise heading here first as queues build up quickly. AAAAA+ The gift shop offers a great variety of souvenirs.

BRITTIP

Not sure what to do first at KSC? Visit the Information Center just to the left before the main turnstiles and they can provide a schedule for the day, working on your arrival time and what you'd like to see.

Space Shuttle Atlantis

© Kennedy Space Center

Orlando's Other Attractions
And Main Shopping Outlets

Daytona

Wekiva Island

94

ALTAMONTE SPRINGS

92

Altamonte Mall

Mount Dora

Sanford-Central Florida Zoo

4

Toll road (from 50c to $5)

436

90

Lake Apopka

429

441

Winter Park

88

OCOEE

87

Leu Gardens

417

WINTER GARDEN

50

Amway Center

Orlando City Soccer Stadium

WEST COLONIAL DRIVE

84

Winter Garden Village

EAST - WEST EXPRESSWAY

83

Downtown Orlando

Lake Eola

408

82

Camping World Stadium

FLORIDA TURNPIKE

KIRKMAN RD

79

80

SEMORAN BOULEVARD

WINDERMERE

78

Mall at Millenia

441

429

Universal Studios

Universal Citywalk

77

76

Islands of Adventure

Orlando International Premium Outlets

Cocoa Beach

Volcano Bay

75

74B

Port Canaveral

74A

Pirates Dinner Adventure

SAND LAKE RD

Florida Mall

528

BEACHLINE

Sleuth's Mystery Dinner Shows

TURKEY LAKE RD

73

INTERNATIONAL DRIVE

Orlando Watersports Complex

Orlando International Airport

Magic Kingdom

535

435

72

ORANGE BLOSSOM TRAIL

BOGGY CREEK ROAD

71

SeaWorld

Hoop-Dee-Doo Musical Revue

4

423

JOHN YOUNG PARKWAY

WESTERN BELTWAY

Lake Buena Vista

Orlando Vineland Premium Outlets

EPCOT DRIVE

Disney Springs

Epcot

69

Buena Vista Watersports

CENTRAL FLORIDA GREENEWAY

Disney's Hollywood Studios

Fantasia Gdns Mini-golf

BOGGY CREEK ROAD

Animal Kingdom

Winter-Summerland Mini-golf

417

The Loop & Loop West

Lake Buena Vista Factory Stores

BOGGY CREEK ROAD

MainGate West

WORLD DRIVE

Island H2O Live

65

Toll road

Old Lake Wilson Rd

64

OSCEOLA PARKWAY

KISSIMMEE

63

Old Town

Osceola County Pioneer Museum

Celebration

Capone's Dinner Show

Osceola County Historical Museum

East Lake Tohopekaliga

61

Medieval Times

192

Silver Spurs Arena

Orlando Tree Trek

Kissimmee Paddling Center

IRLO BRONSON MEMORIAL HIGHWAY

60

Downtown Kissimmee

Champions Gate

Kissimmee Airport

Kissimmee Lakefront Park

FLORIDA TURNPIKE

58

17

Dinosaur World

ST CLOUD

Tampa, Clearwater, Gulf Coast

Boggy Creek Airboat Rides

Wild Florida

Lake Tohopekaliga

Miami

N

0   5 miles

© Steve Munns 2022

Kennedy Space Center at a glance

Location	Off State Road 405 in Titusville
Size	Visitor Complex 70 acres/28.3ha
Hours	9am–5 or 6pm seasonally
Admission	Under-3s free; 3–11 $65; adult (12+) $75; 2-Day Ticket $79 and $89; Atlantis annual pass $120-149, inc free parking and food and retail discounts. Prices do not include tax.
Parking	$10
Lockers	$6 and $8 at Information (to left of main entrance)
Pushchairs	$8-10 at Information
Wheelchairs	$10, ECV $30, with pushchairs
Top attractions	Space Shuttle Atlantis; Shuttle Launch Experience; IMAX films; Astronaut Encounter; KSC Bus Tours, Gateway: The Deep Space Launch Complex
Don't miss	Apollo-Saturn V Center on Bus Tours; Astronaut Memorial; Rocket Garden
Hidden costs	Meals	Burger, chips and coke $15.50 Kids' meal $6–8
	T-shirts	$20-40, Kids $15-25
	Souvenirs	$1.99–12,000
	Sundries	Bus tour photos $15 (single photo) $15–54 Astropass (40% discount in advance online)

Shuttle Launch Experience:
After seeing *Atlantis,* walk up the long gantry for this well-made presentation into a real-life launch, which includes a clever pre-show and paves the way to the 'ready room' for your blast-off. You go through the launch procedure as the vehicle moves into a near vertical position for take-off, and a full 5min launch simulation, with vibration generators, sound effects, cabin movements and screen visuals. You get a taste of the G-forces, the Rocket Booster and External Tank separations, and a moment of 'weightlessness' as you enter Earth's orbit. Finally, the cargo doors open to reveal an awe-inspiring view. There is then a 'space walk' back to Earth via a spiral walkway surrounded by the stars and more satellite views of the planet. R: 3ft 8in/112cm. TTT AAAAA

Forever Remembered: Also inside the Atlantis exhibit is this moving two-part tribute to the astronauts who lost their lives in the *Challenger* and *Columbia* disasters. A short hallway features display cases dedicated to each astronaut, with artefacts, personal belongings and insights. AAAA.

Shuttle Launch Experience

© Kennedy Space Center

Heroes and Legends: This exhibit is part interactive 3-D adventure and part memorial, taking guests along on the earliest space missions and telling the astronauts' stories, for a real you-are-there experience using liberal touches of virtual reality. View the **EVA 23** documentary, which tells the gripping story of Italian astronaut Luca Parmitano's near-fatal spacewalk at the International Space Station. Then, you can interact (virtually) with the inductees into the fabulous Astronaut Hall of Fame. AAAA.

BRITTIP

All of the Shuttle Launch Experience is fully wheelchair accessible, and there is a seat outside for potential riders to test their comfort level. For anyone wary of the full ride (although there is no need to be, unless you are pregnant or have neck or back problems), there is a bypass room where you can experience the attraction without the motion.

Bus tours: The KSC's signature coaches depart every 15mins from 10am and are narrated to provide a full overview of the Space Center. Each tour makes a main stop in addition to driving around much of the working area, including past the massive Vehicle Assembly Building and the former shuttle launch pads.

The main stop is the Apollo/Saturn V Center, one of the KSC's great exhibits, where you can easily spend 90mins. It highlights the Apollo missions and first Moon landing with two impressive theatrical presentations on the risks and triumphs, a full-size 363ft/111m Saturn V rocket and a hands-on gallery of space exploration. A moving tribute exhibit to the crew of Apollo 1 – who were tragically killed during testing in 1967 – is well worth taking in. Allow a couple of hours to do the tour justice but be aware the last bus leaves the Visitor Complex 2½hrs before closing. AAAAA

IMAX films: The big-screen IMAX cinema offers two superb films that feel like you're *in* the action: *Journey To Space,* a 42min review of the Shuttle programme and a look ahead to NASA's future missions, narrated by Sir Patrick Stewart; and *Asteroid Hunters,* a 40min study of the cosmic origins of asteroids and if they're a threat to our planet, narrated by *Star Wars* actor Daisy Ridley.

LEGO Build to Launch: Rediscover the joy of building for fun, but with science-backed concepts courtesy of the LEGO Space Team, as this special exhibit offers an immersive learning experience. With the inside story of NASA's upcoming Artemis I mission and a fab free-build table, it also features some cool photo-ops.

Kennedy bus tour

Planet Play: Also located inside the IMAX building, this children's interactive play area allows young explorers (ages 2–12) to take on gaming and creative challenges, climb through a wormhole, walk along Saturn's rings, map a constellation and slide their way through an asteroid field. Adults can enjoy a beverage at the nearby beer, wine and coffee lounge while watching their youngsters play.

Astronaut Encounter: This engaging feature is a daily talk and Q&A session, with personal observations and stories from various veterans of the space programmes, including Shuttle astronauts. It is held up to three times a day at the Universe Theater. AAAA

Journey To Mars: Explorers Wanted: What will it take to explore deep space? This interactive exhibit inspires thinking through live presentations, interactive games, simulators and a mock-up of NASA's Orion crew capsule. AAAA

Gateway – The Deep Space Launch Complex: New in summer 2022 was this high-tech showcase for the latest innovations in space exploration from NASA and their commercial partners. It features an impressive gallery of modern spaceflight, with recent space-flown modules and rockets from the Orion programme and SpaceX's Falcon 9 booster, plus a full-scale model of the Sierra Space Dream Chaser and various hands-on exhibits. The undoubted highlight, though, is **Spaceport KSC**, a multi-storey motion simulator experience with four astounding journeys – to Mars, around Saturn and Jupiter, the deep-space Trappist-1 system, and through the Cosmic Wonders of various nebulas. The experience is totally futuristic and utterly compelling, and adds a completely new dimension to our view of space travel. **R:** 3ft 3in/99cm. AAAAA

Other exhibits: The **Rocket Garden** showcases a wide variety of spacecraft that have journeyed beyond the Earth's atmosphere since the 1950s, as well as the chance to sit inside replicas of the tiny capsules of the Mercury and Gemini astronauts. Free tours are given up to four times a day (times vary) and are well presented for all ages. Don't forget to stop at the moving **Astronaut Memorial**. AAAA

Cosmic Quest Adventure: This interactive computer game challenges trainees (i.e. you) to test their space knowledge with various missions, culminating in a final Adventure Challenge to decide if they're ready for promotion, or need a bit more training. Four Adventures are located around the Space Center, from building a Martian colony (Journey to Mars building), capturing a rogue asteroid (IMAX), launching a rocket (Apollo/Saturn V Center) or performing experiments on the International Space Station (Atlantis). Doing them all can take several hours, so this is best for a second or third visit ($8.99 for game-activating badge; admission required; best for 8–16s).

Shopping: The Visitor Complex has an excellent **Space Shop** (the world's largest store for space memorabilia and gifts, with some fun interactive elements, including selfies as an astronaut!), **Shuttle Express** in the Atlantis building and **The Right Stuff Shop** at the Apollo/Saturn V Center.

Dining: The **Orbit Café** is a modern counter-service diner with a tempting array of salads, sandwiches, pizza, burgers and kids meals, while the excellent **Rocket Garden Café** serves tasty sandwiches, salads, flatbreads and burgers, plus hot and cold breakfast 9–11am. The new **Space Bowl Bistro** is inside the Gateway complex, featuring protein bowls of various kinds, including quinoa, noodles, barbecued short rib, ahi tuna and even jackfruit. Find hot dogs, crisps and drinks at **Red Rock Grill** and scooped ice cream at **Milky Way**, plus various **Space Dots** (Dippin' Dots) kiosks. **Planet Play Lounge** and **IMAX Snax** are inside the IMAX building and **Moon Rock Cafe** is at the Apollo/Saturn V Center on the bus tour.

BRITTIP

Photographers are stationed at various locations around the Visitor Complex, and it's worth considering the $15–54 **Astropass** for unlimited digital-download photos.

The Center then has additional optional extra tours and features.

KSC Explore Tour: Travel almost within the perimeter security fence of Launch Pad 39-A and get a close-up of the complex, including the flame trench and emergency escape system – with a photo-op stop near the pad. Other sites include drive-by views of Launch Pad 39-B, the Vehicle Assembly Building, mobile launch platforms and a stop at the Apollo/Saturn V Center ($25 adults, $19 for 3–11s).

Cape Canaveral: Early Space: If you want to learn more about NASA history, try this 3hr+ guided tour (Thurs–Sun only) into the early days of space exploration around the older part of the facility. Highlights include the Air Force Space & Missile Museum, Mercury launch sites and Memorial, original astronaut training facility and several active launch pads, all of which are otherwise off-limits. For this tour, international guests (including children) must have a valid passport at check in with the visitor complex security officers

Planet Play

9–11am ($25 and $19). Reserve online or call 1866 737 5235.

Astronaut Training Experience (ATX): This 4–5hr simulator, virtual reality and high-tech, hands-on experience features astronaut 'training' based on a mission to Mars. Participants will 'land' on Mars, walk and drive on the surface of the planet, feel what it's like to "live" on Mars, and experience microgravity, through a series of 35–40min stages (ages 10 and up only, $175). Companion programme **Mars Base 1** includes working in the Plant Lab, operating robotics and taking on the engineering challenges real astronauts will one day face on the Red Planet. This day-long adventure is made all the more realistic through the use of floor-to-ceiling 4K screens that create an entirely convincing atmosphere (5–7 hours, ages 10 and up only, $150). Or try one of three **ATX Training Stages** – Microgravity Simulator, Land And Drive on Mars, and Walk On Mars – for a 30min session for $30, with KSC admission (early booking advised).

BRITTIP

The Space Center still has an active rocket launch programme; see full details at **nasa.gov/launchschedule**.

Launch Director Tour: Former launch director Mike Leinbach conducts this 3hr tour around Space Shuttle Atlantis, Launch Complex 39 and Shuttle Launch Experience, plus a tour of the Forever Remembered memorial ($65, includes signed lithograph; subject to availability).

Chat with an Astronaut: For another fully engrossing feature at the Kennedy Space Center, a small group gets to meet and ask questions of the star of the daily Astronaut Encounter twice a day. It is accompanied by either a continental breakfast (for the 10am group) or a selection of chef's culinary samplings (with the 2pm group), plus one drink per person (alcoholic for those 21 and over) and a commemorative gift and lithograph ($50 adults, $30 children).

LEGOLAND Florida

Children aged 2–12 – plus their parents and even grandparents – will all enjoy this bright and expansive park, which opened in 2011, with the addition of the adjacent Peppa Pig theme park in 2022. In a beautiful lakeside setting on the site of the former Cypress Gardens – and including the old tropical gardens – it offers 150acres/60ha of guaranteed fun with its extensive main park and water park. In fact, while the typical LEGOLAND age range is 2–12, the Floridian version probably appeals to kids as old as 14 with its bigger rides and water flumes. There is plenty to do, with no fewer than 23 rides, two main shows, an extensive adventure play area, the amazing Miniland, LEGO Friends area, LEGO Movie World and new Pirate River Quest adventure. It has two LEGO-themed hotels and the **LEGOLAND Beach Retreat**. There is also great shopping, and their two-day ticket is terrific value. Even the dining options are fresh, healthy and appealing, and there are plenty of quiet corners and gardens in which to chill out.

It requires a lot of legwork to see it all, as it sprawls round the southern shore of Lake Eloise and, when it's hot, there are few places in air-con cool, but there's something for all but older teens and we enjoy the clever landscaping and fun use of LEGO characters and features.

LEGOLAND Florida at a glance

Location	Off State Road 540 in Winter Haven
Size	150 acres
Hours	10am–6 or 7pm in high season (Easter, summer, Thanksgiving and Christmas), 10am–5pm low season weekdays (10am-6 or 7pm weekends); Water Park 10.30am–5 or 6pm in peak season; 11am or noon–4 or 5pm off peak (closed some weekdays)
Admission	Under-3s free; $100 (1-day ticket); $125 (1-day plus water park or Peppa Pig theme park); $127.50 (2-day ticket); $157.50 (2-day plus water park or Peppa Pig theme park), also on Eat & Play Card
Parking	$25; Preferred parking $40
Lockers	$15–20
Pushchairs	$20–30
Wheelchairs	$20, ECVs $80
Top attractions	The Dragon, Coastersaurus, Driving School, Boating School, The Great LEGO Race, Wave Racers, Royal Joust, Ninjago The Ride, Masters of Flight
Don't miss	LEGO Movie World, Miniland, Fun Town 4-D Theater, Brickbeard's Watersports Stunt Show, Cypress Gardens, Pirate River Quest
Hidden costs	**Meals** — Burger, chips and coke $15 / Kids' meal $7.50
	T-shirts — $19–28 kids, $25–35 adults
	Souvenirs — $1.50–400
	Sundries — Face Painting $15–21; Photo Digipass $30, $10 second day

Location and tactics

LEGOLAND Florida is in Winter Haven, about 45mins south-east of the Disney/Kissimmee area.

The parking fee is $25 and then you walk to the entrance. The Preferred Parking area (closer to the entrance; $40) features solar panel technology that provides power to local homes. At 150acres/60ha, the park spreads things out well but still sees queues at peak periods, so head for LEGO Movie World, LEGO Kingdoms and Land of Adventure first, returning to DUPLO Valley, Fun Town and Miniland later on. If your kids love the Ninjago characters, go to Ninjago World first. For a second day, start with your favourite rides, then cool down in the water park (which closes an hour before the main park). Once through the gates, here's what you'll find, moving in an anti-clockwise direction (advisable). NB: All ratings are indicated for younger children rather than adults!

Shorten your wait times at 24 attractions with **Fastrack Unlimited**, which bypasses the main queue ($60/person), or enjoy a one-time front-of-line pass for top rides The Great LEGO Race, The Dragon and Coastersaurus with **Fastrack 3 Pack** ($24–30).

The Beginning: This offers the ticket centre, Guest Relations and functional elements like the lockers, pushchair and wheelchair hire.

Shopping and dining: Immediately to the left of the entrance is **The Big Shop** (one of the largest LEGO merchandise stores in the world). Find a quick-bite counter and coffee bar across from The Big Shop, and pizza, salads and drinks at next door's **Pepper & Roni's Pizza Stop** ($8.25). Also watch for **Refresh And Refill** stations around the park. Purchase a refillable cup at $16 ($15 for 2, $14 for 3) and refill all day. Return visit refills $7.50 per day.

—**BRITTIP**
LEGOLAND employees are called Model Citizens, and each wears at least one Mini-Figure on their name badge. Bring along (or buy) your own mini-figure and they'll trade with you!

Fun Town: Enter a classic LEGO village, with a 4-D cinema, **The Grand Carousel** (TT; under 4ft/122cm must be accompanied by adult) and **Planet Legoland** immersive build experience on a huge globe. **4-D Theater** features four all-action 12min 4-D films.

The LEGO Movie 4D: A New Adventure: This features the further madcap exploits of Emmet, Wyldstyle, Unikitty, Benny and Metalbeard as they encounter evil villain Risky Business; **LEGO NINJAGO: Master of the 4th Dimension** offers kids the chance to be part of the action as they join the ninjas in saving the universe; and **LEGO City 4D: Officer in Pursuit**, a special effects-filled romp around the LEGO metropolis hot on the trail of a thief! Each are good family fun, and kids can meet their favourite characters at meet-and-greets outside the theatre after the show. **LEGO Mythica: Journey to Mythica:** follow the exploits of Bob, a brave alicorn, who has to escape Chimera, team up with Maximus the Sky Lion and splash along with Duo the Hydra on adventures through enchanted forests and mysterious caves. TTT

—**BRITTIP**
Plan your visit to 4-D Theater during the hottest part of the day for a break in blissful air-conditioned comfort.

Dining: Granny's Apple Fries serves up the park's signature dessert (apples, cinnamon and a creamy sauce, also served a la mode), and **Fun Town Slushies** offers great cold treats. **Pizza & Pasta Buffet** is a value-conscious choice for feeding the whole family, and the **Ice Cream Parlor** adds more sweet delights.

DUPLO® Valley: Turn right out of Fun Town to the perfect place for toddlers to let their imaginations run wild as they explore a toddler-size village, featuring a junior-sized train that winds through the country, passing farms, camps and fishing holes. They'll love helping the farmer find missing animal and plough the fields, then cool down in the water play area. TTTT under-6s.

LEGO Movie World: This immersive 'land' is themed as Bricksburg, Emmet's home town from *The LEGO Movie*, and features characters and experiences from the original film and its sequel. Let kids loose in **Benny's Play Ship** play structure, or brave three new rides. The feature attraction is **The LEGO MOVIE: Masters of Flight**, a dynamic 3D 'flying theatre' with wind, mist and scent effects that takes riders on a madcap chase through Bricksburg on Emmet's Triple Decker Flying Couch. The sense of movement comes from on-screen visuals more than the actual movement, but it's a powerful sensation none the less. R: under 3ft/101cm and under age 3; 3ft–4.3ft/101–132cm; and age 3–8 with companion age 14 or up; 4.3ft/132cm and age 9 and up can ride alone. TTTT. **Unikitty's Disco Drop** is a cute 35ft drop tower that gives youngsters a thrill as it rises to 'Cloud Cuckoo Land', then bounces and spins on its way down. R: under 3ft/101cm and under age 3; 3–4ft (101–122cm) and age 3–6 with companion age 14 or up; 4ft/122cm and age 7 and up can ride alone.

TTT Water ride **Battle of Bricksburg** offers the chance to get wet while defending Bricksburg from DUPLO alien invaders. Kids love firing the water cannons from their boat – and shore-side onlookers love firing back! R: Ages 6 and under or less than 4ft (122cm) must ride with companion age 16 or up. TTTT

Shopping: The Awesome Shop carries merchandise themed to Emmet, Wyldstyle and friends.

Dining: Taco Every Day serves chicken or beef tacos and drinks.

Other Entertainment: Kids will find their favourite characters from The LEGO MOVIE at **Emmet's Super Suite** meet-and-greet and photo opportunity.

Planet Legoland

© Legoland

LEGO Kingdoms: The next large-scale land features three major rides and a cool play area. Climb aboard **The Dragon** for a backstage view of life in an enchanted castle, then take off on a thrilling flight as this scenic dark ride becomes a dynamic outdoor coaster! R: 4ft/122cm or 3ft 4in/102cm with adult. Child Swap and ride photo available. TTTT Then, saddle up on LEGO-themed horses for **The Royal Joust**, where youngsters gallop through an enchanted forest, jousting with LEGO knights along the way. R: 3ft/91cm; max 12 yrs and 170lb/76kg. TT Another climbing structure, **The Forestmen's Hideout**, lets kids climb, slide and swing off extra energy. Also here is **Merlin's Challenge**, a standard but quite whizzy fairground circular ride (4ft/122cm or 3ft 4in/102cm with adult). TTT AAAA There are also the **Jester's Games** ($5–10).

Shopping: The Kings Market carries suitably themed gifts.

Dining: Dragon's Den serves sausages and giant turkey legs while **Kingdom Cones** has soft serve ice cream.

Land of Adventure: This BIG land has two major rides and three other great kiddie attractions. The excitement continues at **Lost Kingdom Adventure** as you hunt for treasure while fighting off baddies with laser blasters. Youngsters will want to ride several times to better their score. R: 4ft 6in/137cm or 2ft 10in/86cm with adult. TTT

Another top thrill comes with **Coastersaurus**, a classic wooden coaster that zips through a prehistoric jungle and past life-sized LEGO dinosaurs. R: 3ft/91cm or 4ft/122cm with adult. TTTTT Then you can just let young 'uns loose at **Pharaoh's Revenge** multi-level climbing structure, with the added fun of being able to shoot soft foam balls at each other. **Beetle Bounce** shoots riders 15ft/4.5m high on this kid-friendly tower ride R: 3ft/91cm; TTTT **Safari Trek** is the classic children's car ride, through a clever LEGO-themed African savannah full of lurking animals. R: 2ft 10in/86cm,

or 4ft/122cm with adult, max age 12; TTT **Adventure Games** are more fairground side-stalls for an extra few dollars.

Dining: Build your own sandwich or mac & cheese bowl at **Ultimate Sandwich Builder** food truck.

Ninjago World: This extensive area is set up around the characters and exploits of the Ninjago warriors from the TV series, which spun off the LEGO sets. It features four outdoor experiences, designed to test visitors' balance and agility before they venture to the main event. **Ninjago – The Ride** is an indoor interactive 4-D adventure that sets up a battle to test your ninja skills in a series of 13 animated Dojo challenges. Using only hand and arm gestures, you fire lightning bolts, fireballs, shockwaves and ice at various targets, building up to a battle with the Great Devourer and the chance to earn full Spinjitsu Ninja status. R: Riders under 4ft/122cm must be accompanied by a responsible rider 4ft or taller. TTTT Kai and Nya have a meet-and-greet here, too.

Shopping: Check out the 22 Ninjago building sets – and more – at **Wu's Warehouse**.

LEGO City: This popular area features some of the most classic attractions, themed like a real working town, starting with **Rescue Academy**, where families race each other to 'put out the fire'. But these fire trucks only move when you pump the levers! R: 4ft/122cm or 2ft 10in/86cm with adult; guests in wheelchairs must transfer. TTT LEGOLAND's ultra-popular **Ford Driving School** (ages 6–13), **Ford Jr Driving School** (3–5s) and **Boating School** (4ft/122cm or 2ft 10in/86cm with adult) are all here too, giving kids the chance to navigate electric cars and small boats to earn official LEGOLAND driving licences. TT–TTTT For something more dynamic, try **Flying School's** suspended steel coaster, one of the biggest thrills in the park and a major hit with coaster fans. R: 3ft 8in/111cm or 4ft 4in/130cm with adult. TTTTT

There is an indoor **Tot Spot** play area here, too.

Shopping: Pick up some souvenirs at the **Driving School Store**.

Dining: Grab a tempting chicken lunch or dinner at **Kick'n Chicken Co**, a tasty burger at **Burger Kitchen,** sweet treats from **Firehouse Ice Cream**, or something from the **Traffic Snack Cart**.

> **BRITTIP**
> See LEGOLAND's website for periodic discounts. They sometimes offer up to $15 off ALL tickets if booked in advance for a specific day.

LEGO Technic: This area is packed with fun and thrills for older children as it offers three super rides. The **Great LEGO Race** is the big attraction, a tall, fast-turning steel coaster that is distinctly quicker and steeper than it looks! Loosely themed as a road rally, it starts with a series of hairpin bends and then goes into various drops and rapid turns from a height of 50ft and speeds up to 35mph for 90sec of junior thrills. R: 4ft/122cm or 3ft 6in/99cm with adult. TTTTT Ride the waves and dodge soaking blasts of water on the airboat-style **Aquazone Wave Racers**, a ride so cool you'll want to queue up straight away for another go! R: 4ft 4in/132cm or 3ft 4in/102cm with adult; TTTT). Kids can also try the more sedate **Technicyle** (TT), while toddlers will gravitate to **Technic Tot Spot** soft play area.

Dining: The **Funnel Cake Factory** kiosk sells sweet, fried pastries.

Imagination Zone: Next up is the creative heart of the park, where kids put their imagination to work at eight hands-on indoor play areas. They include the chance to try out touch-screen technology in the **Water Zone**; invent crazy aerial creations in **Flight Zone**; build and test race cars in the **Wheels Zone**; build on the walls of the **Creation Zone**; and conjure up loose-brick creations at **Building Zone**. Then there are the latest LEGO video games in **GameSpace** and computer-controlled robots in the **LEGO Mindstorms** area. Outside, the **Kid Power Towers** then burn off excess energy as kids (and adults!) use ropes and pulleys to ascend colourful towers – and let go for a 'free fall' back down. R: 4ft/122cm or 3ft 4in/100cm with adult; TTT Child swap available, guests in wheelchairs must transfer.

Dining: Try **Panini Grill** for a tasty toasted sandwich, salad and drink.

Cypress Gardens: The beautiful gardens this park was originally known for are now lovingly restored and a haven for strolling, complete with beautiful gazebo, tropical displays and banyan tree. AAAA

Pirates Cove: Come back out of the Gardens and you'll find the place where swashbuckling meets water in an exciting skills challenge on the 'high seas' in **Brickbeard's Watersports Stunt Show**. LEGO characters and a life-sized pirate ship add to the fun of this jaw-dropping water stunt show, with wakeboarding, barefoot skiing, incredible flyboarding feats, a classic ski pyramid and other stunts that visitors of all ages will not want to miss. AAAA

Pirate River Quest: using the former Cypress Gardens waterways, this gentle boat ride, which was due to open late in 2022, has the added bonus of a scavenger-type treasure hunt that also features some mischievous monkeys. AAAA

Heartlake City: This area is dedicated to the LEGO Friends, with

Heroes Weekend

© Legoland

Mia's Riding Adventure offering junior-sized horse-themed fun on a back-and-forth disk coaster. **The Heartlake Stepping Tones Fountain** is another interactive feature with LEGO instruments that play music. **Heartlake Hall** adds periodic live entertainment from the LEGO friends, as well as interactive building workshops.

Shopping: Pick up all the latest LEGO Friends collections and accessories at the **Heartlake Mall**.

Miniland USA: Completing the tour brings you to the park's other crown jewel, an iconic, fully covered area featuring eight superbly themed US locations in miniature. **Florida** shows off some of the state's gems, with separate areas devoted to the **Kennedy Space Center** (complete with Shuttle countdown!) and the huge **Daytona Speedway**. **Las Vegas** boasts the glittering resorts and other icons of Nevada's most famous city while **Washington DC** re-creates the White House, US Capitol, Smithsonian museum and the Washington and Jefferson monuments. **New York City** includes Rockefeller Plaza (with squirt fountains!), Times Square, Lady Liberty, the Empire State building, Bronx Zoo and Grand Central Station. **California** features icons including the Golden Gate Bridge and the Hollywood Bowl. Finally, there is a section devoted to the ever-popular theme of **Pirates**.

Miniland's detail is amazing, so you can easily spend an hour browsing to spot the riot of visual gags and fun touches (like the surprised gent in the loos at Grand Central!).

Water Park: Tailor-made for families, this spread of watery fun is not as large as Disney's Blizzard Beach or SeaWorld's Aquatica, but it is designed completely with young children in mind. It offers lockers, changing rooms, towel rentals and a gift shop (with swimming costumes for sale if you make a late decision to try it), plus **Beach-n-Brick Grill**, complete with shaded Tiki Bar for tired parents! There is also an ice

Haven dining

There are two great locals' choices in Winter Haven. **Harry's Old Place**, on Cypress Gardens Rd, fronting Lake Ned (left out of Legoland, then second right) features classic Floridian style and cuisine, including some excellent seafood and daily specials, with large portions, a friendly welcome and hand-crafted cocktails (lunch and dinner, Tues–Sun only; **harrysoldplace.com**). **Manny's Chophouse** is on Highway 17 (3rd Street SW; left out of Legoland, go 3mls/5km then turn right on to 3rd St SW), with its signature steaks, chops and ribs, plus lively style and eclectic decor. With a good kids' menu and full bar service, it is easily the equal of its Brit-friendly Highway 27 counterpart and, while they don't take reservations, waits rarely top 20–30 mins (**mannyschophouse.com**).

cream kiosk and **Beach Street Tacos**. Cabaña hire is $79–99. There are six main areas and it will require at least half a day of your time. As ever, have plenty of high-factor, waterproof suncream.

DUPLO Splash Safari: This is Toddler Central, featuring small-scale slides and interactive DUPLO creatures, all in just 6in/15cm of water (and within view of the Tiki bar!). AAAA

Joker Soaker: Older children will love this huge watery adventure playground with its slides, fountains, climbs, squirt guns and more, including a 300-gallon bucket that fills and tips periodically! R: 3ft/91cm on 3 lower slides, 3ft 6in/99cm on upper 4; under 3ft 6in/99cm must be accompanied by an adult. AAAAA

Build a Raft River: An imaginative variation on the lazy-river idea, with riders able to build their own floating raft with special LEGO bricks and then complete the 1,000ft/330m-long 3ft/91cm deep circuit. AAA

LEGO Wave Pool: Enjoy some gentle surf fun in this wide, walk-in pool that allows young children to splash happily while their older siblings can brave the 3ft 4in/100cm-plus depths. AAA

Twin Chasers: This raft ride slooshes down double flumes – one open, one enclosed – with a grand splash-down at the end. **R:** 4ft/122cm; **TTTT**

Splash Out: The ultimate thrill-ride for kids, a selection of 3 intertwined body-slides with a drop of 60ft/18m that afford a great view of the surrounding area – before you 'drop in'! **R:** 4ft/122cm; **TTTTT**

Creative Cove: The hands-on Build-a-Boat attraction is where kids can create and race LEGO watercraft through fast-flowing rivers in a setting inspired by the popular LEGO City Coast Guard sets.

Seasonal fun: LEGOLAND adds more entertainment at different times of the year, notably **Red, White & Boom** fireworks (July 2–4), and **Heroes Weekend** fire safety activities (early Sept), **Brick-or-Treat** for the Halloween season (late Sept–Oct 30) with trick or treating, scavenger hunts and a fireworks show; the **Holidays at LEGOLAND**, with festive decorations, a LEGO Santa and sleigh, Master Builder sessions, character appearances and more nightly fireworks; and even a **Kids New Year's Eve**, with the chance to party and celebrate at a more kid-friendly time.

If that's the park, here are some add-ons that may be worth including in your visit.

VIP Experiences: Tour the park with a VIP host, who shares fascinating facts about the park and models. **Red Brick** VIP Experience offers priority access to rides, shows and attractions; a tour of the model shop; lanyard; minifigure; 10% retail discount and park admission (from $300pp); **Silver Brick** adds valet parking; family photo and digital package; and refreshments (from $500pp); **Gold Brick** adds Q&A with a Master Model Builder; building session and take-home build; lunch and all-day snacks; and VIP gift bag (from $700pp). Book VIP experiences on 1855 753 7777 or **legoland.com/florida/tickets-passes/tickets/vip-experiences**

Be Aware: LEGOLAND can close on select Wednesdays in winter. Check in advance on **florida.legoland.com**.

Rooms at the Pirate Island Hotel

© Legoland

LEGOLAND Hotel: Want to stay in the heart of the fun? This is the way to do it. With 152 brightly coloured and themed rooms, there is bags of LEGO style throughout, from the giant dragon at the entrance to dozens of individual pieces in the rooms, where there is a special Treasure Hunt for kids to solve (and find a prize). Choose from Kingdom, Adventure, Pirates, LEGO Friends and THE LEGO MOVIE for the individual room themes, which all feature bunk beds and an entertainment unit for kids, while the two-room suites add a living room, pullout sofa and play area. The VIP Suites sleep up to six. There are king-sized beds for adults, two flatscreen TVs, a mini-fridge and coffee maker in every room. Premium rooms add more LEGO décor and models for kids to play with. The hotel includes a fabulous heated outdoor pool and two dining options for breakfast and dinner, Bricks Restaurant and Shipwreck Restaurant, plus the themed Skyline Lounge, which is open from noon and serves traditional American food. A full breakfast is included in the daily rate, with exclusive Master Model Builder sessions (a major hit with children), early park admission, nightly LEGO building competitions and live entertainment, and there is also a lovely boardwalk on the edge of Lake Eloise. There are interactive play areas for kids throughout the hotel, and it doesn't get much better than walking straight out of the hotel – and straight INTO the park!

BRITTIP

Don't miss the 'Disco Elevators' at the LEGOLAND Hotel – you might not want to get out when it's your floor!

LEGOLAND Pirate Island Hotel: Connected to the LEGOLAND Hotel, this takes the LEGO experience up a notch, adding a massive pirate ship at the entrance, an enormous pool area, themed rooms with in-room Lego building bricks, Master Builder sessions and nightly entertainment. Rooms sleep up to 5 and include a semi-private kids' area with boat-shaped bunks and a trundle bed, a TV in the entertainment centre and in-room puzzles and treasure hunts each day of your stay. A stylish adults area features a king bed, Amazon Alexa, mini-fridge, TV and plenty of USB ports. Kid-friendly bathrooms have a tub and shower combo. Pirate-themed Shipwreck Restaurant serves breakfast and dinner and is designed with little buccaneers in mind, while grown-ups appreciate Skyline Bar for an evening drink. Family-style breakfast, character meet-and-greets, building activities and nightly entertainment are included in the room rate.

LEGOLAND Beach Retreat: This lakefront resort features 83 village-style bungalows for a total of 166 rooms. Along with a cool Lego beach/surfer theme, each of 13 horseshoe-shaped 'coves' of 5–8 duplex-style bungalows is named for a mini-figure. Rooms have a king bed, bunk beds and a trundle bed to accommodate up to five, with a curtain between the kids room and the adults. They are heavily themed and feature a coffee/tea maker, USB ports, LEGO building bricks, safe, mini-fridge and tub/shower combo. Check-in takes place in your car as you enter the property. The resort's central building, The Lighthouse, features a themed pool, sandy 'beach', climbing structure, games and competitions, a gift shop and buffet-style Sandy's Castle Restaurant serving breakfast and dinner, plus evening takeaways to enjoy in your bungalow. Bricks Beach Bar serves beer, wine, and speciality cocktails, with limited food at lunch.

Peppa Pig Theme Park

Fans of the children's TV show will be bowled over by this stand-alone theme park next to LEGOLAND specifically for their age group, with a mix of rides, playgrounds, shows and water–play area. It's small at barely five acres, but that works well for under-5s and little legs, while the theming is bright and fresh and everything is close at hand.

Rides are highlighted by the iconic central **Daddy Pig's Roller Coaster**, which provides big thrills for little 'uns (**R**, 3ft/91cm), while **Grandad Dog's Pirate Boat Ride** is a fun circular bobbing boat adventure and **Grampy Rabbit's Dinosaur Adventure** is a junior-sized ride on the back of a playful dinosaur (**R**, 2ft10in/86cm). **Mr Bull's High Striker** is a scaled-down drop-tower ride (**R**, 2ft10in/86cm), and **Peppa Pig's Balloon Ride** is an aerial carousel. **Peppa's Pedal Bike Tour** and **George's Tricycle Trail** allow youngsters the freedom to pedal their hearts out.

The **Muddy Puddles Splash Pad** adds all the splashing, squirting, sliding fun of an elaborate water playground (swimsuits strongly advised), and **Pirate Island Sand Play** is an over-sized sand pit, complemented by a series of play areas within **Granny Pig's Garden** that include George's Fort and Madame Gazelle's Nature Trail. A series of (free) **Fun Fair Games** provide some simple amusements, and **Mr Potato's Showtime Arena** adds the live entertainment in the form of two 10min shows with Peppa and friends. The **Cinema** is a rare air-conditioned haven in which to sit and enjoy some classic Peppa TV episodes. And that's the sum total of the attractions – you could easily be done in a couple of hours, but most youngsters are happy to repeat the rides and keep returning to the playgrounds.

Shopping and Dining: This is taken care of in typical fashion at **Mr Fox's Shop**, with all manner of Peppa souvenirs, with **Miss Rabbit's Diner** providing fine family fare that includes some imaginative items like rice and veggie bowls, grilled vegetable ciabatta, fresh fruit and salads, as well as sandwiches, flatbreads and fab milkshakes ($7.50–15).

BRITTIP

The park tends to get busy by late morning, which makes it a good time to visit the Cinema or take a break at one of the LEGOLAND hotels.

Peppa Pig theme park is a Certified Autism Center and offers a sensory and accessibility guide to plan visits in advance.

Admission: $35/person (under 3s free); parking $25 (preferred parking $40); annual passes $75–$300; also on Eat & Play Card (**peppapigthemepark. com/florida**).

Daddy Pig's Roller Coaster

© Legoland

Gatorland

For a taste of Florida wildlife, this is as authentic as it gets and is popular with children of all ages. The 'Alligator Capital of the World' was founded in 1949 and is still family owned, so it has a natural, homespun charm few of its big-name rivals can match. And, when the wildlife consists of several thousand menacing alligators and crocodiles in various natural habitats and three fascinating shows – plus a fabulous Zip Line attraction that is disabled accessible – you know you're in for a different experience (although there is a LOT more to Gatorland than just gators – including their Bobcat Bayou). Overall, Gatorland is something you're unlikely to get anywhere else, and the sense of being in the 'real' Florida is terrific.

BRITTIP

If you have an evening flight home from Orlando International, visit Gatorland for half a day on your final day as it is just 20mins' drive from the airport.

Gatorland Express tours: Start by taking the 15min train ride around the park to get an idea of its 110acre/45ha expanse. This has an added fee but is good for multiple rides, is amusingly narrated and is especially fun for kids. You also get a good look at the native animal habitat, which features whitetail deer, wild turkey and quail.

Attractions: Breeding pens, baby alligator nurseries and rearing ponds are also situated throughout the park to provide an idea of the growth cycle of the gator and enhance the overall feeling that it is the visitor behind bars here, not the animals. A nursery exhibit gives close-up views of eggs hatching and baby gators in a special habitat.

Many of the small-scale attractions have been designed with kids in mind and there is plenty to keep everyone amused. **Allie's Barnyard** is a petting zoo, while you can feed some friendly lorikeets at the **Very Merry Aviary**, and view the pink inhabitants of **Flamingo Island**. The **Breeding Marsh Walkway** provides the best overview of the main gator habitat, with a three-storey observation tower for full panoramic effect.

White Alligators: Don't miss this remarkable little "village" housing rare and completely white alligators, which are totally leucistic (without pigment), with startling blue eyes, not pink like albinos.

Bobcat Bayou: This is the place to find Gatorland's two bobcats, while the park also showcases two rare Florida panthers in the **Panther Springs** exhibit. Other animals include owls, turtles, flamingos, giant tortoises, snakes, spiders, emus and deer, while hundreds of wading birds provide a fascinating close-up of their nests from Mar–Aug.

BRITTIP

Lucy and Neiko, brother and sister panthers who live at Gatorland, are at their most lively first thing in the morning when they have been let out of their night quarters – just like any domestic cat!

Shows: The 800-seat **Wrestling Stadium** sets the scene for some real cracker-style feats (a 'cracker' is a Florida cowboy) as Gatorland's resident 'wranglers' catch a medium-sized gator and proceed to point out the animal's features, with the aid of some daredevil stunts that will have you questioning their sanity. The **Gator Jumparoo** is another eye-opening spectacle as some of the park's biggest creatures use their tails to 'jump' out of the water and be hand-fed tasty morsels, like whole chickens! **Up-Close Encounters** is another amusing showcase of creatures, from the expected snakes to less obvious cockroaches and scorpions. Great photo opportunities for brave children!

Gator Gully: This superb little water park features numerous ways for kids to cool down, get wet and generally have fun. The ½acre/0.2ha park features five elements, including a giant jalopy with water jets for spokes and a fountain radiator, an old shack that 'explodes' with water, and giant gators with squirt guns. The neighbouring dry play area and chairs and tables allow parents to sit and watch the kids expend some energy, perhaps with a drink from one of the kiosks.

But wait… that's not all!

Screamin' Gator Zip Line: Gatorland has fixed its eyes firmly on the brave of heart, introducing a first-of-its-kind zipline experience, with four zips soaring high above the park's most notorious residents. At 1,200ft/366m long and up to 56ft/17m high, the lines afford spectacular views of jumping Cuban Crocodiles and the scenic Alligator Breeding Marsh. Start at Tower One, where the 'bunny hill' builds up your courage (and your excitement). Tower Two soars over croc pools (look down – the view is outrageous!); Tower Three is the tallest launch point at 75ft/23m, and its 600ft/182m run zips straight over the breeding marsh at up to 35mph/56kph. Take the walking bridge over to Tower Four where you're met by a thrilling double zipline for a final race to the finish.

---BRITTIP

Reservations are required for Screamin' Gator Zip Line. Capacity is limited to groups of 12 up to 7 times a day and demand is high. Reserve by phone or online.

The experience includes orientation, full equipment check, the zipline and a trek across a swinging bridge. There is a separate fee, but at $69.99/person, it includes all-day admission to the park. A photographer will also chart your journey for purchase back on terra firma! **R:** Min weight 75lb/34kg, max 275lb/125kg. Must be able to climb stairs. Wear closed-toe shoes and trousers or long shorts. Screamin' Gator also includes a brilliant wheelchair-accessible, one-segment zip line for guests with lower-body disabilities (must transfer to specially designed harness), providing a thrilling 350ft/106m glide over the gator marsh.

The hilarious **Stompin' Gator Off Road Adventure** is a 12ft/3.5m high monster buggy ride that takes guests into the wilds of Gatorland for a thrilling excursion through real Florida ecosystems – including a gator pond! It costs extra ($10/person) but is a fun journey into the swampy backwoods hereabouts. Ticketing for all Gatorland's added experiences is at **Gator Joe's Adventure Outpost**.

Gatorland

© Gatorland

Shopping: In addition to three gift stores and the **Gator & Snake** photo opportunity, you should visit the **Gift Shop** complex at the entrance, which incorporates the trademark Gator Mouth entryway.

Dining: Grab a bite or drink at three snack bars: try **Gator Jake's Fudge Kitchen** or dine on fried gator nuggets (as well as burgers and hotdogs) at **Pearl's Good Eats**, with excellent kids' meals at $6.99.

Special events: Some unique options if you really want to get to know your gators are: **Trainer for a Day**, with the chance to work behind the scenes at the park 8–10am, finding out what it takes to handle such dangerous animals, behavioural training and novice gator wrangling ($130 12s and over, max five people; includes park admission); **Gator Night Shine**, which takes guests into the Breeding Marsh after dark for a one-hour tour with a senior gator expert, with torches and gator food to lure the 'locals'. You can then marvel at how gator eyes shine like red beacons in the torchlight and learn more about the habits of these amazing animals – a real family treat, which kids seem to love (dusk, around 8.15pm summer, 6.30pm autumn and winter; $25 all ages; bug spray provided; reservations required); and **Adventure Hour**, a chance to go truly 'behind-the-scenes' in the Breeding Marsh to feed

and pose for photos with the gators here ($12/person). **Meet-A-Gator** is every kid's chance to show his or her bravery and have the picture to prove it ($10 to kneel over a gator's back; extra for the photo). **Admission**: $33 adults, $23 3–12s, $32 over 55s, 10am–5pm, parking free. Annual passes are only $50, $35 and $45 if you plan more than one visit (**gatorland.com**; check website for online savings).

International Drive

The 14½ml/23km tourist corridor of I-Drive (see maps p14 and 206) continues to be an ever-changing source of hotels, restaurants, shopping and fun. There are more than 42,000 hotel rooms, 150+ restaurants and almost 500 shops, as well as 21 attractions, and three mini-golf courses. The I-Ride Trolley links it all in transport terms and the website **internationaldriveorlando.com** highlights all the options. Its Virtual Visitor Guide has an I-Ride map and valuable money-off coupons, which you can download to get you started, plus a hotel booking facility. The I-Ride Trolley section provides 'NextTrolley' info as well as maps and listings of what is near each trolley stop.

Here's a look at the area's attractions (see also Chapter 10, Orlando By Night, and Chapter 12, Shopping, to get the full picture).

Screamin' Gator Zip Line

© Gatorland

ICON Park

This entertainment venue is the BIG attraction on I-Drive as it boasts seven major attractions, including the 400ft/121m The Wheel, 13 bars and restaurants, five shops and free parking. Each attraction has its own gift shop and there is a neat Food Court, making it a well-rounded and enjoyable half or full-day option. The dining choices are excellent (p290), notably the new Gordon Ramsay's Fish & Chips restaurant, and it is beautifully lit at night (**iconparkorlando. com**).

The Wheel at ICON Park: This observation wheel offers a 20min journey in air-conditioned 15-passenger capsules for a panoramic view of Central Florida (as far as the Kennedy Space Center on a clear day. There is narration of the major sights, plus info pads, and the vista is fabulous from the top, including the vast spread of Walt Disney World. It costs $34 adults and $29 4–12s (1–10pm Mon–Thurs, 1–11pm Fri, noon–11pm Sat, 11am–10pm Sun). You can also buy drinks from the Sky Bar to take with you. AAAA

Madame Tussauds: An extensive range of celebrity waxworks allows you to rub shoulders (and take selfies) with famous people, past and present. The experience starts with a meeting with Spanish explorer Juan Ponce de Leon in 1513 as he discovers Florida. There is a quick history tour featuring President Lincoln, Uncle Sam and Martin Luther King, and then the journey continues with famous inventors and innovators (notably the man who brought Mickey to Orlando in the first place!). The Madame Tussaud story is well illustrated at the half-way point, and then the centre really turns on the style with a dazzling range of celebrities such as David Beckham, Elvis, Madonna, Jim Parsons, Jennifer Lawrence and Taylor Lautner. The A-list Party adds mega-stars like Samuel L Jackson, Brad Pitt and Angelina Jolie. But the major appeal here is the **Justice League: A Call For Heroes** interactive area that takes you through Metropolis and Gotham City, helping Wonder Woman, Superman and Batman avert disaster. You'll need at least 90mins to see everything, and taking photos with the 'stars' is actively encouraged ($35 and $30; 11am–7pm Sun–Thurs, 8pm Fri, Sat; also on Eat & Play Card **madametussauds.com/orlando**). AAAA

Kung Fu Panda at Madame Tussauds

© Madame Tussauds

BRITTIP

Check ICON Park websites for current pricing as there are often online discounts for booking in advance.

SeaLife Orlando: The third part of the attraction is a huge indoor aquarium that features some fabulous exhibits and hands-on displays, ideal for children of all ages. The highlight is the 360-degree immersive tunnel through the main aquarium, with fish – including rays and sharks – swimming around you, but there are then a variety of smaller tanks and other underwater scenes, including a Rockpool experience, Stingray Cove and Everglades tableau. In all there are more than 5,000 animals to see and investigate, along with some clever 'Talking Aquarium' interactive talks and animal feedings throughout the day, as well as the chance to see the centre's divers feeding and cleaning at regular intervals. There is a Scavenger Hunt for children to follow along the way, and the different vantage points are geared towards smaller visitors, with a strong eco-friendly message throughout ($35 and $30, under 3s free; 11am–7pm Sun–Thurs, 8pm Fri–Sat). There is a 30min Behind The Scenes tour for an extra $10/person. Combo tickets for two or three of these adventures are priced at $68 and $65; $102 and $97; also on Eat & Play Card (**visitsealife.com/orlando**). AAAA

BRITTIP

Didn't bring a camera to Madame Tussauds? Not to worry – there are photographers at regular intervals to make sure you have great memories of the visit.

Museum of Illusions: Get ready for a series of visual set pieces – including an upside-down room, vortex tunnel, and other illusions – that are designed to trick the eye and amuse all the family. You'll be amazed at the use of forced perspective, as well as the chance to take some mind-boggling selfies to share on social media ($27/adults, $23 3–11s; 10am–10pm daily; combo tickets available with WonderWorks and The Wheel **moiorlando.com**). AAA

In The Game: This high-energy arcade boasts the latest video challenges and activities, including an Escape Room, X-D Motion Theatre and Mirror Maze, plus high-tech variations on familiar games (with prizes to match; $12–25 per activity; 11am–11pm, Mon–Thurs, 11am–midnight Fri–Sun; **inthegame.net/iconpark**).

Next door to ICON Park, look out for two other smart attractions.

Kings Bowl: This upscale bowling centre offers a smart restaurant and bar as well as 22 high-tech bowling lanes in a grown-up atmosphere that is also family-friendly. Its elegant bar and dining room set-up features big-screen TVs, billiard tables, shuffleboard, Foosball and bocce ball while the menu includes burgers, pizza, wings, tacos and great cocktails. The beer list is impressive and the desserts decadent ($17–24/person; noon–12am Mon–Thurs, 1am Fri–Sat, 10pm Sun; **kings-de.com/orlando-fl-venue-features**).

StarFlyer: Towering above I-Drive is this 425ft/129m chair swing ride, the tallest of its kind in the world. Not for the faint-hearted, its 24 double seats revolve at up to 45mph at its full height and it offers a unique view of the surrounding area. Alternatively, you can just sit and watch with a drink at ground level at the Star Bar! (10am–2am daily; $12.50/person, $8 same-day return; **starflyer.com**). TTTTT

The new mirror maze at Ripley's

© Ripley's

Ripley's Believe It Or Not

You can't miss this extraordinary tilted attraction as it's designed to seem as if it's falling into a Florida 'sinkhole'. But once inside you soon get back on the level and, for an hour or so, you can wander through this quirky museum dedicated to the weird and wonderful. Robert L Ripley was an eccentric explorer and collector (a real-life Indiana Jones) who for 40 years travelled the world to assemble a collection of the greatest known oddities. The Orlando branch of this chain features 8,900ft^2/830m^2 of displays in 16 galleries, including authentic artefacts, interactive exhibits, illusions, video presentations and music. The elaborate re-creation of an Egyptian tomb showcases a mummy and three rare mummified animals, while the Primitive Gallery contains artefacts (some quite gruesome) from tribal societies around the world. There are then Human and Animal Oddities, Big and Little galleries, Illusions and Dinosaurs, Weird Florida Gallery and Ripley's Warehouse collection, plus extra interactive elements. The collection of miniatures includes the world's smallest violin and a single grain of rice hand-painted with a tropical sunset. You can also attempt various puzzles and brain teasers, and try the unusual shooting gallery. The new Mirror Maze was due to open in late 2022 ($28 adult, $19 3–11s; 10am–12am, last entry 11pm; **ripleys. com/orlando**). AAA

Titanic - The artefact exhibit

Titanic – The artefact exhibit

Go back in time at this fascinating attraction just north of Sand Lake Road. Guided tours start on the hour and weave through full-scale re-creations of the Titanic's famous rooms, including her grand staircase, first-class parlour suite, Verandah Café, Marconi Room, third class cabin and bridge. Costumed actors portray characters such as Captain Smith and Molly Brown, sharing stories of passengers and crew during the one-hour journey of the famous ship. The 17-gallery attraction features an interactive Underwater Room, including a 15ft/4.5m 'iceberg' and a detailed replica of the vessel as she appears on the bottom of the Atlantic today. More than 300 artefacts and treasures, including memorabilia from James Cameron's blockbuster movie Titanic are also on display here, notably some ultra-rare pieces, including the 2nd-largest piece recovered from the wreck site ($22 adults, $15.75 under 12s, $19.75 seniors; 10am–8pm Sun–Thurs, last tour 7pm, 10am–5pm Fri–Sat, last tour 4pm; **titanicorlando.com**). AAAA Titanic is also included with Orlando Eat & Play Card.

Titanic First Class Dinner Gala: Try this 3hr theatre/dining occasion with the cast of the Exhibit. Starring Molly Brown, Captain Smith, Thomas Andrews and other high-society luminaries, it offers each table a front row seat for the whole Titanic story, setting the scene and delivering a dinner party with a difference, all in period style. Enjoy a sumptuous four-course meal, featuring sirloin steak and chicken, with tea, coffee and soft drinks (extra for beer and wine) in a splendid atmosphere, recreating *Titanic's* first-night sailing each Fri and Sat from 5.30pm ($69 for adults, $42 for ages 3–10; not recommended for under-6s; book online).

Fun Spot America

Just off I-Drive on Fun Spot Way (look for the 250ft/76m SkyCoaster past the junction with Kirkman Road) is this extensive family amusement park. Go-kart thrills come from four challenging tracks, including the enlarged Quad Helix, the triple level corkscrew Conquest, the fiendish Thrasher and multi-level Commander. There are bumper cars and boats, five daring fairground-type rides (including the huge Happy Swing and whizzy Scramblur), one of the largest, most up-to-date video arcades in Florida, a Big Wheel, 10 Kiddie Rides – including a classic two-storey carousel – and a Cadet track for the little ones. Fun Spot also boasts the world's second-largest SkyCoaster (a massive, free-fall swing) and three coasters – the impressive long steel-wooden hybrid of White Lightning, which races along at up to 48mph/76kph with a max drop of 75ft/23m; the tight-turning suspended ride of Freedom Flyer (select seats feature Virtual Reality); the child friendly Sea Serpent. Then there's the high-spinning Enterprise, new 50ft drop-tower ride Firecracker, and children's Splash Pad. The large Food Court serves hotdogs, salads, nachos and the like. Check out **Gator Spot**, a separate area featuring almost 120 residents of Gatorland, including an albino gator, a gift shop and some great photo opportunities ($6/person, photos for extra fee). Parking and admission are free, with a series of ride Passes geared around children's height (above and below 4ft 4in/1.32m), with younger children getting free run of all the rides, and as passengers on the 2-seat go-karts with an adult (Single Day ticket for all 4 tracks, all rides and unlimited Free Play arcade $60; SkyCoaster $40 single rider, $35ea double, $30ea triple, $20ea with Single Day pass; 10am–midnight, 2pm–midnight off-peak; **fun-spot.com/orlando**). TTTT Also with Go Orlando card.

—BRITTIP

ICON Park, WonderWorks, Fun Spot and Andretti Indoor Karting are all open late in high season, long after most theme parks are shut, so you can have a day at the park, then let the kids loose to tire them out completely!

WonderWorks

This interactive fun centre is a three-storey chamber of family fun – all built upside-down (the result of a 'tornado experiment that went wrong'!). Full marks for imagination and there's a lot here, especially for 6–12s. You enter through an 'inversion tunnel' that orientates you the same way round as the building, then progress to various chambers of entertaining and mildly educational hands-on experiences that demand several hours to explore fully. The six WonderZones include natural disasters and Google Earth virtual globe and map; physical challenges (Bubble Lab, Bed of Nails and the chance to make an impression of your body in 40,000 plastic nails at Wonderwall!); Light & Sound challenges; Imagination Lab (more physical and mental challenges); and Space Discovery, where you have the Astronaut Training gyroscope, Shuttle Landers (pilot the Space Shuttle), a Mercury capsule mock-up and Wonder Coaster (a pair of enclosed 'pods' where you design and ride your own coaster). There is also a three-storey glow-in-the-dark ropes course with 20 obstacles, Laser Tag game and the 4D XD Motion Theater with two simulator rides, plus Gift Shop and Café ($36 adults, $27 4–12s; 9am–midnight; $62 and $45 with Outta Control Magic Comedy Dinner Show; **wonderworksonline.com/orlando**). TTT Also on Eat & Play Card.

iFly Orlando

Next door to WonderWorks is this unmistakable blue and red construction housing one of the most fun 'rides' in town, a 'free-fall skydiving adventure' that is clever, addictive, difficult but exhilarating, with the bonus of being a great spectator sport! It's basically a huge upright wind chamber that provides the feeling of a freefall. The standard 1hr programme provides a full briefing with an instructor, then you're given helmet, pads, goggles, earplugs and flight suit, and your group of 8–12 returns to the flight deck, where you get two 1min supervised 'flights' (which seem a lot longer!). It is fiendishly tough to just 'hang' in this 125mph/200kph column of air, but it's a fun, absorbing experience and is almost guaranteed to make you want to try again. There is no fee to watch from the observation area, and you can turn up to see for yourself at any time (2–5 flights, with certificate, $85–160; add a photo or video download for an extra fee; 10am–7pm Mon–Thurs, 8pm Fri, 9pm Sat, 9am–6pm Sun; reservations recommended; also on Eat & Play Card; **orlando.iflyworld.com**). TTTT

Andretti Indoor Karting

This amazing indoor centre features some of the best go-karting in Florida – and a LOT more besides. Billed as the longest indoor track in the world, the state-of-the-art racing is terrific and features three different levels, Adult (at least 15 and 4ft 6in tall), Intermediate (12–15 and 4ft 6in) and Junior (at least 4ft tall). But then there is also 10-pin bowling, Laser Tag, high-tech race-car simulators, a massive array of the latest arcade games, Hologate VR virtual reality game, plus an XD Dark Ride 3-D interactive film experience, which adds a thrilling extra element to the usual shoot-'em-up games against monsters! (Kart races $28 Adult and Intermediate, $12–17 Junior; $13 XD Dark Ride; Bowling $29–36/hour, plus $3.50 shoe rental; Laser Tag $14–15; Racing simulators, Dark Ride, Hologate $13–14; 10am–midnight Sun–Thurs, 1am Fri–Sat; **andrettikarting.com/Orlando**).

BRITTIP

If you're likely to go for multiple rides or visits at Andretti Indoor Karting, consider their $25 Family Membership with discounts on all the activities, plus food at the Andretti Grill.

I Fly Orlando

Helicopter rides

These are another local staple, with half a dozen different operators.

Try **Orlando Heli-tours** for the full overview, with 12 different tours. The Disney Spectacular Tour is their most popular, with 7–9min flights over Walt Disney World. Other tours offer views over SeaWorld, Disney Springs, Universal and Kissimmee, or choose the 18–20min Grand Park Adventure Tour and see the theme parks, water parks and main tourist areas of Orlando (two locations on International Drive, tours from $35–75; **orlandohelitours.com**)

Escape games

There are a variety of these test-your-wits type games centres on I-Drive. Here are two of the best.

The Escape Game: Choose from seven intensely themed games (Prison Break, Gold Rush, The Heist, Mission: Mars, Special Ops: Mysterious Market, The Depths and Playground), then test your ability to solve puzzles and unscramble clues in rooms filled with props and special effects, with a strict one-hour time limit that determines whether you succeed or meet a dire fate, at least symbolically. A Game Master helps out with hints if you get stuck, but there is a real sense of pressure, and ages 13 and up get the most out of the experience. Single players can make up the number with other groups but this is good family fun and also a great place to come in case of bad weather. Booking is highly advisable, but not required. They also list a handy 'degree of difficulty' with each game, so you can judge the level you're happy to tackle ($40/person; 8am–midnight daily; **bit.ly/brit-escape**).

Escapology: This venue on southern I-Drive (in a shopping/office plaza just north of Sheraton Vistana Villages resort) offers a sophisticated style with a 'living room' to encourage visitors to relax before their briefing for one of seven games (which change periodically), and enjoy a complimentary photo and debrief afterwards. Designed for families and friends in private groups of 2–8, the game rooms can even be used for side-by-side games to test each group. The eight 60min games include Under Pressure, Mansion Murder, Narco, Scooby-Doo and the Spooky Castle Adventure, Murder on the Orient Express, 7 Deadly Sins, and Star Trek Quantum Filament. It's a test

Orlando Helitours

of initiative, teamwork and lateral thinking, and each room has a Game Master to monitor progress and provide clues if necessary (11am–11pm daily; $40–45/person; **escapology.com/en/orlando-fl**).

BRITTIP

Players are advised to arrive 15mins early for escape games to allow time for paperwork and briefing. No entry once the clock has started. It's important to select a leader and work as a team. Oh, and visit the loo first!

Chocolate Kingdom: This cute Factory Adventure Tour takes visitors into the story of chocolate making, with fun characters to keep children amused. You can create a customised choccy bar (for an extra $9), while the 45min tours include samples along the way (11.30am–5pm; $19 adults, $15 ages 4–12; **chocolatekingdom.com**).

Mini-golf
For those in need of more holiday fun, don't miss the mini-golf outlets along International Drive (see p289).

Kissimmee
Old Town: This shopping and entertainment attraction in the heart of tourist Highway 192 in Kissimmee has recently undergone a major overhaul. As well as the shopping (p303), it's worth trying the live events, rides and attractions. Look for the high-energy games arcade **Happy Days Family Fun Center** and **Rootin and Tootan's Shooting Alley**, which is great fun for kids (and dads with a competitive streak). More family entertainment is provided by **The Great Magic Hall**, with live 35min magic shows 5–10 times a day ($10/person) and terrifying **Mortem Manor** haunted house with live actors ($15/person, 3pm–8pm Wed–Sun). There is also a classic Carousel, Ferris Wheel, Hurricane coaster and Paratrooper spinning ride, as well as the indoor Xtreme Ninja Challenge (10am–11pm, restaurants 11am–11pm; **myoldtownusa.com**). Old Town also features several iconic car events, notably the **Saturday Classic Car Cruise**, the **Friday Muscle Car Show & Cruise** and **Wednesday Car Show** (**myoldtownusa.com/category/events**).

Ferris wheel at Old Town Kissimee

Fun Spot America: Next to Old Town is another version of this amusement park, with a good selection of rides, including the high-adrenalin **Hot Seat** swinging ride, go-kart tracks and **Mine Blower** coaster. The big daddy of them all is the **SkyCoaster** (or optional **SkySled** harness for those who want to sit upright), a 300ft/90m tower that sends up to three riders at a time on a free-fall plunge that turns into a giant swing – at 85mph/136kph! The more down-to-earth rides consist of two multi-level go-kart tracks, the labyrinthine **Chaos** and **Vortex**, with its challenging banked bowl section. The other 14 rides are almost as much fun, like the fairground **Fun Slide, Happy Swing,** junior-sized **Kiddie Coaster** and the giant swing of **Headrush 360**. More swinging fun is provided by the **Screaming Eagles** and **YoYo**, while standard **Tilt-A-Whirl** and **Bumper Kars** add to the line-up. There's a well-stocked indoor **Snack Bar** when you need to cool down, as well as an **Ice Cream Kiosk,** while kids will gravitate to the **Midway** and **Arcade** (perfect for a wet or super-hot day), plus the thrilling **Galaxy Spin** wild mouse coaster. The big ride is **Mine Blower**, a unique, tight-turning wooden coaster that includes a rare barrel roll and steep 115-degree overbanked turn that adds real thrills for adrenalin junkies (Single Day ticket for both tracks, all rides and unlimited Free Play arcade $60; SkyCoaster $40 single rider, $35ea double, $30ea triple, $20ea with Single Day pass; 10am–midnight, 2pm–midnight off-peak; **fun-spot.com/kissimmee**).

──────**BRITTIP**──────

To visit Orlando's Discover Downtown information center, take exit 82B off I-4 and there are four multi-storey car parks, including the Library (take 4th right on Central Boulevard). Or take 2nd right, Church St, go across Orange Ave and left into the Plaza multi-storey, more expensive but more central.

DOWNTOWN ORLANDO

The last few years have seen a major revitalisation of Orlando's city centre ('downtown'), with new offices, apartments, shops and restaurants. This makes it a tourist attraction in its own right and it is well served by Discover Downtown on Orange Avenue (10am–5pm, Mon–Fri; **downtownorlando.com**). Start here to get a full overview, with a 3-D city model, gift shop and ultra-helpful staff (plus free wi-fi). They can provide free maps of the area, several self-tour guides (including food, cocktails, and art tours) and info on riding the free LYMMO bus service around downtown. Much of the former Church Street Station area is also vibrant again, **churchstreetdistrict.com**.

Orange County History Center

This smart part of the downtown scene offers an imaginative journey into central Florida history, from the wildlife and Native Americans to today's tourists and the space programme. The accent is on hands-on exhibits and audio-visual presentations, and it is very much a journey through time, starting with the Natural Environment and First Peoples and moving on to the 1800s, with an authentic pioneer 'cracker' home, tales of Florida's ranching days, a Seminole settlement, and tourism pre-Disney. Aviation explores World War II bombers to the outer reaches of space and the Theme-Park Era explores the opening of Walt Disney World and beyond. An exhibit on African American history and a series of travelling exhibits round things off (10am–5pm Mon–Sat, noon–5pm Sun; $8 adults, $7 seniors (60+), $6 5–12s; **thehistorycenter.org**).

Getting around: Everywhere is walkable downtown, but the free Lymmo bus service connects the central area along Magnolia Avenue, from South Street and City Hall up to the Centroplex area.

Theatre and more

Orlando boasts world-class theatre these days, most notably at the dazzling **Dr Phillips Center for the Performing Arts**, which features touring Broadway shows, ballet, concerts and more. It includes the new (in 2022) Steinmetz Hall, one of the most acoustically perfect venues in the world, with the ability to change its shape to provide different acoustic profiles (**drphillipscenter.org**). Then there's the amazing Amway Center, home to the Orlando Magic basketball team, Orlando Predators Arena League outfit and Orlando Solar Bears minor-league ice-hockey team, plus major concerts (**amwaycenter.com**). Improv comedy is on offer at **SAK Comedy Lab** in the 250-seat Eola Capital Loft on S Orange Avenue (**sakcomedylab. com**), while **CityArts Factory**, based in the historic 1886 Rogers Building, showcases the thriving Downtown Arts District and its multiple venues, which include the innovative **Snap! Gallery** of digital and augmented reality photography (**downtownartsdistrict.com**).

Dining: The restaurant/bar choice is superb here, too. Take your pick from **Wall Street Plaza** (a lively collection of bars and lounges that are the heart of downtown nightlife), the upscale **Kres Chophouse**, and Church Street Station, the remains of the old entertainment district, which still includes a cluster of fine restaurants and bars, notably the fun **Harry Buffalo** and outrageous **Hamburger Mary's Bar & Grille**, plus the first US outlet of the famous **Ace Café**. See more in Orlando By Night (p259).

Lake Eola: Once you have sampled the downtown hustle, head out to this gem, with more restaurants and shops, plus a lakeside walk, children's play area, swan paddle-boats, artwork and a peaceful ambience. There are regular open-air concerts at the **Walt Disney Amphitheater** and the **Orlando Farmers' Market** (around Lake Eola, 10am–3pm Sun) features local artists as well as fresh produce.

Dining: Stop for a great meal at any of **310 Lakeside** (**310restaurant.com**), **Soco,** with its gourmet twist on traditional southern comfort food (**socothorntonpark.com**), the wine bar chic of **Eola Wine Company** (**eolawinecompany.com**), upscale style of **Anthony's Thornton Park** (**anthonyspizza.com**), polished elegance of bar/restaurant **RusTeak** (**rusteakthorntonpark.com**) and fab comfort food of **Mason Jar** (**masonjarprovisionsorlando.com**).

---BRITTIP

Don't miss the annual Spring and Fall Fiestas around Lake Eola, with hundreds of vendors, live entertainment and fun for kids, the first weekend in April and Nov (**fiestainthepark.com**).

Orange County History Center

Loch Haven park

Continue north and you travel the 'Cultural Corridor' to Loch Haven Park and the area's fine collection of theatres and museums.

Orlando Science Center: Family fun and education are the stock-in-trade here. Its hands-on experiences and habitats entertain as well as inform, and school-age children in particular benefit greatly from it. It has nine permanent exhibits, periodic travelling ones, a night sky observatory, café, Science Store and giant screen cinema, plus exciting new nature and conservation exhibit **Life!** in 2023, adding three environments of animal habitats that highlight diversity and conservation.

The main exhibits include the prehistoric world of **DinoDigs**, the geology and geography of **Our Planet**, the pure science of the **Kinetic Zone**, the human technology of **Bionic Me** and the sustainability of **Tiny Green Home**, as well as the play-time fun of **KidsTown** for under 8s. Additional experiences include **Dr Dare's Lab**, with open experiments periodically, the immersive cockpit simulator of **Flight Lab**, and the **Observatory**, Florida's largest public refractor telescope. The centre has several programmes in **Dr Phillips**

Orlando Science Center

ORLANDO SCIENCE CENTER

CineDome, a 310-seat cinema that surrounds its audience with large-format films and digital planetarium shows, while the **Digital Adventure Theater** adds educational films and Science Live! interactive programmes ($24 adults, $22 seniors and students with ID, $18 2–11s; includes a CineDome film Fri–Sun); parking $5; 10am–5pm daily, closed public holidays; **osc.org**) AAAA Each Jan also sees the fun **Otronicon**, a four-day expo celebrating the latest tech developments, from surgical robots to immersive virtual reality.

Other must-see venues include the extensive **Orlando Museum of Art** (**omart.org**) and the diverse **Mennello Museum of American Art**, with a permanent collection by painter Earl Cunningham (**mennellomuseum.org**). For something different, **Orlando Shakespeare Theater** produces classic, contemporary and children's plays in partnership with the University of Central Florida. Their high-calibre productions include *A Christmas Carol*, *Henry V* and *Kinky Boots* in 2022–23, providing an innovative theatrical experience while showcasing Shakespeare's legacy (**orlandoshakes.org**).

Parents should also note the superb **Orlando Rep**, which specialises in family theatre, youth academies, summer camps for kids and special sensory-friendly shows. Recent works include *High School Musical 2*, *The Colored Museum* and *Dog Man: The Musical* (**orlandorep.com**). Highly recommended.

Dining: nearby Ivanhoe Village offers excellent choices, including the new **The Hall on the Yard** (p296), vibrant **Bites & Bubbles** (**bitesbubbles. com**) with its rooftop terrace, traditional cuisine of **The Greek Corner** (**thegreekcorner.net**), the tapas splendour of Santiago's Bodega (p296) and fine dining of **Russell's on Lake Ivanhoe** (**russellsorlando.com**)

THE WATER PARKS

Florida specialises in elaborate water parks, and Orlando boasts the very best. Disney's duo are the biggest, but Universal's Volcano Bay is a brilliant addition, and SeaWorld's Aquatica may be the most laid-back. Lockers are provided for valuables and you can always hire towels. However, be aware the water parks CAN close for a day or two in winter during serious cold snaps (usually below 15C).

Disney's Typhoon Lagoon Water park

When Typhoon Lagoon opened in 1989, it was the biggest and finest in Florida. And, although it has since been superseded, in high season it is still the busiest, so be prepared for queues. Arrive half an hour early if possible as entry often begins before the official opening hour. The park's 56acres/23ha are spread out around the 2½acre/1ha lagoon fringed with palm trees and white-sand beaches. It is extravagantly landscaped and the walk up Mount Mayday provides a terrific overview. However, you need to arrive early to bag a decent spot. Or, for $70 extra, you can reserve

two beach loungers, two towels, an umbrella and a small table by stopping in at High 'n Dry Rentals (or calling in advance). Really want to splash out? Opt for a Beachcomber Shack (cabaña), which includes a locker, drinks mug, cooler with ice, bottled water, towels, loungers and table, and waiter service. Full day rental for up to eight guests will cost $340. Reserve in advance on 407 939 7529 (we're fans of arriving early and getting your loungers for free!).

Admission: $69 adults, $63 3–9s (under-3s free); included with Disney Magic tickets; lockers $10–15; parking free; 11am-6pm, hours vary seasonally. TTTT AAAAA

BRITTIP

Take water-shoes or socks to all the water parks. They are cheap in local supermarkets.

BRITTIP

Water parks provide both a great way of cooling down and an easy way of getting sunburn. So don't forget the high-factor **waterproof** suncream, and reapply often.

Andy Murray visits Typhoon Lagoon

© Disney

Beating the crowds: To avoid the worst of the summer crowds (when the park often reaches its 7,200 capacity), Monday morning is best (steer clear of weekends at all costs) and, on other days, arrive either before opening or in mid-afternoon, when many decide to dodge the daily rainstorm. Early evening is also pleasant when the park lights up.

BRITTIP

Want to learn to surf? Typhoon Lagoon offers Surfing School 2hrs before park opening every day. Call 407 939 7529 in advancc to book at $199/person.

Slides and rides: The park is overlooked by **Mount Mayday**, on top of which is perched the luckless Miss Tilly, a shrimp boat that legend has it landed here during the typhoon that gave the park its name. Watch out for the water fountains that shoot from Miss Tilly's funnel at regular intervals, accompanied by a blast from the ship's siren, signalling another round of BIG waves in the **Surf Pool** (and they are big; take care with toddlers). Circling the lagoon is **Castaway Creek**, a 3ft/1m deep, lazy flowing river offering the chance to float along on rubber rings.

The slides and rides are all clustered around Mt Mayday and vary from the breathtaking body slides of **Humunga Kowabunga** that drop you 214ft/65m at up to 40mph/48kph down some steep inclines (make sure swimming costumes are securely fastened!) to **Ketchakiddee Creek**, which offers a selection of slides and pools for youngsters under 4ft/122cm. In between, you have the **Storm Slides**, body slides that twist through caves, tunnels and waterfalls, **Mayday Falls**, a wild 460ft/140m single-rider inner-tube flume down a series of banked drops, **Keelhaul Falls**, a more sedate tube ride, and **Gangplank Falls**, a family ride inside rafts that take up to four people down 300ft/90m of

mock rapids. **Crush 'n' Gusher** is a fabulous trio of 'water-coaster' tube rides, plus a large heated pool with zero-depth entry (great for toddlers) and an extensive sandy beach.

Miss Adventure Falls is another family raft ride to rival Crush 'n' Gusher. It features a long lift hill and then a wild white-water adventure over the 'Falls' in a bid to spot some of the treasures acquired by the ocean-going Captain Mary Oceaneer. At two minutes long, it is longer than any other Disney water park ride.

Keeping out of the sun can also be a problem as there's not much shade. A quick plunge into Castaway Creek usually prevents overheating but do remember your sunscreen. There are height restrictions (4ft/122cm) on Humunga Kowabunga and Crush 'n' Gusher and they're not suitable for anyone with a bad back or neck, or expectant mothers.

Shopping: You can buy anything you have forgotten – even a swimsuit – at **Singapore Sal's**. You CAN'T bring your own snorkels, inner tubes or rafts, but inner tubes are provided on Castaway Creek.

Dining: Lowtide Lou's and **Let's Go Slurpin'** both offer snacks and drinks, while **Typhoon Tilly's** and **Leaning Palms** serve a decent mix of sandwiches, burgers, salads and ice-cream. **Happy Landings Ice Cream** offers tasty root beer floats, sundaes and other treats. Avoid main mealtimes if you want to eat in relative comfort. You can bring your own picnic (unlike the main parks), although no alcohol or glass.

Disney's Blizzard Beach Water Park

Ever imagined a skiing resort in the middle of Florida? Well, here it is. This park opened in 1995 and is still the largest, with all 66acres/27ha arranged as if it were in the Rocky Mountains rather than the subtropics! That means snow-effect scenery, Christmas trees and waterslides cunningly converted to look like skiing pistes and toboggan runs. The same 'premium' offer at Typhoon Lagoon applies here for two beach loungers, two towels, an umbrella and a small table for $70. Or, if the price doesn't scare you off completely, you can hire a Polar Patio (cabaña), which includes a locker, drinks mug, cooler with ice, bottled water, towels, loungers and table, and waiter service. Full day rental, accommodating up to eight, is $340 (admission not included). Reserve in advance on 407 939 7529.

Admission: $69 adults, $63 3–9s (under-3s free); included with Disney Magic tickets; lockers $10–15; parking free; 11am-6pm, hours vary seasonally. TTTTT AAAAA

BRITTIP

Adjacent to Blizzard Beach are the amazing Winter Summerland Miniature Golf Courses (where Santa's elves hang out!), with two elaborate courses that are a great diversion for children (p250).

Slides and rides: Main features are **Mount Gushmore**, a 90ft/27m mountain down which all the main slides run. A ski chair-lift operates to the top, providing a magnificent view. Don't miss the outstanding rides, including the world's tallest free-fall speed slide, the terrifying 120ft/37m **Summit Plummet**, which rockets you down a 'ski jump' at up to 60mph/97kph. For those not quite up to the big drop, the brilliantly named **Slush Gusher** is a slightly less terrifying body slide. Then there is **Teamboat Springs**, a wild family inner-tube adventure and arguably the best of all the water rides; **Runoff Rapids**, a choice of three tube plunges; **Snow Stormers**, a daring head-first 'toboggan' run; and **Toboggan Racers**, the chance to speed down the 'slopes' against seven other head-first riders. All four

provide good-sized thrills without overdoing the scare factor. The side-by-side **Downhill Double Dipper** tubes send you down 230ft/70m tubes in a timed race, with a real jolt half-way down! **Tike's Peak** is a kiddie-sized version of the park's slides and a mock snow-beach, and **Ski-Patrol Training Camp** is a series of challenges and slides for pre-teens.

Melt-Away Bay is a 1acre/0.4ha pool fed by 'melting snow' (actually blissfully warm), and **Cross Country Creek** is a lazy-flowing 1½ml/800m river round the whole park that also floats guests through a chilly 'ice cave' (look out for the ice-water waterfalls!).

Shopping and dining: There is a 'village' area with a **Beach Haus** shop and **Lottawatta Lodge** fast-food restaurant (pizzas, burgers, salads and sandwiches), offering a grandstand view of Mount Gushmore. Snacks are also available at **Avalunch** (ouch!), the **Warming Hut**, **Polar Pub** and **Frostbite Freddie's Frozen Refreshments**.

Volcano Bay
This Universal park boasts a clever South Seas theme and a novel range of attractions and experiences, plus the free TapuTapu queue-beating system that allow guests to reserve a return time for most rides.

Admission: $109–159 adults, $104–154 3–9s seasonally (under-3s free; included with the UK 3-Park Explorer Ticket); 10am–6, 7 or 8pm daily. TTTTT/AAAAA

Crowned by the iconic Krakatau, the 28acre/11.3ha park features four main areas, with a huge central lagoon and an outstanding mix of attractions. The centrepiece is a 200ft/60m volcano, which erupts with 100ft/30m jets of water throughout the day. More than anything, though, this is a scenic triumph, and it offers many places just to sit back and enjoy the view (with a choice beverage or two!).

Every guest gets a TapuTapu wristband, and you use this to secure ride times at all the main attractions, with the band letting you know when it is time to ride. While you wait, you are free to play in the wave pool or lazy rivers, go for a drink or something to eat, or just chill out on the beach. Like with Universal's theme parks, you can also buy the skip-the-main-queue Universal Express pass for most attractions for $20–130.

Slides and rides: The **Volcano** area features the headline ride of **Krakatau Aqua Coaster**, four person 'canoes' that zoom into and around the volcano; the 70-degree trap-door drop of **Ko'okiri Body Plunge**; the **Kola and Ta Nui Serpentine Body Slides,** which drop two riders at a time down a pair of intertwined tubes; and **Punga Racers**, a four-lane mat plunge through underwater sea caves.

BRITTIP

There are lots of stairs to the entry to most slides, and much of the queuing is not covered, so apply high factor waterproof sun cream often.

No water park would be complete without a lazy river, and Volcano Bay boasts two. **Kopiko Wai** provides a lush, tropical float past pretty scenery and partially hidden lounge areas, while **TeAwa The Fearless River** is a fun, faster-moving river, with rapids and sudden waves to navigate.

Rainforest Village is the biggest area of the park, with four main attractions, including **TeAwa**, and **Taniwha Tubes**, a series of four flumes (two Tonga and two Raki) with crazily twisted tracks and mischievous statues that spray water at riders. The main attraction is the six-person **Maku Puihi Round Raft Ride**, while the **Ohyah** and **Ohno Drop Slides** each end with a significant drop into the pool below!

River Village offers water-play areas, **Tot Tiki Reef** and **Runamukka Reef**, with child-sized slides and pop-jets to keep the young 'uns happy. Finally, **Wave Village** features **Waturi Beach** wave pool and **The Reef** serene pool, to round out the offerings. Oh, and don't miss the chance to use your TapuTapu to activate a variety of interactive moments, from firing water cannons at riders on the lazy river to taking selfies at a tiki photo booth.

You can hire tiki-hut style cabanas with towels, locker, loungers, fruit and snacks, and mini-fridge with water starting at $160 single cabana (up to 6) or from $600 for a family suite (up to 16), per day. Cabanas also come with a handy tablet that allows you to book and modify your ride times rather than having to visit them individually. You can also hire two loungers with a shade canopy and lockbox for $30–140. To save time, sign up in advance for the Universal Orlando Resort App so you can add paying privileges to your TapuTapu wristband (**bit.ly/ brit-uni**).

Shopping and dining: Each Village has its own high-quality dining outlet, and there are two themed boat bars with cocktails and craft beers (including Volcano Blossom tropical fruit pilsner). Signature restaurant **Kohola Reef**, and tropical **Whakawaiwai Eats**, **Bambu**, and **The Feasting Frog** serve healthy island-inspired dishes, notably a coconut chicken curry with plantains. Four smart shops complete a pretty picture.

Taniwha Tubes at Volcano Bay

© Universal Orlando Resort

Aquatica by SeaWorld

This eye-catching water park has a wonderful range of children's attractions and facilities, innovative rides and an all-you-can-eat-meal option, spread over 59acres/24ha of South Seas-inspired landscaping.

Admission: $95 ages 3 and up; 2-Park Ticket (with SeaWorld) $190; (discounts with online booking; included with UK 2-and 3-Park tickets); parking $30, preferred parking $40, locker rental $15 and $20, towels $7; 9am–8pm (summer) or 10 or 10.30am–5pm (winter, spring and autumn; **aquatica.com**) TTTT AAAAA

Additionally, you can get **QuickQueue Unlimited** (priority boarding on the most popular rides at peak periods for $49–79) and **Unlimited Plus** (unlimited boarding plus a one-time QuickQueue on Ray Rush and Walhalla Wave for $59–99). The **Commerson's Close-Up** tour then adds a chance to join the park's zoological experts for a one-of-a-kind meeting with the playful Commerson's dolphins ($40–70).

Slides and rides: Aquatica's signature attraction is the new **Reef Plunge** (4ft/122cm), a twin body slide that sends riders down 330ft/100m of tubes past an underwater habitat featuring playful black-and-white Commerson's dolphins, sharks and fish. You can then view the Dolphins at the end of the ride through the huge lagoon window. Another standout attraction is **Ihu's Breakaway Falls,** with three enclosed tubes featuring break-away floors (complete with heartbeat effect while you're waiting for the drop!) and one outrageous non-breakaway tube that is every bit as scary. Each offers a completely different slide. **Whanau Way** is a quadruple raft ride with two distinct variations that twist and turn before landing with a resounding splash, while **Tassie's Twisters** are double bowl rides that send riders down single or double tubes into giant bowls before splashing back into the **Loggerhead Lane** lazy river (which also has a coral reef viewing section). **Taumata Racer** (3ft 6in/107cm) is a fast-paced mat slide set up like an

eight-lane racing toboggan run, partly enclosed and then with a double drop into daylight (queues can look long here but they usually move quickly). Family raft ride **Walhalla Wave** features a winding, enclosed section before a big splash finale while **Ray Rush** is a thrilling family raft ride in three distinct sections, featuring a fast-launch start followed by a massive water sphere and then a hilarious plunge into an open-air half-pipe before the final splashdown (**R.** 3.5ft/104cm).

Omaka Rocka features two high-speed single-rider tube flumes, each with three sets of funnels that send you coursing up one side and down the other with a sensational 'feel it in your tummy' weightlessness before final splash-down. New in 2019 was **Karekare Curl** double raft ride that plummets down an enclosed tube, then climbs a massive vertical "wave" wall on its way to the splash-down zone (4ft/122cm). **Big Surf Shores** wave pool offers big dynamic waves, while sister wave-pool **Cutback Cove** features gentler rolling surf. A huge sandy beach offers a large array of sun loungers and umbrellas, and private cabañas (from $79–349 in low season, depending on location, to the Ultimate Cabaña, including upgraded furniture, dining table and a second cabana with couch, coffee table and additional seating for up to eight, at $199–899 seasonally). Call 407 545 5550 to book or go online.

New in 2021 was **Riptide Race**, the world's tallest duelling race slide, featuring two-person rafts atop a 68ft tower that speed down a pair of side-by-side flumes. The slides offer a series of tunnels, twists and turns, allowing racers to duel it out all the way to the splashdown (**R.** 3ft 6in/107cm).

BRITTIP

Head for the Beach area when you first arrive to stake out a place to base yourselves and try to grab one of the bigger fixed umbrellas that offer the most shade.

As well as the gentle **Loggerhead Lane** (under 4ft/122cm must wear life vest), you should try the dynamic **Roa's Rapids** (under 51in/129cm must wear a life vest), which provides a helter-skelter whirl along this river feature, with a series of fountains, jets and other watery boosts to keep you bobbing along with no effort.

Free life vests are on offer here and it is worth trying one for the feeling of floating along in high style!

Kids' features: The big success of the park, though, is its extensive features for children, from the youngest to young teens. **Kata's Kookaburra**

Cove is an exclusive area for those under 4ft/1.2m tall, with a whole range of scaled-down slides, rides, pools and fountains to provide a gentler experience for the young 'uns. By contrast, **Walkabout Waters** is a vast and frenzied 60ft/18m-high water play structure with every kind of climb, slide and water eruptions and outpourings, including two giant buckets that fill and dump in spectacular fashion over those below.

Shopping and dining: The imaginative **Kiwi Traders** is the biggest of the shops, but **Adaptations** is also worth a look for jewellery, accessories and apparel. For dining, try **Waterstone Grill** (chicken sandwiches, burgers, salads and wraps), **Mango Market** (hot dogs, chicken tenders, salads and sweet treats), **Papa's Cantina** (empanadas, wings) or **Banana Beach Cookout** buffet (BBQ ribs, burgers, pulled port and chicken, plus desserts, drinks and kid's meals; All-Day Dining Deal $45 adults, $25 ages 3–9). There are also two bars serving cocktails and beer.

Aquatica features unique elements in Roa's Rapids, Ray Rush, Riptide Race and Kookaburra Cove. And, if you buy the two-park ticket with SeaWorld, it's great value in summer, with the day in Aquatica and then the sister park for the evening.

That's the large-scale attractions, but let's explore some alternatives to the mass-market experience ....

Reef Plunge at Aquatica

© Universal Orlando Resort

8 Off the Beaten Track

Or, When You're All Theme-Parked Out

Orlando's main attractions are undoubtedly a lot of fun, but they can also be tiring and you may need a break from all the hectic theme-park activity. Or you may be visiting again and looking for a different experience. Either way, this chapter is for you.

This chapter could easily be subtitled 'A Taste of the Real Florida', as it introduces the towns of Winter Park, Winter Garden, Celebration and Mount Dora, plus natural delights like the state parks, day-trips and eco-tours.

ORLANDO/Orange County

Winter Park: Foremost among the 'secret' hideaways is this elegant northern city suburb, little more than 30mins yet a world away from the frenzy of I-Drive. The 'real' Orlando in many ways, with museums, art galleries, boutique shops, restaurants, a delightful 50min boat ride around the lakes and, above all, a chance to slow down. The dining and shopping are all one-offs, there are superb annual festivals and a great sidewalk café vibe (**cityofwinterpark.org/visitors**).

Morse Museum of American Art: A must for admirers of American art pottery, American and European glass, furniture and other decorative arts of the late 19th and early 20th centuries, as this beautiful museum includes the world's foremost collection of works by Louis Comfort Tiffany. It also has special Christmas exhibitions and periodic family programmes. (**morsemuseum.org**).

Park Avenue: The heart of Winter Park is a classy street of restaurants, shops and a shaded park. For shops both unique and fun, look for **Lilly Pulitzer** (women's clothing), **Ten Thousand Villages** (international arts and crafts), and the **Writer's Block** bookshop, plus **Peterbrooke Chocolatier**. Street parking allows 3hrs free, but the Truist Plaza car park on E. Lyman Ave is a good all-day option.

> **BRITTIP**
>
> Want to see gators in the wild? Lake **Apopka Wildlife Drive** offers a great look at local wetlands with its many gators and abundant birdlife. It takes a good 1hr to complete the drive and there are plenty of stopping points. Open Fri–Sun dawn to dusk; free (**sjrwmd.com/lands/recreation/lake-apopka**).

Scenic Boat Tour: On East Morse Boulevard, this offers a charming 50min narrated tour for a fascinating look at the local lakes, canals and fabulous houses (several of which top $10m!). Tours run every hour 10am–4pm daily (not Christmas), cash only (**scenicboattours.com**).

A dining delight

Winter Park boasts some of Orlando's finest dining. **310 Park South** is the epitome of elegant, European café culture while pavement bistro **Briarpatch** (breakfast and lunch) and Italian-style **Pannullo's** are worth sampling. The gorgeous **Ravenous Pig** has a wide-ranging choice, from its fine microbrewery to steaks and seafood (**theravenouspig.com**). Or try neighbourhood bar-kitchen-market **Boca** (**bocawp.com**) and the fun Southern-style fast-food joint of **The COOP** (**asouthernaffair.com**). For more variety, seek out any of **Garp & Fuss** (**garpandfuss.com**), or **Prato**, a wildly popular Italian 'gastropub' with superb home-made pastas and pizza (**prato-wp. com**). **Hamilton's Kitchen** at the ritzy Alfond Inn combines fresh food and creative cuisine for a great lunch or dinner (p295). **Hillstone** is also an elegant choice (p297); and local barbecue institution **4 Rivers Smokehouse** is practically essential (p295). Find more at **winterpark.org/list/ql/restaurants-food-beverages-22**.

Winter Garden: A taste of small-town America 18ml/28km north of Disney, its historic district along Plant Street consists of boutique shops and cafés, plus the chic Garden Theatre (**gardentheatre.org**). There are two small museums, an art centre, splash fountains for children to play in, walking and cycling paths on the West Orange Trail and Farmers' Market every Sat (8am–1pm). For dining, Urban On Plant, **Moon Cricket Grille**, vegetarian-friendly **Market To Table**, **Thai Blossom** and the **Chef's Table at The Edgewater** are all highly recommended, along with the new **Hangry Bison** and **Mangoni's Italian Market**, while **Plant Street Market** boasts the fab **Crooked Can Brewing Co** among a variety of fresh food and crafts kiosks (**plantstmarket.com**). Parking is free and there is a lot for the casual wanderer to enjoy (**cwgdn.com**).

MOUNT DORA/Lake County

To the west and north of Orlando is this large, rural county, home to unspoiled Florida charms.

Mount Dora: This smallish town on beautiful Lake Dora is one of Florida's hidden gems. Renowned as a festival city, with 19 annual galas, check your dates on **mountdora.com** (4 July and Christmas are notable, while the April Sail Boat Regatta is one of Florida's finest). Start with a stroll around the quaint shops, cafés and bars in the compact centre. Antique hunters are spoiled for choice but should visit **Village Antique Mall**, with more than 80 vendors, and **Renninger's Vintage Antique Center** (weekends only).

Premier Boat Tours: See more via the *Captain Doolittle* from the Lakeside Inn for a fascinating eco-tour of the beautiful lakes and Dora Canal. Along with gators, you may see raccoons, turtles, otters, birds of prey and other nesting birds, with narrated 2hr tours daily and 1hr Sunset Tours (bring your favourite beverages; reservations required; **doracanaltour.com**).

More info: mountdora.com.

Lake Louisa State Park: Another gem just off Highway 27 (at the west end of Highway 192), the park offers lovely countryside with lakes and rolling hills. There are miles of hiking trails, a picnic pavilion, swimming in Lake Louisa (with lifeguards late May–Aug), plus 20 cabins, sleeping up to six (**floridastateparks.org/park/Lake-Louisa**). Further up Highway 27 is the **Citrus Tower**, built in 1956, with panoramic views from its 22-storey glass observation deck (**citrustower. com**); and **Lakeridge Winery**, which produces some award-winning wines, with free tours and tastings (**lakeridgewinery.com**).

Revolution Adventures: Perfect for families seeking to enjoy the real Florida, this is set in 220acres/89ha

Mount Dora dining

Try a leisurely lunch at the excellent **Copacabana Cuban Café** or **One Flight Up**. **Village Coffee Pot** is the place for coffee and the **Windsor Rose** is an English tea-room. For something stronger, visit **Tremain's Tavern** or **Magical Meat Boutique**. All also offer dinner, but our top four – especially at sunset – are **Pisces Rising**, a lovely Key West-themed restaurant, with a grandstand view of sunsets over Lake Dora, plus fresh Florida seafood and steaks (**piscesrisingdining. com**); sister restaurant **Back Porch Pizza Bar**, for fresh poke bowls, pizza and cocktails (**backporchpizzabar.com**); the charming **Goblin Market** bistro tucked away in a quiet corner of town (**goblinmarketrestaurant.com**); and **1921**, a modern gourmet take on classic Floridian fare with a genuine farm-to-table philosophy, all set in a converted 1920s home (**1921mountdora.com**).

of glorious countryside with a private lake. Whatever the weather, you'll get dirty, so wear old clothes and close-toed shoes or trainers. Central Florida's top off-road adventure park, the fishing lake was also named as one of the top 10 private lakes. Their signature self-drive, guided **ATV** (quad bike) and off-road **Buggy** tours (18 or older with photo ID to drive, but no licence required) start with a safety briefing, then it's off over the sandhills and grasslands on dirt trails and tracks. On the self-drive **Mucky Duck** tour, the amphibious vehicles seat up to four passengers and include training in the Argo UTVs, then a drive around the trails and into the main lake. Drivers must be at least 18 with a full licence, and passengers as young as 2 (with safety vest; must sit upright unaided). You can also take to the water on a 45-minute **Sea Doo** jet ski session (with life vest; 3 jet skis on the lake at one time; ages 16 or older with valid ID). They also feature **Archery Tag**, **Target Archery** on an Olympic range, **Clay Shooting**, for over 15s, and **Fishing** for large trophy bass. Reservations required on 352 400 1322 or **revolutionoffroad.com**.

OSCEOLA COUNTY

Here's where to find some of Kissimmee's most scenic natural attractions.

Balloon trips

You'll often see hot air balloons in Osceola County. The smooth lift-off is breathtaking, and the tranquillity and stunning views are awesome. It's not cheap, but it is appealing to all but young children or those with a fear of heights. It can also be highly personal, with baskets starting at four people.

Bob's Balloons: With more than 20 years' experience, Bob's Balloons fly every day, weather permitting, covering much of central Florida including parts of Disney. The experience lasts roughly 3hrs, with a 1hr flight and champagne brunch on landing. Baskets carry 4–6 people, and hotel pick-ups can be arranged. There are discounts for children and rebookings are offered for all cancellations, while owner Bob Wilamoski is even licensed to perform pre–flight weddings! (**bobsballoons.com**).

Airboat rides

Like flying at ground level, these can be experienced on many of Florida's waterways, but especially in Osceola County. You can explore areas otherwise inaccessible to boats, skimming over the marshes to give you an alternative, close-up view. It can be loud (you will be given ear protectors) and sunglasses are also a good idea to deter stray flies. In summer, a good insect repellent is essential.

BRITTIP
Bring your own good sunblock for any outdoor activity, even in winter.

Winter Park Scenic Boat Tour

© Scenic Boat Tours

Boggy Creek Airboat Rides: About a 35min drive down Poinciana Boulevard, **Southport Park** feels a million miles from the tourist areas and you can also enjoy the authentic Native American Village and Boggy Bottom BBQ restaurant and Tiki Bar. Boats every 30mins so no need to book (bcairboats.com).

Wild Florida: A superb operation on tranquil Cypress Lake, this airboat ride and wildlife reserve features 30min, one-hour and night-time rides from their purpose-built dock (a great place for wildlife watching) with the chance to see gators, turtles, birdlife and even snakes from the safety of their six and 17-passenger airboats. It also features a 13acre/5.2ha **Alligator Park** home to their growing collection of lemurs, sloths, raccoons, bobcats and more, as well as the feature crocodiles and alligators, including two rare albino gators. You can feed some of the animals (for a small fee) and there is an excellent gift shop, in addition to an aviary and a peaceful cypress swamp walk. The yummy **Chomp House Grill** is then ideal for a snack or lunch. The must-see element these days, though, is the 270acre/109ha drive-through **Safari Park**, featuring 100+ exotic animals like zebras, giraffes and watusi cattle all rubbing shoulders with local white-tail deer and cracker cattle, beside a gator pond (with nuisance gators relocated by the Florida Fish & Wildlife Conservation Commission). And you can enjoy it from the comfort of your car!

Riding with the Lazy H Ranch

BRITTIP

For a real Florida dining experience after visiting Wild Florida or the Lazy H (see below), Take Highway 192 in St Cloud to The Catfish Place, a locals' hotspot serving specialities like catfish, gator and turtle (plus steaks, chicken and shellfish). It's as authentic as it gets – see thecatfishplacestcloud.com.

Booking is advisable but they do go out regularly from 9am–4:30pm Mon–Sat (closed Sun). We're big fans of Wild Florida's dedication to providing a home for rescued animals, and their commitment to showcasing wildlife with a conservation message (wildfloridairboats.com).

Paddling, climbing and horse-riding

Kissimmee Paddling Center: Get up close with Osceola County nature, with kayaks, canoes and paddleboards here on Highway 192. Shingle Creek forms the headwaters of the Everglades and is a peaceful haven, perfect for a 1hr or half-day paddling adventure. You can just turn up but it's better to book (paddlingcenter.com).

Orlando Tree Trek: Adventure-seekers will want to try this challenging aerial ropes course in a forest south of Disney. There are two kids' courses and four for ages 12+, from beginner to advanced, plus a giant zipline to finish. There is a full instruction session, then it is off into the treetops for obstacles ranging from short ziplines to cargo nets, ladders, cable bridges, Tarzan swings and more (orlandotreetrek.com).

Lazy H Ranch: For a horse-back view of the Osceola County countryside, head to this wonderful family-owned ranch in rural Kissimmee. It can accommodate up to six, by reservation only, for trail rides of 1–1½hrs. You may even spot a gator or two lurking in the lake! The trail rides operate year-round (see website for age and weight restrictions; lazyhranch.net).

A cause for Celebration

Dining in Celebration is a real highlight. Spanish-Cuban **Columbia** uses unique combinations of authentic ingredients (**columbiarestaurant.com**); **Celebration Town Tavern**, a casual ambiance, featuring New England seafood; **Ari Sushi** for sushi and hibachi dishes; and the **Imperium Food & Wine** is an excellent option for fine wines and cocktails, plus tempting light bites, (**facebook. com/imperiumfoodandwine**). Also try the **Lakeside Bar & Grill** at the Bohemian Hotel, a contemporary steakhouse with old-world charm; and **Kilwins** is great for chocolate and ice-cream.

Celebration

In 1994, Disney set out to build a 'new urban' neighbourhood, a model community with a friendly spirit and strong traditional values. The result was Celebration, where picture-perfect homes and smart town-houses mingle with an array of shopping, dining and entertainment options. On Disney's southern border off Highway 192, enter at the water tower via Celebration Ave, then follow signs to the Bohemian Hotel in the centre.

BRITTIP

For all the Celebration festivals and special events, be sure to look online at **https://celebrationtowncenter.com/** and see the latest Shopping and Dining options.

Market Street: Look out for delightful boutiques, miles of bike and walking paths with a pretty lakefront setting, children's play area and periodic festivals. A huge event is held on American Independence Day, July 4, with picnics, entertainment and face-painting, while the Christmas period also sees festive events and nightly snowfall on Market Street. Parking for big events is at the town entrance, with a park-and-ride bus.

Osceola County History Center & Pioneer Village

Highway 192 (just by Marker 15) features the **Osceola County Welcome Center** and **History Museum**, a collaboration between the County and Historical Society, providing a small-scale but engaging look at the area's history and nature. There is a 'steamboat' entryway inside, then a tour of local history from 1867 to the present, through the four main 'habitats' with tableaux and nature exhibits that depict central Florida nature, plus the original Indian tribes. Outside, you can wander along Shingle Creek, the headwaters of The Everglades. Free admission.

Then, head for nearby **Pioneer Village**, off Highway 192 on Babb Road. This delightful discovery pays homage to 19th-century Florida life, with a preserved 'cracker' homestead, blacksmith shop, Seminole Village and buildings portraying how settlers lived in the 1880s. Tours are self-guided, or with a volunteer, providing a fascinating view of life more than 130 years ago (**osceolahistory.org**).

Cracker house at the Pioneer Village

© osceolahistory.org

POLK COUNTY

Head south from Kissimmee/Osceola County and you head into Polk territory, another of Florida's oldest-established and most authentic areas. It is home to the large-scale attractions of LEGOLAND Florida (p211) but also has its share of off-the-beaten-track experiences.

Bok Tower Gardens

This national monument and garden centre at Lake Wales, 50ml/80km south-west of Orlando, boasts one of the most unusual attractions in the state – a majestic 205ft/62.5m pink-and-grey marble Carillon Tower. Set in 50acres/101ha of parkland, the Singing Tower, a 1920s-built carillon, is the centrepiece and concerts are given every day at 1 and 3pm.

Gardens: Around the Tower is a wide moat, a pond and semi-formal gardens with a wildlife observatory, nature trails, endangered plant exhibit, butterfly and woodland gardens and pine forests. There is a children's garden, plus brass rubbing and family-friendly guided tours.

Pinewood Estate: For an additional fee you can tour the Mediterranean-style architecture in this 20-room mansion, built as a winter retreat for a Pennsylvania steel tycoon in the early 1930s (**boktowergardens.org**).

Lake Wales

Continue on to the Lake Wales area after Bok Tower Gardens and you encounter some other local gems.

Westgate River Ranch: In rural Polk County is this superb ranch and activity centre that boasts great accommodations (including 'glamping' for those who like to camp in style, plus Luxe Tepees and stand-alone Saddle Club Rail Cars) and the chance to try horse-riding, fishing, airboating, trap shooting and archery, as well as take in the Saturday night **Westgate Rodeo** in the 1,200-seat arena or sample fine dining Cattle Company steakhouse. Visit just for the day to try any of the activities or the weekly rodeo (followed by live music, line dancing and a family-friendly Street Party), but the accommodations are excellent and you can sample the River Ranch Saloon without having to drive afterwards – guaranteed family fun and a taste of Florida's genuine cowboy country (**westgatedestinations. com** and click on Menu, then River Ranch, FL).

Westgate River Ranch swamp buggy

SEMINOLE COUNTY

Orange County's northern neighbour boasts the historic city of Sanford plus a wide array of options to get you well off the beaten track. If you want to finish your holiday with a day or so in the area, there are many good hotel choices (often significantly cheaper than their big-name rivals elsewhere) and, after all the hectic theme-parking, you can catch your breath here in Orlando North, as they like to call it!

Adventures in Florida: Get into the wilds with this specialist company that features kayaking tours along the picturesque Econlockhatchee and Wekiva rivers with expert guides. They offer 2–5hr trips, all-day tours and even night-time paddles, manatee encounters and bioluminescent tours. You may encounter gators, manatees, turtles and all manner of birdlife, but must book in advance (**adventuresinflorida.com**).

Central Florida Zoological Park: This private, non-profit organisation is a natural zoo, set in a wooded 116acres/47ha of unspoilt countryside with boardwalks and trails around more than 100 species of animal, with weekend feeding demonstrations, giraffe feeding and children's barnyard zoo, plus a train ride, carousel and Tropical Splash Ground water play area. Also try **Seminole Aerial Adventures,** a separate series of eco-friendly rope bridges, ziplines, guide wires and other aerial challenges through the Zoo's treetops. (**centralfloridazoo.org**).

BRITTIP

Keeper Chats and Demonstrations take place daily throughout Central Florida Zoo, with fun insights into the park's animals, including rhinos, cheetahs, warthogs, gators and more.

Sanford: The heart of Seminole County, this quaint town on Lake Monroe boasts a historic centre full of brick-paved streets, antique shops, a sophisticated array of dining and several great micro-breweries. Part of its heritage is on display with the

St John's Rivership Co, an authentic sternwheel paddle-boat that offers 3–4hr lunch cruises (and some Sat evenings), with a huge array of food and live music (**stjohnsrivershipco.com**). In the evening, stop for a bite on First Street, with its many restored turn-of-the-century buildings. **Hollerbach's Willow Tree Café** is a German diner featuring traditional food, beers and live music (**willowtreecafe. com**). **The Imperial** is an antique store by day and a fabulous bar by night, with cocktails and craft beers (**imperialwinebar.com**). There are also five brew-pubs or micro-breweries, of which the **Sanford Brewing Company** is a great example on S. Sanford Ave (**sanfordbrewing.com**).

The second Thurs each month (not July and Aug) in Sanford features the **Alive After Five** street party 5–8pm on First Street, with music, street artists, restaurant samples and more. Admission is free, food and drink extra.

Elev8 Fun: New in 2022, this huge indoor entertainment centre boasts go-karts, 10-pin bowling, arcade games, ropes course, laser tag, mini-golf and more (**elev8fun.com**).

State Parks: Get back to nature at one of the splendid parks and enjoy their well-marked trails. **Wekiva Springs State Park** offers bike rentals, hiking, canoeing, swimming, picnic areas and shelters, and **Little Big Econ** state forest has 5,048acres/2,045ha of scenic woodlands and wetlands. **Spring Hammock Preserve** offers 1,500acres/607ha of wilderness and the **Lake Proctor Wilderness Area** has 6ml/10km of equestrian, hiking and biking adventures.

Wekiva Island: This fabulous outdoor recreation area is almost a rustic resort in its own right, gorgeously located right on the Wekiva River, with a bar, food servery, and kayak, canoe and paddle-board rentals. The paddling along this stretch of the river is truly serene. It is popular right through the summer, especially at weekends, so aim for weekday mornings (**wekivaisland.com**).

More info: doorlandonorth.com.

WEST VOLUSIA COUNTY

Between Seminole County and Daytona Beach is this enticing piece of Florida real estate with a growing range of attractions and eco-tours, plus an eclectic mix of shops, restaurants and breweries. It makes for a great day-trip from Orlando (or an even better over-night stay), less than an hour along I-4.

Start in the quaint town of **DeLand**, with its historic downtown, museums, boutiques and brew-pubs (notably Persimmon Hollow Brewing Co), plus a great series of annual events (**mainstreetdeland.org**). **Blue Springs State Park** is home to more manatee encounters, plus fishing, boating and kayaking, while eco-adventures are also on offer at **DeLeon Springs State Park**, which boasts the Old Spanish Sugar Mill (p253). For something completely different, the spiritualist camp of **Cassadaga** is a true original (**cassadaga.org**), and fab 19th-century treasure **Stetson Mansion** is open to the public (reservations required on **stetsonmansion.com**).

St Johns River Eco-Tours: At Highbanks Marina & Camp in Debary is this wonderful chance to experience the beautiful St Johns River, with a 2hr pontoon boat ride. You will gain expert insight into the flora and fauna as well as seeing birdlife, gators, turtles and even manatees. There is free bottled water and a restroom on board (**stjohnsriverecotours.com**). You can also enjoy dining at the fun **Swamp House Riverfront Grill**, with an elevated view of the river and marina and the chance to sample catfish and gator nuggets (**swamphousegrill.com**).

More info: visitwestvolusia.com.

BRITTIP
While the **Stetson Mansion** is superb at any time of year, it is jaw-droppingly stunning for the Christmas period (early Nov to mid–Jan), when the whole house is decorated in the most elaborate and spectacular fashion.

CITRUS COUNTY

For a great day out, we heartily recommend visiting this area on the Gulf Coast, and especially the city – and wildlife – of Crystal River.

Crystal River Preserve State Park: Just north of Homosassa Springs, the Crystal River is home to the endangered manatee and it is possible to go swimming with these wonderful creatures, either on a self-guided or an organised tour. Mid-November to the end of March is manatee 'season', but the park offers year-round adventure, with hiking and biking trails, kayaking, canoeing and fishing – or just pack a picnic lunch and enjoy a relaxing afternoon amid the natural beauty. The park hosts the annual **Florida Manatee Festival** each Jan, with an impressive variety of family-friendly activities and events (**gomanateefest. com**). You can also catch a relaxing and educational ride with **Heritage Eco-Tours** aboard the 24-passenger *Monroe* for a unique 1½hr look at local history and wildlife (seasonally, Sept–May, weather permitting; cash only; call to confirm on 352 228 6028).

Admission into the park is free (**floridastateparks.org/parks-and-trails/ crystal-river-preserve-state-park**).

BRITTIP
Manatees are protected and there are heavy fines, strictly enforced, for disturbing or harassing them.

For something really different in Crystal River, try **Scalloping**. From July to late September, visitors can snorkel along the extensive grass flats in 4–6ft/1.2–1.8m of water and collect scallops with a net. It is a unique experience, and they also make for great eating! **River Safaris** are a top company for scalloping tours, among a fab range of eco-adventures (**riversafaris.com**).

Homosassa Springs Wildlife State Park: This park also showcases the manatee (via its underwater observatory), plus whooping cranes, deer, bobcats, black bear and even a hippopotamus among an active display of rehabilitating animals. There are daily programmes on its wildlife, plus a hands-on children's education centre. The park's 210acres/85ha take in some of the state's loveliest landscape, plus the headwaters of the Homosassa River, which is extremely popular in the spring (**floridastateparks.org/parks-and-trails/ellie-schiller-homosassa-springs-wildlife-state-park**).

Where to stay: In the heart of Citrus County is the **Plantation on Crystal River**, a mansion-esque resort in Kings Bay right on the river, featuring lovely rooms, great dining, golf and its own manatee eco-tours, as well as lashings of Southern hospitality. (**plantationoncrystalriver.com**).

More info: discovercrystalriverfl.com.

BREVARD COUNTY

Out on the Atlantic coast is Cocoa Beach's Thousand Islands, where tranquil canals wind past mangrove stands and wildlife flourishes in the still waters. Indian River Lagoon Estuary is one of the most biodiverse eco-systems in the world.

Cocoa Beach Dolphin Tours: Formerly Island Boat Line, this family-owned enterprise offers eco-tours, fishing and the wonderful *Indian River Queen* dinner boat, recalling Mark Twain's tales of paddleboats and peaceful gentility. A relaxing 2hr **In Search of Wildlife** eco-tour on Coast Guard-certified pontoon boats departs from the Sunset Waterfront Bar & Grill on Highway 520. Here you may spot bottlenose dolphins, manatees and coastal birds. There is a daily **Sunset Cruise** from 7–8.30pm (**islandboatlines.com**).

Indian River Queen: Also used for private events, this beautiful triple-deck paddlewheel riverboat is open to the public at weekends, with an elegant **Dinner Cruise** one Fri each month featuring live music, dinner buffet and full bar. Owners Penny and John provide authentic Southern hospitality. Boarding begins at 6.30pm, sailing from 7–9.15pm. The **Sunday Scenic River Cruise** offers 2hr tours with live music, select dates only, 2pm boarding, 2.30–4.30pm sailing (booking required on 321 302 0545 or **indianriverqueen.com**).

The scenic Indian River Estuary on the Cocoa Beach Dolphin Tours

© Space Coast Office of Tourism

EXCURSION OPERATORS

For those without a car, there are tours and day trips visiting as far afield as the Everglades, Miami, Florida Keys and even the Bahamas. You can see a lot if you don't mind a long day (up to 16 hours). However, if the main attraction of a trip to the Everglades is the airboat ride, you are better off going to Wild Florida (p242).

BRITTIP

Use the promo code on the back cover for your exclusive 15% discount with all **Brit Guide** partner Gray Line excursions.

Gray Line Tours: Orlando's biggest excursion company and a *Brit Guide* partner, offering 15% off all tours, from transport-only trips to Kennedy Space Centre to all-day tours to the Everglades or limo pick-ups for Disney character dining; all with air-con coaches and knowledgeable guides. See options at **graylineorlando.com**.

Kennedy Space Center: The KSC can be combined with an airboat ride, Dine With An Astronaut experience, or Small Group VIP Experience for maximum access to the centre. **1-Day Miami:** Long day-trip to Florida's biggest city. **Wild Florida:** Combine the tour in different ways, from transport and airboat ride, to Drive-Thru Safari Adventure admission and Ultimate Package. **City Tour of Orlando:** Enjoy the highlights of downtown, Lake Eola, Winter Park – with boat ride – Disney Springs and more on this epic 6.5hr tour. **St Augustine:** Great day-trip to the Colonial Quarter; see Castillo de San Marcos from a boat tour and ride the hop-on, hop-off trolley. **Clearwater Beach:** A day-trip to one of Florida's best beaches plus the Clearwater Marine Aquarium, dolphin cruise, Captain Memo's Pirate Cruise or Sea Screamer powerboat. **Swim where the Manatees live:** A rare opportunity to swim and snorkel among the manatees of Crystal River.

City Sightseeing Orlando: This British-owned company offers several dozen tours, notably swimming with manatees, Gatorland and airboats, and beaches. No. 1 is the **Florida Adventure Tour:** Breakfast, a 2hr pontoon trip (with snorkel to see the manatees), picnic lunch, airboat ride and trip to Homosassa State Wildlife Park (**citysightseeingorlando.com**).

Real Florida Adventures: A new company in 2020, they specialise in signature adventure experiences like air-boating with Wild Florida and swimming with manatees, plus trips to the Kennedy Space Center (with five different options) and Clearwater Beach (six distinct choices, including a beach-plus-deep-sea-fishing possibility). They also feature sports events like Orlando Magic (basketball) and Jacksonville Jaguars (American football) games. All their guides are certified for first aid, and they operate to high health and safety standards (**realfloridaadventures.com**).

Original Orlando Tours: Enjoy a private tour of Orlando filled with history, tastes and exceptional local knowledge. Among the Sights & Eats Walking Tours are Flavors of ICON Park, Ghosts of Winter Park and Peacocks, Presidents and Puzzles. Year-round tours include Old Florida Roadside Attraction Day, Historic Fort Christmas, plus boat rides, beach visits, and much more. Their seasonal tours are extremely popular (**originalorlando.com**).

You can also have a great day-trip just by heading for the beaches in your hire car (see Chapter 9).

Take a tour of the city and see the sights

© Grayline Tours

SPORT

In addition to virtually every form of entertainment known to man, central Florida is one of the world's biggest sporting playgrounds, with a huge range of opportunities to either watch or play your favourite sport.

Golf

Florida's No.1 sport, with hundreds of courses, offers numerous packages for golfers of all abilities. Winter is high season, hence more expensive, but many courses are busy year-round. Some courses pair golfers with little thought for age, handicap, etc, so if two of you turn up, you may be paired with strangers.

—BRITTIP
Golf balls are cheap so there's no need to bring them. Good-quality clubs are always available for hire, too

Edwin Watts Golf on Turkey Lake Rd carries clubs and accessories. **Tee-Times USA** (**teetimesusa.com/ orlando-tee-times**) offers excellent advice and a reservation service. Visit Florida has its own golf section at **visitflorida.com/golf**. Website **golfnow. com** is also a great source of tee times all over Central Florida, and usually at reduced rates. New on the scene is the massive **TopGolf** floodlit driving range on Universal Boulevard (**topgolf. com/us/orlando**).

Here are a few notable courses to consider:

Walt Disney World: Disney has three high-quality courses, including the Palm, rated by Golf Digest in its top 25, plus a nine-hole course, Oak Trail, which also offers foot-golf (the combo of golf and football). Call 407 939 4653 for tee-times.

—BRITTIP
Some of the best tee-times at Walt Disney World golf courses are reserved for those staying at a Disney resort.

ChampionsGate: Two magnificent Greg Norman-designed courses and coaching from the renowned David Leadbetter Academy (**championsgategolf.com**).

Dubsdread: The oldest public course in Orlando and the only municipal one, offers a testing 18 holes featuring narrow fairways and 'postage stamp' greens, plus superb The Tap Room bar and restaurant (**historicaldubsdread.com**).

Shingle Creek: World-class facility at the five-star hotel, set among beautiful oaks and pines, plus the excellent Brad Brewer Golf Academy (1866 996 9933, **shinglecreekgolf.com** and **bradbrewer.com**).

Also consider **Falcon's Fire** (**falconsfire. com**); **Grande Lakes Orlando** (**grandelakes.com**); **Hawk's Landing** (**marriottworldcenter.com**); **Hyatt Grand Cypress** (**golfgrandcypress. com**); **Mystic Dunes** (**mysticdunesgolf. com**); and **Orange Lake Country Club** (**orangelakegolf.com**).

Disney's Magnolia Golf Course

© Disney

Be sure to ask if fees are negotiable. There are often reductions for seniors but check the dress code, as they can vary. Typically, you need a collared shirt, Bermuda shorts and no denim.

Fans: For those keen to see the stars in action, the big annual event is the Arnold Palmer Invitational at the Bay Hill Club each March, a major tournament on the US PGA tour (**arnoldpalmerinvitational.com**).

Mini-golf

Not exactly a sport, but Orlando's many extravagant mini-golf centres are a big hit. Several attractions and parks offer mini-golf as an extra, but for the best try the self-contained centres.

Disney's Fantasia Gardens: Just off Buena Vista Drive is a two-course challenge over 36 holes, themed from classic film *Fantasia*. Fantasia Fairways is a cunning putting course, complete with rough, water hazards and bunkers, and 18 holes can take more than an hour.

International Drive: Try the 18-hole **Congo River** in front of the Four Points by Sheraton or **Pirates Cove**, with a whole Pirate 'village' at its entrance. **Putting Edge** has indoor glow-in-the-dark mini-golf next to the Cinemark cinema at the top of I-Drive and **Gator Golf & Adventure Park** has a variety of gator shows daily, plus some challenging mini-golf.

Kissimmee: Look for **Congo River Golf & Exploration Co** on Highway 192; **Pirates Cove**, next to Old Town; and **Mighty Jungle Golf**, on Highway 192.

Universal's Hollywood Drive-In Golf: This creative set-up at Universal's

CityWalk has *The Haunting of Ghostly Greens*, a 1950s mock-horror themed 18 holes that includes putting through a cemetery and a giant spider's lair, and *Invaders From The Planet Putt*, 18 holes of sci-fi humour that feature an alien spaceship and 30ft/9m robot. And, while it looks good during the day, it sparkles at night and stays open long after the theme parks have closed (**hollywooddriveingolf.com**).

Winter-Summerland Mini-Golf: At the entrance to Blizzard Beach is a half beach, half snow-themed 36 holes that are great fun to play (Blizzard Beach admission not required).

Water sports

There's all manner of watery fun here!

Buena Vista Watersports: Jet-skis, water-skiing, wakeboard, tube rides, canoes, kayaks, paddle-boards, and pontoon boats on Little Lake Bryan, Highway 535 (**bvwatersports.com**).

Nona Adventure Park: the heart of this impressive outdoor adventure complex in Lake Nona (just south of Orlando Airport) is a massive aqua park, with all manner of obstacles, slides, and fun! (**nonaadventurepark. com**).

Orlando Watersports Complex: Just off the Beachline Expressway (528) near Orlando Airport, this features wake-boarding and water-skiing, by boat and suspended cable, for novices and experts, plus a family-friendly bouncy aquapark (**aktionparks.com**).

Walt Disney World: There's a variety of boats for rent, plus activities like surfing (at Typhoon Lagoon; p233) and fishing. Boat rentals are first come, first served.

Spectator events

American sport is great entertainment. From the Orlando Predators of the Arena League (an indoor version of American football) to National Cheerleading championships at Disney's ESPN Wide World of Sports, all sports are represented.

Silver Spurs Rodeo

Basketball: Try the Orlando Magic of the National Basketball Association (NBA) Nov–May (with exhibition games in Oct). The 18,500-seat Amway Center (on W Church Street, exit 82B off I-4) can sell out, so contact the Magic (407 440 7900, **amwaycenter. com**) for tickets (from $15 in upper seats to $1,500+ courtside), or StubHub (**stubhub.com** or 1866 788 2482).

BRITTIP

You don't need to understand the game to experience some real Americana. Just turn up and enjoy the family-friendly fun.

American football: Local NFL teams are Tampa Bay, 75ml/120km west, Miami, 3–4hrs' down the Florida Turnpike, or Jacksonville, a 3hr drive on I-4 and I-95 past Daytona to the east coast. Ticket prices and dates from StubHub (Sept–Dec). Tampa offers 75min tours of the impressive Raymond James Stadium for much of the year (813 350 6500, **raymondjamesstadium.com/behind-the-scenes**).

Baseball: St Pete has the **Tampa Bay Rays** at Tropicana Field (Apr–Sept). Tickets are usually available for the big indoor stadium.

Orlando City Soccer Club: Soccer is Orlando's other big sport thanks to our MLS team, playing Mar–Oct at their 26,000-seat stadium in downtown Orlando. Games have a superb atmosphere, with tailgating (a big car park party) at surrounding venues, food trucks and live music before kick-off (**orlandocitysc.com/tickets**). Church Street is great for pre-game excitement, the weekly 'March to the Match', post-game celebration and Watch Parties for away games.

ESPN Wide World of Sports™

Disney's big sports development is an impressive 220acre/86ha state-of-the-art complex, featuring 30 sports. It boasts a 9,500-seat baseball stadium, softball quadraplex, 10-court tennis complex, 5,000-seat indoor facility, athletics and extensive sports fields.

The centre's extensive fields cater for soccer, lacrosse, baseball and softball, and college and school teams often offer some keen action. ESPN is off Osceola Parkway, on Victory Way (**espnwwos.com**).

Run Disney: Half and full marathons, 10k and 5k fun-runs are popular, with great spectacles up to six times a year and up to 55,000 runners taking part. Most include all four Disney theme parks and can cause daily disruption. Check dates on **rundisney.com**.

Rodeo

An all-American pursuit, the **Silver Spurs Rodeo** is staged twice a year at the 8,300-seat Silver Spurs Arena. The biggest event of its kind in the south-east, it is held in Feb and early June (321 697 3495, **silverspursrodeo. com**). There is also a weekly Saturday Night Rodeo at *Westgate River Ranch* (p244).

Motor sport

Race fans will find big-league thrills at **Daytona International Speedway**. Highlights are the **Rolex 24** (a 24hr sports car event, late Jan), famous **Daytona 500** (Feb), and **Coke Zero 400** (early July). The Speedway also provides great daily tours, from the basic 30min Speedway Tour to a 1hr All Access Tour and 2.5hr VIP Tour. A huge gift shop and café complete the set-up while the **Motorsports Hall of Fame** (**mshf.com**) offers more fascinating fun, even for non-race fans (**daytonainternationalspeedway. com**). The Richard Petty Driving Experience is a great opportunity to sample NASCAR racing first hand, either as passenger or driver, with a range of different on-track experiences (18 or over for all but the Ride-Along and Junior Ride-Along; **drivepetty.com**).

OK, that's the local area sorted out; now let's take you further afield…

9 The Twin Centre Option

or, To Orlando – and Beyond!

While Orlando continues to get bigger and better, it is equally true there is a LOT more to see in the rest of Florida. From St Augustine in the north-east to Key West in the south, it's easy to find glorious beaches and superbly authentic experiences.

Heading north-east first, here's what you find.

St Augustine

A 2hr drive up I-4 and I-95 brings you to America's oldest city. Founded by Spanish conquistadors in 1565, St Augustine is full of authentic buildings and signs of the original settlement around the imposing Castillo de San Marcos. Much of the original walled city still remains and 18th and 19th-century Mediterranean influences are everywhere. Walk the narrow, uneven streets of the Restoration Area to discover colonial architectural treasures, now home to gift shops, cafés, antique shops, quaint B&Bs and more.

Tours: To see as much as possible, hop on a horse-drawn carriage, the **Red Train Tours** sightseeing train or the **Old Town Trolley Tours** for a narrated tour. For a spookier experience, walk the streets with **Ghost Tours of St Augustine**, with your guide in period costume. The **Old Jail Tour** – by day or night! – is another fascinating insight into the 19th century period.

Other attractions: Florida railroad history is on offer at the **Lightner Museum**, formerly Henry Flagler's ornate Hotel Alcazar, and **Flagler College**, the magnificent 19th century Ponce de Leon hotel, with tours daily (**legacy.flagler.edu/pages/tours**).

Restaurants: These range from **The Spanish Bakery & Café** and the famous, family-owned **Columbia Restaurant**, to a modern microbrewery, **A1A Ale Works**.

Where to stay: The premier hotel is historic **Casa Monica** (**casamonica. com**), while the boutique **St George Inn** (**stgeorge-inn.com**) is also a good choice, as is the **Sebastian Hotel** (**radissonhotelsamericas.com/en-us/hotels/radisson-individuals-sebastian-hotel**).

More info: St Augustine Visitors & Convention Bureau (**floridashistoriccoast.com**).

BRITTIP

Florida's new All-American Road runs from Ponte Vedra Beach in the north-east to Flagler Beach 72 miles south and is tailor-made for a great driving experience, with a free audio tour App to accompany the route (**scenica1a.org**).

Volusia County

Travel south from St Augustine and you arrive in this famous beach area.

Daytona Beach: 1hr from Orlando along I-4 east, this family-friendly area is busiest mid-June to mid-Aug.

At the southern end is the **Ponce de Leon Inlet Lighthouse**, America's second tallest lighthouse (**ponceinlet. org**), where **Ponce Inlet Watersports** offers fishing, parasailing, kayaks, paddleboards and great dolphin eco-tours (**ponceinletwatersports.com**). The **Marine Science Center** is a chance to explore the local sea habitats, with a turtle rehab facility, artificial reef aquarium, boardwalk and nature trail (**marinesciencecenter.com**).

Daytona Speedway: This is one of the biggest draws (p251), with three great tours of this amazing facility.

Where to stay: Any of **The Daytona** (**thedaytona.com**), **Hilton Daytona Beach Oceanfront Resort** (**daytonahilton.com**), **The Shores Resort & Spa** (**shoresresort.com**), or **Hard Rock Hotel** (**hardrockhotels. com/daytona-beach**) provide first-rate accommodations.

Cook-it-yourself breakfast

Just north of DeLand in DeLeon Springs State Park is the unique local institution of the Old Spanish Sugar Mill grill and griddle house, famous for hearty cook-it-yourself pancake breakfasts (**oldspanishsugarmill.com**). You can then try the park facilities, which include canoes, kayaks, hiking trails and boat tours (**bit.ly/3MK9Ra7**).

More info: Daytona Beach Area CVB (**daytonabeach.com**).

The Space Coast

Further south on the Atlantic seaboard is the 'Space Coast', home to the iconic Kennedy Space Center (p205).

BRITTIP

For info on Kennedy Space Center rocket launches and public viewing spots, see **spacecoastlaunches.com**.

Cocoa Beach: Barely 50mins east of Orlando, this area has two excellent public beaches, plus shopping at iconic Ron Jon's Surf Shop (**cocoabeach.com**). For activities, try **Midway Airboats** on the St John River (**airboatridesatmidway.com**), or Cocoa Beach Dolphin Tours (p247). Be aware the sea can be chilly from Nov–Apr.

Cocoa Village: This little town on the intracoastal waterway offers an array of unique shopping and dining (**visitcocoavillage.com**).

Titusville: Don't miss **Merritt Island National Wildlife Refuge**, a self-drive tour adjacent to Kennedy Space Center, and **Dixie Crossroads**, a locals' spot for fine Florida seafood (**dixiecrossroads.com**).

Aviation fans will enjoy **Valiant Air Command Warbird Museum**, with dozens of vintage warplanes and guided tours through the exhibits and history of military aviation, as well as their dedicated restoration programme (**valiantaircommand.com**).

Cocoa Beach and Pier

© Space Coast Office of Tourism

Melbourne: Family-friendly **Brevard Zoo** is well worth a visit, with almost 500 animals in six themed areas (**brevardzoo.org**).

Where to stay: The must-try new hotel is the **Courtyard Titusville**, featuring the iconic rooftop Space Bar with grandstand views of launches from the Space Center (**marriott.com/en-us/hotels/tixcy-courtyard-titusville-kennedy-space-center**).

More info: visitspacecoast.com.

Tampa

Going west from Orlando brings you down I-4 to the bright city of Tampa, right on a major sea bay and with some excellent attractions of its own (including Busch Gardens, p191).

Dinosaur World: Right on I-4 as you head to Tampa (Exit 17) is this family-run attraction ideal for 3–8s. With several hundred life-sized dinosaurs in a natural setting, plus walking trails, picnic area, play-ground and gift shop (**dinosaurworld.com/florida**).

Florida Aquarium: In the heart of Tampa is this superb child-friendly draw with a series of galleries and The Splash Pad water-play area (**flaquarium.org**; also on Tampa CityPass).

BRITTIP

Book online using the Florida Aquarium's Plan Ahead Pricing to save on general admission.

ZooTampa at Lowry Park: Rated one of America's top zoos, this lush 60acre/24ha spread showcases more than 1,000 animals, water-play areas, educational shows and rides. (**zootampa.org**; also on Tampa CityPass).

Museum of Science and Industry: More family fun (especially for 4–12s) can be found at this entertaining science centre, with three floors of educational exhibits, Sky Trail Ropes Course and Saunders Planetarium, with tours of the night sky several times daily (**mosi.org**; also on Tampa CityPass).

Ybor City: Tampa's historic district can be found in the rejuvenated Cuban quarter of the city, where a fine mix of shops and restaurants provides a lively day and night vibe.

BRITTIP

Don't miss Columbia Restaurant in Ybor City. Opened in 1905, it covers a whole city block that was slowly absorbed into this Spanish/Cuban bar-diner. Ask if they can give you a tour (**columbiarestaurant.com**).

Brewery Central: Tampa is a major centre for breweries and craft beer, with more than 30 breweries producing high-quality ales, lagers, ciders and more. Many offer tours and samples of their wares.

Where to stay: Distinctive hotels include the **Epicurean Hotel**, with gourmet restaurant Elevage (855 829 2536, **epicureanhotel.com**), upscale **Le Meridien**, (813 221 9555, **bit.ly/brit-lemeridien**) and the **Grand Hyatt**, in a quiet corner of Tampa Bay and offering a terrific array of activities and dining (813 874 1234 **bit.ly/brit-grandhyatt**).

More info: visittampabay.com.

BRITTIP

The Tampa Bay CityPass card offers BIG savings on attractions like Busch Gardens, Clearwater Marine Aquarium, Florida Aquarium and ZooTampa (**citypass.com/tampa**).

Zoo Tampa at Lowry Park

© Zoo_Tampa

St Pete/Clearwater

Continue west for the gorgeous Gulf Coast, a 2hr drive down I-4 and through Tampa on I-275 south to St Pete Beach (105ml/169km) or Clearwater Beach (110ml/177km), all featuring white-sand beaches, water sports and lots of wide, open space. The sea is warmer and calmer on this side of Florida so is more suitable for small children. The long stretch from St Pete to Clearwater represents the heart of the Sunshine State beach experience and is a popular two-centre option.

BRITTIP

Do the 'stingray shuffle' in the sea from Apr–Oct. Move your feet through the sand without lifting them up to alert the odd stingray to your presence, then they will move away. Neosporin is a good antiseptic if you are stung.

St Petersburg: This city, just across Howard Frankland Bridge from Tampa, is a glorious mix of old and new, with an impressive Art District (10 museums, dozens of galleries and counting) and a real café society feel. Take time for the world-renowned **Dali Museum** (**thedali.org**), and the **Chihuly Collection**, a superb showcase of the American glass artist (**moreanartscenter.org**).

Beaches: You are spoiled for choice, from **Fort De Soto Park** in the south to stunning **Caladesi Island State Park** in the north (regularly voted in America's Top 10). Treasure Island, Sand Key and St Pete Beach all receive awards for cleanliness and safety. Visit **John's Pass Village** for eclectic shopping and restaurants, plus the fun **Pirate Cruise**, a replica sailing ship offering a 90min party cruise and 90min **Dolphin Quest** tour (**boattoursjohnspass.com**). Parasailing, jet-skiing, fishing, boat rentals and tours are also popular (**johnspass.com**).

Dolphin Landings: Don't miss the chance to take a 2hr trip along the calm inland waterway for close-up dolphin-watch cruises and sunset sailings; a 4hr trip around beautiful Egmont Key; or a 3½hr trip to Shell Key, with up to 2hrs on the beach (**dolphinlandings.com**).

Clearwater Beach: Continue north to acres of clean, white sands and the must-visit **Clearwater Marine Aquarium**, a wonderful non-profit organisation that rescues and rehabilitates injured dolphins, turtles, river otters and more (especially good for under-12s). There are 17 main exhibits, along with dolphin presentations that highlight their behaviour and care (not 'shows' as such) and interactive animal encounters, plus a Dolphin & Animal Care Assistant programme, behind-the-scenes tours and 2hr Sea Life Safari (great for kids) that cruises the coastal waterway (**cmaquarium.org**; also on Tampa CityPass, p254).

The Beach Walk: The heart of the area is a winding beachside promenade linking a long stretch of resorts, shops and restaurants to **Pier 60**, which holds a daily sunset celebration. Also here is the marina home of the 2hr **Captain Memo's Pirate Cruise** (**captainmemo.com**) and fab **Sea Screamer** power boat that goes out into the Gulf and often attracts dolphins jumping in its wake (**seascreamer.com**).

Restaurants: The area boasts 2,000 restaurants, of which the Key West style of the five **Frenchy's Cafes**, **Crabby's Dockside** (Clearwater Beach marina) and **RumFish Grill** (St Pete Beach) are all worth visiting.

Where to stay: Upscale hotels include family-friendly **Tradewinds Island Resorts** on St Pete Beach, (**tradewindsresort.com**); the superb **Sandpearl Resort**, a four-star choice on Clearwater Beach (**sandpearl.com**); and **Hyatt Regency Clearwater Beach Resort & Spa**, an all-suite hotel at the heart of Beach Walk (**bit.ly/hcclearwater**). More modest choices on the seafront in St Pete Beach are the chic motel style of **The Postcard Inn** (**postcardinn.com**) and funky **Bilmar Beach Resort**, with self-catering rooms (**bilmarbeachresort.com**). The **Vinoy Resort** (in St Petersburg) is a

1920s treasure for its Spanish Revival style (**bit.ly/brit-marriott**).

More info: visitstpeteclearwater.com.

The South-west

Bradenton/Sarasota: Around 2hrs' drive from Orlando is this artsy area (take I-4 then I-75), which features the superb beachfronts of Anna Maria Island (charming and secluded beaches), Longboat Key and Venice ('the shark tooth capital of the world' and great for fossil hunters).

In Sarasota, visit **Ringling Estate and Museum of Art**, including the unique Circus Museum and Tibbals Learning Center (the world's largest scale model of a classic circus). The dazzling **Ca d'Zan Mansion**, grounds and gardens are also part of the entry fee (**ringling.org**). There is superb shopping at **St Armand's Circle** in Lido Key.

Where to stay: Anna Maria Island is full of small-scale B&Bs and beach-front inns, plus **Zota Beach Resort** (**zotabeachresort.com**). Sarasota offers the smart **Hyatt Regency Sarasota** (**bit.ly/hrsarasola**).

More info: Sarasota, **visitsarasota.com**; Bradenton and Anna Maria Island, **bradentongulfislands.com**.

Fort Myers/Sanibel: If there was an area that caught the full force of deadly Hurricane Ian in 2022, it was this beautiful stretch of south-west coastline. The storm left a colossal trail of destruction. This included the highly popular resort destinations of Fort Myers Beach, Pine Island, Sanibel, Captiva and Bonita Springs. The local economy and attractions of the region will need a LONG time to recover, hence we can only refer you to the tourism website for this area for information on when it will be possible to visit them once again.

More info: fortmyers-sanibel.com.

Where to stay: There is a good mix of vacation homes and cottages in Fort Myers Beach and Sanibel,

while the top hotels are **Lovers Key Resort** (**loverskey.com**), **Sanibel Harbor Marriott Resort & Spa** (**marriott.com**), and **Hyatt Regency Coconut Point** (**bit.ly/3Tuk9gQ**).

BRITTIP

Some attractions still require date-specific reservations *and* pre-purchase of tickets online prior to visiting. Be sure to check websites for current entry requirements.

Paradise Coast: Continue south to the magnificent 'Paradise Coast' of Naples and Marco Island. Naples is a fresh, modern city with plenty of attractions, notably **Corkscrew Swamp Sanctuary** (**corkscrew.audubon. org**), plus ultra-chic shopping, as well as great beaches. Try the **Old Naples Pub** for fine food in a relaxed ambience. On Fifth Avenue, each of **Ocean Prime** steaks and seafood, Parisian **French Brasserie Rustique** and **Osteria Tulia**, with its rustic Italian vibe, offer memorable dining.

BRITTIP

Naples and Marco Island were also badly affected by Hurricane Ian, so you should consult their website for the latest info on the area's recovery.

Where to stay: Pick from **JW Marriott Marco Island** (**jwmarco.com**), **Marco Beach Ocean Resort** (**marcoresort.com**) and **Naples Grande Beach Resort** (**naplesgrande.com**), or the ultimate indulgence of **The Inn On Fifth**, on ritzy Fifth Avenue (**innonfifth.com**).

More info: paradisecoast.com.

Miami nice

If you see nothing else in Miami, do spend time in South Beach (or SoBe) and über-cool Ocean Drive, full of open-air cafés, art galleries and nightclubs. Tranquil during the day, non-stop at night, this is where the beautiful people hang out, or just cruise in their Ferraris.

Treasure Coast

Returning to the Atlantic Coast, heading south on Highway 1 brings you to an often-overlooked gem, Vero Beach. Nicknamed the Treasure Coast for its history of shipwrecks, it boasts the intriguing **McLarty Treasure Museum**, **Pelican Island National Wildlife Refuge** and **McKee Botanical Garden**. Vero Beach is on the barrier island of North Hutchinson but spreads to the mainland, with art galleries, smart shops, restaurants, resorts and beach parks, including a boardwalk atop the dunes.

Go south again for the **Palm Beaches**, with the barrier island town of Palm Beach, one of Florida's most chic hangouts. A playground of the rich and famous, the fab **Flagler Museum** is a highlight, while the many restaurants are places to go celebrity-watching and **Worth Avenue** is one of America's most iconic shopping streets. Dine at Italian-style **Bice** (bice-palmbeach.com), tapas-style **Buccan** (buccanpalmbeach.com) or celebrity bistro **Ta-boo** (taboorestaurant.com).

Where to stay: Hutchinson Shores Resort on Hutchinson Island (hutchinsonshores.com), or Palm Beach's blissful **Eau Palm Beach** (eaupalmbeach.com), iconic **The Breakers** (thebreakers.com), or **The Colony**, a 1960s haunt of the Duke and Duchess of Windsor (thecolonypalmbeach.com).

More info: thepalmbeaches.com.

Miami and Fort Lauderdale

From Palm Beach, you reach Delray Beach, chic Boca Raton, Deerfield Beach, Pompano Beach and **Fort Lauderdale**, one of Florida's most upmarket destinations.

Top things to see are **Old Fort Lauderdale Village & Museum** (historyfortlauderdale.org/museum) and **Las Olas Boulevard**, full of boutiques and restaurants. Shop at **Sawgrass Mills**, Florida's largest mall. This is also a perfect stay for a few days before or after a cruise.

Where to stay: Check out the fun of **Margaritaville Beach Resort** (margaritavillehollywoodbeachresort. com), five-star **Ritz-Carlton** (ritzcarlton. com/en/hotels/florida/fort-lauderdale) and **Marriott Harbor Beach Resort** (marriott.com/hotels/travel/fllsb-fort-lauderdale-marriott-harbor-beach-resort-and-spa/). For self-catering, **Beachwalk Resort** has suites with full kitchens (beachwalkresortfl.com).

More info: sunny.org.

Miami: Some 230ml/370km south of Orlando is Florida's biggest city, with superb high-rise resorts, miles of open beaches, funky **South Beach,** with its Art Deco District, fantastic shopping, sports, restaurants and nightlife. A boat tour from Bayside Marketplace shows off the mansions of the rich while other attractions are ornate **Vizcaya Museum** (https:// vizcaya.org/) and **Miami Seaquarium** (miamiseaquarium.com). Find fashion-conscious shopping at **Bal Harbor Shops**, **Aventura Mall**, funky **Lincoln Road**, **CocoWalk** shopping district, or the **Shops at Merrick Park** in Coral Gables.

Dining: Consider the Latin American cuisine of **Ola Miami** (olamiami.com); Northern Italian trattoria **Salumiera 104** (salumeria104.com); and swish **Casa Tua** (casatualifestyle.com/miami).

Where to stay: The Beacon on Ocean Drive (beaconsouthbeach.com) or **Miami Beach Edition**, a chic conversion of the 1950s Seville Hotel (editionhotels.com/miami-beach). **More info**: miamiandbeaches.com.

Corkscrew Swamp Sanctuary

Florida Keys

Leaving Miami on Highway 1 brings you to the amazing Keys, a loose archipelago of 1,700 islands that arc down into the Caribbean. This is the laid-back 'Conch Republic', with its 'Floribbean' culture and some of the world's best coral reefs, including **John Pennekamp Coral Reef State Park** (**pennekamppark.com**) and **Vandenberg Artificial Reef**.

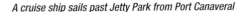

BRITTIP

The Keys offer Florida's other All-American Road experience, running 110 miles from just north of Key Largo to Key West (**scenichighwayflkeys.com**).

Eclectic **Key West** is a mix of the laid-back and outrageous, with street performers, sidewalk artists, cafés and bars, plus the former home of Ernest Hemingway. You should also see **Key West Aquarium** (**keywestaquarium.com**) and **Key West Shipwreck Museum** (**keywestshipwreck.com**), and the wonderful shops. You must be on the harbour front for the daily Sunset Celebration, when the party is in full force. The other great Key West feature is its myriad ways to get around – you can try the **Conch Tour Train**, **Old Town Trolley Tours**, pedicabs and bicycles. Just don't expect your stay to be sedate!

Where to stay: Guest houses, inns and B&Bs are plentiful, like the chic **Marquesa Hotel** (**marquesa.com**) in Key West's Old Town. Or go for epic style at **Casa Marina**, a Waldorf Astoria hotel that links back to Henry Flagler's era (**casamarinaresort.com**). For something special, try **Hawks Cay Resort** in secluded Duck Key (**hawkscay.com**), luxurious **Isla Bella Beach Resort** in Marathon (**islabellabeachresort.com**) or Key West's tropical island hideaway **Parrot Key** (**parrotkeyhotel.com**). **More info:** fla-keys.com.

Cruise-and-stay

Taking a cruise is increasingly popular with an Orlando stay and there are well-priced 3, 4, 5 and 7-day sailings out of **Port Canaveral** (**portcanaveral.com**), **Tampa** (**porttb.com**), **Fort Lauderdale** (**porteverglades.net/cruise**) and **Miami** (**miamidade.gov/portmiami**). From here, you can visit the Bahamas, the Caribbean, Mexico, Central and South America.

Now on to all the night-time entertainment …

A cruise ship sails past Jetty Park from Port Canaveral

or, Burning the Candle at Both Ends

If Orlando and the parks are hot during the day, they positively sizzle at night, with yet more diverse and thrilling entertainment, most of it family friendly. Disney and Universal lead the way, but there is much to enjoy throughout the area.

The full range runs from purpose-built entertainment complexes and an amazing variety of dinner shows to a unique array of bars and nightclubs. The choice is widespread and almost always high quality. Downtown Orlando has some great offerings, as does International Drive, while Disney has two entertainment centres and Universal features its CityWalk district of live music, dining and fun.

Disney's Electrical Water Pageant

© Disney

> **BRITTIP**
> Many bars and restaurants added outdoor seating over the last 2 years, so, if you prefer to dine outside, you'll find plenty of options, some comfortably heated in winter.

DISNEY SPRINGS
Disney's big shopping, dining and entertainment district is a four-part adventure, made up of the original Marketplace and West Side, plus The Landing and Town Center, featuring iconic restaurants, bars and venues (see also Dining, p278; Shopping, p300).

> **BRITTIP**
> Photo ID is essential for all bars and clubs, even if you happen to be the 'wrong' side of 30. No ID equals no alcohol, and there are no exceptions. For Disney, a photocopy of your passport ID page is needed, along with your driving licence.

The Landing
Raglan Road: This pub features traditional live Irish music each night in its Grand Room 5:30pm–11pm Mon–Sun, plus Irish dancing 5pm–10:30pm daily. Enjoy its full bar, ample collection of genuine Irish whiskey, nine European beers, three beer flights, plus local brews, great bartenders and even better menu (p279; **raglanroad.com**).

The Boathouse: This bar-restaurant venue offers live music, 8pm–midnight Fri–Sat, but the real feature is the Amphicar rides. Each land-to-water car accommodates up to three guests and a Car Captain (provided driver), with 20min rides costing a whopping $125, but it's a unique opportunity. Tickets can be purchased at The Boathouse. For the best spectator value, watch the Amphicars on the lake from the comfort of the waterside Boathouse bar. Tours run 10am–10pm, weather permitting.

BRITTIP

If your tipple is vodka and lime, ask for vodka and a dash of lime cordial. For port and lemon, ask for port and Sprite. Otherwise you'll get a slice of citrus fruit with your alcohol.

The Edison: This massive 1920s-style 'Industrial Gothic' destination offers a funky menu featuring classic American food, craft cocktails, beer and wine plus live music and various acts, from stilt walkers and dancers to aerialists. Eclectic? You bet! One of Disney's best night-time venues? No doubt about it! Ages 21 and up only after 10pm.

Jock Lindsey's Hangar Bar: Indiana Jones fans will love this wonderfully themed bar named for the pilot of the Indy films. There is a boat-themed patio and aeroplane memorabilia, plus reminders of the former Adventurer's Club at Pleasure Island, as well as a range of craft beers, cocktails and a small-plate dining menu.

Paddlefish: Housed in a replica paddleboat, this seafood-themed offering boasts a superb rooftop lounge and bar with a magnificent view, plus live music Fri–Sat, 9pm–midnight. Perfect for enjoying the sunset with an excellent craft beer or handcrafted cocktail (also see Dining p279).

Paradiso 37: This expansive, split-level bar-restaurant offers a fine array of food from Latin America plus a Tequila Bar featuring over 50 varieties. Live music adds to its picturesque waterfront location (p279).

STK Orlando: The latest outlet of this über-chic international steakhouse has a high-energy vibe that features an in-house DJ and a fabulous rooftop patio with great views over Disney Springs – ideal for cocktails and people-watching.

Enzo's Hideaway: Tucked away in a former underground tunnel for Cast Members, this speakeasy-style lounge is one of our favourites for small-plate, late-night bites and superb classic cocktails (11.30am–10pm daily).

The Edison

© Disney

West Side

AMC® Dine-In Theaters Complex:
With 24 screens and 6,000 seats plus a huge choice of snacks, drinks and even its own bar, this superb cinema multiplex shows first-run films in state-of-the-art surroundings, including the Enhanced Theatre Experience (a bigger screen, with 3D technology, 12-channel audio and digital projection) and a Dine-In option, with six of the auditoriums converted to serve meals and drinks while you watch. The menu includes starters like chicken tenders and rice bowls, then salads, sandwiches, flatbreads, burgers and milkshakes, plus wine, beer and cocktails (tickets $11–18, prices vary by show; food and drink extra; call 407 827 1308 for show times; under 18s must be accompanied by an adult in Dine-In theatres; **amctheatres.com**). Disabled accessible; assisted listening devices available at Guest Services.

BRITTIP

Some films have added features, such as enhanced sound, larger screen, or 3-D that will increase your ticket price. However, you can save up to 30% on tickets at the AMC® cineplex by visiting daytime shows (hours vary).

Cirque Du Soleil: New show *Drawn To Life* opened in 2022, with the original story of an animator's daughter drawn into the magic and fantasy of Disney animation, and it has immediately made the latest Cirque performance THE show to see in Orlando. From the opening act, where unexpected objects come to life, to the grand finale, featuring a series of jaw-dropping acrobatic feats between two huge pendulum swings, this is an exercise in pure balletic grace and daring. Synchronised acrobats jostle with dramatic wheel performers and breathtaking stilt-walkers to weave an artistic narrative of visual excellence, all undertaken with hints of classic Disney that never take you out of the Cirque wizardry. Elegance, bravura and supreme showmanship combine to create a 90-minute masterpiece, all underpinned by live music and eye-popping stage effects. Cirque calls it "a love letter to Disney animation interpreted through Cirque du Soleil's acrobatic performances," but we simply think it is utter brilliance from start to finish ($85–$185; **cirquedusoleil.com/drawn-to-life**).

BRITTIP

Although the start time for *Drawn To Life* may indicate 5.30 or 8pm, you will want to be in your seat at least 15min early to enjoy the amusing pre-show featuring an animated pillow. Yes, really, and it is pure genius.

House of Blues: Free live music every night at the Front Porch bar, with full concerts at the separately accessed music venue next to the restaurant. The main venue offers a mix of big-name headliners, up-and-coming bands and local acts. Standing only. Tickets required, no discounts for children ($20–250 and up; **houseofblues.com**).

Splitsville: An imaginative venue in which to 'dine, dance, drink – and bowl'. But with a difference. Built in best 1950s period style, this twin-level entertainment palace offers 30 lanes of bowling, multiple bars, billiard tables and a full-service restaurant, plus elegant indoor and outdoor seating, including a 1st-floor patio for a great view over Disney Springs. Walk-in rates are $20/person Mon–Fri 10.30am–4pm and $24 from 4pm; $24/person all day Sat and Sun 10pm-close, with Early Bird specials until noon. Book a lane in advance by calling or online (11am–11pm Sun–Thurs; 11–11.30 Fri–Sat; **splitsvillelanes.com**).

© Disney

Drawn to Life

Town Center

While this is primarily a shopping area, with a few smart dining outlets like D-Luxe Burger, Wolfgang Puck's and Blaze Pizza, there are a couple of worthy candidates for evening fun.

Coca-Cola Store: Another iconic building, this is home to Coke products, gift items and memorabilia, and features a glamorous rooftop tasting bar.

Planet Hollywood Observatory: This smart venue features a futuristic space observatory theme to go with its celebrity style. As well as the main restaurant, there's the Stargazers outdoor terrace and bar with live entertainment.

Marketplace

This area is again primarily about shopping and dining but there are still a couple of nice spots to stop for a drink, notably the **Lava Lounge** (beside the Rainforest Café and with a view over Crescent Lake), and **Dockside Margaritas**, an open-air terrace facing the water that also serves great cocktails.

Other entertainment: The evening sees a variety of live music performers throughout Disney Springs, from flamenco guitarists to classical quartets and more. Look for them in all four sections.

Disney's Coronado Springs Resort

© Disney

Disney Resorts

Disney's Boardwalk: Disney's other big entertainment offering is part of its impressive BoardWalk Resort, where the waterfront district contains several notable venues (not counting the excellent micro-brewery and restaurant of **Big River Grille and Brewing Works** and five star **Flying Fish** Café), plus the new (in 2023) **Cake Bake Shop** for an elegant afternoon tea. **Jellyrolls** is a variation on the duelling piano bar, with the pianists conjuring up a lively evening of audience participation (7pm–1.45am, music from 8pm; $18 cover charge; 21 and over only) while **Atlantic Dance Hall** features mainly modern dance music with house and guest DJs, plus occasional live music, a huge dance floor and a great bar service and ambience (8pm–1am; closed Mon–Weds; strictly 21 and over). The Boardwalk also features amusing live entertainers, like magicians and jugglers.

Coronado Springs Resort: A hidden gem here is the **Rix Sports Bar & Grill** with an elegant setting for a sports bar. It's stylish, lively and features hand-crafted cocktails and craft beers along with classic bar food, while multiple TVs show all the major sports (7am–11pm).

Electrical Water Pageant: This is another nightly (and free!) alternative, a 'parade' that circles Bay Lake and the Seven Seas Lagoon. It lasts just 10mins, but it's almost a waterborne version of a typical Magic Kingdom parade, with thousands of twinkling lights on a cavalcade of pontoons, all set to music. The 2022 schedule was 8.45pm at the Polynesian Resort, 9 at Grand Floridian Resort (get a grandstand view at Narcoosee's restaurant), 9.30 at Wilderness Lodge, 9.45 on the shores of Fort Wilderness Resort and 10 at Contemporary Resort. It can also be seen outside the Magic Kingdom at 10.20pm during extended hours.

UNIVERSAL'S CITYWALK

As part of the big Universal Orlando development, this 30acre/12ha spread offers a bustling expanse of restaurants, snack brratars, shops, open-air events, escape games, mini-golf and nightclubs. It offers a huge variety of cuisines, from fast food to fine dining, an unusual blend of speciality shops and an eclectic bar/nightclub mix. For dining, see p283.

Bob Marley – A Tribute to Freedom: A clever re-creation of Marley's Jamaica home is turned into a courtyard music venue and restaurant. The bands are excellent, the atmosphere authentic and the place comes alive at night (4pm-midnight).

Pat O'Brien's: This version of the famous New Orleans bar-restaurant features classic Cajun and Creole food, a lively bar – serving the signature Hurricane cocktail among others – and a duelling piano lounge that follows its Bourbon Street heritage (4pm-midnight).

> **BRITTIP**
> Park in Universal's multi-storey car park for all CityWalk venues – free after 6pm (except during special evening events).

Hard Rock Live: A massive mock-Coliseum styled 2,500-seat theatre with high-tech staging and sound, big-name artists are on stage several times a week (Collective Soul, Joe Satriani, Flaming Lips and the fab Classic Albums Live have all appeared in recent times; **hardrock.com**).

Jimmy Buffet's Margaritaville: Live music, both on the main stage indoors and outdoors on the Porch of Indecision, plus an extensive menu, which includes the classic Cheeseburger in Paradise, and four bars, including two outdoors (11am–11pm).

Universal's Great Movie Escape: Due to open in late 2022, this elaborate escape game replaces the old Groove nightclub with a series of specially designed rooms that take their cue from blockbuster films *Jurassic World* and *Back To The Future*. Designed by the creative team behind Universal's Halloween Horror Nights programme, the games feature state-of-the-art missions and intricately detailed sets that challenge guests to solve clues in a multi-sensory experience. No prices or opening times were announced when we went to press, so look up **universalorlando**.com for the latest details.

Rising Star Karaoke: It's karaoke taken to the next level and is hugely entertaining, with a live band, back-up singers, a large selection of songs and a host who makes every singer feel like a star. There is a full bar with speciality cocktails and appetisers (7pm–midnight nightly; 18 and over Thurs–Sun).

NBC Sports Grill & Brew: For a sports bar raised a level, this is perfect for live sporting events (or just a good meal or a drink at one of the two bars). The atmosphere is lively, its own brewery offers great beers and the many HD TV screens feature multiple views of the action. The food is well above usual sports bar cuisine, though, and even non-sports

Orlando's 'Districts'

One of the biggest developments in Orlando in recent years has been the growth of hip, trendy 'Districts' that are great locals' hangouts as well as interesting places to explore. From SoDo, or 'South Downtown' (home to the Pulse Memorial) to Ivanhoe Village and College Park to Curry Ford West, there are 12 distinct 'main street' neighbourhoods of shops, cafés, bars, breweries and nightlife, all of which have real tourist appeal if you're looking for an authentic local experience. They offer a more urban take on places like Winter Park and Winter Garden, and feature original dining, boutiques (notably antiques in Ivanhoe Village) and community events. You should definitely try the Mills 50 district, with its strong Asian influences (like Vietnamese restaurant Little Saigon), and the Milk District, where 7Bites restaurant is a regular award winner, the Tasty Takeover is a Tuesday night Food Truck Block Party, and The Plaza Live offers great live music. Look up more at **orlandomainstreets.com**.

fans should feel comfortable with the more sophisticated style. We especially like the Midwest Ribs, Cedar-Planked Salmon, Bang-Bang Chicken and succulent barbecue dishes (10.30am–1am daily).

Coca-cola Store in Disney Springs

© Disney

Toothsome Chocolate Emporium & Savory Feast Kitchen: This temple to all things sweet is a work of art, with its steampunk décor and built-in gadgetry, as well as actors playing the roles of Penny Toothsome and robot companion Jaques. The entertainment value is high but the range of milkshakes, sundaes and desserts is dazzling. Look out for the Chocolate x 5 (with five different kinds of chocolate ladled into a milkshake), the Thrilla in Vanilla and the Espresso Buzzzz. The restaurant also serves excellent burgers, steak, pasta and seafood, but we're betting you're coming for the sweet stuff! There is also a gift shop (10.30am–1am daily).

Not breathless yet? Well, there's still the 20-screen **Universal Cineplex** with a capacity of 5,000 and Luxury Loungers and an XD auditorium for the latest in movie comfort. And, of course, there's the Hollywood Drive-In Golf (p250).

POINTE ORLANDO
This development on I-Drive, almost opposite the Convention Center, is a mix of shops, cinema, restaurants, live entertainment and the WonderWorks fun centre (with its magic-themed dinner show). The Pointe has day and night appeal.

Dockside Margaritas at Disney Springs Marketplace

© Disney

Blue Martini: This was Tiger Woods' favourite hang-out when he lived in Orlando, a high-energy cocktail lounge featuring DJs, live music, signature drinks and a tapas menu, plus an extensive daily Happy Hour (**orlando.bluemartini.com**).

Cuba Libre Restaurant and Rum Bar: Offers live Latin music on Fri and Sat nights, starting at 10pm (**cubalibrerestaurant.com**).

Main Event Entertainment: For active fun, this high-quality indoor complex – with state-of-the-art 10-pin bowling, ropes course, story rooms, mini-golf, karaoke, laser tag, multiball and video games – takes some beating. Especially clever is their multi-player virtual reality centre that pits guests in active, free-roaming challenges against zombies, robots and more. Another highlight is the extensive indoor/outdoor bar and dining room, with a great drinks menu and New American cuisine (noon–midnight Mon–Fri, 10am–midnight Sat, 11am–midnight Sun; **bit.ly/brit-mainevent**).

Orlando Improv Comedy Club and Fat Fish Blue: The Improv pulls in top US comedians, with shows ranging from risqué to raucous. The intimate theatre makes it easy for entertainers to interact with guests (often with hilarious results) and it is a terrific change of pace for a grown-up night out. All shows 21 and over, with two performances Fri and Sat. Connected to the Improv, bistro-style Fat Fish Blue serves American fare with a New Orleans accent. Full bar, a good range of speciality beers, and live music up to five nights a week (**theimprovorlando.com**).

Regal Cinema: State-of-the-art 21-screen movieplex (with IMAX screen) boasting stadium seating and the latest 4DX immersive technology (**bit.ly/brit-regal**).

Taverna Opa: A lively Greek option, with belly-dancing, other live entertainment and a great ouzo bar! (**opaorlando.com**).

For more info go to **pointeorlando.com** or p290 for restaurant choices.

DOWNTOWN ORLANDO

Church Street is the epicentre of this nightlife hub, part of the City District, with a wide variety of dining choices, from the distinctive supper-club of **Kres Chophouse** and its elegant bar, to the all-American burger bar frenzy of **Graffiti Junktion**. Add in high-energy bars **Latitudes, Cahoots** and **Chillers**, plus cabaret, theatre and live music, and this is Party Central at weekends. It's fairly lively Wed and Thurs, too. **Harry Buffalo** appeals to sports fans, while **Hamburger Mary's** takes some beating, with its outrageous drag acts and live comedy (distinctly non-PG but lots of fun), to complement its great burgers, sandwiches, decadent desserts and cocktails. They feature Twisted Sisters Bingo on Thurs, the Dining With The Divas Friday Show ('an interactive drag show'), Leigh Shannon's Cabaret on Sat and a Broadway Brunch on Sun (shows variously 6.30–7.30pm, 11am Brunch, booking highly advised; **hamburgermarys.com/orlando**).

Nearby, **Wall Street Plaza**, between Orange Ave and N Court Ave, is equally lively Thurs–Sat as the locals bar-hop the seven bar venues, which include live music for special events (**wallstplaza.net**). More downtown entertainment can be had at **The Social**, an indie club staging eclectic bands most nights, plus a busy bar; the **Bosendorfer Lounge**, for great live jazz inside The Grand Bohemian Hotel; and **The Beacham**, a nightclub and concert venue next to The Social. The Speakeasy phenomenon can also be found here, with the 1920s 'hidden bar' style well evidenced by **Hanson's Shoe Repair** (call in advance on 407 476 9446 and they will contact you with the nightly password!) and **The Treehouse** (**thetreehouseorlando.com**). New in 2021 was **Haos on Church**, a unique dining and entertainment venue featuring a wide array of acts, from burlesque to visual artists, as well as an impressive menu and trendy Sunday brunch (**haosonchurch. com**).

The City District also includes the rapidly-expanding Creative Village, and other exciting developments, and you can look up the latest info on **citydistrictorlando.com**.

Downtown Orlando at night

DINNER SHOWS

Dinner shows are an Orlando phenomenon: live entertainment coupled with dinner and free soft drinks in a fantasy environment, where even the waiters and waitresses are in costume. They have strong family appeal and you are usually seated at large tables where you get to know other people, but at $32–69, they are not cheap (especially with taxes and tips). Be aware, too, of the attempts to extract more from you with photos, souvenirs and upgrades.

BRITTIP
American cinema popcorn is invariably SALTED. Sweet popcorn in the US is usually called Kettle Corn.

BRITTIP
Most dinner shows can be quite chilly, especially those with animals, like Medieval Times, so bring a jacket or sweater to beat the air-conditioning.

Hoop-Dee-Doo Revue

Disney's dinner show offering is this wildly popular nightly presentation at the Fort Wilderness Resort, extending the resort's Western theme and adding typical food (all-you-can-eat ribs, fried chicken, salad, baked beans, corn bread and strawberry shortcake, plus unlimited beer, wine, sangria and soft drinks). Especially popular with children, it features the amusing song and dance of the Pioneer Hall Players in a merry American hoedown. We're slightly biased but we love this show as it's been running since 1974 and remains a Disney tradition, full of genuine wit and humour, plus a hugely energetic cast that keep things fresh every night. The Revue plays at 4, 6.15 and 8.30pm at the authentic Pioneer Hall, Category 1 seating (main floor centre) is $74/adult, $44/under-10; Cat 2 (back and balcony) $69 and $40; Cat 3 (side balconies) $66 and $39 (under-3s free; prices include tax and gratuity) and the show lasts almost two hours. Reservations are ALWAYS necessary and can be made up to 180 days in advance (full payment at booking). NB: Disney closed its Spirit of Aloha luau show at the Polynesian Village Resort in 2022.

Medieval Times

Spain in the 11th century is the entertaining setting for this two-hour extravaganza of medieval pageantry, falconry and robust horseback jousts. It's worth arriving early to appreciate the clever mock castle design as you are ushered into the pre-show hall before being taken into the arena. The show features jousting, sword-fighting and hand-to-hand combats, plus some superb horsemanship, with the basic idea of cheering on one of the Knights of the Realm in the six colour-coded sections. The weapons are all real and used with great skill, and there are some neat special effects. You need to be in full audience participation mode as you cheer on your knight in the traditional good-v-evil scenario, but kids (and many adults) get a huge kick out of it and they'll also love eating without cutlery (the soup bowls do have handles, though!). The elaborate staging is backed up by a succulent chicken dinner, with tomato soup, garlic bread, potatoes and corn, plus dessert (vegetarian meal available) and the serfs and wenches who serve you make it a fun experience. A basic Royalty Package upgrade for $15/person includes priority access, preferred seating, and a knight's cheering banner. The Queen's Royalty Package adds VIP first or second-row seating in the centre seating area, plus a framed group photo

Hoop-Dee-Doo Revue

© Disney

($25); and the birthday Celebration Package includes a group photo per person, VIP seating, banner, lanyard, personalised announcement during the show and a slice of cake ($20 more). Doors open 90mins prior to show time (times vary seasonally; $65 adults, $39 3–12s; **medievaltimes. com**). The Castle is on Highway 192, 5ml/8km east of the junction with I-4 between Markers 14 and 15.

Pirates Dinner Adventure

One of the most spectacular settings, this features a life-size pirate ship 'anchored' in a huge indoor lagoon – and a full pirate crew to fill it! It delivers good value with a pre-show, plentiful food and soft drinks. The hearty main meal features soup or salad, chicken or surf and turf with mash and seasonal vegetables, or vegetarian pasta, plus dessert. The story revolves around your invitation to the Governor's Ball, where you will meet a magical mermaid who possesses the legendary Serpent's Eye jewel. But evil Captain Sebastian the Black is plotting revenge, and it all devolves into chaos when he and his pirate crew stage a kidnapping that includes Princess Anita, the mermaid and YOU. That's the cue for duels, acrobatics, fights and trapeze acts, with plenty of audience participation. A Treasure Upgrade adds 3rd-row seating, bandana or eye patch, unlimited soda and beer or two glasses of wine during the show, 50% off parking, and gift shop discount ($25 adult, $20 child); a VIP Upgrade ($37 adult, $27 child) adds exclusive pre-show lounge, bar and restrooms, first or second row seating, appetisers, unlimited beer and soft drinks or two glasses of wine during the show, upgraded dessert, eye patch and bandana, 50% off parking, group photo, plus meet and greet with the cast. It is located on Carrier Drive between I-Drive and Universal Boulevard, and runs at 7.30pm Tues–Sat; 6pm Sun. Appetisers are served for 45mins prior to seating ($68 adults, $42 3–12s, includes two rounds of beer during the show; see website for savings; parking $8; **piratesdinneradventure.com**). Watch for themed Pirates Christmas and Halloween shows in December and October.

Sleuth's Mystery Dinner Shows

This is a live version of Cluedo acted out before your eyes in hilarious fashion while you enjoy a substantial meal with a main course choice of Cornish hen, lasagne with or without meatballs (or, for $6 extra, prime rib) or a vegetarian meal, and unlimited beer, wine and soft drinks. You can choose between various plot situations (some of which have amusing British settings), including Squire's Inn, Roast 'Em & Toast 'Em and Lord Mansfield's Fox Hunt Banquet (mayhem at an English banquet), that add up to some elaborate murder mysteries. The action takes place all around you and members of the audience can take some cameo roles. The quick-witted cast keep things moving and keep you guessing during the theatrical part of the 2½-hour show, then during the main part of dinner you think up questions for interrogation (but the real murderer is allowed to lie!). Solve the crime and you win a prize, but that is pretty secondary to the overall entertainment and this is a show we enjoy a lot, plus it's a terrific choice with teens ($68/adult, $/3–11; times vary; Sleuth's is in the plaza just past Ripley's Believe It Or Not on I-Drive, with three theatres, a smart pre-dinner bar area and gift shop.

Sleuth's

© Disney

Outta Control Magic Comedy Dinner Show

This smaller-scale dinner show is at WonderWorks on I-Drive (at Pointe Orlando). A novel mixture of improvised comedy and magic, with all-you-can-eat pizza, salad, and dessert, plus beer, wine and Coke. Set in the intimate Shazam Theater, it features illusionist (and funny guy) Tony Brent serving up one-of-a-kind close-up sleight of hand with plenty of audience participation, especially if you sit close to the stage. Nightly at 6 or 8pm, it costs a good-value $33/adult, $23/4–12 and seniors. A VIP Combo for the show and an All Access ticket to WonderWorks (open 9am until midnight, p226) is $61/$42 (407 351 8800, **wonderworksonline.com**).

Capone's Dinner & Show

Enter Miss Jewel's 1930s Prohibition-era Chicago speak-easy, where gangsters, dames and mobsters gather – and hapless Detective Marvel might make YOU part of his efforts to close the joint down. A mix of comedy and song and dance numbers tell the slapstick-style story, while a huge Italian-American 4-course dinner ensures no-one goes home hungry. Unlimited Bud Light, a selection of wines and cocktails, plus soft drinks, juice and Kiddie Cocktails round out the hearty menu ($70/adult, $46/4–12, 3 and under free; **alcapones.com**). At face value, this is one of the most expensive dinner shows, but there is usually an online discount of up to 50 per cent.

Disney's Typhoon Lagoon after hours

© Disney

LIVE MUSIC

Orlando's live music scene is lively and always changing but several venues can be relied on for quality entertainment. As already noted, the House of Blues and Hard Rock Live provide regular big-name concerts, while international acts appear at the state-of-the-art **Amway Center** in downtown (as well as the Orlando Magic, Orlando Predators and Orlando Solar Bears sports teams). Recent performers include Michael Buble, Roger Waters and The Killers (**amwaycenter.com**).

The **Dr Phillips Performing Arts Center** also features big-name concert performers as well as touring Broadway performances and the Orlando Ballet company (p231).

SPORTS BARS

The sports bar is an American invention. If you'd like to sample the way the locals follow their sport (American football is the biggest at weekends Sept–Jan, but basketball is also popular along with baseball and ice-hockey), try these locations.

Buffalo Wild Wings: This popular national chain has nine Orlando locations (notably on I-Drive, in Kissimmee, and at ICON Park), where masses of chicken-based dishes (watch out for the Blazin' sauce – it's seriously hot!) are served up in a casual, lively atmosphere, highlighted by its Buzztime Trivia System at each table and multiple big-screen TVs (**buffalowildwings.com**). Be like the cool kids and call it 'B-Dubs.'

Miller's Ale House: Among the multitude of sports bars, one of our favourites has fine examples on Kirkman Road, opposite Universal Studios at Lake Buena Vista on Highway 535 near Disney Springs, on I-Drive, at Champions Gate and the Kissimmee location on Highway 192. The Ale Houses feature more than 30 TVs (each!), classic American bar food, including their signature spicy 'chicken zingers' and an above-average range of beers (**millersalehouse.com**).

Other options: Look out for the **Uno Chicago** chain (**unos.com**) or any **TGI Friday's, Graffiti Junktion** or **BJ's Brewhouse** outlet. Then there are **The Pub** and the **Main Event**, both at Pointe Orlando (p290). **Universal CityWalk** boasts **NBC Sports Grill & Brew**, with more big-screen TV style and fab food in an elegant, comfortable atmosphere. **Walk-Ons Sports Bistreaux** is new in town, with locations on International Drive and Highway 192 in Kissimmee, and it features all the sports action with the taste of Louisiana's Cajun cuisine. Or, for possibly the most impressive TV screen, **Wreckers Sports Bar** at the Gaylord Palms resort takes some beating (as does its food). Or try **Frankie Farrell's Irish Pub** at Lake Buena Vista Resort & Spa (next to the Factory Stores).

SOMETHING DIFFERENT

ICEBAR: Spend 45mins surrounded by 50 tons of carved ice while sipping a chilled vodka beverage, then warm up in the Nordic-inspired Fire Lounge, at this fun venue on I-Drive just north of WonderWorks. Coats and gloves are provided or you can upgrade to a glam mock fur coat for $10, and entry fee is $21 (drinks not included; watch for discounts online).

ICEBAR Orlando

Open 5pm–12am Sun–Thurs, 5pm–2am Fri–Sat, with the first ICEBAR entry time at 5.15pm; ages eight and up allowed 5pm–9pm only. No cover charge for Fire Lounge (which also features DJs), but no children. Happy Hour daily, and Experience Package at $43.95 (online discount saves 27%), including one premium drink in ICEBAR and one in Fire Lounge (**icebarorlando.com**).

Howl at the Moon: If you're looking for a serious party, try Howl at the Moon on I-Drive, where the live music doesn't stop until the wee hours! An energetic piano-playing duo pound out a rockin' good time, highlighted by 'Showtime', when the whole bar joins in a choreographed dance-fest. Cocktails are available by the glass or the bucket(!), with drink specials nightly (21 and over only; 7pm–1.45am Thurs-Sat; cover charge $5 Mon–Wed, $7 Thurs, $10 Fri–Sat; **howlatthemoon.com**).

Ole Red Orlando: Join the country-music-tinged party scene at this impressive ICON Park venue (p290) for nightly live music, video fun and more, with a cracking Tennessee-style menu (closed Mon; **https://olered.com/orlando**).

Mango's Tropical Café: This restaurant/nightclub offers a vibrant taste of the Latin-fuelled Miami Beach night-time vibe. Mango's features a colourful multi-storey setting for its array of shows, dancers and live music, with signature performances including the Samba, Cuban Conga and a Michael Jackson Tribute act, as well as DJs and themed nights. The evening entertainment style is aimed at adults (21 and up) but the restaurant and Sidewalk Café are open to all-comers, and the carnival atmosphere keeps going until 2am Thur–Sun (cover charge $10–30 after 9pm; **https://mangos.com/mangos-orlando/**).

Now you'll want to know a lot more about where, when and how to tackle that other holiday dilemma – where to eat. Read on…

11 Dining Out

or, Eat, Drink and Eat Again!

Orlando dazzles with its attractions, delights with its quality and bewilders with its quantity and variety. And that is also true when it comes to dining. There has never been more choice, in more ways and more alternatives than ever before. Hold on to your waistbands, we're going in....

Variety

The diversity of food on offer, from fast-food counters to five-star gourmet experiences, is now Orlando's speciality, especially as the city picked up its first Michelin-starred restaurants in 2022.

Chain restaurants are seemingly everywhere, and you need to know your Applebees from your Red Robins. But, at the same time, there are a range of one-off restaurants of all kinds that maintain the local tradition for convenience, value and superiority.

As a rule, food is plentiful, relatively cheap, available 24 hours a day, and nearly always appetising and filling. You will find an increasing number of fine-dining possibilities, but the basic emphasis is on value, so unless we have marked somewhere as 'pricey', you'll find prices are fairly consistent. Portions are large, service is efficient and friendly, and it's hard to come by a bad meal. The one real exception is

if you dine mainly at fast-food places and the likes of Denny's and Co, you won't find much fresh veg. But you can always ask for the vegetable option instead of fries or potatoes for a more balanced choice. Plus, salads are almost always on the menu.

BRITTIP

As a general rule, Orlando is not somewhere that has a late dining scene (like, say, Spain). That means if you prefer a late dinner, you need to check how late a restaurant stays open.

Exceptional deals

Most restaurants tend towards the informal (T-shirts and shorts are nearly always acceptable) and cater readily for families; you will always find a kids' menu, and many have activity packs. Many hotels and restaurants offer Kids-eat-free deals (from under-10 to under-14), provided parents are also dining. The age limits vary. The all-you-can-eat buffet (some served, some self-serve) is another common feature, where you can probably eat enough at breakfast to keep you going to dinner! Some places offer early-bird specials for dining before 5.30pm as 5.30–7.30pm is peak time for most restaurants. You may have a wait if you arrive between 6 and 8pm.

Don't be afraid to ask for the leftovers 'to go' and don't hesitate to say if something isn't right; the locals will readily complain (politely) if they are not happy, so restaurants are keen to ensure everything is to their diners' satisfaction. And, please, don't forget to tip; the basic wage for waiters and waitresses is low, so they rely heavily on tips as part of their income and are taxed on an assumed level of tips. Unless service really is shoddy (in which case mention it), the usual tip rate is 10% of your bill at buffet-style restaurants and 15–20% at full-service restaurants. Check if service is already added to your bill, though this isn't common. The big shopping malls all offer good-value food courts.

You will encounter a huge range of food types. Florida is renowned for its seafood, which comes much cheaper than in the Mediterranean: crab, lobster, shrimp (what we call king prawns), scallops and oysters, as well as several dozen varieties of fish, many unusual (like mahi mahi and grouper; take note, dolphin on a menu is dolphin fish, not the mammal!). Latin-style cuisines, notably Cuban and Mexican, are common, and the South American influences mean the delicious citrus-marinated seafood called ceviche is often featured. There is also plenty of Asian fare, from Chinese and Indian to Japanese, Thai and Vietnamese. 'Cracker' cooking is original Floridian fare, and the speciality is alligator, either stewed, barbecued, smoked, sautéed or braised. Fried gator tail 'nuggets' are a local favourite, as are catfish and frogs' legs. And do try key lime pie!

Paddlefish at Disney Springs

© Visit Orlando

Belly up to the bar!

If you'd like just a snack or sample of a restaurant's fare, many places offer a bar or appetiser menu, including Bar Louie, Big Fin Seafood, Bonefish Grill, Capital Grille, Carrabba's, Eddie V's, Fishbones, Fleming's, Hillstone, House of Blues, Kres Chophouse, Moonfish, Morton's, The Oceanaire, Old Hickory, Paddlefish, Rainforest Café, Ravenous Pig, Roy's, Seasons 52, Texas de Brazil, T-Rex Café and Brio Tuscan Grille (weekdays only, in the bar), Landry's Seafood House (3.30–5.30pm Mon–Fri), The Palm at Universal Orlando's Hard Rock Hotel and the fab Nomads Lounge at Animal Kingdom.

Vegetarian options

In a country where beef is king, vegetarians often find themselves hard done by. However, there are some bright spots. Most good-quality restaurants should provide a veggie option and are usually happy to provide something even if it's not on the menu. All Disney's full-service restaurants will be able to oblige, and most at Universal, too. Full vegetarian restaurants include **Woodlands** (Indian cuisine) on S Orange Blossom Trail (**woodlandsusa.com**); Indian street food of **Honest** (**honestrestaurantusa. com**; closed Mon); Winter Park's **Ethos Vegan Kitchen** (**ethosvegankitchen. com**); **Winter Park Biscuit Co** (biscuit meaning American savoury scone) in Winter Park (**winterparkbiscuitco. com**) and the bohemian **Market On South**, in Orlando's Milk District (**marketonsouth.com**).

The **Panera Bread** chain also offers some decent veg options (and free wi-fi).

BRITTIP

Portions are often so large, you can save money by sharing a main course. Your waiter or waitress should be happy to oblige (but keep their tip up to the full rate).

Drinking

Looking for a good beer or cocktail? Orlando definitely has you covered. You can run a tab in the majority of bars and pay when you leave. But be aware US licensing laws are stricter than ours and you MUST be 21 to drink alcohol in a bar or lounge. You'll often be asked for proof of age before you are served (or allowed into a club), so take your passport or photo driving licence. No arguing: no photo ID, no beer!

Ice: Drinks usually come with a LOT of ice. If you want your whisky (or vodka, etc) without ice, ask for it 'straight up'. If you prefer soft drinks without the usual iceberg, ask for 'no ice' or 'light ice'.

Spirits: Called 'liquor' in the US, these come in a large selection, but beware of ordering just 'whisky' as you'll get bourbon. Specify if you want Scotch or Irish whiskey.

Cocktails: There is a massive choice of cocktails and most bars and restaurants have lengthy happy hours with good prices.

Wines: Good-quality Californian wines are better value than European.

Soft drinks: If you stick to 'sodas' or coffee, most bars and restaurants give free refills.

Dollar Off Drinks Card: This programme does exactly what it says – provides a dollar off drinks (beer, wine, cocktails, sodas, tea and coffee) at more than 70 bars and restaurants around Orlando. It costs $15 for a card that can be used up to 30 days and is valid on all full-priced drinks (not happy hour or other specials), and can be used with *every* drinks order, so you could save $41 if you used it just four times a day for two weeks (potentially a lot more with greater use or a longer visit). Look up more at **dollaroffdrinks.com**).

Breweries

There's a huge craft beer scene in the US, with new breweries popping up all the time. Big-label beers (Budweiser, Coors and Miller Lite) leave a lot to be desired in taste terms, hence there has been big growth in national alternatives like Sam Adams, Leinenkugel's, Yuengling, Goose Island, Blue Moon and Kona. The state's brewery scene has mushroomed in recent years, with more than 30 craft breweries in Central Florida alone. The following provide an excellent cross-section, and most offer flights, or tasting selections. There's also the **Orlando Ale Line** that runs a brewery bus loop each Saturday (**orlandoaleline.com**).

Broken Strings Brewery: Just two blocks from Orlando City soccer stadium, this brewery is hugely popular with fans and offers a great variety in their taproom, with beers like Purple Mane that pay homage to the team (2–8pm Tues–Thurs, 2–10 Fri, noon–10pm Sat, 2–8pm noon–6pm Sun, closed Mon; **brokenstringsbrewery.com**).

Bowigens Beer Company: This Casselberry brewery and taproom offers 19 drafts and more than 20 bottled beers, including staples like a Citrus Pale Ale, 7 Layer Stout and Daytime Tangerine (2–10pm Mon–Wed, 2–11pm Thurs, noon–11pm Sat, noon–8pm Sun; **bowigens.com**).

Crooked Can: In Winter Garden's Plant Street Market is this signature brewery, producing a wide range from a Belgian Golden Ale to Chocolate Stout and Hefweisen. The taproom is open 11am–11pm Sun–Thurs and 11am–midnight Fri and Sat, with food available from the neighbouring market stalls. Tours Sun noon–4pm ($5/person, includes a pint of your choice; **crookedcan.com**).

Crooked Can Brewing Company

The Hourglass Brewery: Established in 2012 in the suburb of Longwood, this brewer has a reputation for unique beers – notably a barrel-aged selection – as well as flagship, year-round ales like the GoneMild! and Frankie Rock hefeweizen (11am–11pm Mon–Thurs, 11am–1am Fri and Sat, noon–10pm Sun; **thehourglassbrewery.com**).

Orlando Brewing Co: The oldest and biggest brewer in town was forced to move from downtown in 2022, but they hoped to be in a new home at 5638 International Drive by the end of the year. Be sure to check **orlandobrewing.com** for the latest details.

Redlight Redlight: A Winter Park success story, with a regularly changing array of beers, lagers, cider and even barley wine (3pm–midnight Mon–Thurs, 3.30–2am Fri, 1pm–2am Sat, 1–11pm Sun, **redlightredlightbeerparlour.com**).

Ten10 Brewing: This lively brewer is in the heart of the Mills 50 district, hence popular with the locals for its tempting range, including a tasty Sundae Best brown ale and Black Gold Stout. Their small-plate menu is good, too (noon–10pm Mon–Thurs, noon–11pm Fri–Sat, noon–8pm Sun; **ten10brewingcompany.com**).

Brew-pubs

These are also extremely popular and can be found in growing numbers, offering their own craft beers and surprisingly good food. The pick of the bunch include **Big River Grille & Brewing Works** at Disney's Boardwalk Resort; **NBC Sports Grill & Brew** at Universal's CityWalk; **BJ's Restaurant & Brewhouse** in five Central Florida locations (**bjsrestaurants.com**); **The Yard House** at ICON Park; and the chic **Whisper Creek Farm: The Kitchen** at the JW Marriott hotel at the Grande Lakes Resort.

— BRITTIP

If there are several of you drinking beer, ordering a pitcher will work out cheaper than buying it by the glass.

Magical dining

Orlando has become a foodie's paradise in recent years and, to celebrate, the period from late Aug to 2 Oct is officially **Magical Dining**, with a selection of more than 120 top restaurants offering a three-course prix fixe menu at $40/head, a great saving on regular prices. These have included A Land Remembered (Rosen Shingle Creek), Seasons 52, and the superb Hamilton's Kitchen. Check out more at **bit.ly/brit-dining**.

The Cheesecake Factory at Mall at Millenia

Who's who

Despite the emerging foodie culture, most restaurants in the main tourist areas will still be the big chains, so here is a run-down of who they are (apart from the obvious fast-food places like McDonalds, KFC, Subway, Wendy's, etc).

Fast food: A few notable US additions to the burger scene, with a more distinctive touch, include BurgerFi, Five Guys Burgers & Fries, Fuddruckers, Steak 'n Shake, Sonic and newcomers White Castle and Portillo's.

Breakfast-style: Serving throughout the day but with a speciality for breakfast, and none of them serving alcohol: Bob Evans, Cracker Barrel, Dennys, Friendly's, IHOP, Panera Bread, Perkins, Waffle House and our recommendations of **First Watch** (**firstwatch.com**) and **Keke's Breakfast Café** (**kekes.com**).

BRITTIP

American bacon is always streaky crisp fried, and sausages are chipolata-like and slightly spicy. Very different from the British versions.

Buffet style: The all-you-can-eat options that tend to be cheap and cheerful: CiCi's Pizza, Golden Corral, Ponderosa and Shoney's.

Bar-restaurant style: The full American dining experience, with typical bar food and drinks: Applebee's; Bahama Breeze (with a Caribbean twist); BJ's Brewhouse (wide-ranging menu and craft beers); Buffalo Wild Wings and Miller's Ale House (both in sports bar territory); Cheesecake Factory (a huge menu, and decadent desserts); Chilis and Chuys (with Tex-Mex flavours); Hooters (with their 'Hooter Girl' waitresses); Hurricane Grill & Wings (above average bar food and great wings); Manny's Chophouse (a local favourite); Red Robin (for some of the

Jiko at Animal Kingdom

© Disney

best burgers in town); Shake Shack (a lot more than just great milkshakes!); TGI Friday's (eclectic American style); Uno Pizzeria & Grill (with a more upmarket touch).

Steakhouse style: Where you'll get a really good steak, but also fish, chicken and salads: Capital Grille (the fancy touch); Charley's Steakhouse (also with a deluxe ambience); Logan's Roadhouse; Lone Star Steakhouse; Longhorn Steakhouse; Morton's Steakhouse (the sophisticated touch); Outback Steakhouse (Brit-popular and consistently good value); Ruth's Chris Steakhouse (another superb upmarket choice); Saltgrass Steak House (equally smart and classy); and Sonny's Real Pit Bar-B-Q (with the accent on barbecue everything).

Italian flavours: With classic Italian menus: Brio Tuscan Grille (one of the best); Carrabba's; Macaroni Grill; Maggiano's Little Italy; Olive Garden.

Seafood specials: Where you can indulge in the full range of Floridian specialities like grouper and stone crabs: Bonefish Grill (with an upmarket touch); Boston Lobster Feast (pile 'em high!); Joe's Crab Shack (family-friendly style); Red Lobster.

Where to eat

That gives you the inside track on HOW to eat and drink like the locals. Now you need to know WHERE. There are 4,000-plus restaurants in the area, so the following selection covers the main ones, grouped by area.

As with most things Orlando, we start with Walt Disney World.

DISNEY DINING

Having said how Orlando is dominated by chain restaurants, you'll find little evidence of that in Walt Disney World, apart from one McDonalds near the All Star resorts; Earl of Sandwich, Starbucks, Planet Hollywood and House of Blues at Disney Springs; and niche upmarket names like Morimoto, Wolfgang Puck, Todd English and Shula's Steakhouse. Some of the most distinctive dining is from Disney's own creative team around the resorts, and we strongly recommend trying at least one of them.

Animal Kingdom Lodge: Jiko is one of Disney's finest dining choices, with a creative new world fusion cuisine boasting hints of Africa, India and the Mediterranean, as well as a superb South African wine list. **Sanaa** has similar African-Asian influences, but with more accent on Indian food and a couple of great curry dishes, all with a view over the animal savannah. For families, **Boma** is the ideal buffet choice, with a fabulous array of different dishes, both exotic and more familiar, and it's a great opportunity to sample more unusual offerings.

Contemporary Resort: The **California Grill** is the classic high-rise dining experience, with spectacular Pacific-coast flavours, including superb sushi and an amazing Sunday Brunch (with the price tag to match); **Steakhouse 71** opened in Oct 2021, offering a casual setting for all-day dining but with an upscale dinner menu and signature cocktails.

Disney's Boardwalk Inn: There is more wonderful seafood on offer at the **Flying Fish,** with eye-catching décor and superb cocktail lounge, where the culinary team serve up some of the best seafood in Orlando; **Trattoria al Forno** features classic Italian cuisine with regional specialities like Parmigiana di Pollo and Pettini di Mare, plus great desserts and an all-Italian wine list.

Our Disney Hotel Top 10

Ideal for a special occasion

1. Jiko
2. Bluezoo
3. Victoria & Albert's
4. California Grill
5. Shula's Steakhouse
6. Narcoossee's
7. Artist Point
8. Yachtsman Steakhouse
9. Sanaa
10. Flying Fish

Citricos at the Grand Floridian

© Disney

Grand Floridian: First-class seafood is on offer at gorgeous waterfront restaurant **Narcoossee's**, which is a great special-occasion choice, if a touch pricey; **Citricos** offers fine dining with a Mediterranean-infused twist; and **Victoria & Albert's** is Disney's crème-de-la-crème, a superb gourmet experience with white-glove service and New American cuisine.

Polynesian Village Resort: The full South Seas dining experience is on display at **'Ohana**, where food is served family-style, with large plates of food for the whole table, and as much as you can eat; **Kona Café** also offers a Polynesian and Asian-tinged menu but with a more sophisticated ambience.

Riviera Resort: Atop the new DVC resort, **Topolino's Terrace** is a refined venture into cuisine from the French and Italian rivieras, with a classic retro vibe and decadent steak, seafood and pasta dishes.

Swan and Dolphin: The choice here is dazzling, from the elegant supper-club style of **Shula's Steakhouse** to the classic Italian of **Il Mulino**, an upmarket New York trattoria with lashings of style. Japanese cuisine and excellent sushi is on offer at **Kimonos**, with an interesting sushi menu, and there is also karaoke nightly. Todd English's **Bluezoo** is another sumptuous seafood choice, both for the décor and the cuisine, as well as another wonderful bar

area and wine list, while the new Swan Reserve offers the succulent Mediterranean flavours of **Amare**.

Wilderness Lodge: A great fine-dining experience is on offer at **Artist Point,** where steaks and seafood are superbly cooked and presented in elegant surroundings with a Pacific North-West culinary touch; **Whispering Canyon Café** is a rowdy, family-style restaurant, where the food has an Old West vibe and is served family-style.

Yacht & Beach Club: Fine dining is on offer at the **Yachtsman Steakhouse**, where succulent steaks are the order of the day, as well as fine seafood and gracious service. It's not cheap but the quality is unarguable. **Cape May Café** is themed like a New England beachfront, with quality seafood to match, served buffet style.

That is Disney's signature resort dining, but there are other gems worth noting. Caribbean Beach Resort has **Sebastian's Bistro**, where American favourites are given a Caribbean twist and the quality is well above average. Coronado Springs has **Maya Grill,** a Latin-infused menu that elevates dining beyond the norm, and fabulous new rooftop option **Toledo–Tapas, Steak & Seafood**; and Port Orleans has the eye-catching **Boatwrights** serving tastes of Louisiana, including jambalaya and catfish, in its heavily themed interior.

Character dining at Topolino's Terrace

© Disney

Disney Springs

Dining here is now a huge adventure in all four areas. Just remember you're paying for the scenery and ambience as well as the food!

The Landing

The Boathouse: This is nautically themed, with the obvious focus on great seafood, but also excellent chicken, chops, salads, raw bar and some of the best steaks in Florida. A well-presented kids' menu is also available, and the presentation is stylish. There are three bars, outdoor dining, live music, gift shop, boat rides and a water view from each dining room, which makes for memorable dining, but with the price tag to match (11am–11pm, **theboathouseorlando.com**).

—BRITTIP
Maria & Enzo's features an excellent weekend brunch menu from 11.30am–3.30pm on Saturdays and Sundays **patinagroup.com/maria-enzos**.

The Edison: This imposing 1930s-style nightclub/restaurant scores highly for its cabaret and live music, plus stilt-walkers and aerialists, but it also has an enticing range of artisanal snacks, small plates, flatbreads, sandwiches, charcuterie and desserts (don't miss the big-enough-for-two milkshakes!) to go with great handcrafted cocktails (**theedisonfla. com**).

Maria & Enzo's Ristorante: This enormous split-level southern Italian offering serves up soups, salads, pasta, fish and meat in surroundings themed as a 1930s airport terminal, and with magnificent lakeside views. Again, desserts are a highlight (5–10pm Mon–Fri, 11.30am–10pm Sat–Sun; **patinagroup.com/maria-enzos**).

Enzo's Hideaway: The 'sister' restaurant to the Ristorante, this is part Speakeasy-type bar and part clandestine restaurant, serving a delicious selection of prohibition-era cocktails and Italian culinary favourites. In its 'hideaway' location, it is excellent for a quiet lunch or a romantic dinner (11.30am-10pm, **patinagroup.com/enzos-hideaway**).

Chef Art Smith's Homecomin': Celebrity chef Art Smith brings true Florida cooking (and moonshine!) to this elaborate rustic setting, with an excellent bar and show kitchen. Smith specialises in old-time 'Cracker' fare, with a modern twist and fresh local ingredients. Try his cheese-laced drop biscuits, fried chicken, and shrimp and grits, plus the signature cakes and fresh fruit cobblers for dessert. The adjacent Shine Bar offers wonderful coolers, cocktails and punches (11am–10pm Mon–Fri, 9am–10pm Sat–Sun; **homecominkitchen.com**).

Jock Lindsey's Hangar Bar: This Indiana Jones-themed lounge bar is packed with eye-catching novelties, as well as great cocktails, but it also serves up some excellent small-plate meals, like the Snakebite Sliders, Club Obi Wan Chicken Wings and Tuna Tacos (noon–11pm Mon–Thurs, 11.30pm Fri, 11am–11pm Sat–Sun).

Morimoto Asia: We're big fans of the Pan-Asian style of Chef Masaharu Morimoto (of TV's *Iron Chef* fame), which puts the emphasis on Japanese cuisine, seafood and elaborate sushi offerings in a sleek two-storey setting. Exhibition kitchens, a contemporary cocktail lounge and patio dining add to the ambiance, while the menu features classics such as Orange Chicken and Dim Sum, plus plenty of contemporary twists. A 'Street Foods' patio window also serves small-scale tastes (4.30am–9pm Mon–Thurs, 10pm Fri, noon–3pm and 4.30–10pm Sat, 12.30–3pm and 4.30–9pm Sun; **patinagroup.com/morimoto-asia**).

—BRITTIP
Make sure you taste Morimoto's Spare Ribs, deep-fried with a hoisin sweet chilli glaze – even if you only sample them from the Street Foods window. They are truly delish and ideal for sharing, either as a half-rack starter or full-rack main course.

Paddlefish: The former Fulton's Crabhouse has an excellent seafood menu, which includes Crab guacamole and a shellfish-stuffed cod, plus steaks and burgers. It's not cheap but the rooftop lounge is worth visiting just for a drink (noon–11pm daily; **paddlefishrestaurant.com**).

Paradiso 37: This 'Taste of the Americas' offers a wide variety of foods, much with a Latin-tinged flavour, and live music nightly. A tempting menu includes Argentinean skirt steak, Baha Fish Tacos, cocktails and tequila. The lively style, split-level restaurant, chic bar area (inside and out) and lakeside setting mark this out for a relaxing lunch or upbeat dinner (11am–11pm Sun–Thurs, 11.30pm Sat–Sun; **paradiso37.com**).

Terralina Crafted Italian: This replaced the old Portobello with even more authentic Italian flair under award-winning chef Tony Mantuano. It is built around a show-kitchen, with a broad range of Italian regional specialities, notably an antipasti tower, house-made pastas, artichoke chicken and artisanal wood-fired pizza, plus a kid's menu and a genuine, laid-back vibe (**terralinacrafteditalian.com**).

Raglan Road: This Irish-themed pub, with lively music and a genuine Emerald Isle style, is where you really can enjoy the food as well as the craic. Much of the restaurant's interior was shipped over from Ireland (including four reclaimed bar-tops dating back to the 1870s), establishing an authentic backdrop to an original menu. Fresh, simple ingredients with an imaginative twist: shepherd's pie, drunk mussels, Salmon Boxty, Irish sausages, plus a range of original sandwiches at lunchtime and a healthy vegan Shepherd's Pie. Great weekend brunch and special dining events, and it's not too taxing on the wallet (11am–11pm Mon–Thurs, 11.30pm Fri, 9am–11.30pm Sat, 9am–11pm Sun **raglanroad.com**).

STK Orlando: This fabulous take on steakhouse chic brings a vibrant, edgy style to a traditional area, combining restaurant and lounge (with great cocktails). Instead of dark, brooding and formal, STK goes for playful and innovative (including a live DJ), with a creative touch to the décor and a decadent depth to their flavours. Rooftop dining – perfect for warm Floridian evenings – is another feature, along with trendy menu items that include Maine lobster linguine, jalapeno pickled shrimp cocktail, and Baby Gem Caesar, along with large, medium and small steaks, plus some sizzling signature cocktails (11am–10.45pm Mon–Thurs, 11am–11.15pm Fri, 9.30am–11.15pm Sat, 11.30am–10.45pm Sun; happy hour from 3–6.30pm, **bit.ly/brit-STK**).

Wine Bar George: This sparkling offering is the work of local master sommelier George Miliotes, who helped create Disney's California Grill and Seasons 52 restaurants. A rustic two-storey creation, it features delicious small-plate bites – like Grilled Octopus and Crispy Mac and Cheese – as well as huge 'sharing' dishes (don't miss the luscious Skirt Steak), plus a superb Wine Country Brunch at weekends. There is a dazzling array of 140 wines, by the ounce, glass or bottle, including some well-priced wineries sourced by George himself, plus signature cocktails, craft beers and ciders. And the Olive Oil Cake for dessert is to die for! (noon–11pm Mon–Thurs, 11.30pm Fri, 10.30am–11.30pm Sat, 10.30am–11pm Sun, brunch 10.30am–2pm Sat–Sun, **winebargeorge.com**).

Other choices: To one side of Raglan Road is **Cookes of Dublin**, a chippie serving up real chips, beer-battered fish, gourmet battered sausages and

Jock Lindsey's Hangar Bar

© Disney

scrumptious chocolate brownies. Fabulous Italian-style ice cream is on offer at **Vivoli Il Gelato** (direct from Florence) or head to **Joffrey's Coffee & Tea Co** for a really good cuppa. Massively popular **Gideon's Bakehouse** is the place for giant cookies, cakes and cold brews. The quick-service **Pizza Ponte** next to Maria & Enzo's adds great pizza, Italian sandwiches and pastries.

BRITTIP

For reservations at any Disney restaurant, call 407 939 3463 (407 WDW DINE), or book online at **disneyworld.co.uk.**

The Marketplace

While the Marketplace is largely a shopping area (p299) it also offers tempting dining.

Rainforest Café: In a safari-style setting under a volcano belching fire and smoke, fill up on platefuls of chicken, pasta, steak, seafood and burgers, surrounded by audio-animatronic animals and periodic 'rainstorms', with an excellent kids menu. The Lava Lounge features small-plate appetisers, great cocktails and drink specials in a lakeside setting (11am–10pm Sun–Thurs, 11pm Fri and Sat; **rainforestcafe.com**).

T-Rex Café: Enter a vast series of themed areas, like the Jurassic Forest, home to all manner of roaring dinos, with meteor strikes and thunderstorms too! The food is straightforward (with wacky names like Boneyard Buffet) but portions are large and you can also pop in just for a drink (11am–10pm Sun–Thurs, 11pm Fri and Sat; **trexcafe.com**).

Other choices: Ghirardelli Ice Cream & Chocolate Shop is a great option for dessert or a milkshake. **The Earl of Sandwich** serves superb sandwiches and lighter meals, and **Wolfgang Puck Express** has quick-service Californian cuisine, while there are quick-bite counter service offerings at **The Daily Poutine** (Canadian-style French fries with different toppings), and **BB Wolf's Sausage Co** (tempting artisan sausages with a variety of toppings).

BRITTIP

We think the best value at Disney Springs is the excellent Earl of Sandwich, where one of their hot sandwiches is often enough for two.

West Side

Back in the more hip night-time district of Disney Springs are another four options.

House of Blues®: Enjoy some rock 'n' roll as you dine in 'backwoods Mississippi' style, plus a signature Gospel Brunch on Sun that offers fab food with a full gospel show (10.30am; $49/person). The main restaurant offers excellent Cajun and Creole specialities, notably seafood jambalaya and crawfish etouffee, and live music (11.30am–11pm Mon–Fri, 10am–11.30pm Sat, 10am–11pm Sun; **houseofblues.com/orlando**).

Splitsville: OK, so it's a bowling alley, but the food and drink are good, so you might want to consider this as a dining option on its own. Fresh sushi is their speciality, but the menu also offers gourmet burgers, sandwiches, pizza, entrée salads and main-course dishes like taco bowl, fish 'n' chips, Ahi Tuna, grilled salmon, and chicken fried rice. Try their Super Sundae for dessert and the cocktail menu is extremely tempting (11am–11pm Sun–Thurs, 11.30pm Fri–Sat; **splitsvillelanes.com**).

Jaleo: This authentic taste of Spain from influential Chef José Andrés features an extensive menu of tapas, cured meats, paella, cheese dishes, shellfish and favourites such as *carne asada* and chorizo. Beer, wine and cocktails continue the Spanish influence and desserts are markedly Catalan, including a scrummy Flan with cream and orange (11.30am–11pm daily; **bit.ly/brit-jaleo**).

City Works Eatery & Pour House: This sports bar and brew pub offers three bars, large-screen TVs,

90 craft beers on tap, plus an open-air patio and tempting menu, notably for weekend brunch (11am–11pm Mon–Thurs, 11.30pm Fri, 10am–11.30pm Sat, 10am–11pm Sun; **cityworksrestaurant.com/disneysprings**).

Other choices: Grab a snack at **Wetzel's Pretzels**, pretzels, hot dogs and lemonade; **YeSake's** Asian bowls and wraps; try **Haagen-Dazs** ice-cream; **Everglazed** donuts, cold brews, sandwiches and milkshakes are some of the best you'll find (**everglazed.com**); grab a coffee at the inevitable **Starbucks**; or try the **Food Truck Park**, with a series of trucks offering local favourites like tacos and Mac & Cheese. New in 2022 was the heavenly ice cream inspiration of **Salt & Straw**, with a wildly creative menu. New concept **Summer House on the Lake** should open in 2023, offering California-inspired cuisine in a chic lakeside setting.

Town Center

This area of Disney Springs is focused firmly on shopping, but there are still several tempting food offerings, and the return of a stylish Californian brand.

Blaze Fast-Fire'd Pizza: For counter-service artisanal pizza, plus salads and desserts, this is another fresh choice, and at a lower price than many. Everything is flash-cooked in their 'blazing hot' ovens, so beware biting too soon! (11am–10pm Sun–Thurs, 11pm Fri–Sat).

Chicken Guy!: Looking for fast-food chicken with a twist? Visit celebrity chef Guy Fieri's latest creation, with Chicken Tenders, signature Sandwiches and Salad Bowls all given a fresh burst of flavour, and enhanced by Guy's choice of 22 (!) sauces to go with them (**https://chickenguy.com**).

D-Luxe Burger: You'll need both hands for these huge gourmet burgers, each prepared to order from a relatively simple (but delicious) selection. Fries are separate and come with four dipping sauces, and there are magnificent milkshakes and soda floats for dessert (11am–10.30pm Sun–Thurs, 11pm Fri–Sat).

BRITTIP

For a drink with a kick, try the alcoholic shakes at D-Luxe Burger, including a Smoked Bourbon and Bananas Foster. A cocktail and dessert in one!

Frontera Cucina: Here's more celebrity chef style, with TV's Rick Bayless presenting his modern version of traditional Mexican cuisine in another imaginative setting. As well as tacos and his famous tortas (sandwiches), there are luscious chicken and shrimp dishes, plus a heavenly Carne Asada – red chilli-marinated Black Angus steak. For smaller tastes, there is a grab-and-go window (11am–11pm; **fronteracocina.com**).

Planet Hollywood Observatory: The largest and busiest of this worldwide chain, a sleek, sophisticated observatory in keeping with the Disney Springs story. The menu focuses on familiar foods with an upscale twist, including long-time favourite World Famous Chicken Crunch, L.A. Lasagne, bbq ribs, and Sirloin Steak, along with salads, sandwiches and gigantic burgers designed by Guy Fieri. Save room for one of their outrageous desserts! Beer, wine and speciality cocktails are all available, and there are three bars, including outdoor Stargazers Bar, (11.30am–11pm, bar until 1am).

BRITTIP

Planet Hollywood's ground-level **Stargazer's Bar** offers possibly the best-value drinks in Disney Springs, with a daily Happy Hour from 4-7pm and bargain prices on beer, wine and cocktails. It also offers Karaoke on Wednesdays and live music on Fri and Sat (7–11pm).

Sprinkles: All the cupcakes (and cookies and ice-cream sundaes) you could imagine, in regular and mini sizes, served up with immense style in this modern bakery but, again, with prices to match! (10am–11pm Sun–Thurs, 11.30pm Fri–Sat; **sprinkles.com**).

The Polite Pig: This delicious counter service addition, from the owners of Winter Park fave The Ravenous Pig, specialises in wood-fired fare straight from the smoker, such as pork ribs, shoulder and brisket, plus hearty sandwiches (try the Fried Chicken or Southern Pig) and scrumptious sides. Healthy salads and decadent desserts round out your meal, with beer, wine and a bourbon bar. Kid-friendly meals available (11am–11pm Sun–Thurs, midnight Fri–Sat; **politepig.com**).

Wolfgang Puck Bar & Grill: Back in Disney Springs with a new 'farmhouse inspired' California concept, this tempting choice puts an emphasis on Puck's signature dishes highlighted by Mediterranean flavours. From homemade focaccia to artistic pizzas, burgers, salmon and ribeye steak, the

© Universal Orlando Resort

Amatista Cookhouse at the Sapphire Falls Resort

menu is delightfully refined. Don't miss some delicious desserts, plus their Gelato Tasting. Handcrafted cocktails, craft beer and wine round out some impressive offerings (11am–10pm Sun–Thurs, 11pm Fri, 10am–11pm Sat, 10am–10pm Sun; **bit.ly/brit-puck**).

UNIVERSAL ORLANDO

Universal also has a terrific array of hotel dining, many of which are worth trying even if you're not staying there.

Aventura Hotel: This relative newcomer features superb rooftop dining 17 storeys high in **Bar 17 Bistro**, offering classic fare paired with custom-crafted cocktails, all with an amazing view – ideal at sunset.

Hard Rock Hotel: The Palm is a signature New York steak-and-lobster supper club restaurant, hence slightly more formal by Florida standards. The celebrity caricatures on the walls pay tribute to the original restaurant's roots in the Manhattan newspaper district, while the food features Nova Scotia lobster, prime cuts of meat and Italian specialities. **The Kitchen** epitomises more of the rock-star style with a livelier atmosphere and imaginative menu featuring New York strip steak, burgers, pasta, excellent fish dishes and comfort foods like roast chicken and gourmet mac and cheese.

Portofino Bay Hotel: The jewel in the crown here is **Bice**, a superbly presented formal restaurant with genuine Italian flair and tastes. For a special night out it takes some beating, and their antipasto, pan-

Our Disney Springs Top10

You'll definitely be in for a treat at this selection of fine-dining choices:

1. Wolfgang Puck's Bar & Grill
2. The Boathouse
3. Raglan Road
4. Morimoto Asia
5. Jaleo
6. Chef Art Smith's Homecomin'
7. STK Orlando
8. The Edison
9. The Polite Pig
10. Planet Hollywood Observatory

The Boathouse

seared Branzino and roasted rack of lamb are divine. **Mama Della's Ristorante** is more Italian style, but with a more traditional touch in the fish and pasta dishes (still not cheap, though). **Trattoria del Porto** is more brasserie style, with sandwiches, salads and a great pasta selection.

Royal Pacific Resort: The **Islands Dining Room** is a good choice for dinner, with Wok specials and other Asian-influenced dishes, like Korean Bulgogi Ribeye.

Sapphire Falls Resort: Just one main restaurant at this hotel, but it's a highlight, with **Amatista Cookhouse** featuring a Caribbean-inspired menu, a show kitchen and views over the central lagoon, plus the lure of the adjacent **Strong Water Tavern** with its rum-based cocktails and excellent small-plate Caribbean cuisine.

BRITTIP

Toothsome Chocolate Emporium (p284) serves beer, wine and creative hand-crafted cocktails in the surprisingly grown-up atmosphere of their upper-floor lounge. An excellent way to unwind after a day in the parks.

Universal CityWalk

Citywalk provides Universal's other great concentration of dining opportunities, with wonderful variety.

Antojitos Authentic Mexican Food: This cavernous party restaurant offers bags of Mexican style and atmosphere, from their own Mariachi band to fabulous cocktails. The

Antojitos Authentic Mexican Food

© Universal Orlando Resort

menu is equally good, running the culinary gambit from street food (tacos, enchiladas, fajitas) to refined twists on traditional dishes such as Mahi Mahi and Mole-braised short ribs, along with 203 authentic tequilas (4pm–1am Sun–Thurs, 2pm–1am Fri–Sat).

Bob Marley: Jamaican cuisine in a funky setting, featuring entrées such as curry shrimp, oxtail stew and Jamaican Jerk Chicken (4pm–2am daily; 21 and up after 9pm).

Bubba Gump's Shrimp Co: This has the full *Forrest Gump* theme, and is heavy on seafood but also includes chicken, sandwiches, ribs, salads and more, with catchy names like Shrimper's Heaven and Ping Pong Chicken (gluten-free menu available; 11am–11pm Sun–Wed, midnight Fri–Sat; **bubbagump.com**).

BRITTIP

Mention you are celebrating a birthday at Bubba Gump's and you'll find yourself the centre of attention!

The Cowfish: Fresh and innovative, this claims to be the world's first restaurant to feature great sushi AND burgers (hence their trademark 'Burgushi'), with a wide variety of both in an eclectic, lively setting. Spiked milkshakes, premium sakes, craft beers, wine and exotic martinis add to the temptations here, along with a great pure sushi bar (11am–1am Sun–Thurs, 10am–1am Fri–Sat; **thecowfish.com**).

BRITTIP

Looking for a pastry experience with a difference? Try the Voodoo Doughnut, with a dazzling array, including many vegan and gluten-free options. The Texas doughnut is big enough for 4!

Our Universal Top 10

For a memorable meal, choose any of our Universal favourites:

1. Bice
2. The Toothsome Chocolate Emporium
3. Vivo Italian Kitchen
4. The Palm
5. Bigfire
6. The Cowfish
7. Antojitos
8. NBC Sports Grill & Brew
9. Amatista Cookhouse
10. The Kitchen

Rock Café: The largest one of this worldwide chain, with its rock 'n' roll memorabilia (including a pink 1959 Cadillac) and full concert venue, is hugely popular, so get in early for lunch or dinner, with their signature burgers, steaks, fajitas, ribs and sandwiches (8am–midnight, Rock Bar until midnight; **hardrock.com/cafes/orlando**).

BRITTIP

Take a fascinating look 'backstage' at Hard Rock Café with their Backstage & Burgers Tour. View unique memorabilia, hear the history of the Café (which began in London), and take a look inside the John Lennon-themed VIP room, with lunch included. Book online. Tours 10am Sat and Sun only ($12.95–29.95).

Margaritville

© Universal Orlando Resort

Hot Dog Hall of Fame: All kinds of hot-dogs, frankfurters and stuffed dumplings from around the US, with hundreds of condiment variations make this a fun offering (11am–1am daily).

Jimmy Buffet's Margaritaville: An island homage to Florida's laid-back musical hero, with 'Floribbean' cuisine (a mix of Key West and Caribbean), with the Volcano Bar, which 'erupts' margaritas periodically (11am–10pm daily, live music nightly; **margaritavilleorlando.com**)

NBC Sports Grill & Brew: Sophisticated and large scale, with more than 100 TV screens, an excellent menu and its own range of beers. Two bars and most of the food comes from huge custom-made gas grills in the main show kitchen. The outdoor stadium-style screen sets the scene and there are a lot of smart touches inside, not least with the menu that includes Cedar-Planked Salmon, Bang-Bang Chicken and succulent pulled pork, as well as standards like burgers (11am–1am Sun–Thurs, 10.30am–1am Fri–Sat).

Pat O'Brien's: This is a reproduction of the famous New Orleans bar and restaurant with its Flaming Fountain courtyard, main bar and duelling piano bar. Excellent Cajun food and world-famous Hurricane cocktails. (4pm–midnight Sun–Thurs 2am Fri–Sat, with a $7 cover charge after 9pm; 21 and over only; **bit.ly/brit-obrien**).

Red Oven Pizza Bakery: Authentic artisan pizza at this chic restaurant, with some imaginative flavours all baked in their signature 900° Red Oven (11am–2am daily).

Bigfire: This open-fire cooking concept serves American 'campfire' favourites such as steak, bison burger and lake trout in a lakeside summer-house setting from a custom wood-fired grill. The smoky aromas are good enough on their own, but the 16oz Cowboy Ribeye is superb and the speciality S'mores, prepared tableside, are a must-try (4pm–midnight Sun–Thurs, 2pm–midnight Fri–Sat).

Toothsome Chocolate Emporium & Savory Feast Kitchen: This funky Steampunk-style venue is ice cream parlour, gift shop and spectacular restaurant in one. The vast menu features soups, salads, burgers, quiche, waffles and crêpes *before* you get to the entrees. Specialities include Signature Filet Mignon, Chicken Bourguignon and Brisket and Wild Mushroom Meatloaf. Start with their Warm Chocolate Almond Bread, but save room for dessert, massive milkshakes and killer cocktails (10.30am–1am daily).

Vivo Italian Kitchen: Fine Tuscan dining with fresh ingredients served from an open kitchen that offers a customisable menu for its pasta and other featured dishes. Everything is made from scratch and includes freshly pulled mozzarella, house-cured meats and slow-cooked ragu. Excellent wine and cocktail list (2pm–midnight daily).

Other choices: Try **Menchie's** for fab frozen yoghurt, **Bread Box** for great sandwiches, **Cinnabon** for cinnamon pastries, **Cold Stone Creamery** for indulgent ice-cream creations, **Bend The Bao** for bao buns and Asian fusion delights, **Voodoo Doughnut** for 'sinfully delicious' doughnuts, and **Starbucks** for coffee. **The Top of the Walk** food court adds **Burger King Whopper Bar, Panda Express,** and **Moe's Southwest Grill**. **bit.ly/brit-citywalk**.

> **BRITTIP**
> If the CityWalk restaurants are full, take a boat to the Hard Rock Hotel for The Kitchen, or to Portofino Bay for Trattoria del Porto or Mama Della's.

Vivo Italian Kitchen

© Universal Orlando Resort

INTERNATIONAL DRIVE
We divide this into I-Drive North, Sand Lake Road, I-Drive South, Pointe Orlando and ICON Park.

I-Drive North
North of Sand Lake Road is largely, but not all, fast-food and buffets.

> **BRITTIP**
> A hearty breakfast at any of Denny's, IHOP, Keke's, Perkins or First Watch should keep you going until tea-time and is an excellent way to start a theme-park day.

Fast food: Burger King, Dairy Queen, Del Taco, Dunkin' Donuts, Fuddruckers, KFC, McDonalds, Panda Express (Chinese), Pizza Hut, Pollo Tropical (Latin American), Popeye's (fried chicken), Starbucks (Orlando Premium Outlets), Sonic, Subway, Taco Bell, and Five Guys (Orlando Premium Outlets).

Breakfast style: Denny's, IHOP, Perkins.

Applebee's, Buffalo Wild Wings, Chili's, TGI Friday's.

Steakhouse style: Black Angus.

Seafood specials: Red Lobster.

Individuals: Look for **Hash House A Go-Go**, for an inspired, fresh take on classic dishes like burgers, salads, meatloaf, chicken and waffles, and *huge* portions (8am–2pm Sun–Thurs, 8am–7pm Fri and Sat; **hashhouseagogo. com**); and the spectacular upmarket Brazilian steakhouse **Texas de Brazil**, which features a set-price all-you-can eat menu, with a huge salad bar and fresh-cut meats. Pricey but worth it (lunch 11.30am–3pm Thurs and Fri, noon–3.30 Sat and Sun dinner 5–9pm Mon–Thurs, 5–10.30pm Fri, 4–10pm Sat, 4–9.30pm Sun; **texasdebrazil.com**). New in 2022 was **Camelo Pizzaria**, Brazil's own version of the pizza restaurant (dating back to 1957), with some original flavours and toppings, and its own unique style (5–11pm Mon–Thurs, 5–12pm Fri and Sat; 5–10pm Sun; **camelopizzaria.com**).

Sand Lake Road

West of the I-Drive Junction is an area that has more notable one-off restaurants than almost anywhere in town and is called 'Restaurant Row'.

Fast food: Chick-fil-A, Chipotle (more Mexican), Jimmy John's (sandwiches), McDonalds, Starbucks, Tijuana Flats (fresh Mexican style).

Breakfast style: First Watch, Panera Bread.

Steakhouse style: Ruth's Chris.

Seafood specials: Bonefish Grill, and the beautifully upmarket **Ocean Prime** for a special dinner occasion.

Amura: Some of Orlando's best sushi is in this eye-catching Japanese restaurant that also features Asian table barbecue, plus flavourful beef and chicken dishes and first-class seafood. 'Fresh, healthy and delicious,' they promise, and we agree (11.30am–2.30pm and 5–9.30pm Mon–Thurs, 11.30am–2.30pm and 5–10pm Fri, 5–10pm Sat, noon–9.30pm Sun; **amura.com**).

Cedar's: Lebanese cuisine with some of the best chicken and lamb in town. A family-run Middle Eastern delight, it offers the full range of kebabs, falafel and hummus as well as specialities like pan-seared halibut, grilled quail and fried kibbeh. A different alternative and an aromatic treat (noon–9pm Sun–Thurs, noon–10pm Fri, noon–midnight Sat; **cedarsorlando.com**).

Eddie V's: Supper-club style venue featuring succulent seafood with live jazz most evenings. A stylish option but with a more informal V Lounge that is first-come, first served. The menu is a mouth-watering collection of fresh fish and shellfish, as well as fine steaks. Superb wine list and signature cocktails (4–10pm Mon–Sat, 9pm Sun; **eddiev.com**).

The Melting Pot: Every night is fondue night at this smart dining experience, which features seasoned vegetables, fresh-cut meats and artisan cheeses (5–10pm Mon–Thurs, 5–11pm Fri, noon–11pm Sat, noon–10pm Sun; **meltingpot.com/orlando-fl**).

Rocco's Tacos: Wildly eclectic but quality-conscious Mexican offering, great for a fun lunch or lively evening. Follow their table-side guacamole, with a signature Molcajete dish – a sizzling fajita in a lava rock bowl with fresh flour tortillas. Their taco choice is equally tempting, as is the array of margaritas and speciality drinks from their Tequila! (11.30–11pm Mon, Wed, and Sun, 11.30am–2am Tues and Fri, 11.30am–midnight Thurs, 11am–2am Sat; **roccostacos.com**).

Saffron: Smart and stylish Indian with fab-value lunch deals, weekend tableside buffet and classic fine-dining dinner menu. All spice levels can be adjusted and the Chicken Xacutti and Saffron Lamb Curry is worth coming in for alone (11.30am–2.30pm Mon–Fri, 11.30am–3pm Sat–Sun, 5–10pm Sun–Thurs, 10.30 Fri–Sat; **saffronorlando. com**).

Seasons 52: A trendy national chain, with 10 outlets in Florida, we think this offers some of the best dining, with a creative, seasonal, health-conscious menu. All appetisers salads and soups range from 100–250 calories, and all mains are less than 475 calories. The 'mini indulgence' desserts are ideal to finish a meal in style. The bar and outdoor terrace are equally stylish, ideal for a romantic occasion, and fab value for happy hour 3–6pm Mon–Fri (11.30am–10pm Sun–Thurs, 11pm Fri–Sat; **seasons52.com**).

The Whiskey: Great burgers, killer cocktails and almost 150 whiskies, ryes and bourbons are on offer at this chic bistro-pub, with its friendly welcome, keen service and excellent small-plate choices alongside succulent burgers, chops, salmon and salads (noon–midnight Sun–Mon, noon–2am Tues–Sat; **downatthewhiskey.com**).

Vine's Grille & Wine Bar: This upmarket restaurant and wine shop features live jazz and a tempting menu from grilled octopus and oysters to excellent salads, fine steaks and fresh seafood. Another special occasion night out (11.30am–midnight Mon–Thurs, 2am Fri, 11am–1am Sat, 11pm Sun; **vinesgrill.com**).

Sand Lake Road – Dr Phillips Plaza

Staying on Sand Lake Rd but moving into the Dr Phillips Plaza, there are:

Fast food: Chipotle, Pizza Hut, Starbucks, Subway, Toojay's Deli (excellent sandwich choice).

Breakfast style: Keke's.

Steakhouse style: Morton's.

bartaco: A lively tapas-style restaurant in an urban-casual setting, their mini tacos, rice bowls, tuna poke and fab chicken soup are all worth trying, while kids meals, desserts, beer, wine and signature cocktails are all reasonably priced. Be sure to start with the guacamole! (11am–1pm Sun–Wed, midnight Thurs–Sat; **bartaco.com**).

Bosphorous: Why not sample some Turkish flavours with a delicious range of authentic breads, hot and cold appetisers, salads, soups, pides (Turkish pizzas), kebabs and specialities like moussaka and baklava? Dine royally without breaking the bank. Try babaganoush (char-grilled aubergine with fresh herbs and spices), feta plate, lamb sauté or chicken adana (11am–10pm; **bosphorousrestaurant.com**).

Christinis: an upmarket, formal Italian restaurant that has been around for half a century and remains as stylish and traditional as ever, with a classic menu. Reservations usually required (6–11pm; **christinis.com**).

The H Orlando: This Turkish/Mediterranean offering specialises in charcoal oven dishes for a rich array of smoky delights, from meze dishes to steaks, plus tempting traditional desserts (4pm–midnight Sun–Thurs, 2am Fri, noon–2am Sat, 11am–3pm Sunday Brunch; **thehorlando.com**).

Sand Lake Road – Dellagio complex

Moving on to the final part of Sand Lake Road is the **Dellagio** complex, with several more upscale options.

Big Fin Seafood: One of Orlando's most imaginative seafood options, Big Fin is refined but relaxed, a big-scale experience that offers special-occasion atmosphere. The main dining room features a grand salon style but two smaller rooms are more intimate, while the Trophy Bar is ideal for a pre-dinner drink. The menu features sushi, sashimi, oysters and ceviche; classic salads and chowders; steak, chops and chicken; crab and lobster dishes; fresh fish and tempting pastas. Happy Hour is 5–7pm daily at the Bar with $7 drink specials and a reduced-price menu (5–9pm Sun–Thurs, 10pm Fri–Sat; **bigfinseafood.com**).

Dragonfly: Get ready for a Japanese taste sensation from the super-hot *Robata* grill that produces delicious fish, beef, chicken, shrimp and pork. Dragonfly also specialises in fresh sushi and sashimi, as well as its own cocktails and sake for an authentic dining experience (5–10pm Sun–Thurs, 11pm Fri–Sat, **dragonflyrestaurants.com**).

The H Orlando

Fleming's: Award-winning steakhouse serving succulent cuts of the best meats, fish and chicken, notably a divine Prime New York Strip Steak. All can be enhanced with rubs, toppings and sauces for steak aficionados, but this is a premium experience, with all side dishes extra (4–10pm Mon–Sat, 9pm Sun; **flemingssteakhouse.com**).

Peperoncino Cucina: Authentic – and stylish – traditional regional Italian cuisine with a modern twist, served up by passionate chef Barbara Alfano. Daily specials jostle with favourites like lasagna and gnocchi, all from house-made pasta, plus periodical wine-pairing dinners (noon–10pm Mon–Sat, 9pm Sun; **facebook.com/peperoncinoorlando**)

Slate: A smart upmarket restaurant at the far end of the Dellagio complex (just past Trader Joe's), featuring wood-grilled cuisine, with indoor and open-air dining. Imaginative menu offers pizza, pasta, salads, seafood and steaks with a lighter touch, plus a fab weekend brunch (4.30–10pm Mon–Thurs, 11pm Fri–Sat, 9pm Sun; **slateorlando.com**).

International Drive South

Heading back to I-Drive south of Sand Lake Road, you'll find a dazzling range of choice.

Fast food: Checkers, Domino's Pizza, Dunkin' Donuts, Firehouse Subs, McDonalds, Starbucks, Subway.

Breakfast style: Friendly's, Denny's, Panera Bread.

Buffet style: CiCi's Pizza, Golden Corral.

Bar-restaurant style: BJ's Brewhouse, Bahama Breeze, Buffalo Wild Wings, Chuys, Hooters, Red Robin, Miller's Ale House, TGI Friday's, Twin Peaks, Uno Pizzeria & Grill.

Steakhouse style: Charley's, Longhorn, Saltgrass Steak House.

Italian flavours: Olive Garden.

Seafood specials: Boston Lobster Feast, Joe's Crab Shack, Red Lobster.

Café Tu Tu Tango: A wonderful tapas-style menu is boosted by live music and local artists at work in this Bohemian-style cafe. Vegetarians are well catered for, and you can try succulent pizzas, seafood, salads and soups, plus imaginative Mexican dishes and a thoughtful kids' menu (11am–midnight Mon–Fri, 10am–midnight Sat, 10am–11pm Sun; **cafetututango.com**).

Cooper's Hawk: Wine lovers are spoiled for choice here, with a massive range in their Tasting Room to complement an excellent wide-ranging menu that runs the gamut from burgers and flatbreads to seafood and prime steaks (11am–9pm; **coopershawkwinery.com**).

Del Frisco's Double Eagle: I-Drive's standard for fine steaks and stylish dining, with an amazing array of fresh-cut meats, plus seafood, chicken and great cocktails, but with the price to match. There are two gorgeous bars and a picturesque patio (5–9pm Mon–Thurs, 4–10pm Sat, 4–9pm Sun; **delfriscos.com**).

Everglades: Tucked away inside the Rosen Centre Hotel is this beautiful Florida speciality restaurant, specialising in great steaks and fine seafood. Don't miss the Thai Curry Seafood and melt-in-the-mouth Filet Key Largo (5.30–10pm; **evergladesrestaurant.com**).

Twenty Pho Hour: Decorated to resemble a black-and-white comic, this new option features Japanese-inspired gg rolls, dumplings, summer rolls, pho bowls, stir-fry noodles and build-a-bowl (11am–10pm Mon–Wed, 11am opening on Thurs, then open 24hrs Fri–Sat, closing at 9pm Sun; **twenty-pho-hour.com**).

BRITTIP

For a great lunch or dinner alternative, visit Fogo de Chao and just sample their 30-item Market Table at $15 (lunch) or $30.95 (dinner). It is WAY more than just salad, with the likes of aged Parmesan, Italian salami and smoked salmon, and is wonderfully fresh and appetising.

Fogo De Chao: This Brazilian churrascaria is superbly authentic and flavourful, with an enchanting mix of elaborate serving style and succulent cuts of meat, all cooked on the traditional 'churrasco' skewer grill. It is a set-fee lunch or dinner, ($41.95–58.95) for the full churrascaria experience, including a buffet-style Market Table (noon–2.30pm and 5–10pm Mon–Thurs, noon–3pm, 5.30–10.30pm Fri, 11.30am–10.30am Sat, noon–9pm Sun; **fogodechao.com**).

Spencer's: The Hilton by the Convention Center is home to this beautiful restaurant that features magnificent steak, chops and seafood. Steaks are all pasture-raised without hormones or antibiotics, aged for 21 days and cooked in a custom-made grill (6–9.30pm Tues–Sat; **thehiltonorlando.com**).

ICON Park

This extensive entertainment complex is also a restaurant destination in its own right.

Fast food: Ben & Jerry's (ice cream), iCafe de Paris.

Bar-restaurant style: Buffalo Wild Wings, Shake Shack.

Steakhouse style: Outback Steakhouse.

Italian flavours: Carrabba's.

Gordon Ramsay's Fish & Chips: New in August 2021, this is great news for fans of Britain's celebrity chef, with a tempting line-up of fish, shrimp, lobster, chicken and sausage served with various types of chips (including jalapeño and truffle), plus tempting sweets and shakes. Terrific style and quality (**gordonramsayrestaurants.com**).

iLounge Istanbul: Enjoy a glass of wine, a hookah and a snack (cheese platter, chicken nuggets or wings, antipasto) at this trendy indoor/outdoor lounge (4pm–2am; **iloungeistanbul.com**).

BRITTIP

The legal age to purchase or smoke tobacco, or use tobacco-related devices in Florida is 18.

Sugar Factory: An 'American brasserie' catering to those of a sweet-toothed persuasion, it still serves pasta, burgers, salads, flatbreads and sandwiches, but really dazzles with its ice-cream-based desserts, milkshakes and candy-inspired cocktails. Don't miss the coffee and milkshake window (11am–11pm Mon–Thurs, 1am Fri, 10am–1am Sat, 11pm Sun; **sugarfactory.com/orlando**).

BRITTIP

The Covid-era bonus with many Florida restaurants is the option to dine outside. This is a real feature at ICON Park and is strongly encouraged.

Tapa Toro: Classic and contemporary Spanish specialities with a focus on tapas and paella, plus live music and tableside flamenco dancers in this elegant and multi-faceted restaurant (1–10pm Mon–Thurs, 11am–11pm Fri–Sat, 10pm Sun; **tapatoro.restaurant**).

Tin Roof: Country music fans will love the live entertainment here, with a smattering of rock, soul, Americana and pop. The menu features Tex-Mex favourites, and specialities include chicken tenders and wings, tacos, quesadillas and burgers. Full bar, funky style, and a somewhat raucous atmosphere after 10pm (noon–2am Mon–Fri, 11am–2am Sat–Sun; **tinrooforlando.com**).

Yard House: With a huge selection of beers on tap and a wonderfully inventive menu, this isn't your typical bar. Its air of comfortable refinement is also family-friendly, and the menu is several steps above the norm, featuring twists on bar favourites, plus other gourmet offerings. There is a good selection of healthy/vegetarian dishes, along with steaks, pizza, seafood, pasta and a kids menu (11–11.30am Sun–Thurs, 1am Fri–Sat; **yardhouse.com**).

Uncle Julio's: Get genuine made-from-scratch, Mesquite-grilled Mexican favourites with modern Tex-Mex twists at this lively bar/restaurant. Look out for their Swirl Margarita – layered with home-made sangria – among a great array of beers and cocktails, plus signature smoke-grilled fajitas, shrimp brochettes and salsas (11.30am–10.30pm Sun–Thurs, 11.30pm Fri–Sat; **bit.ly/brit-julios**).

Ole Red Orlando: Country music superstar Blake Shelton's Ole Red, offers a 'laid-back, irreverent' evening featuring live bands, Southern cookin' (try the Tater Tot Poutine, Pulled Pork BBQ Sandwich, or Hillbilly Bones ribs) and 'Blake-approved' signature cocktails (11am–2pm Mon, 11am–11pm Tues–Thurs and Sun, 1.30am Fri–Sat; **https://olered.com/orlando**).

Sloppy Joe's: Step into Key West style with this traditional bar-restaurant that comes direct from the former home of Ernest Hemingway (and was his favourite watering hole). Enjoy classic seafood, signature burgers (including the essential Big Sloppy), tropical-inspired cocktails and an excellent range of beers at this laid-back Floridian institution (noon–11pm Mon–Thurs, midnight Fri–Sat, 10pm Sun; **sloppyjoesorlando.com**).

▶BRITTIP

Looking for a great burger? Look no further than the Capital Grille (at Pointe Orlando and Mall at Millenia). Although it's an upmarket steakhouse, their lunch menu features a Kona-Crusted Wagyu Burger at $17 that is truly heavenly.

Pointe Orlando

Head to this other I-Drive entertainment complex, and you'll find more great dining options.

Bar-restaurant style: Marlow's Tavern (above-average menu and live music).

Steakhouse style: Capital Grille.

Italian flavours: Maggiano's Little Italy.

Blue Martini: Upmarket bar with 42 signature martinis, plus beer, wine and cocktails. Light fare, flatbreads and signature dishes such as Shrimp Martini and Beef Tenderloin Sliders. Live music nightly, plus a good happy hour 6–8pm each day (6pm–2am Wed–Sat; **bluemartinilounge.com**).

Cuba Libre: This bar/restaurant adds a touch of 1940s Havana, featuring Latin-inspired cuisine with an exciting twist, from tasty tapas and ceviche to grilled skirt steak – and wicked cocktails! (5pm–10pm daily, bar and nightlife 10pm–2am Fri, 2.30am Sat; **cubalibrerestaurant.com**).

The Oceanaire: Step back in time at this relaxed, stylish seafood room. The decor, reminiscent of a classic 1930s ocean liner, and mood music lead you into a fish and shellfish wonderland, complete with a superb oyster bar, as well as superb steaks and chicken. The raw bar alone is dazzling and the fish dishes are some of the best in town. Service is equally top-notch (5–9pm Sun–Thurs, 10pm Fri–Sat; **theoceanaire.com**).

The Pub: This huge pub-style offering features a wide variety of cosy seating nooks, a fantastic mix of UK and US beers (including the Orlando Brewing Co), a sharp menu and multiple TV screens for sports fans. The unique 'Pour Your Own Beer Walls' are a fun feature, as is Happy Hour Mon–Fri 3–6pm (11am–midnight Mon–Fri, 10.30am–midnight Sat, 11pm Sun; **experiencethepub.com/orlando**).

Rodizio Grill: A Brazilian steakhouse featuring gaucho servers and plenty of fresh-grilled meats served directly from skewers. Choose the Full Rodizio (unlimited meats, salads and sides) or Unlimited Gourmet Salads only (5pm–9pm Mon–Fri, noon–10pm Sat, noon–9pm Sun; **rodiziogrill.com**).

Taverna Opa: Lively Greek option, with an appetising menu, from hot and cold meze to moussaka, souvlaki, kebabs and signature lamb chops, but much more besides, like fine steaks, fresh seafood and a great ouzo bar. Watch for belly dancing and napkin throwing! (noon–10pm Sun–Thurs, 11pm Fri–Sat; **opaorlando.com**).

Hampton Social: This coastal-inspired spot goes all-in on seafood sharing plates, including lobster rolls and linguine with clams, landlubber options such as short ribs, wings and burgers, plus pizza, soups and salads. Indulge in handcrafted cocktails and an intriguing 'Rosé All Day' selection of 15 rosé wines. Sat and Sun Brunch is served until 3pm. (3pm–11pm Mon–Wed, 11am–midnight Thurs, 1am Fri, 10am–1am Sat, 10am–11pm Sun; **thehamptonsocial.com/orlando).**

Kava's Tacos & Tequila: Large and vibrant Tex-Mex restaurant by celebrity chef Roberto Treviño, also featuring a wide selection of tequilas and live entertainment (due to open autumn 2022; **kavastacos.com**).

─BRITTIP

There is free valet parking at some Pointe Orlando restaurants if you're dining there, so ask about validation. Just pull in at the drop-off point next to Capital Grille (but don't forget to tip the valet when you pick up your car).

LAKE BUENA VISTA

At the junction of I-4 and Highway 535 (Apopka-Vineland Rd) is this busy area of hotels, shops and restaurants – lots of restaurants. It falls into two sections, east of I-4 and west of the motorway.

─BRITTIP

Join the free Landry's Select Club and earn rewards points toward a $25 gift voucher each time you dine at a Landry's location, including Yak and Yeti restaurant in Disney's Animal Kingdom.

Lake Buena Vista West

Fast food: Burger King, Domino's Pizza, Dunkin' Donuts, KFC, Qdoba Mexican Eats, Pizza Hut, Starbucks, Steak 'n Shake, Subway.

Breakfast style: Denny's, IHOP, Waffle House.

Buffet style: Hokkaido (Asian).

Bar-restaurant style: Chili's, Giordano's (pizza), Hooters, Miller's Ale House, Twin Peaks.

Steakhouse style: Black Angus Steakhouse, Kobe.

Italian flavours: Macaroni Grill, Olive Garden.

El Patron: Reliable and great value-for-money Mexican choice, with good traditional dishes given a contemporary twist, like the Seafood Veracruz and grilled skirt steak, plus great artisan tacos (11am–10pm **elpatronorlando.com**).

Four Flamingos, A Richard Blais Florida Kitchen: Located inside the Hyatt Grand Cypress Resort is this pleasingly quirky offering from celebrity chef Richard Blais, featuring fabulous seafood and succulent meats with a vintage-Floridian twist and some wonderfully creative cocktails. The smart-casual ambiance is ideal for a special occasion dinner or just a chance to splash out (5pm–10pm; **fourflamingosorlando.com**)

Taverna Opa

Join The (Curry) Club!

Viceroy Chipshop Curry Club is a new venture taking typical flavours into existing restaurants for a Curry Night several times a month. It costs $22/person and provides a set meal with a choice of entrée, with rice, naan, onion bhaji, samosa and vegetables. It is the brainchild of Paul and Jennie, a British couple who have run several successful dining ventures in Orlando. Book via **facebook.com/viceroycurry/** and order in advance. One of their regular locations is El Patron in Lake Buena Vista, and we are keen customers!

Sofrito Latin Café: Simon's favourite place for a quick lunch or dinner, serving traditional authentic South and Central American dishes. You order at the counter then wait at your table for the fresh-cooked meal, with tapas-style plates and main courses. No recommendations – just try anything! They also have local craft beers and wine, and a breakfast menu (8am–9pm Sun–Thurs, 10pm Fri–Sat; **sofritocafe.com**).

O-Town West: Go up Palm Parkway from Lake Buena Vista and discover a major new restaurant/shopping development. Hot dog specialists **Portillo's** (from Chicago) and northern burger chain **White Castle** opened in 2021, followed by Dunkin' Donuts, BurgerFI, Tijuana Flats, Wendy's and World of Beer, plus our breakfast fave, Maple Street Biscuit Company, with more due in 2023.

Lake Buena Vista East

Fast food: Chick-fil-A, Dunkin' Donuts, Panda Express, Starbucks, Subway, Wendy's.

Breakfast style: Panera Bread.

Buffet style: CiCi's Pizza, Golden Corral.

Bar-restaurant style: Applebee's, Bahama Breeze, BJ's Brewhouse, Cheesecake Factory, Ford's Garage.

Steakhouse style: Longhorn Steakhouse, Outback Steakhouse (opposite Orlando Premium Outlets), Saltgrass Steak House.

Italian flavours: Carrabba's.

Frankie Farrell's: Inside the Lake Buena Vista Resort Village & Spa is this pub-style restaurant and bar with an imaginative menu, good range of beers and live entertainment (noon–1pm; **frankiefarrells.com**).

Landry's Seafood: This big-name company boasts an elegant touch, featuring fresh daily seafood platters and excellent salad bowls, with top-notch service and wine list. For a special occasion, the Crawfish Étouffée and Seafood Platters are superb (3.30–9.30pm Mon–Thurs, 10pm Fri, noon–10pm Sat, 9pm Sun; **landrysseafood.com**).

Cheesecake Factory: Part of the ever-expanding dining options in Vineland Pointe, just off Palm Parkway, is this American style eatery with a massive menu and portion sizes to match. If you want it, they probably have it, and their desserts are big enough to feed a family (11am–10pm Sun–Thurs, 11pm Fri–Sat, 10am–10pm Sun, Happy Hour 4–6pm daily; **thecheesecakefactory.com**).

Hyatt Regency Grand Cypress

© Hyatt Regency

KISSIMMEE

Heading east and west of I-4 into Highway 192, you are largely in fast-food territory, but there are some notable individuals.

Highway 192 East

Fast food: Arby's, Burger King, Checkers, Chick-Fil-A, Chipotle, Domino's Pizza, Dunkin' Donuts, Five Guys, Jimmy John's, KFC, McDonalds, Panda Express, Pizza Hut, Starbucks, Steak 'n Shake, Subway, Taco Bell, Wendy's.

Breakfast style: Cracker Barrel, Denny's, IHOP, Panera Bread, Perkins, Waffle House.

Buffet style: CiCi's Pizza, Golden Corral, Ponderosa.

Bar-restaurant style: Applebee's, Chili's, TGI Friday's, Uno Pizzeria & Grill.

Steakhouse style: Black Angus, Charley's Steakhouse, Longhorn Steakhouse, Logan's Roadhouse, Sonny's BBQ.

Italian flavours: Carrabba's, Macaroni Grill, Olive Garden.

Seafood specials: Joe's Crab Shack, Red Lobster.

Old Hickory Steakhouse: A five-star, Everglades-themed steakhouse in the Gaylord Palms Resort, the house speciality of certified prime-aged beef is cooked to perfection. There are a few alternatives, such as fish, chicken and veggie, but all sides are extra and this is a pricey but memorable experience (5.30–10pm; 407 996 2385).

MOOR: Old Hickory's seafood-focused sister restaurant at Gaylord Palms, with fabulous fresh Florida fish dishes to go with hand-crafted cocktails, plus a signature Key Lime Pie dessert that is worth coming in for on its own (5–10pm Mon–Tues, Thurs–Sun, closed Wed; 407 586 1101; **marriott.com/en-us/hotels/mcogp-gaylord-palms-resort-and-convention-center/dining**).

Smokey Bones: With a rustic, log-cabin touch and succulent BBQ, this eye-catching venue serves up fire-grilled steaks, salmon, chicken, burgers and salads. Try the BBQ platters and rib combos. Sports fans can also enjoy a huge array of TVs (11am–1am Sun–Thurs, 2am Fri–Sat; **smokeybones.com**).

Highway 192 West

Fast food: Burger King, Chick-Fil-A, Culver's (burgers), Domino's Pizza, Dunkin' Donuts, McDonalds, Panda Express, Pizza Hut, Pollo Tropical, Starbucks, Subway, Taco Bell, Wendy's.

Breakfast style: Bob Evans, Cracker Barrel, Denny's, IHOP, Panera Bread, Perkins.

Buffet style: CiCi's Pizza, Golden Corral, Ponderosa.

Bar-restaurant style: Applebee's, Bahama Breeze, Buffalo Wild Wings, Chuys, Giordano's, Flippers Pizza, Hooters, Miller's Ale House, On The Border (Mexican Grill and Cantina), Red Robin, TGI Friday's.

Steakhouse style: Black Angus, Logan's Roadhouse, Longhorn, Outback, Texas Roadhouse.

Italian: Carrabba's, Olive Garden.

Seafood specials: Bonefish Grill, Joe's Crab Shack, Red Lobster.

Wildside Texas BBQ: Dive into superb barbecue at this iconic location. It serves up signature steaks and seafood, as well as burgers and sandwiches, but the real speciality is their delicious home-smoked pulled chicken and pork, beef brisket, St Louis ribs and baby back ribs (4–10pm Tues–Sun; **wildsiderestaurant.com**).

Salt & The Cellar: New in 2022, this exciting concept by Michelin-starred chef Akira Back has stirred up LOTS of local interest, as much for its setting in the unique ette Hotel (p73) as for its novel Mediterranean-Asian menu and wildly flavourful non-alcoholic cocktails. It's completely out of place in this part of Kissimmee but is a welcome addition to the restaurant scene (11.30am-2pm and 5.30-11pm; 407 288 1919; **https://saltandthecellar.com**).

─── BRITTIP ───

For something truly original, try **Salt & The Cellar's** Afternoon Tea presentation, with some of the most luscious sandwiches and pastries on the planet.

─── BRITTIP ───

The huge Cheesecake Factory at Mall of Millenia is a firm Brit favourite for its extensive (and sophisticated) menu and huge portions. See more at **cheesecakefactory.com**.

The Promenade at Sunset Walk

Part of Kissimmee's huge Margaritaville Resort, Sunset Walk consists of Island H2O water park and dining/entertainment section The Promenade, featuring 15 places to eat. They include counter-service **Burger Fi**, **Coldstone Creamery** and **Bahama Buck's** (shaved ice), Mexican **El Jefe Tequila Cocina & Cantina** and **Bento Asian Kitchen + Sushi**. Then there's the "neighbourhood burger and beer joint," **Ford's Garage**, the all-British **Yeoman's Cask & Lion** pub (when you need Shepherd's Pie and bangers and mash in an eclectic pop-art setting) and the rockin' good fun of **Rock And Brews**, with an immense craft beer list and a comfort food menu featuring signature wings, salads, seafood and pasta. Chic restaurant/nightclub **Estefan Kitchen** features a fresh take on Latin and Cuban flavours with the music – and dancing – to go with it, while **Lizzie's Memphis Style BBQ**, and **The Wharf** seafood and oyster bar add even more to the flavour profile on offer here (**sunsetwalk.com**).

Mall at Millenia

There's more temptation around the upmarket Mall at Millenia.

Fast food: Jimmy John's, Krispy Kreme Doughnuts, McDonalds, Moe's Southwest Grill, Panda Express, Pollo Tropical, Subway, Wendy's, Zaxby's Chicken.

Breakfast style: Keke's.

Bar-restaurant style: BJ's Brewhouse, Cheesecake Factory, Johnny Rockets, TGI Friday's.

Steakhouse style: Capital Grille.

Italian flavours: Olive Garden.

Brio Tuscan Grille: Inside the Mall (and at Winter Park Village), this stylish Italian makes for a superb casual lunch or romantic dinner, with steaks, creative pastas and regional specialities like chicken limone and lamb chops, plus daily specials. Tuscan country-style ambience and fresh kids' menu (11am–10pm Sun–Thurs, 11pm Fri–Sat; **brioitalian.com**).

Earls Kitchen & Bar: Also in Mall at Millenia, try an upscale burger or one of their Black Angus beef steaks, plus fresh choices like sushi, rice bowls, ribs, chicken, plant-based options, steaks and more (11.30am–10pm Mon–Thurs, 11.30am–midnight Fri, 10am–midnight Sat, 10am–10pm Sun; **bit.ly/brit-earls**).

PF Chang's China Bistro: Inside the Mall, this mixes classic Chinese fare with American bistro style that makes fans of virtually all who sample it. Try the Chang's Spicy Chicken, Oolong Chilean Sea Bass and Miso Glazed Salmon. There is also a good veggie selection (11am–10pm Sun–Thurs, 11pm Fri–Sat, **pfchangs.com**).

Brio Tuscan Grill

ChampionsGate

This burgeoning area west on I-4 is now filling up with dining options, most of the fast food kind, but with a few notable individuals.

Fast food: Dunkin' Donuts, Jersey Mike's Subs, McDonald's, Planet Smoothie, Subway, Tijuana Flats, Wendy's.

Breakfast style: First Watch, Panera Bread.

Bar-restaurant style: Chilis, Miller's Ale House, Red Robin.

Steakhouse style: Longhorn.

Italian: Olive Garden.

4 Corners Tavern: A locals' sports bar and restaurant featuring some imaginative touches and menu choices beyond the obvious (noon–2am Mon–Sat, noon–midnight Sun, **4cornerstavern.com**).

Blue Coast: Asian cuisine is the prime fare here, with some excellent sushi, for dine in or take away (11am–10pm Mon–Thurs, 11am–11pm Fri, noon–11pm Sat, noon–10pm Sun; **bluecoastcg.com**).

Osteria: Dive in to some original and tasty Italian fare, with classic dishes like Chicken Parmesan, Shrimp Alfredo and Spaghetti and Meatballs (noon–9pm Mon–Thurs, 10pm Fri–Sat, 8pm Sun; **osteriaitalian.com**).

The Fish & Chip Shop: Get a taste of home with traditional fish and chips, home-made pies, daily special and beer and wine (11am–8pm Tues–Thurs, 9pm Fri–Sat, closed Sun and Mon; 321 401 4111).

Zen: For great Asian dining, the Omni Orlando Resort (p74) features a stylish restaurant, sushi and saki bar. An oasis of relaxed charm, highlights include the Szechwan-style Beef Tenderloin and Sautéed Shrimp in Black Pepper Sauce and Spinach (6–10pm; **omnihotels.com/hotels/orlando-championsgate**).

Finally, just up Highway 27 from ChampionsGate is **Best of British,** another all-British style café and bar that caters to those in need of a full English breakfast, pies, pasties, Scotch eggs, and a pint of Magners, Boddingtons or Harp. Or try their take-away chippie next door (9am–10pm Mon, Wed–Sat, 8pm Sun, 6pm Tues; **bestofbritish.net**).

EAT LIKE A LOCAL

A short drive to the more residential areas means you can sample off-the-beaten-track choices.

4 Rivers SmokeHouse: Annually rated the best barbecue in Central Florida, this Winter Park original (with 12 more Florida locations) draws long queues at peak times, but it's worth the wait for their succulent pulled pork, brisket, ribs and chicken (11am–8pm Mon–Sat; **4rsmokehouse.com**).

Dixie Cream Café: When we want a 'home-cooked' breakfast or lunch, we head to this charming café/bakery/coffee shop in the heart of the ritzy suburb of Windermere and enjoy a variety of Southern comfort food, burgers, sandwiches and salads (8am–2.30pm; **dixiecreamcafe.com**).

East End Market: Perhaps the ultimate local dining experience, the Market in the Audubon Park district features a tempting collection of small-scale outlets like Gideon's Bakehouse (now at Disney Springs – p280), Olde Hearth Bread Company, Hinckley's Fancy Meats (great sandwiches) and creative noodle dishes of Domu (8am–7pm Mon–Thurs, 9pm Fri–Sat, 6pm Sun; **https://eastendmkt.com**).

Hamilton's Kitchen: For a stylish lunch or when we're feeling fancy, we head to Winter Park for the chic, artsy feel of the Alfond Inn. The signature restaurant is a treat and the food fresh and inventive (Brunch 7am–2pm Mon–Fri, 8am-2pm Sat, 3pm Sun, Dinner 5pm–9pm Tues–Sat; **bit.ly/brit-alfond**).

Orlando Top 10

Here's our 'Best Of' list for the Orlando area in general.

1. A Land Remembered (p298)
2. Capa (Four Seasons) (p297)
3. Knife and Spoon (p298)
4. Slate (Dellagio) (p288)
5. Hamilton's Kitchen (p295)
6. The Ravenous Pig (p298)
7. Highball & Harvest (p297)
8. The Boheme (p297)
9. Kres Chophouse (below)
10. Yellow Dog Eats (p297)

BRITTIP

For something special, try Hamilton's Kitchen's Brunch, then shop along Park Avenue to stroll it off.

Kres Chophouse: For an elegant night-on-the-town, this is a great choice in downtown Orlando, in the busy Church Street area. Ideal for pre-dinner cocktails, a late-night nightcap or a full, elegant dinner, Kres features signature steaks, chops and seafood, plus a supper-club style that is genuinely classy (11.30am–11pm Mon–Thurs, midnight Fri, 5pm–midnight Sat, 5pm–10pm Sun; **kresrestaurant.com**).

Luke's Kitchen & Bar: In the suburb of Maitland (north of downtown), this smart-casual contemporary American showpiece features a seafood-heavy menu that focuses on fresh local ingredients, all compiled in an eye-catching open kitchen (4–9pm Mon–Tues, 11.30am–10pm Wed–Thurs, 11.30am–10.30pm Fri–Sat, 11am–9pm Sun, **eatatlukes.com**).

Maxine's On Shine: The locals flock to this downtown spot for the superb weekend brunch (Fri-Sun), as well as dinner Weds-Sun. Lively, eclectic and with extensive outdoor seating, Maxine's features a generous Happy Hour (Wed-Fri), live music and a real community vibe (5–9pm Wed–Thurs, 10am–9pm Fri–Sat, 10am–3pm Sun, **https://maxinesonshine.com**).

Santiago's Bodega: Tapas dining at its finest at this downtown beacon of Spanish/Mediterranean flair, with a superb outdoor patio and eye-catching weekend brunch (11am–2am Mon–Fri, 10am–2am Sat–Sun, **santiagosbodega.com**).

Shakers American Café: Voted Orlando's best breakfast, this unassuming café in the College Park district has been serving plenty of wholesome fare since 1993 and is renowned for its home-made soups, salads and sandwiches (6.30am–2.30pm Mon–Sat, 8am–2pm Sun; **shakerscafe.com**).

Taste of Chengdu: Simply the best Chinese restaurant in town, with superb traditional Sichuan cuisine given a modern, spicy, twist (11.30am–9.30pm Tues–Thurs, 10.30pm Fri–Sat, 9.30pm Sun; **tasteofchengdufl.com**).

The Glass Knife: Ready for dessert? This is the place to go in Winter Park, with a mouthwatering array of cakes, pastries, doughnuts and sandwiches, for breakfast, brunch or afternoon tea/coffee (8am–10pm Sun–Thurs, 11pm Fri–Sat; **theglassknife.com**).

The Hall on the Yard

The newest dining concept in town is this eclectic indoor/outdoor food hall in downtown's Ivanhoe Village district. Consisting of nine diverse restaurants, plus cocktail bars and event spaces, it features Indian, Greek and Japanese cuisine along with contemporary fusion flavours and vegetarian creations, and it attracts keen foodies and locals looking for that 'something different' factor. Like a food court with sit-down service, it's fun, lively and serves up terrific food, ideal for a grown-up night out (11am–11pm Mon-Thurs, 11–2am Fri and Sat, 9am–9pm Sun, **thehallontheyard.com**).

The Taproom at Dubsdread: Yes, Dubsdread is a golf course (just west of downtown), but it boasts a great clubhouse restaurant with some of the best burgers in town. There are also great steaks, seafood and truly decadent desserts (11am–10pm Mon–Sat, 10am–9pm Sun; **taproomatdubsdread.com**).

Yellow Dog Eats: Just past Windermere in rural Gotha is this eclectic deli-restaurant-country store with a hugely appealing mix of salads, sandwiches, tacos, nachos and veggie offerings, plus their succulent barbecue specialities and kids' menu. There is also a good beer and wine selection, plus Happy Hour 2–6pm and live music 6pm–10pm Thurs–Sat (11am–9pm, **yellowdogeats.com**).

DELUXE DINING

This selection is when you really have something to celebrate.

Boca: This eye-catching Winter Park favourite features fresh, local seasonal ingredients with a cosy, European ambience. Salads, flatbreads, sandwiches, seafood and daily specials all feature, but there is plenty of imagination (and organic produce) in dishes like 60-Spiced Chicken, Bronzed Sea Scallops and their Brie and Apple Flatbread (11am–10pm Mon–Thurs, 11pm Fri, 9.30am–11pm Sat, 10pm Sun; **bocawp.com**).

The Boheme: Tucked away inside the Grand Bohemian hotel in downtown is this elegant restaurant that's ideal for a special occasion. Boasting fabulous seafood, decadent steaks and exquisite cocktails, all with a New American cuisine twist, it also features a Sunday jazz brunch (**bit.ly/brit-boheme**).

The Boheme

Cala Bella: A proven winner at the stylish Rosen Shingle Creek Resort, Italian-influenced Cala Bella is heavy on pasta and seafood, with signature dishes like its sensational Cala Bella Lamb, Veal Chop Milanese and Seafood Pescatore. The pastry chefs are among the best in America (5.30–10pm; **calabellarestaurant.com**).

Capa: The signature rooftop restaurant at the Four Seasons hotel is tops for elegance, style and views of the Magic Kingdom fireworks. Even better is its contemporary Spanish steakhouse cuisine, with dishes from delightful small plates, freshly shucked oysters and Florida seafood to succulent steaks from the wood-burning grill (5–10pm; **bit.ly/brit-capa**).

Highball and Harvest: This chic choice in the Ritz-Carlton hotel features Southern cuisine with an upmarket twist. Menu faves include Shrimp and Grits, Roasted Napa Cabbage, an aged charcuterie plate and succulent 14oz ribeye steak. Head to the bar for a handcrafted cocktail and Bar Bites menu (4–5.30pm), and don't miss the Coconut Cream Pie for dessert! (7am–10pm; **highballandharvest.com**).

Knife and Spoon: Another Ritz-Carlton gem, this is the preserve of award-winning chef John Tesar and his decadent steak-and-seafood extravaganza. The King Crab Scampi and Bucatini are magnificent, but the Bone-In Ribeye steaks go a whole lot further 5.30–10pm Wed–Sun, **ritzcarlton.com/en/hotels/florida/orlando/dining/knife-spoon**).

Hillstone: This lakeside location in Winter Park provides a relaxed but upmarket choice for a casual lunch or full-scale dinner. Where the locals go for a 'power lunch,' it is also an evening oasis, with the chance to enjoy a drink on their pier or grab a patio table with a wonderful view of Lake Killarney. The menu varies from simple burgers and salads to epic fresh fish dishes, rotisserie chicken and succulent steaks (11.30am–9.30pm Sun–Thurs, 9.30pm Fri–Sat; **hillstone.com**).

The Michelin Awards

Florida achieved the distinction of its first Michelin Guide in 2022, with restaurants in Orlando, Miami and Tampa earning coveted stars and Bib Gourmand awards. Four Orlando restaurants received Michelin stars, seven were honoured with the Bib Gourmand label for quality and value, and another 23 were commended. The fab four were Capa, Knife & Spoon, Soseki and Kadence, while the super seven included The Ravenous Pig. See more at **guide.michelin.com/en/us/florida/orlando/ restaurants**.

A Land Remembered: Inside the golf clubhouse of the Rosen Shingle Creek Resort (but open to non-residents), this is a superbly refined venue boasting exquisite service and an outstanding wine list. The fish, chicken and smoked short rib are outstanding, but the all-natural prime black Angus beef is out of this world. Various cuts of steak, including a Tomahawk for Two, are among the most succulent meat dishes you will find and, while it is pricey, we believe it is worth every cent (5.30–10pm; **landrememberedrestaurant.com**).

BRITTIP

Check out our good friend, restaurant critic and foodie Scott Joseph for the latest dining news, views and insights. His 'Flog' (food blog) is essential reading, plus he offers coupons and special deals at local restaurants. Find his essential Orlando Restaurant Guide at scottjosephorlando.com.

The Ravenous Pig

Ravenous Pig: Staying in Winter Park, local restaurateurs James and Julie Petrakis have crafted the British gastropub idea into a cosy hideaway that oozes style, whether you want great pub food or the full gourmet experience. Superb craft beer is supplied by their own Cask & Larder micro-brewery. Bookings are highly advisable though, as its popularity is widespread (4–10pm Tues–Thurs, 11pm Fri, 11am–11pm Sat, 7pm Sun, happy hour 4–6pm; **theravenouspig.com**).

And finally…

Soseki and **Kadence:** These two sumptuous Japanese omakase selections in Audubon Park and Winter Park respectively earned Michelin stars in 2022 for their individual style and distinction. Seating just ten diners at a time, they specialise in sushi and hot dishes with a true 'chef's choice' touch that changes almost daily. Both have a (high) set fee for dining and you need to book well in advance for either one (**sosekifl.com** and **kadence.com**).

OK, that's enough eating for now – on to another of our favourite topics – shopping…

Disney Springs

© Disney

12 Shopping

or, How to Send Your Credit Card into Meltdown

As well as being a theme park wonderland, this vast area of Florida is a shopper's paradise, with a dazzling array of specialist outlets, malls, flea markets and discount retailers. New centres spring up all the time, from smart malls to cheap gift shops – and you can't go a few paces in the tourist areas without a shop insisting it has the 'best bargains' of one sort or another.

With so much good shopping to be had for UK visitors, there's a danger of exceeding your baggage allowance for the flight home – or your duty-free allowance. American stores are genuinely fun just to browse, let alone splash out in and real bargains are to be had in jeans, trainers, sports equipment and cosmetics. Almost everywhere offers free, convenient parking, while shop assistants are polite and helpful.

Sales tax: Be aware of the hidden extra costs of shopping. Unlike our VAT, Florida sales tax is NOT part of the displayed purchase price, so you must add on 6% or 7% (it varies by county) for the final price. Also, some shops will ask for photo ID with credit card purchases, so have a photo driving licence or photo ID with you.

Allowances: Your limit in the catch-all duty category of 'gifts and souvenirs' is only £390 per person. If you exceed that, you need to keep your receipts and go through the 'goods to declare' channel (though paying the duty and VAT can still be cheaper than buying the same items at home). Some items, such as clothing and footwear for children, do not incur a VAT rate. However, restrictions apply to all reduced-rate VAT items, so be sure to check details with HM Revenue & Customs. Your ordinary duty-free allowances from America include 200 cigarettes and 4 litres of spirits or 9 litres of fortified wine or sparkling wine and 18 litres of still wine.

> **BRITTIP**
>
> Don't buy electrical goods in the US – they won't work in the UK without a converter. Most games systems (notably X Box, Wii and Playstations) are also NOT compatible with UK players. Hand-held games are fine.

Zara at Disney Springs

© Disney

Up, up and away!

In Disney Springs West Side, across the bridge from The Landing, is Aerophile, a wonderful tethered balloon ride that gently soars up to 400ft/122m high carrying up to 30 at a time in a 19ft/5.7m gondola on 6min rides. It provides a fab panorama of much of the huge extent of Walt Disney World and is a great photo opportunity by day or night (9am–11pm). It costs $25/adult and $20/3–9s. In certain weather conditions the number of passengers is limited, while it is grounded in high winds or heavy rain.

Customs duty: You pay duty (which varies depending on the item) on the total purchase price (i.e. inclusive of Florida sales tax) once you have exceeded £390, plus VAT at 20%. You CANNOT pool your allowances to cover one item that exceeds a single allowance. Hence, if you buy a single item that costs £700, you have to pay the duty on the full £700, and then VAT on top of that. However, if you have several items that add up to £390, and then another that exceeds that, you pay the duty and VAT only on the excess item (and customs officers usually give you the benefit of the lowest rate on what you pay for). Duty rates are updated regularly and vary from 2.5 to 14%. You pay 2.5% for goods worth up to £630, and then it depends on the type of goods above £630. For more info, contact the Customs and Excise National Advice Service on 0845 010 9000, **gov.uk/duty-free-goods**.

Alligator products constitute those of an endangered species (to UK authorities) so require an import licence. Consult the Global Wildlife Licensing and Registration Service for more info.

►BRITTIP ◄

If you're anything like Simon's parents, just going in to shops like Walgreens, Walmart and Target is all part of the Orlando holiday experience, so don't be afraid to branch out and explore – you just might find your new favourite in **Bed, Bath & Beyond, Best Buy or World Market!**

Disney Springs

This shopping and dining district splits into: Marketplace, The Landing, Town Center and West Side. Imaginative architecture and one-off elements make shopping a pleasure. There are 103 shops and 65 dining options, and a free water-taxi links each end, as well as Disney's Old Key West, Port Orleans and Saratoga Springs Resorts.

Disney Springs can be found off exits 67 and 68 of I-4 and is well signposted (exit 68 can be congested at peak periods). There are three new multi-storey car parks featuring clever technology to indicate every empty space on each floor (look for the green lights).

Marketplace: Don't miss the **World of Disney** store, the largest of its kind, with a mind-boggling array of Disney merchandise, from clothing to home goods. Equally impressive are **The LEGO Store** (an interactive playground and shop), the amazing **Art of Disney** and the **Marketplace Co-Op** (a number of small shops under one roof). **Once Upon a Toy** is a gigantic toy emporium complete with a host of classic games, many with a Disney theme, for kids to try. There's also **Bibbidi Bobbidi Boutique,** where youngsters can have hair, make-up and nails done in Princess style (and priced to match!). The Knight Package ($20) offers a gel and confetti hairstyle, plus a sword and shield. Other worthwhile one-offs are the blissful **Basin** (for toiletries) and **Disney's Wonderful World of Memories** (for all scrapbook fans).

►BRITTIP ◄

Beware! The Bibbidi Bobbidi Boutique is hideously expensive. Packages range from $20–450 (plus tax!). The adult version, Character Couture, at several Disney salons, runs from $50–120.

Princess Parade: Young girls in the princess mood may want to take part in the daily parade from the Bibbidi Bobbidi Boutique at 1–2pm (weather permitting). It marches around the Marketplace, finishing at the

Carousel, where all children get a free ride. Kids can dress up (or not) and there is NO fee.

Arribas Brothers is a big, attractive gift store, while those keen on pin-trading should check out **Pin Traders**. Then there's **Star Wars Trading Post**, **Tren-D**, a cutting-edge Disney fashion store for women, **The Spice & Tea Exchange** (tea, food, housewares), **Pearl Factory** (clothes) and **Disney's Days of Christmas**.

Dancing fountains and squirt pools (where kids tend to get seriously wet) and the lakeside setting all add to the appeal. **Build-A-Dino** and **Dino Store** can be found inside T-Rex Café. There are several kiosk-style shops as well.

The Landing: Browse a variety of imaginative shops like **The Art of Shaving** (toiletries), **Chapel Hats** (funky/vintage hats), **Havaianas** (flip-flops), **Oakley** (apparel and accessories), **Sanuk** (shoes) and **Erin McKenna's bakery NYC** (a range of vegan/gluten-free baked goods). For dining, see chapter 11 (p278), while **Raglan Road** also has its own Irish-themed gift shop here.

West Side: This area offers the superb **AMC 24** cinema complex (p261), plus another 13 retail and dining outlets, notably **Disneystyle** and **Pelé Soccer**. **Pop Gallery** has collectable artwork while **Disney's Candy Cauldron** is a big hit with kids. Others include **Super Hero Headquarters** (apparel and collectables), **Star Wars Galactic Outpost**, **Sunglass Icon** and the huge, immersive **M&M's** candy wonderland (sweets, apparel and more). There are also gift shops for **House of Blues** and **Splitsville**, and this is where to find the **Food Truck Park** (p281).

Town Center: The final part of Disney Springs is more like an upmarket mall, with nice touches in the architecture and story of Disney Springs itself. The water features are eye-catching and there are great back-stories at **Amorette's Patisserie** and **D-Luxe Burger** in particular (the former of which serves decadent cakes and pastries). The stores are those you'll find in most good malls including **Everything But Water, Tommy Bahama, Lilly Pulitzer, Kate Spade, Under Armour, Coach** and **Lacoste** for the latest fashions and sportswear. Jewellery shops include **Vera Bradley, Alex and Ani** and **Pandora,** while footwear and cosmetics notables include **UGG, Sperry**, **Sephora** and **L'Occitane. Sugarboo** features arts and crafts while the **Coca-Cola Store** has a fab array of products. The new **Art Walk** adds a genuine artistic element here, with murals, seasonal exhibitions and other touches from international artists for a lively, extra-colourful visual flourish.

Disney Springs shops are open 10am–11pm. For more details, see **disneysprings.com**.

Disney Springs Town Center at Christmas

© Disney

International Drive

This core tourist area is awash with shopping of all kinds, from the cheapest and tackiest plazas full of tourist gift shops, to four purpose-built centres. Some of the shops just north of the Sand Lake Road junction are best avoided, while the northern end of I-Drive has undergone a major redevelopment. This area is also renowned for discount outlet shopping – a local speciality – offering name brands at heavily reduced prices.

Orlando International Premium Outlets: At the top of I-Drive, this attractive 175-shop 'lifestyle centre' has gone all out for the big, semi-open-air style that encourages people to wander the long promenades full of shop fronts and big-name brands.

Boasting a landscaped canal running through the centre, outdoor seating, cafés, a Market Place food court and a Guest Services centre, it provides a luxury touch. Major brands include **Kate Spade New York, Calvin Klein, Lacoste** and **Michael Kors**. Other familiar names include **Nike Factory Store, Tommy Hilfiger, Dooney & Bourke, Banana Republic, Bath & Body Works, Aeropostale** and **Brooks Brothers,** plus, inevitably, a Starbucks. With its attractive food court, including the popular Five Guys Burgers, Sundial Brazilian Café, and Sbarro pizza, plus Italian restaurant Vinito, you have one of the area's brightest shopping centres that is also at the top of the I-Ride Trolley route; (**bit.ly/brit-premium**).

Pointe Orlando: In the heart of I-Drive, this is a good choice for an evening out with some retail therapy. With 8 smart stores, you can indulge your passion for fashion at **Hollister** or stock up on gifts and souvenirs at **One For the Road, Design By U, Moon Dance, Redi to Pedi, Bowe's Signature Candles** and **Tharoo & Co** jewellery. For the lowdown on places to eat at Pointe Orlando, see p290. Parking is in the multi-storey car park, but some restaurants will redeem your parking

A Kissimmee tradition

Old Town is home to some weekly events that appeal to both locals and tourists alike. The Saturday Nite Cruise at 8.30pm is a trademark drive-past of 300-plus vintage and collector cars (the biggest in America; viewing starts at 1pm). A Friday Nite Muscle Car Cruise features cars built since 1964 (viewing from 3pm, with the cruise starting at 8.30pm), while the Wednesday Themed Car Show runs from 5–11pm. There is live music, fairground stalls and prizes, and it can get fairly raucous later on, with plenty of alcoholic llbations (witness the Sun on the Beach bar!).

ticket if you shop there (11am–9pm; later at the bars and restaurants; 407 248 2838, **pointeorlando.com**).

BRITTIP
Popular comic book and fantasy gaming store **Gods and Monsters** can be found in Orlando Crossings Plaza on upper International Drive (**godmonsters. com**).

ICON Park: This entertainment and dining complex (p223) has a selection of shops, including the big chemist and general store **Walgreens, Caleoni Sunglasses, Wheelhouse Gift Shop** (ICON Park souvenirs) and **Build-A-Bear**.

Universal CityWalk: The mega new **Universal Studios Store** offers a wide range of park souvenirs and gifts, including the biggest array of Harry Potter merchandise, while the companion **Universal Legacy Store** features Universal's 30-year history of films and rides in a warehouse-type setting. **Quiet Flight** is the place for all your beach-wear, sunglasses, apparel and more, while **Hart & Huntington Orlando Tattoo Shop** offers a chance to get a tattoo or buy signature clothing and accessories.

Bass Pro Shops: The big sports and camping equipment store is located on north International Drive, along with **Cinemark** multi-screen cinema.

Kissimmee

Along the tourist territory of Highway 192, you will again find a complete mix of outlets, with a profusion of the cheap and cheerful, but also several highly enticing possibilities.

---BRITTIP

Brit Guide readers receive a FREE Florida Mall Destination Passport and a special tote bag with the cut-out ad on the back flap of this book. Take advantage of this exclusive opportunity for added savings on your holiday shopping.

Old Town: This is Kissimmee's version of the purpose-built tourist shopping centre, an Old Florida style offering with an eclectic mix of shops, restaurants, bars and fairground attractions set out along brick-lined streets. The shops range from standard souvenirs and novel T-shirt outlets to sportswear and collectibles (check out the **Old Town General Store** for a step back in time, or the **Old Town Portrait Gallery** for period-style photos). The individual style of **Out of This World Embroidery** offers a 'you name it, we'll stitch it' service, while, **Filthy Rich** jewellery, **Wild Billie's Gifts** and **Lucky Mouse** are all great for gifts. There are also 15 restaurants or snack bars. For lunch or dinner, try **Shoney's**, **Southern Breeze** or the fun style of **Froggers Bar & Grill**. **Flippers Pizzeria** and **El Borrego** are also worth trying, while there are other snack outlets, with offerings from popcorn to candy and the wonderful **Sweet Dreams Ice Cream Café**. **Sun on the Beach** is a good nightclub in the evening (until 2am). Parking is free (10am–11pm daily; **myoldtownusa.com**).

Downtown Kissimmee: This offers the more local, authentic face of shopping in Florida, with the charming Main Street area featuring antique shops, one-off boutiques, cafés and restaurants. Much attention has been paid to the historic district in recent years, and it is now a relaxing place for a wander and a meal. **The Welcome Station** on Main Street (formerly an old-fashioned petrol station) is a great place to start, and even has local crafts, keepsakes, and books focusing on Floridian history (9am–5pm Mon–Fri). Then look into the likes of local landmarks **Lanier's**, **Makinson Hardware** (the oldest hardware store in Florida), and **Echoes of Yesterday** antiques. Try the casual sports-bar style of **Broadway Pizza**, or the smart **3 Sisters Speakeasy** wine bar and café, which has **Trivia Night Tuesdays** (**3sisters-speakeasy.com**), and the **Kissimmee Valley Farmers Market** on the first Fri every month (**kissimmeemainstreet.org**). For a truly charming local experience, be sure to check out **Diane's Tea Room** on Broadway, while there is usually free parking available on E. Deakin Avenue and Pleasant Street.

---BRITTIP

For something different, don't miss **Abracadabra Ice Cream Factory**, just outside Kissimmee town centre (on North Main Street). Here, they mix fantastic creamy creations using a wonderful variety of ingredients – and flash freeze it all with liquid nitrogen for a true taste sensation! It's open 11am–10pm daily.

The Loop and The Loop West: Apart from Old Town and Downtown, the Kissimmee area is largely short of quality shopping, but head to the Osceola Parkway (at the junction with John Young Parkway), running parallel to Highway 192, to find these extensive developments. They offer an enticing mix of shopping and dining, plus a 16-screen Regal Cinema in a pedestrian-friendly setting, with the shops grouped around two large car parks. Many of the shops may be unfamiliar but are worth visiting. Of note at The Loop are **Ross** (a huge discount warehouse of clothes, shoes, linens, cosmetics and more), **Kohl's** (a well-priced department store), **Bed, Bath & Beyond** (household), **Old Navy** (clothing), **Michaels** (arts and crafts), **Famous Footwear** (discounted shoes) and a hairdresser, nail salon and chemist (**CVS**). At The Loop West, look for the big department stores of **JC Penney** (clothing and housewares) and **Sketchers** (footwear), plus **Ulta** (cosmetics), **TJ Maxx** (clothing) and **DSW** (shoes), plus several other shops.

The extensive dining choice includes classic 1950s diner **Johnny Rockets**, **Ben & Jerry's** ice cream, the counter-service of **Pei Wei Asian Diner**, Mexican choice **Abuelo's, Noodles & Company** and the big-name chains of **Chick-Fil-A, Chili's, Panera Bread, Bonefish Grill** and the distinctive **BJ's Brewhouse** offering great burgers, sandwiches, salads and steaks, plus an impressive beer choice (407 932 5245, **bjsbrewhouse.com**). The shops are open 11am–9.30pm Mon–Sat, 11am–6pm Sun, later at the restaurants and cinemas (**experiencetheloop.com**).

> **BRITTIP**
>
> Free parking is limited at Vineland Premium Outlets. It is $12 to valet park and the multi-storey car park is $10.

Lake Buena Vista

The Lake Buena Vista area offers two of the best discount outlet centres, with a great range and prices.

Orlando Vineland Premium Outlets: High on your 'must visit' list, this is a huge hit with UK visitors. With a fresh look and ambience, and a legion of big-name designers, it is the sister centre of the I-Drive version, with a number of similarities but also its own style and range of shops. It can be found on Vineland Avenue between I-Drive and I-4 (just south of SeaWorld; or exit 68 off I-4).

In all, it offers more than 150 stores of well-known brand names (like **Diesel, Armani Exchange, Perry Ellis, Banana Republic, Coach, Kate Spade** and **Calvin Klein**) in a semi-covered pedestrian plaza, with free open-air parking and the convenience of being at the south end of the I-Ride Trolley. Other signature shops are **Samsonite Company Store, OshKosh B'Gosh** (baby/toddler clothes), **Crocs** (footwear) and **Perfumania**. Watch out also for big Disney bargains at the **Disney Outlet**, which offers the previous season's items. The adjoining expansion of The Promenade adds 12 more stores, including a two-storey **Sak's Fifth Avenue Off 5th** and **Forever 21**. The

food court is quite tempting, too, with 11 outlets, from **Five Guys** and **Shake Shack** burgers to **Starbucks** and **Häagen-Dazs**, with full-service **Ford's Garage** restaurant next to The Promenade.

The Lynx bus service stops here, while **Mears Transport** has taxi stands. Premium Outlets is open daily 11am–8pm Mon-Thurs, 10am–9pm Fri-Sat, 11am–7pm Sun (**bit.ly/brit-premium**).

> **BRITTIP**
>
> Want to see a REAL shopping frenzy? Visit either Orlando Premium Outlets centre for Midnight Madness on the Fri after Thanksgiving when they open at midnight and stay open for 24 hours – and thousands pour in to shop!

Lake Buena Vista Factory Stores: Get ready for more big-name products at discount prices here, from **Fossil, Gap Outlet, Reebok, Tommy Hilfiger, OshKosh B'Gosh** superstore and (the better-priced) **Carter's For Kids**. It is another open-air plaza, with 44 stores spread over 6acres/2.5ha and with plentiful parking. It's slightly off the beaten track and therefore not quite as busy as some of the others.

Another option is **Disney Outlet** for Disney gifts and apparel. Some of the names may not be well known to us, but the likes of **Old Navy** (excellent-value casual clothing), **Crocs** (super-comfortable shoes), **The Toy Company** and **Rack Room Shoes** are worth discovering. **World of Coffee** is an internet café with good coffee, an outdoor terrace and bird cages (plus British snacks and chocs!). There's a a decent food court with a pleasant outdoor deck and kids' playground. Worth noting at the neighbouring Lake Buena Vista Resort Village and Spa are the fab **Reflections Spa** for a bit of pampering after a day's shopping, and **Frankie Farrells Irish Pub** (p292).

The Factory Stores are on SR 535 (2ml/3km south off exit 68 on I-4) and are open 11am–7pm (noon–6pm Sun, later in peak season). Their shuttle service picks up at 60 hotels and condos in a 10ml/16km radius (**lbvfs.com**).

Malls

Head out slightly beyond the main tourist territory and you will discover the further choice and style of the area's many malls. They contain a huge range of shops and, if you take advantage of their periodic sales, you will be firmly back on the bargain trail. The top two locally are the Florida Mall and the Mall at Millenia, and both offer a contrasting experience.

Florida Mall: The largest in central Florida, this features more than 230 shops, with four large department stores and a huge food court, plus a children's play area, and the popular fresh offerings of **Nature's Table** and hearty **Buca di Beppo**. Located on the South Orange Blossom Trail, on the corner of Sand Lake Road, this spacious and smart mall is open 11am–8pm Mon–Thurs, 10am–9pm Fri–Sat, 11am–7pm Sun. Highlights are the department stores, led by the upmarket **Macy's**, plus **JC Penney**, **Sears** and **Dillard's**. Other shops worth looking out for are **Bath & Body Works**, **Gap, PacSun** (beachwear and more) and the **Build-a-Bear Workshop** and **Game Stop**. Also here is the massive **Crayola Experience** (interactive fun and design for kids; **crayolaexperience. com/orlando**). Guest services offers a discount booklet with a handy international size chart, while there is also free wi-fi throughout the mall, free wheelchair use, pushchair rental and foreign currency exchange. **JC Penney** even has a hair styling salon (**simon.com/mall/the-florida-mall**). The Mall also benefits from the integral **Florida Hotel**, with **Cricket's Bar**.

Mall at Millenia: If the Florida Mall is the biggest shopping venue, this is the smartest. Just off I-4 to the north

of Universal Orlando, it is among the most dramatic centres in Florida, with famous New York department stores **Bloomingdale's** and **Macy's** among top-name boutiques like **Louis Vuitton**. The entrance features a huge glass rotunda with a water garden theme and a concièrge desk (valet parking is available). As well as five restaurants, it also offers a high-quality food court featuring **Chickpea's Mediterranean Grill**, **Firehouse Subs**, **Sbarro**, the Mandarin-style of **Chinatown**, **Chipotle Mexican Grill** (salads, tacos and burritos) and **Häagen-Dazs** ice cream, plus **Chick-Fil-A** (chicken sandwiches, soups, salads, shakes).

The grand architecture is also focused on five separate courts along a flattened, serpentine S-shape, topped by an arched glass roof. On two airy levels (three in Bloomingdale's and Macy's) and with eight Juliet balconies connecting the two sides, the mall consists of a colossal amount of glass, plus a stunning Grand Court, featuring a dozen 20ft/6m columns capped by curved plasma video screens. And, while around 20% of the 150 stores are upmarket (**Jimmy Choo, Burberry** and **Gucci**), there are regular-priced shops like **Urban Outfitters**, **Apple**, **MAC Cosmetics**, **Anthropologie**, **Abercrombie & Fitch**, **Hollister**, **Gap**, **Banana Republic** and **Victoria's Secret**. The five main restaurants are also first class: **The Cheesecake Factory**, **Earl's Kitchen + Bar**, **PF Chang's China Bistro**, the stylish **Brio Tuscan Grille**, and the swanky **Capital Grille**. On top of that there is the excellent fresh sandwich style of **Charlie's Philly Steaks**, the **California Pizza Kitchen** and a

Johnny Rockets diner. This is also the only mall with a US post office inside (NB: Standard postcards to the UK cost $1.40). A currency exchange is available, as are international phone cards (11am–8pm Mon–Thurs, 11am–9pm Fri 10am–9pm Sat, 11am–7pm Sun; **mallatmillenia.com**).

Other malls: The **Altamonte Mall** is on Altamonte Avenue in the suburb of Altamonte Springs (take exit 92 off I-4 and head east for ½ml/800m on Route 436, then turn left); **Seminole Towne Center**, just off I-4 to the north of Orlando on the outskirts of Sanford (exit 101C off I-4); and **Oviedo Mall**, to the east of Orlando (right off exit 41 of Central Florida Greeneway, 417). The Altamonte Mall is the best of the bunch and well off the beaten tourist track, featuring 111 speciality shops, three major department stores – **Dillard's**, **JC Penney**, **Macy's** – and 21 eateries, including the fun and swanky **Seasons 52** (p286), plus an 18-screen cinema and children's soft-play. Open 11am–8pm Mon–Thurs, 11am–9pm Fri–Sat, noon–6pm Sun, the Customer Service Centre offers a VIP savings book to visitors (**altamontemall.com**). During the week you'll feel as if you have it to yourself!

Winter Garden Village: A final recommendation, 10ml/16km north of Walt Disney World on Highway 535 at the junction with toll road 429, Winter Garden Village is primarily a locals' centre but still has visitor appeal. The expansive open-plan design is set around key stores like **Super Target**, **Best Buy**, **Ross**, **Marshall's**, **Home Goods** and **Beall's** and features a mix of the big names and smaller boutiques, with notable speciality stores like **World Market**, as well as an array of 21 cafés and restaurants.

Look for the upmarket seafood choice of **Bonefish Grill**, the elegant **Longhorn Steakhouse**, family-style **Chili's**, **Cracker Barrel**, **UNO Chicago Grill** and **First Watch**, or the counter-service options like **Five Guys Burgers**, **Panda Express**, **Coldstone Creamery** and **Chick-Fil-A**, and our favourite burger restaurant, **Red Robin** (**https://wintergardenvillage.com**).

Specialist shops

Wal-Mart: This popular warehouse-like store sells just about everything. There are 25 Wal-Marts in central Florida, 16 of which are 24hr Supercenters. The main tourist area stores are on Highway 27 (just north of 192); Highway 192 by Medieval Times (between markers 14 and 15); Osceola Parkway (at Buenaventura Lakes); John Young Parkway (at Sand Lake Road); on Kirkman Road (north of Universal Boulevard); by Highway 535 and Osceola Parkway; on Old Lake Wilson Road at the junction with Highway 192; and on Turkey Lake Road.

Other supermarkets: There are many other choices, including local chains **Publix** and **Winn-Dixie**, plus **Aldi** and organic newcomer **Sprouts**. Then there are the upscale **Whole Foods Market** stores (with a branch on Turkey Lake Road), including excellent fresh produce, salad bar and hot-food counter (**wholefoodsmarket.com**). Equally, **Fresh Market** (with five Central Florida locations) is a top choice for high-quality grocery shopping (**thefreshmarket.com**).

For clothes, DIY, home furnishings, electrical goods, household items, gifts, toys and groceries, visit **Target** (its superstores on Highway 192 just west of Highway 535, near Mall at Millenia and Winter Garden Village are fine examples). The big chemists ('drug stores') of **Walgreens** and **CVS** also carry a wide range of goods.

Individual outlets: Ross (10 in Orlando, see **rossstores.com**) carries a huge range of discounted brand-name clothes, shoes, linens, towels, etc (hours vary by store, roughly 9am–11pm), while **Marshalls** (five in Orlando, **marshallsonline.com**) and **TJ Maxx** (also five, **tjmaxx.com**) are similar. For American sports gear visit **Academy Sports** stores (**academy.com**), while golfers should visit **Edwin Watts Golf** (including the Turkey Lake Road clearance centre; **worldwidegolfshops.com**). You can pick up some great deals on golf clubs in particular.

But now the shopping is done, it's time to think about going home…

After all the fun of Central Florida, it's time to face the bane of all holidays – the journey home. But fear not. Orlando's airports are usually a breeze to navigate, and make the return journey as straightforward as possible.

The car

Returning the hire car can take time if you used an off-airport firm, so allow an extra half hour if you did. The on-airport options are much easier and quicker. Most airlines require check-in 3hrs before an international flight, so don't be tempted to leave it until the last minute. As we went to press, the off-airport check-in for Virgin Holidays at Disney Springs (by the Cirque du Soleil theatre) was still suspended, so be sure to check if it is working again in advance if this pre-flight bonus is important to you. Here is a guide to the two main airports.

Orlando International

Timing: Orlando's biggest airport is 46ml/74km from Cocoa Beach and 54ml/87km from Daytona Beach on the east coast, 84ml/135km from Tampa and 110ml/177km from Clearwater and St Petersburg to the west, 25ml/40km from Walt Disney World and 10ml/16km from Universal Orlando, so always allow plenty of time for the return journey, check-in and security procedure. The Beachline Expressway (528) can get congested in late afternoon, for example, and the Central Florida Greeneway (417) is often better.

Should you have more than 3hrs to spare, it's worth taking the 15min taxi ride to the Florida Mall.

The car: A convenient 'quick turnaround' area for hire cars allows most of the big hire companies to have onsite locations, a huge boon especially when returning the car.

Facilities: One of America's biggest and rated top for passenger satisfaction, this modern airport typically handles around 50 million passengers a year, which is more than Gatwick and San Francisco. It can get busy at peak times, but it usually handles crowds with ease, and this is one of the most comfortable airports you could find. It boasts great facilities and its wide, airy concourses make it feel more like an elegant hotel (one end of Terminals A and B is actually the airport-owned Hyatt Hotel). The new $2.7billion Terminal C opened in September 2022 and adds more convenience and lustre to the airport's appeal, with bright, high-tech facilities, green spaces and plentiful food and beverage offerings. It is connected to Terminals A and B by an automated tram and has its own short-term parking (Car Park C). It also features an array of environmentally friendly enhancements.

Facilities for the disabled: Ramps, restrooms, wide lifts and large open areas ensure easy wheelchair access, and there are features like TDD and amplified telephones, wheelchair-height drinking fountains, Braille lift controls and companion-care restrooms for any travellers with disabilities.

BRITTIP

You are advised to leave all luggage unlocked (no combination locks or padlocks) when you check in for your flight, as the TSA security staff open a LOT of bags during screening and have the right to access any case, locked or not. TSA approved locks are suggested, if you prefer to lock your cases.

Landside A & B

As with all airports, there is a division between LANDSIDE (for visitors) and AIRSIDE (where you must have a ticket). There are three levels to Terminal A and B's Landside: Level 1 is for ground transportation, tour operator desks, parking, buses and car rentals, plus the Virgin Atlantic baggage claim; Level 2 is for main Baggage Claim and private vehicles meeting passengers; Level 3 holds all the check-in desks, shops and restaurants.

Level 3 is further divided into interconnected sections:

Terminal A: This is the check-in for Gates 1–29 and 100–129, including Air Transat, Southwest, Frontier, Spirit (international) and Virgin Atlantic (though Virgin departs from Gates 70–99).

Terminal B: The check-in for Gates 30–99 and American Airlines, Air Canada, Caribbean, Delta, United, WestJet and Spirit (domestic).

Shopping: Once checked in, you can explore the East and West Halls of the Level 3 concourse, which house a tempting mix of restaurants and shops, while the Hyatt Hotel is in the East Hall. The East and West Halls are linked by restaurants, shops and services. In total, there are 132 places to shop and eat, including the food court, and it's almost like being in a smart shopping mall.

Many shops feature outstanding design and even photo opportunities: see the **Disney, Universal** (two of each!), and **SeaWorld** stores. Other notable shops are **Desigual** and **Mango** apparel, **Brookstone**, **Ron Jon Surf Shop**, **Lids** (sports hats and clothes) and **Hudson News**.

Dining: Another pleasure here, the eight-counter food court features **Carvel** ice-cream, **Sbarro** pizza, **Qdoba Mexican Grill**, **McDonalds**, **Panda Express** and **Chick-Fil-A**. **Macaroni Grill** is a tasty full-service Italian restaurant, while **City Pub** adds a multi-screen football bar themed to Orlando's teams. Upstairs at the West Hall is **Chili's Too**.

The East Hall is more picturesque as it is dominated by the eight-storey Hyatt Hotel atrium. Up the escalator is the main entrance, and, to see out your visit in style, **McCoy's Bar & Grill** (up and turn right) is a smart bar-restaurant with a superb airport view and a menu that includes a **Sushi Bar** and fresh salads, sandwiches, flatbreads and small plates (7am–12am, Sushi Bar 4–11pm; **orlandoairport.regency.hyatt.com**).

To go really upmarket, take the lift to 9th-floor **Hemisphere** restaurant (dinner only). You'll have an even more impressive view, and its made-for-sharing small-plate menu is packed with flavour, from grilled octopus to chicken mole (5pm–10pm Tues–Sat).

BRITTIP

If the queues at security for Gates 70–99 look long, you can use the other side, for Gates 100–129, as you end up in the same place after screening. Just remember to get the tram to Gates 70–99.

Airside A & B

Once it's time to move to your departure gate, be aware of the four satellite 'arms' that make up Airside. This is where you will probably need to queue as the security screening takes time, and you should allow AT LEAST 30mins. The arms are divided into Gates 1–29 and 30–59 at the West end, and 70–99 (for Virgin Atlantic and Delta) and 100–129 (other US domestic flights) at the East. There are more boutiques and cafes here, too.

The four satellites are each connected to the main building by an automated tram, so you need to be alert when it comes to finding your departure gate. There are no Tannoy announcements for flights, so check your departure gate and time when you check in. The usual gates are:

1–29: Frontier, Spirit and Silver Airways.

30–59: American, Spirit and United.

70–99: Air Canada, Bahamasair, Delta and Virgin Atlantic.

100–129: Southwest and Alaska Air.

Airside is clean and efficient. There's just as much choice as Landside, and there are two duty-free shops (your purchases are delivered to the departure gate for you to collect as you board). Both stores include designer sunglasses, jewellery, handbags, fashion watches, perfumes and a selection of travel retail exclusives.

BRITTIP

Orlando International Airport offers free WiFi throughout its main concourse and satellite arms.

Gates 1–29: Here you'll find the first duty-free shop, **Hudson News** (newsagent), **ZaZa Cuban Café**, **On the Border Mexican Cantina**, and a mini food court with **Starbucks**, **Burger King**, **Cold Stone Creamery**, **Famous Famiglia**, **UrbanCrave** street food and **Le Grand Comptoir** bar.

Gates 30–59: These have **Qdoba Mexican Grill**, **Manchu Wok**, **Nature's Table**, **Wendy's**, **Freshens Treats**, **ZaZa**, full-service **Ruby Tuesday**, the fresh grab-and-go or bar style of **Camden Food Co** and **Hudson News** (books and gifts) and **Natalie's Candy**.

Gates 70–99: The satellite arm for Virgin and Delta offers a good duty-free shop, currency exchange, **Stellar News & Gifts,** and **XpresSpa**. A food court contains **Nathan's Hot Dogs**, **Carvel, Starbucks** and fresh deli style of **MCO/MKT**, plus the full-service **Outback Steakhouse** and bar, tropical **Bahama Breeze Island Grille**, and a small **Cibo Express** grab-and-go and bar.

Gates 100–129: This revamped satellite offers a food court with **Asian Chao**, **Green Leaf's & Bananas** (salads, smoothies and frozen yoghurt), **Jersey Mike's Subs**, **Chipotle**, **McDonalds**, **Starbucks**, **Villa Italian Kitchen** and the grab-and-go **The Market by Villa**. Even better is a full restaurant from **Cask & Larder**, one of Orlando's best gastropubs, plus eight shops and the **Terminal Getaway Spa**.

Melbourne Orlando International Airport

© Walt Simpson

Terminal C

Orlando's dazzling new terminal – which includes the **Brightline** train station with high-speed service to Palm Beach, Fort Lauderdale and Miami, plus more car hire and ground transport options – is now the gateway for British Airways, Aer Lingus, Emirates, Norse, Lufthansa and Icelandair, plus several others. Passengers will have glimpsed this high-tech facility on arrival, but there is MUCH more to enjoy on departure. It serves **Gates 230-249**, so if you don't see your gate at Terminals A or B, you need to take yourself and your luggage on the automated tram (next to Gates 70-99) to the new facility and follow signs for Terminal C. You arrive in the main level (past multi-storey Car Park C) and **Town Square**, with its towering video screens, ticketing and check-in desks, and several food and beverage outlets, including **Harvest & Grounds** for coffee, pastries and sandwiches, and organic options at **Raw Juce**.

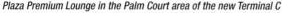

BRITTIP

If you are flying with a Terminal C airline and have a hire car to return, be sure to follow signs for Terminal C Rental Cars, or you will have to use the automated tram from Terminals A and B.

After Security, passengers reach the signature **Palm Court** area, a huge three-storey courtyard featuring more than 20 shops, restaurants and cafes, as well as live palm trees. This is the place for a good pre-flight meal, craft beer or final shopping, with **Disney**, **Universal** and **SeaWorld** all having outlets here, plus the gifts and apparel of **Brighton**, **Sunglass Hut** and **City Arts Market**, and an impressive **Duty Free** shop. As well as national outlets **Starbucks**, **Shake Shack**, **Chick-fil-A** and **Auntie Anne's**, there are premium local dining options like **Wine Bar George** (a new outlet of the Disney Springs bar-restaurant), **DeSano Pizzeria**, **Cask & Larder Bar** and **Provisions**, the health-conscious salads and bowls of **Greenbeat**, **Olde Hearth Bread Co**, and full-service dining at **PGA Tour Grill** and **Summer House** (Florida fresh food and drinks). Finally, there is more to enjoy at the departure gates, notably the fab **Sunshine Diner** of Chef Art Smith (another Disney Springs star), craft beers at **Orange County Brewers** and **Orlando Brewing**, the Italian cuisine of **Cucina & Co**, **Replenish** (coffee and tea) and **Main Street Market** (grab-and-go items).

It's a heady mix, and should ensure your Orlando farewell experience is as enjoyable as your stay.

More info: See orlandoairports.net, with live flight details and a handy airport App to aid in navigation.

Plaza Premium Lounge in the Palm Court area of the new Terminal C

Melbourne Orlando

TUI moved to this regional airport in 2022, opening a new option for UK visitors and initiating a grand, $61million expansion to accommodate an influx of passengers and TUI's 787 Dreamliner aircraft. It's further from Orlando's tourist centres but closer to the beaches and Port Canaveral (for TUI's Marella Cruises, and others, 40min to the north).

Those on fly-drive holidays will need to allow 2hrs for the return journey in case of any traffic hold-ups from Orlando, unless you're driving from Kissimmee, in which case you should allow 90min. Melbourne is 90 miles south of Daytona Beach and 40 miles north of Vero Beach. If your arrival was at this airport, you may not have seen much of it on your way through, so here's how it looks for the return flight.

Dropping off the hire car is straightforward, right next to the main terminal and purpose-designed Welcome Center that greeted TUI customers on arrival. The TUI check-in is inside the terminal to the right and is highly visible. The airport's efficient service is aimed at processing passengers quickly and with minimum fuss. A new four-lane security checkpoint uses the latest screening technology and funnels passengers up to the spacious departure lounge, which has been built specifically to facilitate TUI's international operations.

Once upstairs, passengers will find a bright, airy departure lounge with plenty of seating, a full-service restaurant, the **Butcher Block** grab-and-go option, a **Duty Free** shop and a newsagents/gift shop, **Coastal 2**. Further along the corridor to the domestic departure gates there is a coffee shop and a bar-lounge, so there is no shortage of amenities. TUI's Premium customers also have the benefit of a smart **VIP Lounge**, with its own large bar and buffet-style food service (the likes of hot dogs, macaroni and cheese, and pulled pork sandwiches), children's play area and outdoor terrace for smokers. For non-Premium passengers, the Lounge can be paid for on the day for $40/adult or $20 children 6–16 (subject to availability).

The main dining option in the departure lounge is the **Tap Room** bar-restaurant, which features four local craft breweries, including Melbourne's Intracoastal Brewing Company and the Space Coast's Playalinda Brewing Co, as well as a full menu offering pizza, sandwiches, fresh fish specialities and a kids selection. It boasts plenty of tables and chairs as well as the option to sit at the bar. Food can also be delivered anywhere in the Departure Lounge using the airport's app, which locates you via your phone.

The airport also participates in the **Hidden Disabilities Sunflower Program**, providing lanyards for guests who may require additional support. Finally, the aircraft gates are only a short walk away along the dedicated international flight jetway, which can accommodate three Dreamliners at a time.

Be sure to check for the latest info, news and videos online at **mlbair.com**. The airport is keen to make a good first impression with visitors and will welcome your feedback on their social media.

If you arrive back at the airport with *too* much time to spare, **Melbourne Square** indoor shopping mall is less than 10min away, boasting Dillard's, Macy's and JC Penney department stores, plus Hollister, PacSun, Pandora, Champs Sports, American Eagle, Yankee Candle and Bath & Body Works among more than 80 shops (**melbournesquare.com**). Or treat yourself to a final drink on the beach at **Sand On The Beach** bar/restaurant, just 20min away (**http://sandonthebeach.com**). The fine dining of **Chart House** restaurant, with a gorgeous view over the intracoastal waterway, is only 15min away (open from 4pm Mon–Sat, 11am Sun; **chart-house.com/location/chart-house-melbourne-fl**).

From either airport, your return flight will be about 1hr shorter than the journey out, thanks to the Atlantic jetstreams. But you'll get home more jetlagged because the time difference is more noticeable. Avoid alcohol on the flight if you will be driving when you land. By far the best way to beat Florida jetlag is to enjoy the memories from this trip – then start planning your next Orlando holiday! Believe us, the lure of this wonderland is hard to resist – you WILL be back!

Your chance to give something back

After a wonderful trip, you might be interested in two charities that help children with serious illnesses to have an equally memorable holiday.

Give Kids the World Village is an amazing organisation in Kissimmee, working with wish-granting foundations worldwide to provide an unforgettable week's holiday for children with life-threatening illnesses and their families. It is set up as a resort and includes meals, accommodation, transport, themed venues, donated park tickets and other thoughtful touches in a magical setting. It's a charity we support ourselves and we hope you will, too. You can donate via its website, **gktw.org**.

Dreamflight takes seriously ill and disabled children from the UK on a 'Holiday of a Lifetime' to the theme parks of Orlando, bringing fun and joy into the lives of children whose illnesses and treatments have brought pain, distress and disruption to their lives. Each October, Dreamflight takes 192 children aged 8–14 from all over the UK. For many, it will be their first time away and most will require medical treatment or supervision. One adult accompanies every two children, a high proportion from the medical professions. Helpers in Orlando accompany each child in the parks on a one-to-one basis.

Since 1987, thousands of children have enjoyed what in many cases is a life-changing experience. Priority is given to children who would not otherwise be able to have such an opportunity. They meet others with similar experiences, form many long-term friendships and return with increased confidence and self-esteem. For further information or to make a donation please see **dreamflight.org**.

Thanks in advance for any contributions to these worthwhile organisations.

Only here for a week? Here's our suggestion for an action-packed 7 nights in Orlando:

Day 1: Arrive; visit EPCOT in evening for the nighttime show

Day 2: Up early for Magic Kingdom

Day 3: All day at Universal and Islands of Adventure

Day 4: EPCOT for the day; Disney's Hollywood Studios for evening

Day 5: Disney's Animal Kingdom for a full day

Day 6: SeaWorld with mid-day break at Aquatica

Day 7: Hollywood Studios for the day, Magic Kingdom evening

Day 8: Shopping and return flight

Example: 2 weeks with Disney's 7-Day Ultimate, Universal 3-Park Explorer & SeaWorld 3-Park Tickets

Disney's Ultimate Tickets give 7 or 14 days of unlimited admission at their 4 main theme parks, plus visits to Blizzard Beach, Typhoon Lagoon and ESPN World Of Sports™, valid for 7 or 14 days from first use. Universal 3-Park Explorer Ticket is valid for all 3 parks – including Volcano Bay – and CityWalk for 14 days from first use. SeaWorld 3-Park ticket includes SeaWorld, Busch Gardens and Aquatica for 14 consecutive days.

Day	Our Example	Your Planner
1 (Mon)	Arrive 4.40pm local time, Orlando International airport; transfer to resort – check out local shops and restaurants	
2 (Tues)	Start with a full day at SEAWORLD	
3 (Wed)	Start day at UNIVERSAL STUDIOS for Wizarding World of Harry Potter; then VOLCANO BAY	
4 (Thur)	Morning at MAGIC KINGDOM; take a break and return for Disney Enchantment fireworks at 9pm	
5 (Fri)	Rest day – take in some shopping and have afternoon at SeaWorld's AQUATICA water park	
6 (Sat)	All the fun of DISNEY'S HOLLYWOOD STUDIOS; stay for evening shows	
7 (Sun)	Enjoy Universal's ISLANDS OF ADVENTURE park; evening at CityWalk or VOLCANO BAY	
8 (Mon)	Take a trip to WILD FLORIDA; evening at leisure (dinner show or ICON Park)	
9 (Tues)	A day at BUSCH GARDENS; consider evening at SEAWORLD if back in time	
10 (Wed)	A full day at Disney's EPCOT park, with the nighttime show at 9pm	
11 (Thur)	An early start for all the Pandora attractions at DISNEY'S ANIMAL KINGDOM; enjoy Tree of Life Awakenings after dark	
12 (Fri)	A Disney chillout day – spend time between TYPHOON LAGOON and Disney Springs	
13 (Sat)	The best of UNIVERSAL STUDIOS and ISLANDS OF ADVENTURE; or Kennedy Space Center	
14 (Sun)	Back to our favourite Disney parks – perhaps ANIMAL KINGDOM and MAGIC KINGDOM	
15 (Mon)	Gatorland/Back to airport; return flight at 5.30pm	

Index